Introduction
to ADVENTIST
Mission

Gorden R. Doss

Department of World Mission
Seventh-day Adventist Theological Seminary
Andrews University
Berrien Springs, Michigan

Institute of World Mission
General Conference of Seventh-day Adventists
Silver Spring, Maryland

Published by

Institute of World Mission
General Conference of Seventh-day Adventists
Silver Spring, Maryland

Department of World Mission
Seventh-day Adventist Theological Seminary
Andrews University
Berrien Springs, Michigan

The views and opinions expressed in this book are solely those of the author and
do not necessarily represent those of Andrews University nor the Seventh-day
Adventist Theological Seminary.

This book is available on Amazon.com as a paperback or Kindle book.

Copy Editing   Linda Bauer and Bonnie Beres
Graphic Design   Amy Rhodes
Cover Design   Amy Rhodes

Library of Congress Cataloging-in-Publication Data

Doss, Gorden R.
   Introduction to Adventist Mission
   Includes biographical references.
   ISBN 978-0-9960305-6-4
      Library of Congress Control Number: 2018953116

COVER

John Nevins Andrews, with his children, Charles and Mary, went as missionaries to Switzerland in 1874. They were the first Adventists to be sent as missionaries by the General Conference beyond the shores of North America. The former Emmanuel Missionary College, established in 1874, was renamed Andrews University in their honor. Today, the Andrews family is remembered by a sculpture at Andrews University. The sculpture portrays the family as they might have appeared at Boston Harbor, waiting to board the ship to Europe. Angeline Stevens Andrews, the wife and mother of the family, was deceased and her absence is noted by the empty place next to Mary. The sculpture was created by Alan Collins.

A farewell prayer, written by Andrews, was published in the *Review* as they departed. The prayer, now referred to as the "J. N. Andrews Benediction," is used at Andrews University for commencement services and other special occasions.

"And now, as we set forth, we commit ourselves to the merciful protection of God, and we especially ask the prayers of the people of God that his blessing may attend us in this sacred work."
—*Advent Review and Sabbath Herald*, September 22, 1874.

CONTENTS

ACKNOWLEDGMENTS

Many friends and colleagues deserve thanks and appreciation for advising, supporting, and facilitating the lengthy writing project that produced this book. My colleagues in the Department of World Mission, led by Bruce Bauer and then Wagner Kuhn, provided time for writing, taught some classes for me, and reviewed the manuscript. The Institute of World Mission, led by Cheryl Doss, provided support for some contract teaching that gave time to write. Special thanks to Cheryl for reading and re-reading the manuscript and giving constructive suggestions. Seminary Dean Jiří Moskala gave constant support and encouragement. Colleagues Denis Fortin and Jerry Moon gave detailed responses to certain sections. John Wesley Taylor read the final draft and provided detailed suggestions. Linda Bauer was a careful and patient proof reader and Amy Rhodes did the excellent graphic design.

Most of all, I praise and glorify the Triune God whose love, mercy, compassion, and justice led him to plan and implement the redemption of humanity. He graciously called my family and me to participate in his mission and there is no greater privilege.

Gorden R. Doss
Andrews University
August 2018

DEDICATION

To my missionary family

Gorden and Alpha (Faul) Oss
Norman and Florence (Oss) Doss
Victor and Alma (Cummings) Brown
Cheryl (Brown) Doss
Kristi (Doss), Adam, Zachary, and Julie Kîs
Richard, Hadassah (Rodriguez), Zivah, and Zahra Doss

ABBREVIATIONS

OT Old Testament
NT New Testament

Books by Ellen G. White:

COL Christ's Object Lessons
DA   Desire of Ages
ED   Education
GC   Great Controversy
LS   Life Sketches
MH   Ministry of Healing
PK   Prophets and Kings
PP   Patriarchs and Prophets
SC   Steps to Christ
SD   Sons and Daughters of God
SR   Story of Redemption
1-9T Testimonies, vols. 1-9

Chapter 1

Introduction to the Study of Mission

~•~

Adam and eve, patriarchal period, history of Israel, The time of the messiah, the church, the end.

The story of God's mission to lost humanity is the greatest story ever told. The story begins in the OT immediately after the Fall of Adam and Eve and continues through the patriarchal period and the history of Israel. The Gospels record the central event of God's mission—Christ's birth, ministry, atoning death, resurrection, and ascension. The biblical story continues in the book of Acts and the Epistles with the launching of the Christian church and ends with the apocalyptic climax of God's mission in Revelation. God's mission is the central narrative of the whole biblical canon from Genesis to Revelation.

The story of Christian mission through the different eras of church history takes many twists and turns as the church has faced challenges within itself and in the world. There have been periods of great zeal and faithfulness to God's mission and other periods of less faithfulness; yet, God's active engagement with his redemptive plan has never wavered.

Adventist mission was born with a deep calling to obey the Great Commission (Matt 28:19-20) in the context of the messages of the three angels of Revelation 14:6-12. The story of Adventist mission is one of steadily broadening vision, from a limited North American focus, to the sending of J. N. Andrews to Switzerland in 1874, and onward to the development of a global mission engagement.

As this is written, the Seventh-day Adventist Church claims more than 20 million members in 215 nations. The mission that began as an America-to-the-world movement is now an everywhere-to-everywhere movement. The privilege and responsibility for Adventist global mission that once rested on just a few thousand members in the North American Division (NAD) is now shared by a much larger membership spread around the world. The missional capacity now available within the church to be used in the hands of God gives cause for joyful praise, doxology, and optimism. God is on his throne, directing his mission to humanity, empowering his servants through the Holy Spirit, and joyously planning the soon return of Jesus Christ in glory.

what is the mission to preach views of the 1844 distinctive message?

At the same time, the challenge of the unfinished task of mission is constantly before the church. Obeying the Great Commission requires constantly refocusing the church's vision of the unfinished task even as the church gives praise for its growth. Focusing on the unfinished task should not be misinterpreted as negative thinking. On the contrary, focusing on how best to bring the Gospel to unevangelized people groups is the most positive thing the church can do. From a human perspective, the unfinished task of evangelization is daunting for several reasons.

First, the world population has grown dramatically. When the Adventist church was born in the mid-nineteenth century, only about 1.7 billion people inhabited the planet but today the total is over 7 billion.

Second, the composition of today's growing world population is very challenging. The portion of the population that claims to be Christian has remained more or less steady for 150 years at about one-third. However, the historically Christian nations of the West have become secularized, regular participation in church activities has declined, and biblical literacy has declined. Nations that were once the hubs of Christianity and missionary activity have become challenging mission fields themselves. The Christian center of gravity has shifted southward toward Sub-Saharan Africa and Latin America, regions that have their own challenges.

The non-Christian two-thirds of the population, almost 5 billion people, are composed of adherents of other world religions and non-religious people. The world religions of Islam, Hinduism, and Buddhism make up almost half of humanity.

Third, the Adventist capacity for evangelization that resides in its membership (missional capacity) is distributed unevenly. About 75% of Adventists live in the Americas (North, Central, and South) and Sub-Saharan Africa but only about 25% of the global population is located in these two world regions. On the other hand, only about 25% of Adventists live in Europe, Asia, the Middle East, and North Africa where about 75% of the world's population is located. Further complicating the task of mission, these massive global regions are where the religions of Islam, Hinduism, and Buddhism are centered; where the mega-nations of China and India are located; and where secularized people are numerous. The people groups in these regions have been relatively unresponsive to any form of Christian evangelization. Thus, the global Adventist church has only a small fraction of its membership living among the peoples who have historically been the most challenging to reach.

Humanly speaking, the easiest period of Adventist mission may be in the past and the most challenging just ahead. In the Americas and Sub-Saharan Africa, Adventists have encountered mostly Christians of other denominations and the followers of various traditional religions who have been comparatively receptive. However, in the other world regions Adventists have encountered people groups who have been comparatively unreceptive. How can the world church best engage the more challenging people groups in mission?

The strategic missional challenge for the world church in this century has two dimensions: (1) to maintain and enhance Adventist mission in the Americas, Sub-Saharan Africa, and some parts of Asia where the membership is concentrated; (2) to give added priority to Adventist mission among people groups who have been less receptive and where the Adventist membership is comparatively small.

The challenges of the unfinished mission task mean that the church cannot travel forward on missional auto-pilot, depending only on its hunches, habits, and favorite methods. Rather, mission must be approached as a subject to be studied and understood as deeply as is humanly possible. Creative new methods and approaches need to be tried. The church needs to give itself permission to be bold and sometimes to fail. God initiated his mission and he will complete it, but his servants must engage all of the gifts he has given them to work as creatively, diligently, and intelligently as they possible can. This book is presented prayerfully as a small contribution to the systematic study and implementation of the Adventist mission to the world.

Definitions

As with all areas of study, the study of Christian mission has a set of words used in particular ways that are helpful in pursuing a deeper understanding.

Biblical Words

The word "mission" and its related forms is not found in English Bible translations, although some paraphrases might include it. The Greek New Testament (NT) words that best correspond to "mission" and its variations are *pempo* and *apostello*, both of which refer to "sending." Scripture says that God sent prophets (Luke 11:49), John the Baptist (John 1:6), and Jesus Christ (John 4:30); Jesus sent the Twelve and the church (Matt 10:5; John 20:21); and the Father and Jesus sent the Holy Spirit (John 14:26).

The English word "mission" was derived from the Latin words *mitto* ("to send") and *missio* ("sending"). The Latin word mission, which later became the English word, came into general usage in the seventeenth century (Ott and Strauss 2010:xiv). Thus, "sending" or "being sent" is the basic biblical concept of mission.

Missiology

The word "theology" is used both for the broad study of biblical beliefs and for the specific study of the nature of God. The pattern of dual usage is also found in mission studies. "Missiology" can refer to the all-inclusive study of Christian missions and also to the theological principles undergirding missions.

> Missiology is the conscious, intentional, ongoing reflection on the doing of mission. It includes theory(ies) of mission, the study and teaching of mission, as well as research, writing, and publication of works regarding mission. (Moreau, Netland, and Van Engen 2000:633)

Missiology is an inter-disciplinary discipline that draws on and blends the disciplines of theology, history, and cultural anthropology. The discipline of theology, including biblical and systematic theology, provides the foundational principles for doing missions. The study of history offers valuable lessons from the past to guide contemporary missions. Cultural anthropology provides concepts, insights, and skills to enhance cross-cultural mission. The blending of theology, history, and anthropology produces a kind of conversation that is new to some people. The lens of missiology provides a way of viewing the church, the world, and the task of mission in very helpful ways.

Missiology is one of the disciplines that make up pastoral-theological education. At times the study of mission has been located in the church history or practical theology departments of a seminary. There are at least two good reasons to place missiology in a separate department: first, the discipline of missiology blends the other seminary disciplines (Old Testament, New Testament, Church History, Theology and Philosophy, Christian Ministry, etc.) with selected social science disciplines in a unique and helpful combination; second, the massive challenge of the unfinished mission task requires a strong and intentional emphasis on mission studies for those studying theology.

Adventists started including the formal study of missiology in pastoral-theological and missionary education in the mid-1960s when the Department of World Mission was opened at the Seventh-day Adventist Theological Seminary, Andrews University. Prior to that, some occasional training had been offered for missionaries. In recent years, the discipline of missiology has greatly expanded to offer masters and doctoral level programs on a number of campuses.

Paul wrote of Israelites who had a zeal not based on knowledge (Rom 10:1-2). Christians can fall into the same trap, especially given the complexity of missions in these times. Under the slogan of "just get out there do something," zealous believers can be unproductive or even counterproductive in their mission endeavors. Missiology can add a depth dimension to mission zeal that makes it more effective. One of the important contributions of missiology is developing the skill of missiological reflection. There are different levels of thought about the church's missionary task.

Doctrinal-evangelistic thinking asks: "How can the church conduct more evangelistic efforts among Hindus in India (or among any other group) to teach Adventist doctrines?" This question is good and proper but more depth is needed.

Doctrinal-evangelistic-theological thinking asks: "How can the church conduct more evangelistic efforts among Hindus in India to teach the deeper meaning of being a Christian as expressed in Adventist doctrines?" This question is an improvement on the last one because Hindus would not simply be taught the externals of Adventist belief but would go deeper to understand theological meanings. For example, the teaching would go beyond keeping Sabbath from sunset Friday to sunset Saturday to the deeper meaning of the Sabbath rest in Jesus Christ and how it blesses humanity. But there is yet a deeper level.

Missiological reflection asks: "What cultural, religious, economic, political perspectives, and personas do Adventists bring with them when they go to work among Hindus in India? What is the cultural, religious, economic, educational, political, and historical context of the particular people group where they will work? Based on what Christians bring with them and what they learn about the receptor audience, what methods and approaches will be most effective? In what order shall they teach Adventist beliefs and lifestyle? What parts of the Adventist message need special emphasis for this people group? What parts of traditional Hindu Indian culture, belief, and practice are biblically innocent and should be retained, which modified, and which rejected to become true disciples of Jesus?" These questions illustrate the missiological concepts of worldview-level contextualization that will be developed in coming chapters.

Mission

Given the prominence of missions in the history of the Christian church, one might expect that defining the word "mission" and related words would be quite easy. Instead, mission is a disputed and ambiguous word, with many different nuances and usages. A quick look at the mission shelf of a library or a few minutes listening to a small group discussion about missions will quickly confirm the complexity of the mission concept. One frequently heard remark is, "Well, that all depends on how you define missions."

The very nature of Christian mission is what makes defining mission difficult. Mission is about crossing boundaries of faith, language, culture, or geography and sometimes crossing all of these boundaries at the same time. Crossing boundaries removes a person from familiar reference points and adds layers of complexity to life and ministry. A Korean (Chilean or Kenyan) pastor (teacher, dentist, or accountant) serving as a missionary in a Muslim (Hindu, Buddhist, or secular) country not only faces the challenges of their profession but also of working in an unfamiliar and sometimes hostile environment. "Mission outreach has always disturbed the peace of the church" (Hiebert, in Van Engen 1996:9) because it upsets the status quo of doing things in the same habituated ways. Christians love missions, but doing missions effectively can be very challenging.

Understanding mission is complicated because the many contexts in which the church works are so very different at any given time. Furthermore, the contexts of mission change between historical eras. The twentieth century began in the era of high colonialism, then came World War I, the Great Depression, World War II, and the Cold War. Between the 1940s and 1960s, the former European colonies became independent. In the last half of the century, a bewildering sequence of wars, economic trends, and the birth of the computer age impacted human life. The twenty-first century opened with a bewildering witch's brew of wars and terrorism. Today, human migration is repositioning the human race, taking people groups away from their traditional locations and bringing them to new places. Migration has altered the demographic makeup of almost every nation on Earth.

The definition of mission has created major debates within the church. Different Christian groups spent much of the twentieth century debating about whether or not evangelism and social ministries (healthcare, education, relief and development, human rights, etc.) were both part of mission. Some at the conservative end of the theological spectrum insisted that only evangelism qualified and some at the liberal end said that social action could stand alone. By the late-twentieth century, a consensus had emerged among many Christian groups embracing wholistic mission that includes both evangelism and social ministries. Adventist world mission has been consistently wholistic, even though in various times and places it may not have achieved the ideal coordination of evangelism and social ministry.

In recent decades, a discussion has emerged about whether wholistic mission includes anything and everything the church does. Can doing evangelism and serving on the church board both be called mission? Are routine local church custodial work and operating bush clinics both mission? Should a long-term cross-cultural missionary, who has learned the language and understands the culture where she serves, and a two-week short-term mission trip participant both be called missionaries? Are pastors serving in their cultural homes and pastors serving in very different cultures both missionaries? These questions illustrate the challenge of defining mission.

Timothy Tennent asserts that "the word *mission* [and its variations] needs a twenty-first century renovation" (2010:54). The famed South African missiologist, David Bosch, cautions that people must not try to define mission "too sharply and too self-confidently" (1991:9). This whole book is a work that seeks to understand mission in a biblical way that is appropriate for this century.

Lesslie Newbigin offers a helpful suggestion for defining mission by distinguishing

> between mission as a *dimension* of the Church's whole life, and mission as the primary *intention* of certain activities. Because the Church is the mission there is a missionary dimension of everything that the Church does. But not everything the Church does has a missionary intention. Certain activities can be considered to have a *missional intention* when they are "an action of the Church in *going out beyond the frontiers of its own life* to bear witness to Christ as Lord among those who do not know him, and when the overall intention of that action is that they should be brought *from unbelief to faith*." (in Goheen 2014:82-83, italics supplied)

The distinction between dimensions of mission and missional intentions provides some helpful clarifications. The many parts of the church's inner life and work (church boards, building projects, custodial work, etc.) are what Newbigin calls the dimensions of mission. Activities that move outside the church's inner work and life to cross boundaries of faith, language, culture, or geography are intentional acts of mission. The dimensions of mission within the church are appropriate when they contribute to the church's missional intentions outside the church. The reason for the church's existence is reaching out. The inner life of the church has natural momentum that keeps it moving along, but missional intentionality must be purposefully generated and renewed for the church to move outside itself to cross boundaries.

Some church activities cannot properly be called either dimensions or intentions of mission because they are sidetracks and diversions into mere busyness or entertainment. The church should avoid using mission as a theological seal of approval that authenticates activities of marginal value to its God-given purpose on Earth. The church must invest its resources and energies in the dimensions of mission to the extent that they facilitate the intentions of mission. The ultimate intention of mission is to lead people who do not worship and serve the Creator God to "Fear God and give him glory" (Rev 14:7).

The concept of internal and external mission is related to that of dimensions and intentions. The church has an internal mission to itself that can also be called discipleship. Through its varied ministries, the church leads its members toward mature discipleship at every stage of life, from cradle to grave. At the turning points of life—birth, marriage, parenthood, old age, and death—the congregation loves, guides, and supports its members. A major part of the church's internal mission is to train, support, send, and oversee its members for external mission outside the church.

Ideally, internal and external mission function as an integrated pair because each potentially benefits and empowers the other. The member who grows closer to God through a Sabbath School fellowship group has a more vibrant spiritual life to empower witnessing to non-Christians and members have a more dynamic ministry to fellow members when non-believers are led to Christ through their witnessing.

Short Term Mission (STM) trips are a popular way of combining internal and external mission. As with all intentional forms of mission, the primary motivation must always be for others. If the primary motivation is to benefit those making a trip, the term "iMission" or "selfiMission" may apply. Blessings received from any form of service or mission must always be seen as secondary and derivative. Authentic mission is always God-centered and Other-oriented.

Charles Van Engen's definition of mission gives focus to this book:

Mission is the people of God intentionally crossing barriers from church to non-church, faith to nonfaith, to proclaim by word and deed the coming of the Kingdom of God in Jesus Christ; this task is achieved by means of the church's participation in God's mission of reconciling people to God, to themselves, to each other, and to the world, and gathering them into the church through repentance and faith in Jesus Christ by the work of the Holy Spirit with a view to the transformation of the world as a sign of the coming of the Kingdom in Jesus Christ. (1996:26-27)

Mission and Missions

The words "mission" and "missions" were used synonymously until the 1960s. Terminologies began to change in the 1960s as the world moved out of the colonial era and into the era of political independence. The association of missionary work with colonialism during the modern missionary movement era (c.1750-1950) caused intense self-examination in missionary circles as the colonial era ended. Some church groups in the former colonies called for a complete moratorium on missionary service. On all sides, including in the West, questions were asked about the validity of Christian missions. Was any and all missionary work a continuation of colonialism?

Differing answers were given to the question. Some have adopted the pluralist position that accepts all religions as equally valid spiritual pathways. For them, calling adherents of other religions to become Christians seems like an act of continued colonialism. Others believe that Jesus Christ is the unique source of salvation and that calling non-Christians of every cultural and religious group to become his disciples is a Great Commission imperative.

A consensus emerged among more conservative evangelical Christian groups that, although mistakes were made during the colonial era, there was something in missions far greater than the missionaries and their human errors. That greater factor was God himself, and his "redemptive, historical initiative on behalf of his creation" (Tennent 2010:59).

To capture the concept that the Triune God is the divine Initiator of mission, the term *missio Dei* (mission of God) came into use. The word "mission" (singular) started being used to refer to the divine role in the plan of salvation. "Mission" also came to include a second dimension, the mandate God has given to the church (Ott and Strauss 2010:xv).

The word "missions" (plural) came to be used to refer to the church's various activities of missional intention done in participation with God's mission and in obedience to his mission mandate. The church, as God's primary human agency, performs various "missions." God the Holy Spirit also works directly on human hearts, through dreams and visions, and through general revelation. God's "mission" (singular) is always sovereign over the church's "missions" (plural), which are as fallible as its members. In other words, the church should never think that God's "mission" can be held hostage or controlled by the church's "missions." Neither should God be blamed for the mistakes made by his fallible human agents as they perform the church's "missions."

Missionary

A "missionary" is a "sent one" or an "emissary" who follows in the tradition of the Twelve Apostles, although not having the same historic role in the church as the Twelve. A missionary is one sent by the church to do the work of missions explicitly and intentionally (Ott and Strauss 2010:xvii).

In a broad sense, all believers who use their spiritual gifts for the advancement of God's Kingdom can rightly be called "missionaries" or "ministers" because every believer has a mission and ministry. However, the church uses the word "minister" to identify a person with a specific role in the church. In the same way, the word "missionary" is used for those sent to intentionally cross boundaries of faith, culture, language, or geography.

There is some tension between validating every believer as having a God-given role in the missions of the church and validating the continued essential role of specialized cross-cultural missionaries. The reason for reserving the term "missionary" for a specialized role is that the missionary is more needed now than ever before for missions among today's large people groups who are unevangelized or poorly evangelized.

Among Adventists, there are contrasting thoughts about being called a missionary. Some people who are being sent by the church to serve in another culture resist using the word for themselves, often because they are not pastors. Others declare themselves to be missionaries when they return from a two-week mission trip. Others resist the term because it reminds them of the caricature of "the missionary" of the colonial era. However, when fully understood, the ministry of a cross-cultural missionary remains biblically valid in the church. The continued need for cross-cultural missionaries will be demonstrated in many coming chapters.

Missional

A recent addition to the vocabulary of missiology is the word "missional." Christopher Wright explains that "missional is simply an adjective denoting something that is related to or characterized by mission, or has the qualities, attributes or dynamics of mission" (2013:24). A "missional church" is one that is not only involved and supportive of missionaries but which understands that "the church itself is sent by God with a missionary mandate" (Ott and Strauss 2010:xviii). Such a church uses the dimensions of mission to implement missional intentions of various kinds.

The Mission Field

Many shades of meaning are implied by the term "mission field." Broadly speaking, the mission field can include everything from the family, to the local church, to unevangelized people groups far away. The term frequently implies a sense of neediness, both in a material and spiritual sense.

This book uses the term "mission field" to identify people groups among whom the local Adventist church has high strategic missional need and with whom the world church needs to work in supportive partnership (the implications of this definition are spelled out in chapter 14).

Strategic missional need is made up of two factors: (1) missional capacity is the ability of the local church to evangelize its own community or area; missional capacity includes human and material factors, like the number of members and churches and their tithes and offerings; (2) missional context is the legal, social, religious, and political setting in which the local church functions.

Strategic missional need is low where local missional capacity is high and local missional context is high. In other words, the local conference has many members, meeting in many churches, giving tithes and offerings that are adequate (although leaders always pray for more money), and the context is generally open to evangelization. Such a conference is not a mission field according to the definition used here because it can carry the responsibility for Adventist mission within its own territory.

Strategic missional need is high where local missional capacity is low and missional context is low or unfavorable. For example, in a nation of 50 million people, where the Adventist Church has only fifty members meeting in two small churches and where the environment is unfavorable for Christian mission, the strategic need is high. This nation is a true mission field and the local church needs the supportive partnership of the world church.

Home and Foreign Missions

Seventh-day Adventists used the terms "home missions" and "foreign missions" for many decades. During Sabbath School there was a "mission story" and an offering for foreign missions. Between Sabbath School and the worship service there was the "home missionary period" that featured outreach in the local community. The "Home Missionary Department" was renamed the "Lay Activities Department" in 1967 (*SDA Yearbook* 1968).

Referring to local church outreach as "home mission" was positive because it avoided the common mistake of thinking that "mission is over there" and "evangelism is over here." Whether the general understanding of mission agreed with the terminology is uncertain. In my childhood, when my family served as missionaries in Malawi and we went to America for furlough, we were often called "real missionaries." The unfortunate implication was that the mission of the local American church was less important or authentic than mission in Malawi. Bosch offers this helpful clarification about home and foreign missions:

> The difference between home and foreign missions is not one of principle but of scope. We repudiate the mystical doctrine of salt water, that is, the idea that travelling to foreign lands is the sine qua non for any kind of missionary endeavor and the final test and criterion of what is truly missionary. (1991:10)

In more recent times, the North American church has tried to correct the misconception that "real mission" is somewhere else, across saltwater. The primary role of the local church in mission has been appropriately reaffirmed and emphasized.

Perhaps the contemporary challenge for Adventists everywhere is to have a vision for mission that is broad enough. Mission includes both the local church and the mission field far away across saltwater. The Multi-Focal Mission Vision model (see chapter 14) provides one way to bring the contemporary global mission challenge into focus in its different perspectives.

A Global Missiology

The historical period called the modern missionary movement (c.1750-1950) began when Protestants became fully engaged in world missions and ended when the European colonies became independent and a new era of global Christianity began. During that period, Christian missions moved primarily "from the West to the rest."

In 1800, only about 14% of all Christians lived outside the West. If the whole world was to be evangelized, the 86% of Christians living in Europe and North America had the responsibility to take action. By 2000, the portion of Christians living outside the Western nations had grown to about 58% of the total. Christianity is now a global religion and the Adventist Church is a global church. As this is written, about 93% of Adventists live outside the North American Division.

These shifts in the concentration of Christianity mean that Christian mission no longer moves primarily "from the West to the rest." Instead, mission must move and is already moving from-everywhere-to-everywhere. This means that missiology must have a global focus that educates and guides the church everywhere to fulfill its mission everywhere.

Adventists from everywhere are already serving and witnessing everywhere. Some are officially called by the church to be cross-cultural missionaries, while others are sent by independent Adventist agencies. Many Adventists have migrated away from their homelands, some permanently and others seeking education or temporary employment. These refugees or immigrants attend local Adventist churches in communities very different from their home cultures.

All of the Adventists described above are called to cross the barriers of faith and religion and some to cross barriers of language, culture, and geography. The same basic missiological principles apply to them all and need to be understood by all. To illustrate, the same principles apply to cross-cultural missionaries from Brazil (Kenya or Korea) serving in Mongolia (Lebanon or Malaysia). The same missiological principles apply to Adventist refugees or immigrants from Congo (the Middle East or Myanmar) who find themselves living in England (Canada or the United States). The same principles apply to Adventists living in their native homelands who hear God's call to cross boundaries for him.

Malawi: A Continuing Mission Case Study

Case studies are useful in the study of missions, or any other subject. The story of Adventist mission in Malawi, Africa, is one of amazing growth. David Livingstone explored Malawi (then Nyasaland) in 1859. Anglican missionaries working with the Universities' Mission to Central Africa mission agency arrived in 1861. The first Adventist to reach Malawi was George James, a self-support-ing missionary who arrived in 1893 but stayed only a short time. In 1902, the newly reorganized General Conference, under the leadership of A. G. Daniells, sent missionaries to Malawi to establish Malamulo Mission. When my family arrived in 1954, there were about 10,000 members in Malawi. By 2015, the Adventist membership had grown to almost 500,000 in a population of about 15 million. Among the nations where Adventist mission received a warm welcome, Malawi, the "Warm Heart of Africa," is an excellent case study. Parts of the story of Adventists in Malawi will be a continuing case study.

Limitations of an Introduction

As an "Introduction to Adventist Mission," this book partakes of the limita-tions of every introduction. The field of missiology is so large in every dimen-sion that its topics can only be discussed partially in a single book. Over and over I have felt like adding the caveat that "much more could be said about this topic." Instead, the caveat is hereby made for the whole book. Hopefully, this in-troduction will lead readers into deeper studies of the many great and wonderful aspects of the study of God's mission to humanity.

Author's Perspective

I am a Euro-American born in Lincoln, Nebraska into a missionary family. My maternal grandparents were missionaries in Trinidad. My parents, Norman and Florence Doss, served in Malawi and Zimbabwe for 21 years. I married Cheryl Brown, daughter of Victor and Alma Brown, who were American mis-sionaries in South Africa, Malawi, and the Philippines for 15 years. I grew up in Malawi and met Cheryl at Helderberg College, in South Africa. Cheryl and I served for 16 years as missionaries in Malawi.

Cheryl is director of the General Conference Institute of World Mission. Our two children, with their families, have each served about eight years out-side North America. My professional experience has been mostly in pastoral education in Malawi and teaching mission at Andrews University since 1998. I have earned a Doctor of Ministry degree from Andrews University and a PhD in Intercultural Studies from Trinity Evangelical Divinity School.

My background, education, and experience shape how I think and write about Adventist world mission. I acknowledge my perspective and in doing so put into practice a basic missiological principle. Effective mission requires that one understands and acknowledges the lenses that shape one's view of everything. I have tried to articulate missiological principles that can be applied everywhere, but understand that my own experience shapes the book. Readers will need to make their own applications to their particular contexts.

Chapter 2

The Bible as a Grand Narrative of God's Mission: Old Testament

~•~

Introducing the Theology of Missions

The Need to Articulate a Theology of Mission

The Adventist Church needs a well-articulated theology of mission. There is a de-facto theology hovering behind or implied by what the church thinks and does about missions; but, in my observation, Adventists have an easier time discussing their theology of creation, sin, salvation, Sabbath, and Second Coming than of mission. Perhaps the commendable activist spirit of a church that just wants to "Get out there and obey the Great Commission" explains why they do less theological thinking about mission itself. Wanting to take action is good but the work of mission is greatly enhanced when guided by a thoughtful theology of mission. Theology answers the "why" and "so what" questions that provide guidance for answering the "what," "when," "where," and "how" questions of missions to direct the missionary zeal of the church.

The church needs theology that is missional and missiology that is theological. In other words, theology should not be an abstract discussion of principles and formulations without having mission at its heart. On the other hand, missiology should not be reduced to the discussion of methods and strategies without having theology at its core. Both imbalances are visible at times in the church today.

The NT writers did theology in response to concrete issues they faced in missions. Mission has rightly been called the "mother of theology," while theology has been called "an accompanying manifestation of the Christian mission" (Bosch 1991:16). Paul and the others wrote in an "emergency situation" that grew out of missionary encounters with the world that "forced them to theologize" (16). The cross-cultural mission engagement that brought converted former pagans into the church alongside Jewish believers made the profound theology of Romans, Galatians, and the other books a necessity. If the NT writers were not scholars producing theological works in isolation, neither were they pragmatic field workers merely producing step-by-step strategy manuals for doing mission in every time and place.

In the centuries that have followed, theology and mission have sometimes been divorced from each other. Thus, some believers rush to "get out there" without theological reflection about what they are doing, while others debate doctrine and theology without being engaged in intentional missions. Missional action and theological reflection need to work in partnership and when they do, the church's service in God's mission is enhanced in several ways:

First, a good theological base for what the church does helps it discern God's deep intentions and purposes for humankind and the whole cosmos. The Bible's grand narrative of mission provides an overview of God's work for His lost creation. The faithfulness and unfaithfulness of God's people to his will recorded in Scripture are highly instructive for the church as it seeks to use godly methods in mission. Theology of mission can help believers to discover their personal role in God's grand narrative of mission.

Second, theology of mission helps the church to avoid a strictly pragmatic orientation to missions that approves almost anything that "works." For example, manipulative or even unethical methods can produce short term "successes" that do not nurture mature disciples and further God's Kingdom. Modern marketing strategies need to be used selectively in mission to avoid a manipulative approach.

Third, a theological foundation can help to avoid ethnocentric and paternalistic views of the people groups missionaries work with. Missionaries often work among people groups who are very different from themselves, culturally, educationally, and economically. The insights of cultural anthropology can help missionaries develop positive relationships with very different people groups but a theological perspective is needed to give them godly love for the people they serve.

> Sometimes mission theology has taken a back seat to questions of strategy and methodology...

Fourth, a clear theology of mission is needed to avoid the "de-theologizing of missiology" through an inappropriate use of cultural anthropology and other social sciences (Ott and Strauss 2010:xiii). In other words, the social sciences can be used properly in missions only within a good theological framework. Sometimes mission theology has taken a back seat to questions of strategy and methodology, the social sciences, and various activist issues and agendas and this must be avoided.

Fifth, theology of mission helps the church to avoid a narrow institutional view of mission that focuses primarily on the addition of members for statistical reports and the expansion of territories. The institutional dimension of the church—with its institutions, committees, policies, procedures, and statistics—is valid but human structures need to be servants and not masters of the church's God-given mission.

Finally, the historical and contemporary challenges to the validity of mission can be addressed by a theology of mission. One longstanding challenge comes from the historical association of missions with colonialism. A contemporary challenge comes from the culture of postmodernity that sees converting non-Christians to Christianity as arrogant, bigoted, and intolerant. Postmodernity assumes that all religions are equally valid pathways to God (religious pluralism) and that individuals and societies can properly adopt whatever ethical-moral systems they wish (moral-ethical relativism). The idea of a single, universal, absolute moral-ethical code and a single pathway to salvation based on the Bible is abhorrent to postmodern and secular peoples, who see missionaries as agents of intolerance and destroyers of culture. These challenges can be met with a robust theology of mission.

Sources for a Theology of Mission

Having noted several benefits of having a well-defined theology of mission, the next matter to consider is the various sources to be used when developing a theology of mission. Obviously, the Bible is the primary source, to which all other sources must be secondary and subordinate. This is not to suggest that the Bible contains neat definitions, direct answers to every question, or methodological instructions for every missional task and issue in every time and place. The Bible is an ancient document written by and for people very different from ourselves. That means that the deeper missional meanings and principles of Scripture must be sought.

For Adventists, the writings of Ellen White are a rich resource for thinking theologically and practically about mission. Although her travels did not take her to every continent, she did spend significant time as a cross-cultural missionary in Australia, Europe, and among recent immigrants to America.

The history of missions reveals the strengths and weaknesses of mission thinking and practice through the centuries and is a valuable source for theological reflection. Just as God's missional will was revealed through the life and work of the early church, he uses both the failures and successes of later generations to guide his church.

The voices of the global church are essential for a theology of mission. Although the global north retains a strong influence in theological education and publishing, the global south is now the numerical center of Christianity. Among Adventists, only about 7% of members now reside in North America. This means that the whole church needs to speak and be heard in the work of missiological study. Looking at the task of world mission from the perspectives of Asia, Africa, Europe, and Latin America, in addition to North America, produces essential insights and understanding.

The academic discipline of missiology has a rich library of periodicals, books, and websites that provide excellent resources for studying the theology of mission.

Finally, the social sciences cannot properly be considered a direct source of mission theology, but they do provide valuable insights into the many and varied human contexts of missions. The NT writers developed their missiology from within specific cultural contexts and contemporary missiology must do the same. Cultures have profound differences that shape every part of human life and the responses people make to the Gospel. Cultural anthropology and the other social sciences open windows of understanding to cross-cultural missionaries who can then frame more effective approaches that are culturally informed and theologically truthful.

Characteristics of a Theology of Mission

Having established that a well-defined theology of mission is needed and having examined some sources to be used, what are its characteristics? Charles Van Engen outlines the following characteristics of a mission theology (1996:15-27).

First, mission theology is multidisciplinary. In other words, it draws on all of the disciplines of pastoral-theological studies, including biblical studies, philosophy, systematic theology, church history, and practical theology. The social sciences (notably cultural anthropology) are secondary disciplines for missiology, used for placing theological reflections on mission into varied human contexts.

Second, mission theology is integrational. In other words, it uses all of the disciplines named above to integrate or draw together the three elements always involved in mission: (a) The different contexts of the Bible, including the authors, the original recipients or readers, the surrounding cultures of the times, and the position of particular passages in the biblical canon; (b) the cultural, historical, political, and economic context of missions among contemporary people groups; and, (c) the church community, in its own cultural, historical, political, and economic context, with its human and material resources.

Third, theology of mission is definitional. As already noted in chapter 1, missiological definitions are inherently difficult because of the boundary-crossing, out-of-habituated-comfort-zone character of missions. Much of this book involves defining and redefining elements of mission.

Gerald Anderson defines mission theology as "the basic presuppositions and underlying principles which determine, from the standpoint of Christian faith, the motives, message, methods, strategy, and goals of Christian world mission" (Van Engen 1996:18; 29). Another definition says that "'mission theology' is the normative part of mission studies or missiology" (Corrie et al. 2007:237). In other words, mission theology sets the biblical standard for missions.

Fourth, mission theology is analytical. The many components of mission overlap and interact with each other. These components include missions through different human agents, missions taking different forms in the church, missions as it impacts global humanity, the predictable results of missions, and the unpredictable results of missions. Then there are the contexts, agents, motives, means, goals, methods, and results of missions.

Every aspect of Christian mission has theological implications, unlike secular business ventures that focus only on means and methods for increasing market share. A soft drink maker can distribute samples to increase market share, but giving food and drink to attract non-Christians to be baptized raises theological questions. A theology of mission analyzes the factors, means, and methods of missions based on the biblical standard.

To illustrate, what predictable and what unpredictable results might follow if a Nigerian (or Norwegian or Argentinian or Indian) conducted traditional evangelism (or seminar evangelism or small group outreach or coffee house outreach) among Egyptians (or Filipinos or Chinese or Russians) using various approaches? What might be the outcomes for God's mission, the human agents, the church, or global humanity? What are the moral-ethical and theological implications?

Finally, a theology of mission is, and must always be, truthful. The social sciences are descriptive but seldom prescriptive. They collect valid and reliable data about particular people groups but do not ask whether the group beliefs and behaviors conform to a standard of truth. For example, they may describe patterns of biblically forbidden behavior but do not prescribe remedial changes. Missiology is both descriptive and prescriptive because it goes beyond the valid and reliable descriptive data that social sciences provide to asking truth questions. Missiology seeks to understand how God's universal, revealed truth can be faithfully incarnated within a particular people group in a real life context. Every strategy and method used in missions must be more than just effective—it must be truthful. "Missiology, as a branch of the discipline of Christian theology, is not a disinterested or neutral enterprise; rather, it seeks to look at the world from the perspective of commitment to the Christian faith" (Bosch 1991:9).

A Brief History of the Theology of Mission

The writers of the NT thought, taught, and wrote as they interacted with real-life mission challenges in the early church. They were not professional theologians developing theological systems that included a formal theology of mission. As Bosch notes, "In the first century, theology was not a luxury of the world-conquering church but was generated by the emergency situation in which the missionizing church found itself.... In this situation, mission became the 'mother of theology'" (1991:489).

The first generations of missionaries after the Apostles built on the Apostolic writings but did not develop formal theologies of mission. "Whereas the earliest itinerant evangelists and missionary monastic movements had a theological rationale for their undertakings, they lacked an explicit, articulated theological reflection on mission" (Ott and Strauss 2010:xxiv).

There were theologians in the history of the church who had a missiological focus. Augustine (354-430) emphasized "the importance of mission beyond the boundaries of the empire and argued against the generally held view of Eusebius that the Apostles had completed the Great Commission" (Ott and Strauss 2010:xxiv). "The most prolific medieval writer on mission was Raymond Lull (1235-1315), whose primary concern was the conversion of Muslims and training missionaries for that task" (xxiv). Jose de Acosta (1540-1600) was a Spanish Jesuit missionary to the East Indies who wrote theologically about mission. The Sacred Congregation for the Propagation of the Faith produced materials guiding Roman Catholic overseas missions. The religious orders were the main Catholic structures for mission.

The Protestant Reformers were so preoccupied with theological, social, and political conflicts that they had only a minimal focus on world missions. The Great Commission, they said, applied to the Apostles who had accomplished it. Gisbertus Voetius (1588-1676) was a Protestant theologian who tried to make mission a part of theological study. Justinian von Weltz (1621-1668) called for a Protestant missionary movement. However, almost three centuries passed after Luther's Ninety-Five Theses before Protestants became seriously involved in mission theology, initiatives, and structures. Part of the problem was that Protestants did not adopt structures for missions replacing the Catholic religious orders.

The two Great Awakenings (1726-1760 and 1787-1825) had a profound influence on mission thinking. "Jonathon Edwards's thought was the great intellectual and spiritual vein from which missionary theology in the period was mined" (Bosch 1991:277). William Carey published *An Enquiry into the Obligations of Christians to Use Means for the Conversion of the Heathens* in 1792 as a ringing call to global missions. Like Carey, "Many of the earliest Protestant missionaries became experts in local religions and outstanding ethnographers, but few articulated a theology of mission per se" (Ott and Strauss 2010:xxv). Henry Venn (1796-1873) and Rufus Anderson (1796-1880) were mission administrators in England and the United States who developed the "three-self theory." Newly planted churches, they said, should be self-supporting, self-governing, and self-propagating. The three-self theory is a theological statement about the nature of the church that guides how mission is done.

The study of missions as an academic discipline and part of seminary education started in the second half of the nineteenth-century. Gustav Warneck (1834-1910) pioneered Protestant missiology and published *Protestant Doctrine of Mission (Evangelische Missionslehre)*. Joseph Schmidlin (1876-1944) is considered the father of modern Catholic missiology. Roland Allen's (1868-1947) *Missionary Methods: St. Paul's or Ours?* was a provocative work of missiology that challenged missionaries to step beyond approaches heavily influenced by colonialism.

In the twentieth century a series of missionary conferences discussed missions in the setting of two world wars, the great depression, colonialism, the independence of the colonies, communism, and secularization. The Edinburgh Mission Conference of 1910, attended by three official Seventh-day Adventist delegates, brought mission studies to an unprecedented level of development.

Gustavo Gutiérrez (1928-) promoted liberation theology that made social action a priority in mission. Donald McGavran (1897-1990) launched the Church Growth Movement. As the century progressed, conciliar or mainline Protestants with a more liberal theological perspective, and evangelical Protestants, with their more conservative theological perspective, went in different directions in regard to the theology of missions. Roman Catholic understandings of mission were refocused by the Second Vatican Council (1962-65).

Evangelical Protestants gathered for a series of major mission conferences starting in 1974. The Lausanne I Congress on World Evangelization of 1974 met in Lausanne, Switzerland, under the theme "Let the Earth Hear His Voice." Billy Graham (1918-2018) and John Stott (1921-2011) were the main organizers and the conference issued the Lausanne Covenant. This document has endured as a well-balanced theological consensus of Evangelical missiology. The Lausanne II Congress on World Evangelization of 1989 met in Manila, Philippines, with the theme "Proclaim Christ until He Comes: Calling the Whole Church to Take the Whole Gospel to the Whole World." The Lausanne III Congress on World Evangelization of 2010 met in Cape Town, South Africa, and issued The Cape Town Commitment. The archives of the Lausanne conferences are a rich resource (www.lausanne.org).

Another milestone was the Edinburgh Mission Conference of 2010, which was a centennial celebration of the 1910 Edinburgh Conference. As at the 1910 conference, three Adventists were again sent as official delegates in 2010. Like the Lausanne conferences, the Edinburgh conferences (1910 and 2010) issued major missiological documents (www.edinburgh2010.org).

Topics that have occupied missiological reflection in recent decades include the continued challenges of social change and instability, the resurgence of traditional cultures and traditional religions, the challenge of self-identified Christians who are spiritually inactive, women's issues, children's issues, human rights and abuses, globalization, environmental stewardship, religious pluralism, ethical relativism, interreligious dialogue, engagement with Western culture, secularization, postmodernism, the decline of Christianity in parts of the West, the relationship of evangelism and social action, the Kingdom of God and mission, spiritual powers and mission, insider movements and other strategies for specific religious groups. Many excellent works on the theology of mission have been published recently. David Bosch's *Transforming Mission* (1991) is considered the single most influential work of the era.

As already noted, Adventists have not always made a theology of Adventist mission prominent in their scholarship and work. Like many other Protestants, Adventists have been people of action more than theological reflection about mission; however, there is a functional Adventist theology of mission that is discernable. Many of its features are compatible with other evangelical theologies of mission but there are points of uniqueness that will be addressed later.

The Bible as a Grand Narrative of God's Mission

A biblical theology of mission is not to be built on collections of "missionary texts" or "proof texts" but on the whole narrative of the Bible. The Bible is a "redemptive-historical whole," a "literary whole," and altogether a "missional phenomenon" which must be studied to discern the grand narrative or big story of mission (Goheen 2014:37). The Bible should be read using mission as a hermeneutical key to discern the missional character of every passage and then placing it within the big story of God's mission. Just as Bible students seek to discern aspects of God's character or of salvation in a particular text, they should seek to discern aspects of God's mission in all of Scripture.

Adventists speak of the Bible's metanarrative of mission as the "Great Controversy" that has several main movements: (1) God and his cosmos once existed in perfect harmony; (2) sin and rebellion were introduced by Lucifer, who was expelled with his supporting angels from God's presence; (3) Earth and humankind were created sinless; (4) Adam and Eve rebelled and brought suffering and death upon themselves and the whole earthly creation; (5) the Triune God embarked on a comprehensive mission, centered in the work of Jesus Christ, to restore humans, the Earth, and the whole universe to the original perfect state; (6) Satan, sin, and sinners are to be eliminated; (7) perfect harmony is to be restored.

The Bible can be divided into three major sections (Glasser et al. 2003:29-30) that show God pursuing his mission for all humanity in different ways. In the first section, starting in Eden and ending at Babel (Gen 1-11), God works through faithful followers who do not belong to a specific ethnic people group. The second section (Gen 12-Acts 1) sees God selecting Abram and his descendants as a particular ethnic group through whom He will work. In the third section (Acts 2-Rev 22) God works through his church, which is made up of all people groups. The Bible concludes with a prophecy of the eschatological consummation of God's mission.

The Bible's grand metanarrative of mission, in summary, shows God working on a comprehensive project to restore his Earth and his whole cosmos to its original, perfect state. The narratives of the Bible, from Genesis to Revelation, describe aspects of God's cosmic mission project. The overall theme is that the sovereign, gracious, loving Triune God initiated his mission and he will bring it to full completion.

Figure 2.1 shows one outline of the main acts in the grand narrative of God's mission presented in Scripture. Other outlines could be made with equal validity. The discussion of the grand narrative necessarily abbreviates some lengthy time periods, especially of the OT era.

Figure 2.1
Outline of the Grand Narrative of God's Mission

Prelude: Cosmic Perfection Blemished
Act 1: Creation and Fall
Act 2: Patriarchs, Flood, and Babel
Act 3: Call of Abraham and Israel
Act 4: Exodus and Nationhood
Act 5: Exile and Return
Intertestamental Period
Act 6: Jesus the Messiah
Act 7: The Church
Act 8: Special End Time Message
Act 9: Consummation of the Kingdom
Postlude: Cosmic Perfection Restored

Mission in the Old Testament

Prelude: Cosmic Perfection Blemished

Although the biblical narrative is primarily about humans on planet Earth, God's mission is presented in the Bible as having cosmic dimensions. There was a time of complete harmony when no sinful thought or act blemished the cosmos; however, Lucifer's mysterious rebellion introduced evil to the universe. God's first missional act was to separate the loyal angels from the rebellious angels. (See Ezek 28; Isa 14; White PP:33-43.)

Lucifer's rebellion raised the possibility that the humans whom God was planning to create with free choice would be in jeopardy. Before Creation a covenant was made within the Trinity that Jesus would be the Savior of humanity if humans sinned. Jesus Christ "indeed was foreordained before the foundation of the world, but was manifest in these last times for you" (1 Pet 1:20). God "chose us in Him before the foundation of the world, that we should be holy and without blame before Him in love" (Eph 1:4; see Rev 13:8).

God's mission for rebellious humanity was not like the reactive, panicked response of a parent caught off guard.

> The Father consulted His Son in regard to ... [creating] man to inhabit the earth. He would place man upon probation to test his loyalty before he could be rendered eternally secure. If he endured the test ..., he should eventually be equal with the angels.... he did not see fit to place them beyond the power of disobedience. (White SR:19)

The salvation of the human race has ever been the object of the councils of heaven. The covenant of mercy was made before the foundation of the world. It has existed from all eternity, and is called the everlasting covenant. (White 1901. Signs of the Times, June 12, 7)

Act 1: Creation and Fall

Creating humanity was the crowning act of God's creation. God's reigning authority embraced Adam and Eve and all of his earthly creation; however, the Tree of the Knowledge of Good and Evil gave them freedom to obey or disobey. Sadly, they disobeyed and withdrew themselves and all of the creation from God's protective reign. Satan, the deceiver, thus became the temporary, partial master of humanity and the Earth.

God's Edenic mission initiative started by going in search of Adam and Eve and demanding an accounting for their actions (Gen 3:9-13). They did not search for him but he searched for them. Then came God's curses upon the serpent and the ground and a description of the consequences of sin for Adam and Eve (14-19). In the middle of this fearful passage comes the *protoevangelion*, the first Gospel promise, of the destruction of Satan and sin by the Seed of the woman. "And I will put enmity between you and the woman, And between your seed and her Seed; He shall bruise your head, And you shall bruise His heel" (15).

Then God gave them skins of animals to wear and drove them out of the Garden to deny them access to the Tree of Life, which would have perpetuated their sinfulness for eternity (3:21-24). The skins given to Adam and Eve and the sacrifices by Abel (4:4) were the first stages of a system of atonement rituals pointing to Jesus. The altars of worship and sacrifice of the patriarchs (12:7; 31:54; 46:1) continued the Edenic system that Moses later developed more fully in the wilderness sanctuary. Jesus would become the atoning Lamb of God and the great center of God's mission. As they exited Paradise, Adam and Eve had lost more than they could imagine, but God had given humanity its first fresh start and the promise of redemption. God's magnificent mission was underway.

Act 2: Patriarchs, Flood, and Babel

God's mission continued as the human family grew and spread, even though the details are not as abundant as in later parts of the Bible. Hebrews 11 speaks of the godly witness of the patriarchs Abel, Enoch, and Noah. They and the other faithful pre-Flood patriarchs were God's missionaries. Sadly, the story from Genesis 3 to 11 is "an escalating crescendo of human sin alongside repeated marks of God's grace" (Wright 2006:195).

The Flood was a missional act of God that destroyed the irreversibly rebellious majority of humanity and preserved a faithful remnant to continue the human race (6:5-8). The Flood brought judgment for this second collective apostasy and God's covenant with Noah (9:17) marks a second fresh start.

The Table of Nations (Gen 10) reveals God's missional intention for all nations. The list of nations includes the ancestors of those who would become Israel's worst enemies and might have been completely excluded from the list, except that they were included in God's mission for all humanity.

The third collective apostasy took place at the Tower of Babel (Gen 11) when humanity plotted to make a united conspiracy to defy God. God had commanded Noah and his sons to "fill the earth" (9:1) and they did do some "spreading" or "scattering" (9:19; 10:18, 32); however, the migration seems to have stopped at the plain of Shinar (11:2). At Shinar they conspired to build a "tower that reaches to the heavens" for two reasons. First, "so that we may make a name for ourselves;" and second, so that they would not be "scattered over the face of the whole earth" (3-4). The first goal indicated arrogance and contempt for God and the second a resistance to God's purpose for humanity to multiply, migrate, and fill the earth. God's missional response was to confuse their single language, break up their building project, and scatter them to the whole earth (5-8) to prevent a unified conspiracy.

> There is no basis for the "simplistic view that ethnic pluralism is merely God's judgment on human sinfulness."

There is no basis for the "simplistic view that ethnic pluralism is merely God's judgment on human sinfulness" starting at Babel (Glasser et al. 2003:52). Had post-Flood humanity migrated and multiplied as God commanded, they would have developed diverse cultures as they lived in varied environments. God accelerated the normal linguistic and cultural change that would have occurred at a slower rate had they followed his plan. One of the lessons of Babel is that cultural diversity is a potential safeguard of spiritual purity.

The story of Babel does not have a happy ending because kinfolk fought and migrated away from each other. This third apostasy seems to bring humanity to a complete dead end. In "Genesis 1-11 we see the great creative mission of God being constantly thwarted and spoiled in ways that affect not just human well-being but the whole cosmos" (Wright 2006:199). There is a limit to God's grace for particular peoples who are resolutely rebellious. What could God do next in his cosmic mission project?

Act 3: Call of Abraham and Israel

The LORD had said to Abram, "Go from your country, your people, and your father's household to the land I will show you. I will make you into a great nation, and I will bless you; I will make your name great, and you will be a blessing. I will bless those who bless you, and whoever curses you I will curse; and all peoples on earth will be blessed through you." So Abram went, as the Lord had told him. (Gen 12:1-4)

God's call to Abram was his missional response to humanity's third great apostasy at Babel, with its chaos and confusion. Until that time, God had worked for all of humanity through a series of faithful patriarchs like those named in Hebrews 11. With Abram, God chose a special people whose generations would be his mission agents for all of humankind. God's interactions with Israel account for most of the rest of the OT, but his missional intentions for all of humanity are clear.

In Genesis 12 the reader stands "at one of the most important places in a missiological reading of the Bible" (Wright 2006:199). Paul spoke of God's call of Abram as the "gospel in advance" (Gal 3:8). Abram's call has been called the Great Commission of the OT.

Christopher Wright notes that God's call had two imperatives: "Go" and "Be a blessing" (or "you will be a blessing") (2006:201). Abram left Ur to serve as a cross-cultural missionary among peoples he did not know. God's call to Abram involved his gracious offer to enter into a covenant with Abram that was later fully explained and ratified. That covenant had several features:

1. "Through your offspring [Seed] all nations on earth will be blessed" (see Gen 26:4). Both Peter (Acts 3:25) and Paul (Gal 3:16) identified the "Seed" of Abraham as Jesus Christ. Abram was the father of the nation of Israel through whom Jesus the Messiah would come to bless all peoples. Humanity has received no greater blessing than the Messiah.

2. Abram's descendants would have a homeland. Israel, Jerusalem, and the Temple would be the missional center of the earth to which the nations would come to learn of God.

3. God would have a special righteous love for Israel that would be reflected through them to all the nations. All peoples would be either blessed or cursed depending on their relationship with Abraham, his descendants, and his Seed. The work of Jesus Christ is the very heart of God's mission to humanity and the eternal destiny of all people would depend upon their relationship to him (see Acts 4:12).

4. Circumcision would be a constant, visible sign and reminder of Israel's covenant with God.

Abraham's life as a cross-cultural missionary provides a realistic model for contemporary missionaries. He made mistakes, like saying his wife Sarah was his sister; however, he obeyed God's calling and established worship of the true God wherever he went. He interceded directly with God for the pagan people of Sodom. He was open to unexpected encounters with godly people like Melchizedek who were not from within his own spiritual line. Abraham's great-grandson, Joseph, was a highly effective cross-cultural missionary about whom no mistakes are recorded in Scripture.

Act 4: Exodus and Nationhood

"Now there arose a new king over Egypt, who did not know Joseph" (Exod 1:8). God's mission plan for the people of Israel seemed thwarted as they languished in Egyptian bondage, but God did not abandon his special people

> God rescued Israel from bondage to relieve their suffering, but even more significantly to continue his mission to all humanity.

or his mission for humanity. God rescued Israel from bondage to relieve their suffering, but even more significantly to continue his mission to all humanity.

Moses, leader of the exodus, was a cross-cultural missionary. Besides leading his own Israelite people, he led a great multi-cultural, "mixed multitude" (Exod 12:38) that joined the migration. The mixed multitude brought with them pagan practices and beliefs that Moses and the other leaders had to confront. The sanctuary system was an illustrated teaching device to lead both Israelites and non-Israelites to worship the one true God in the right way. The OT sanctuary illustrates the value of practical learning methods for cross-cultural missions.

Before giving his Law on Sinai, God said to Israel, "Although the whole earth is mine, you will be for me a kingdom of priests and a holy nation" (Exod 19:4-6). Peter used the same designation for the church (1 Pet 2:9). Israel "is not a kingdom *with* priests, but the nation itself is a kingdom *of* priests. The role of priest is that of mediation; thus Israel mediates between God and the nations" (Ott and Strauss 2010:9) through the sanctuary system.

The overall method to be used in God's mission by the nation of Israel was described in Deuteronomy 26:19, "He has declared that he will set you in praise, fame and honor high above all the nations he has made and that you will be a people holy to the Lord your God, as he promised." The community would be a highly attractive model of good living based on God's laws. When aliens interacted with or lived among the Israelites, they would be treated with the same moral-ethical laws as the Israelites (Num 9:14; Deut 14:29). The alien would be taught "to fear the Lord your God and follow all of the words of the law" (Deut 31:12). Through this magnetic or centripetal style of mission, Israel was to become a great center of learning about God and how to worship him, first in the wilderness sanctuary and later in the Jerusalem temple.

When Solomon dedicated the temple, he asked God to "do whatever the foreigner asks of you, so that all the peoples of the earth may know your name and fear you, as do your own people Israel, and may [all] know that this house I have built bears your Name" (1 Kgs 8:41). Two prominent examples illustrate the response of Gentiles to the attraction of Israel's worship and lifestyle. The Queen of Sheba came with gifts to visit King Solomon, learned about God, and witnessed Solomon's reputed wisdom (1 Kgs 10). Captain Naaman came to be healed of leprosy and to worship God (2 Kgs 5).

At Sinai, God expanded and contextualized the Abrahamic covenant. The Ten Commandments defined a good relationship with God (1-4) and humanity (5-10) in a way that would give God exclusive allegiance and give Israel spiritual purity and missional effectiveness among the nations. The missional value of the weekly Sabbath can hardly be overstated—both for ancient Israel and today. Tragically, Israel was often guilty of multiple allegiances, to God and to pagan deities. The temple itself was often corrupted with pagan worship and the Sabbath was broken (see Ezek 8).

The OT prophets were part of God's mission to and through Israel. They were God's forth-tellers who spoke, wrote, or role-played God's messages. When true prophets made predications, they came to pass (Deut 18:21-22), and thus, they strengthened God's mission. The prophets called the Hebrews to high moral, ethical, and spiritual living based on God's Law and vigorously condemned sin among both commoners and rulers (see Ps 51).

David, as king, prophet, musician, and poet of Israel (Acts 2:30) also emphasized the "universal dimensions of God's mission. George Peters found over 175 references in the Psalms to the world, the nations, peoples, and all the earth. Some were in the context of Israelites bringing the hope of salvation to them" (Glasser et al. 2003:111).

Elijah challenged Baalism, with its worship of the cycles of nature, within Israel and staged the dramatic confrontation at Carmel (1 Kgs 17-18).

The prophets constantly reminded Israel and Judah that their election was not for privilege but for mission. That was the message of Jonah. In spite of Jonah's failings,

> Jonah is considered the great missionary book of the Old Testament. Though numerous Old Testament prophets were given messages for the nations—usually of judgment—we have with Jonah ... a prophet ... explicitly sent geographically to a Gentile nation as God's messenger. (Ott and Strauss 2010:19)

In spite of his missionary work in Nineveh, Jonah remains an ambivalent missionary model. Jonah's actions at the end of the story (4:1-3) suggest he did not truly share God's desire to show mercy and compassion to a depraved city, even though its inhabitants repented. Jonah had a message challenging exclusivism among the chosen people, but he himself may not have learned the lesson. The book is silent about what happened in Nineveh after God's judgement was averted.

Act 5: Exile and Return

Israel's consumer mentality towards God's blessings, their repeated lapses into polytheism, and their loss of mission vision led God to send his chosen people into the Babylonian Exile (605-539 BC). God's intention was to reform Israel and re-focus their mission vision. They were to multiply as a people who would continue serving God's mission and they were to work for the shalom, or wholistic well-being of their captors. Said Jeremiah, "Increase in number there; do not decrease. Also, seek the peace and prosperity of the city to which I have carried you into exile. Pray to the Lord for it, because if it prospers, you too will prosper" (Jer 29:6-7). Daniel and his three friends and Esther and Mordecai were exemplary missionaries who worked for the peace and prosperity of their captors.

At the end of the Exile, 42,360 captives returned to Jerusalem with Ezra and Nehemiah (Ezra 2:64; Neh 7:66) starting in 538 BC. The returnees became what Glasser calls God's "right hand" in mission, while those who remained behind in Babylon and became part of the Jewish Diaspora were God's "left hand" (Glasser et al. 2003:131). He means that though the returnees were God's main instruments for mission, the unknown number who remained in Babylon were also instruments God used.

Haggai (c. 520), Zechariah (c. 518), and Malachi (c. 425) ministered to the returnees in the last century recorded in the OT canon. The obstacles to God's mission were both internal and external as the Israelites worked on rebuilding the temple and the walls of Jerusalem. Haggai and Zachariah were prophets who worked alongside the people to rebuild the Temple (Ezra 5:1-2). Their manual labor is a model for contemporary missionaries involved in wholistic mission work that sometimes does not seem very spiritual. The continuous opposition of the troublesome Samaritans is reminiscent of the opposition faced by some contemporary missionaries.

The Temple and the walls of Jerusalem were rebuilt, but still the Messianic Kingdom had not come and Malachi ministered to a discouraged and backslidden people. Daniel's 70 week/490 year prophecy (9:24-27) revealed that the Messiah's coming was well into the future, but it is not clear how many Jews knew and understood that prophecy. Malachi ends the OT with an eschatological prophecy about the great day of the Lord, when the "Sun of Righteousness shall arise with healing in his wings." Israel must remember the Law of Moses. Elijah the prophet would come to unite the genders and generations in God's continuing mission (Mal 4:1-6).

Old Testament Mission Themes

Several major mission themes can be seen in the OT.

1. Because God created all nations, his rightful dominion, reign, and glory extend over all nations and he deserves their worship.

For dominion belongs to the Lord and he rules over the nations. (Ps 22:28)

God reigns over the nations; God is seated on his holy throne. (Ps 47:8)

Rise up, O God, judge the earth, for all the nations are your inheritance. (Ps 82:8)

2. The nations do not all worship and glorify God, but he intends to bring them back to a good relationship with himself as his worshipful creatures.

Many nations will come and say, "Come, let us go up to the mountain of the Lord, to the temple of the God of Jacob. He will teach us his ways, so that we may walk in his paths." The law will go out from Zion, the word of the Lord from Jerusalem." (Micah 4:2)

For the earth will be filled with the knowledge of the glory of the Lord as the waters cover the sea. (Hab 2:14)

3. God wants to use Israel and even some Gentiles as his agents to return the nations to himself.

May God be gracious to us and bless us and make his face shine on us—so that your ways may be known on earth, your salvation among all nations. (Ps 67:1-2)

Give praise to the Lord, proclaim his name; make known among the nations what he has done. (Ps 105:1)

Sing the praises of the Lord, enthroned in Zion; proclaim among the nations what he has done. (Ps 9:11)

In that day there will be a highway from Egypt to Assyria. The Assyrians will go to Egypt and the Egyptians to Assyria. The Egyptians and Assyrians will worship together. In that day Israel will be the third, along with Egypt and Assyria, a blessing on the earth. The Lord Almighty will bless them, saying, "Blessed be Egypt my people, Assyria my handiwork, and Israel my inheritance." (Isa 19:23-25)

4. God's mission centers around the Seed of Abraham, the Servant of Yahweh.

Here is my servant, whom I uphold, my chosen one in whom I delight; I will put my Spirit on him, and he will bring justice to the nations. (Isa 42:1)

It is too small a thing for you to be my servant to restore the tribes of Jacob and bring back those of Israel I have kept. I will also make you a light for the Gentiles, that my salvation may reach to the ends of the earth. (Isa 49:6)

5. God's mission has a strong eschatological focus.

All the ends of the earth will remember and turn to the Lord, and all the families of the nations will bow down before him, for dominion belongs to the Lord and he rules over the nations. (Ps 22:27-28)

And afterward, I will pour out my Spirit on all people. Your sons and daughters will prophesy, your old men will dream dreams, your young men will see visions. (Joel 2:28)

This is what the Lord Almighty says: "Many peoples and the inhabitants of many cities will yet come, and the inhabitants of one city will go to another and say, 'Let us go at once to entreat the Lord and seek the Lord Almighty. I myself am going.' And many peoples and powerful nations will come to Jerusalem to seek the Lord Almighty and to entreat him." This is what the Lord Almighty says: "In those days ten people from all languages and nations will take firm hold of one Jew by the hem of his robe and say, 'Let us go with you, because we have heard that God is with you.'" (Zech 8:19-23)

6. Although Israel was called to be a "kingdom of priests and a holy nation" (Exod 19:6) and "my servant, whom I uphold, my chosen one in whom I delight" (Isa 42:1), Israel did not fulfill its God-given missional role. God laments that his servant, Israel, is blind and deaf.

Who is blind but my servant, and deaf like the messenger I send? Who is blind like the one in covenant with me, blind like the servant of the Lord? You have seen many things, but you pay no attention; your ears are open, but you do not listen. (Isa 42:19-20)

A Summary of Mission in the Old Testament

Adventist theology, with its unifying great controversy theme, sees substantial continuity between the Old and New Testaments. The sanctuary system, with its blending of law and grace, foreshadows the atoning work of Jesus at Calvary, which is at the center of the Triune God's mission. Thus, God's missional intention for the nations embraces both Testaments. However, the missional style or methodology of the OT is somewhat different from that of the NT. "The Old Testament was centered on the temple, the priest, the altar, the sacrifice, and the gathered community," or the *kahal* (Tennent 2010:95). The Christian church (*ekklesia*) was a community of house churches empowered by God the Spirit to "go out" from Jerusalem to Judea, Samaria, and all the world (Acts 1:8).

The NT "going out" style, crossing geographic, linguistic, cultural, and religious boundaries to evangelize Gentiles is rarely seen in the OT. There were exceptional individuals, like Abraham, Joseph, Daniel, and Jonah who "went out" in different ways, but that method was not the dominant one.

Israel was to relate to the nations (1) *historically* in terms of incorporation, that is, receiving Gentiles into the community, and (2) *eschatologically* in terms of ingathering in the last days.... Israel was never denounced by the prophets for failing to go to the nations. (Ott and Strauss 2010:22)

Mission in the OT was universal in scope, but mediated through a particular ethnic group of covenant people—Israel (Goheen 2014:48). However, Israel often failed to live the kind of holy lives that would attract the nations to Jerusalem.

Two words clarify the difference between mission in the two Testaments. The primary methodology of the OT was "centripetal," attracting the nations to the center of Israel, the temple, and Zion. In the NT, as will be seen, the "centrifu-gal" movement, going outward from the center of the church, was emphasized. However, mission in the NT was also centripetal. The local congregation went out and attracted converts to come into the fellowship of believers. Instead of attracting Gentiles to Jerusalem to be incorporated into ethnic Israel, believ-ers were to attract non-believers of every ethnicity into the body of Christ, the church. Paul referred to the multi-ethnic composition of the church as a mys-tery. "This mystery is that through the Gospel the Gentiles are heirs together with Israel, members together of one body, and sharers together in the promise in Christ Jesus" (Eph 3:6). Paul and his colleagues went out to plant churches which became hubs for both centrifugal and centripetal mission.

Mission in the Intertestamental Period

The mission of God did not cease during the intertestamental period of four centuries between Malachi (c. 425 BC) and the Messiah, even though there were no canonical prophets. "God was, is, and always will be in control of history" (Glasser et al. 2003:129). "But like the stars in the vast circuit of their appointed path, God's purposes know no haste and no delay" (White DA:32). Thus, God was at work as the time of the First Advent approached.

A succession of empires ruled Palestine, bringing great turmoil and change to Judaism.

During this period Israel developed from a small city-state of agrarian orientation to an urbanized, populous people.... The sequence of political upheavals they experienced, particularly their encounter with Greek thought and culture, made a massive impact on their religious consciousness. Even so, many Jews of the Diaspora were caught up in a growing movement to convert the peoples of the Gentile world to Judaism. The stage was now set: 'the fullness of time' had come. God sent forth his Son (Gal 4:4). (Glasser et al. 2003:163)

Population numbers in antiquity are only estimates. However, the estimates suggest a significant growth of Judaism during the intertestamental period that came from both Jewish births and Gentile conversions.

The world population in 400 BC (Malachi's time) is estimated at 162 million. When Jesus was born the world population had grown to about 225 million, with an estimated 45 million in the Roman Empire (*Wikipedia* 2016).

Ezra reported that 42,360 Jews returned to Palestine in 457 BC (Ezra 2:64) but the number of Jews who remained in Babylon is unknown. At the end of the second century Maccabean Wars the Jewish population was about 180,000. By the time of Christ, there were an estimated 4 to 4.5 million Jews in the Roman Mediterranean (Blauw 1974:57). The Jewish birthrate is unknown but if the Jewish population had grown to as much as 4 million when Christ was born, there must have been some "intensive proselytizing activity" among Gentiles in the whole Mediterranean area (Glasser et al. 2003:129). Jesus referred to aggressive proselytism across "land and sea" (Matt 23:15).

Diaspora Jewish religious life was centered in the synagogue and the study of the Torah. The Greek Septuagint (LXX) gave those who did not know Hebrew access to the OT. The Hebrew faith was attractive to Gentiles because of its high moral-ethical standards, which were visibly superior to practices of the pagan mystery religions. The Diaspora made Judaism less of a national or ethnic religion for Jews only and more of a universal faith open to Gentiles.

Gentile "inquirers" who were attracted to Judaism faced the rites of baptism and circumcision, which taken together, meant "being born again." Those who submitted to both circumcision and baptism became full proselytes and members of the community. Those who declined circumcision but accepted baptism became "worshippers" or "God-fearers," who were associate members of the community. Jewish synagogues, with both Jewish-born and converted Gentile members, became the hubs from which the first Christian churches would grow.

> Apostolic Christian mission was indebted to the proselyting work of intertestamental Judaism.

Apostolic Christian mission was indebted to the proselyting work of intertestamental Judaism for several reasons: (1) The general influences of Judaism were felt in most of the Roman Empire; (2) almost every town had a synagogue where Yahweh was worshipped; (3) the OT and other materials were widely available; (4) synagogue members worshipped on Sabbath and were taught ethical-moral control of their personal lives; (5) in a polytheistic world, an impressive argument was made by Judaism for monotheism and a divine cosmic plan; (6) adherents were taught that sharing their religious convictions was a duty (Glasser et al. 2003:175).

Intertestamental Jewish proselytism did not prepare every convert to accept the Messiah. Jesus referred to Jewish proselytism in very negative terms when he said "Woe to you, scribes and Pharisees, hypocrites! For you travel land and sea to win one proselyte, and when he is won, you make him twice as much a son of hell as yourselves" (Matt 23:15). However, intertestamental Judaism provided a valuable groundwork that God could use to attract spiritually receptive people to accept the Messiah and later in his mission through the NT church.

Chapter

The Bible as a Grand Narrative of God's Mission: New Testament

~•~

Mission in the New Testament

Act 6: Jesus the Messiah

The mission of God that commenced at the Fall (Gen 3:15) and functioned in different ways during the OT and intertestamental periods reached its center-point in the person, teachings, and works of Jesus Christ. The incarnated Jesus of Nazareth is the greatest missionary of the Bible. His work laid the foundation for the missionaries of the early church and ultimately for today's church. The discussion of Jesus' own missionary work and teaching about mission is based on a selection of exemplar texts.

Jesus, the Missionary in Action

Before he went to the cross to do the work of atonement, Jesus was a missionary who worked with a missionary team, on behalf of God's mission to humanity.

> Jesus went through all the towns and villages, teaching in their synagogues, proclaiming the good news of the Kingdom and healing every disease and sickness. When he saw the crowds, he had compassion on them, because they were harassed and helpless, like sheep without a shepherd. Then he said to his disciples, "The harvest is plentiful but the workers are few. Ask the Lord of the harvest, therefore, to send out workers into his harvest field." (Matt 9:35-38)

Several patterns of missionary work emerge from this brief but potent text:
- Jesus felt deep compassion for people lost in the helplessness of sin. His work was driven by this compassion.
- Jesus went to where the people were—towns, villages, sick rooms, synagogues, seaside, and wherever. Besides going to their physical locations, he went to their cultural, social, spiritual, and emotional locations. He was fully present with people as "Immanuel, … God with us" (Matt 1:23).

- Jesus preached the good news of the Kingdom that "the Kingdom of God has come near" (Mark 1:15). The life he called people to live was made possible by what God had already done. Receptive souls felt uplifted by his teaching.
- Jesus was a wholistic missionary, uniting spiritual, emotional, and physical healing in his ministering.
- Jesus focused much attention on people who were marginalized for various reasons, including lepers, adulterers, thieves, poor people, sick people, and women, who were generally treated as second-class citizens.
- Jesus foresaw a great harvest, in spite of the daunting opposition he confronted.
- Jesus looked to the Father to supply the additional workers and resources needed for his mission.
- Jesus was very urgent about his work and wanted God to send more workers urgently.

Instructions for the First Mission Trip

In Matthew 10, Jesus sent the Twelve out on their first missionary journey without him. His instructions included the following, all of which are highly relevant today:

- The Twelve were to heal the sick and cast out demons (10:1). These "power ministries" would later become normative in the NT church.
- They were to plan their mission strategically, adapting their approaches for various people groups, like Israelites, Samaritans, and Gentiles (5). They were to adjust strategy to varying levels of spiritual receptivity (12-14).
- They were to use the very best diplomacy and wisdom to stay out of trouble with the authorities, for the sake of their mission (16).
- If prosecuted or imprisoned they were to depend on the Holy Spirit for the right words to speak (20).
- They were to assume that being Christ's disciples would cause them to receive the same opposition Jesus received (25).
- When suffering as missionaries, the Twelve were to feel constant assurance of God's care because he knew the smallest details of their situations (28-31).
- Being missionaries required them to be willing to surrender loved ones, family, and even life itself for the sake of Christ.
- The mission of the Twelve was actually the on-going mission of Jesus Christ and of God the Father (40).

The Mission Commission

Christianity is a missionary religion because of Christ's intention, from the start of his ministry, that his followers would continue his mission when he was gone. The Apostles, under the supervision and empowerment of God the Holy Spirit, were to continue the mission of God through the church until Jesus would return.

Before he ascended Jesus, gave special instructions for the continuation of his mission. Possibly the most repeated version of Christ's pre-ascension mission commission is the "Great Commission" recorded by Matthew. Sometimes Matthew's version is used as a slogan that is separated from instructions found in the other Gospels and in Acts. George W. Peters wisely suggests that we can best understand Christ's mission commission by studying it as a "composite commission" using all of the versions (1972:174).

> Then the eleven disciples went to Galilee, to the mountain where Jesus had told them to go. When they saw him, they worshiped him; but some doubted. Then Jesus came to them and said, "All authority in heaven and on earth has been given to me. Therefore go and make disciples of all nations, baptizing them in the name of the Father and of the Son and of the Holy Spirit, and teaching them to obey everything I have commanded you. And surely I am with you always, to the very end of the age." (Matt 28:16-20)

> Later Jesus appeared to the Eleven as they were eating; he rebuked them for their lack of faith and their stubborn refusal to believe those who had seen him after he had risen. He said to them, "Go into all the world and preach the Gospel to all creation. Whoever believes and is baptized will be saved, but whoever does not believe will be condemned. And these signs will accompany those who believe: In my name they will drive out demons; they will speak in new tongues; they will pick up snakes with their hands; and when they drink deadly poison, it will not hurt them at all; they will place their hands on sick people, and they will get well." (Mark 16:14-18)

> Then he opened their minds so they could understand the Scriptures. He told them, "This is what is written: The Messiah will suffer and rise from the dead on the third day, and repentance for the forgiveness of sins will be preached in his name to all nations, beginning at Jerusalem. You are witnesses of these things. I am going to send you what my Father has promised; but stay in the city until you have been clothed with power from on high." (Luke 24:45-49)

> But when the Helper comes, whom I shall send to you from the Father, the Spirit of truth who proceeds from the Father, he will testify of Me. And you also will bear witness, because you have been with Me from the beginning. (John 15:26-27)

> As You sent Me into the world, I also have sent them into the world. And for their sakes I sanctify Myself, that they also may be sanctified by the truth. I do not pray for these alone, but also for those who will believe in Me through their word; that they all may be one, as You, Father, are in Me, and I in You; that they also may be one in Us, that the world may believe that You sent Me. (John 17:18-21)

> Again Jesus said, "Peace be with you! As the Father has sent me, I am sending you." And with that he breathed on them and said, "Receive the Holy Spirit. If you forgive anyone's sins, their sins are forgiven; if you do not forgive them, they are not forgiven." (John 20:21-23)

Then they gathered around him and asked him, "Lord, are you at this time going to restore the kingdom to Israel?" He said to them: "It is not for you to know the times or dates the Father has set by his own authority. But you will receive power when the Holy Spirit comes on you; and you will be my witnesses in Jerusalem, and in all Judea and Samaria, and to the ends of the earth." (Acts 1:6-8)

Some of the points in the analysis that follows are direct and explicit and others are implied by Jesus' words. The missional activities seen in the composite mission commission were overlapped and intertwined in the ministries of Christ and his disciples. The analysis seeks a comprehensive view of Jesus' capstone instructions to his disciples.

The Foundation of Mission: Christ's Promises

Christ's promises provide the assurance that his mission will ultimately be victorious. Success in mission does not depend upon his followers whipping themselves up into a frenzy of enthusiasm. His commands or imperatives can be obeyed because he promises the means and power to fulfill them.

The Comprehensive Mission Imperative: Discipleship

The primary imperatives or commands of the composite commission are "make disciples" and "preach the Gospel." Of these two, "make disciples" is primary because it is the end result or goal of "preach the Gospel" and the other imperatives. Christ's very first invitations by the Sea of Galilea started the discipling process that brought all of the Twelve except Judas to the commissioning moment at the end of his earthly ministry. When Jesus ascended, he left behind the most important fruits of his multi-faceted labors who would continue his mission on earth—his disciples.

The second main imperative, "preach the Gospel," is the imperative for evangelization. Jesus was the model evangelist who proclaimed that the Kingdom had come in himself and his ministry (Mark 1:15). He preached to large crowds, taught small groups, and mentored individuals, demonstrating different modes of evangelism. His disciples were to follow his example.

The command to teach full obedience to Christ's teachings is closely linked with preaching and making disciples. Mission that follows Christ's model is very Christ-centered. The disciples recalled, repeated, and wrote his teachings in obedience to this command. Following Pentecost, the apostles emphasized teaching (Acts 2:42).

Baptizing was also an integral part of mission in Christ's model because it publicly symbolized the inner change of repentance and forgiveness. The commission did not indicate that baptism was to be a goal in and of itself or a single marker of success in mission. Rather, baptism was an important step in the process of discipleship that started before baptism and continued throughout life.

The imperative to "Go" is important because it describes missional intentionality. The disciples were not to expect missions to happen on auto-pilot. On the other hand, they were not to run off half-prepared in a flurry of zeal without wisdom, as the commands to wait, pray, prepare, and be filled with the Spirit demonstrate.

Figure 3.1
The Composite Mission Commission

	Matthew 28:16-20	Mark 16:14-16	Luke 24:45-49	John 20:21-23	Acts 1:6-8
Imperatives or Commands	Go, make disciples, teach obedience	Go, preach the Gospel	Wait for the Holy Spirit	Receive the Holy Spirit	Be my witnesses
Authority or Power	Jesus	Jesus' name	Word, Father, Son, Spirit	Father, Son, Spirit	Father, Son, Spirit
Recipients Scope	All nations	All the world, all creation	All nations, beginning in Jerusalem	Anyone, everyone	Jerusalem, Judea, Samaria, ends of earth
Time or Duration	Until the end of age				Until the Kingdom is restored
Task	Baptizing, teaching	Performing signs and wonders, preaching	Giving witness, proclaiming repentance and forgiveness	Teach forgiveness	Witnessing
Message	Christ's commands		Repentance and forgiveness	Forgiveness	Witness of Jesus
Response Sought	Obedience to Christ's commands	Belief, baptism	Repent and be forgiven	Accept forgiveness	
Significance or Gravity		Saved or condemned		Forgiveness or non-forgiveness	
Promises	I am with you always, to the very end	Signs will accompany believers	Repentance and forgiveness will be preached to all nations, you will be clothed with power	Will do greater works (14:12)	Holy Spirit will come upon you

The command to "be my witnesses" expresses a key element of Christian mission. The disciples were to tell what Jesus had done for themselves and others. Mission, in all of its forms, is made most effective by the personal witness of one who can say, "Once I was lost but now I am saved and this is the difference Christ has made for me." Christian witnessing is non-manipulate and non-coercive persuasion that draws its power from biblical truth and the spiritual gifts of the witnessing believer.

Undergirding all of the other imperatives was the command to wait for the infilling of the Holy Spirit. When Christ ascended, God the Holy Spirit became the member of the Trinity who would supervise and empower God's mission through the church until the Second Coming. The disciples needed the Spirit's infilling personally, and the church needed him corporately.

The Authority for Mission: The Triune God

The composite mission commission makes it clear that the Triune God provides the authority for mission. The disciples would not see the commission as a mere suggestion if they understood its authority. Many enemies would challenge the validity of mission without shaking the confidence of the disciples in their task because they worked under the authority of God.

The Recipients of Mission: All Humanity

All ethnic people groups, in every geographic location, on the entire earth were to receive the Gospel message. The expanding reach of mission was to be made strategically—from Jerusalem, to Judea and Samaria, and to the ends of the earth.

The Time Frame of Mission: Until the Second Coming

The disciples were not to speculate or make predictions about the time of Jesus' return. Their responsibility was to faithfully lead the church in mission until Jesus would return at the time set by the Father.

Integral to Mission: Confronting Suffering and Evil Powers

Various power ministries—exorcism, healing the sick, speaking in tongues, and other signs and wonders—were part of Christ's mission model. Both Jesus and his disciples used power ministries extensively in missions.

The Desired Response to Mission: Repentance and Forgiveness

Jesus did not commission or model a take-it-or-leave-it model of mission. He respected the freedom of individuals to resist and reject his message, but he used non-coercive persuasion to draw them to himself. The disciples were to seek a response of repentance and minister the forgiving grace of Jesus to their hearers.

The Significance of Mission: Eternal Destiny

Mark's Gospel highlights the high stakes involved in mission. Those who believe the Gospel and are baptized will be saved and those who ultimately refuse the invitation will be condemned. Eternal destinies are involved in Christian mission. "Salvation is found in no one else, for there is no other name under heaven given to humankind by which we must be saved" (Acts 4:12).

Act 7: The Church

The whole Christ event, from his birth to ministry to death to resurrection to ascension, was the centerpiece of God's mission. Jesus won a decisive victory over Satan and evil. His Kingdom, both as reign or authority and realm or territory, was secured. As Jesus ascended, it was time for the next major movement in God's mission—establishing his church.

The book of Acts and the Epistles are mission documents describing the missionary movement of the early church. They build on the OT and the Gospels to provide the foundation for the church's theology of mission and for principles that guide mission methods and strategies. The NT should not be seen as a detailed manual for church growth methods in every time and place because the context of mission in the first century was very different from today's context.

The book of Acts outlines the major movements of first-century mission, although numerous details are added in the Epistles.

Figure 3.2
Main Events in the Book of Acts

To Jerusalem	Commission and ascension	1:1-11
	Upper room	1:12-26
	Pentecost and earliest church formation	2:1-5:42
	Church leadership expansion, deacons	6:1-7
	Stephen's ministry and death	6:8-7:60
To Judea and Samaria	Persecution and scattering; Philip to Samaria; Ethiopian eunuch	8:1-40
	Conversion and call of Saul	9:1-31
To the ends of the earth	Peter and Cornelius; Gentile conversions; report to Jerusalem	9:32-11:18
	Antioch the new mission center; Barnabas and Saul sent	11:19-13:3
	First missionary journey	13:4-14:28
	Jerusalem Council	15:1-35
	Second missionary journey	15:36-18:22
	Third missionary journey	18:23-21:16
	Paul in Jerusalem and Caesarea	21:17-26:32
	Paul's trip to Rome	27:1-28:31

God the Holy Spirit, Pentecost, and Mission

When Jesus was about to ascend, his disciples asked: "Lord, will You at this time restore the Kingdom to Israel?" (Acts 1:6). His answer (1:7-8) had four elements: (1) There would be an interim, preliminary period before the Kingdom of God would be fully established; (2) the church would continue the work of Jesus ("you shall be my witnesses"); (3) the Holy Spirit would equip the church by giving it a foretaste of the full power of the Kingdom ("you shall receive power when the Holy Spirit has come upon you"); and (4) the church's witness would be "in Jerusalem, and in all Judea and Samaria, and to the end of the earth." When Jesus ascended the Holy Spirit was poured out and the church was launched on its global mission.

The story of the Jerusalem church of Acts 2 is like a "movie trailer" or "prime exhibit" in advance of what the Kingdom of God will be like when it is fully established (Goheen 2014:64). The community formed by the Spirit is a highly relational fellowship that shares material goods generously, enjoys table fellowship regularly, studies truth deeply, listens to the spoken word attentively, prays devoutly, and experiences signs and wonders regularly (Acts 2:42-47).

The "coming of the Holy Spirit at Pentecost marked the great new event in the sequence of God's mighty acts of redemption" (Glasser et al. 2003:261). At Pentecost, God the Holy Spirit assumed the role of presiding over God's mission until the Second Coming of Jesus and the consummation of all things. For the Christian this means that "you never witness or evangelize alone, because you are always accompanied by God the Evangelist, who speaks and works through you by the power of the Holy Spirit" (Tennent 2007:182).

> When we consider the many texts that refer to the work of the Holy-Spirit-in-Mission, we see that this Spirit is the primary agent of mission, and human beings are secondary. "The Spirit of truth," Jesus said, "will testify about me. And you also must testify" (John 15:26-27).... "Do not worry about what to say or how to say it. At that time you will be given what to say, for it will not be you speaking but the Spirit of your father speaking through you" (Matt. 10:19-20). (Glasser et al. 2003:263)

Spiritual Gifts and Mission

As the primary agent of mission, the Spirit spoke directly to human hearts but he also empowered believers to be God's primary human mission agents through the special outpouring at Pentecost and through spiritual gifts and ministry gifts. The dramatic tongues of fire outpouring in the Upper Room (Acts 2:2) was repeated in somewhat less dramatic ways on other occasions (10:44; 11:15); however, the less spectacular but no less empowering provision of spiritual gifts and ministry gifts became a permanent factor in God's mission.

Three passages speak of spiritual gifts (Rom 12:3-8; 1 Cor 12:1-11; Eph 4:1-16) and one passage of the fruit or virtues of the Spirit (Gal 5:22-23). Max Turner (1998:278-279) seems correct when he suggests that the fruit or virtues of the Spirit are best understood as being intertwined with spiritual gifts and ministry gifts for mission.

God the Holy Spirit gave spiritual virtues, spiritual gifts, and ministry gifts (1) for the equipping of believers, (2) for works of service, (3) to build up the body of Christ in the unity in faith, (4) to provide the knowledge of God and spiritual maturity, (5) so that the church would not be tricked by doctrinal error, (6) as they fulfill God's mission. Because these gifts are given to each believer as God wills, no one should feel proud of their role in the church or jealous of another's role.

Figure 3.3
Spiritual Gifts, Ministry Gifts, and Fruit of the Spirit

Romans 12:6-8	1 Corinthians 12:8-10, 28	Ephesians 4:11	Galatians 5:22-23
Prophecy, service, teaching, exhortation, giving, leading, mercy	Wisdom, knowledge, faith, healing, miracles, prophecy, distinguishing spirits, various tongues, interpreting tongues, apostles, prophets, teachers, miracles, healing, administration	Apostles, prophets, evangelists, pastors, teachers	Love, joy, peace, forbearance, kindness, goodness, faithfulness, gentleness, self-control

Spiritual gifts of different types gave believers Christ-like, non-coercive powers of attraction and persuasion. Individual believers with their specific gifts would make up the organically united body of Christ—the church. The church was a new kind of community with a mission to reach all peoples, everywhere, of every ethnicity. Unlike Israel, the church was composed of all ethnic groups. Although the early church did not enjoy unbroken peace and harmony, the degree of harmony they experienced in God's mission was unprecedented. As the church went out in centrifugal mission, its magnetic, centripetal attraction drew unbelievers into the fellowship of the body of Christ.

Quantity and Quality at Pentecost

Luke's account of Pentecost and the church in Jerusalem emphasizes the large numbers of converts and baptisms (Acts 2:41,47; 4:4; 5:14; 6:1,7). However, this emphasis should not be seen as a disregard for spiritual quality and mature discipleship. Neither should the conversions be attributed solely to the events of that amazing day. Many conversions at Pentecost were the delayed fruit of Christ's earlier ministry.

The many positive examples of spiritual maturity among the believers and the painful story of Ananias and Sapphira (5:1-11) show that spiritual quality and mature discipleship were priorities from the very beginning. Following the dramatic events of the day of Pentecost and the baptism of 3,000 souls, the community of believers was "continually devoting themselves to the apostles' teaching and to fellowship, to the breaking of bread and to prayer" (2:42). As the book of Acts continues, accounts of dramatic evangelistic meetings and large baptisms like those at Pentecost are less prominent than the teaching, fellowship, breaking bread, and prayer pattern of discipleship training.

Ananias and Sapphira

The painful story of Ananias and Sapphira is like a dark blot among the wonderful happenings that followed Pentecost (Acts 5:1-11). The inclusion of the story shows how seriously God views the stewardship of resources used in his mission. By withholding their pledged offerings, Ananias and Sapphira potentially withheld the good news of salvation from lost sinners. The story makes it clear that the early church was not populated by sinless members.

Peter and Cornelius: Two Conversions

The account of Acts 10-11 is the story of "two complementary conversions" (Flemming 2005:36). In this narrative, Peter experienced a "missiological conversion," or turning toward Christ's full mission, that made it possible for him to lead Cornelius to conversion to Christ.

Cornelius was neither a pagan, nor a full proselyte (who had submitted to circumcision and Jewish ritual laws), nor was he yet a believer in Jesus Christ. Before his conversion to Christ, "He and all his family were devout and God-fearing; he gave generously to those in need and prayed to God regularly" (Acts 10:2). In a sense, Cornelius was already converted to God, but his encounter with Peter led him to turn explicitly toward Jesus Christ.

Flemming places Cornelius in an early "bridge group" of Gentiles who accepted the Gospel before the great flood of Gentiles that converted later (2005:36). Cornelius represented Gentiles who were truly open to God, but who did not receive the Gospel because of Jewish Christian reluctance to share it with them. He was a cultural, religious middle man whose conversion pointed Peter and the predominantly Jewish church toward the Gentile world.

Peter's many-staged conversion to Jesus Christ as one of the Twelve needed to be followed by a conversion to Christ's mission to all peoples. In some respects, Peter's vision on the rooftop was as dramatic as Paul's vision at Damascus. Peter's rooftop vision convinced him that individuals in every people group could become followers of Jesus Christ while remaining members of their respective ethic, cultural groups (Acts 10:34-35). This is a deeper concept than simply that all people groups could be evangelized. When Cornelius became a Christian, he became a Gentile Christian, retaining his cultural identity. He received a new primary identity as a Christian and his Gentile identity became secondary. As a believer, he was a member of the body of Christ, the new people of God made up of all cultures, whose primary identity was as Christians. This narrative and others (like the Jerusalem Council) provide a theological foundation for contextualization.

Antioch and Ephesus: Decentralization and Diffusion

The book of Acts starts with a mostly mono-cultural church located in Jerusalem and ends with a multi-cultural church spread around the Roman Empire. The early expansion of mission beyond Jerusalem happened through spontaneous, Spirit-directed encounters, and as a response to persecution (Acts 8-10). The church's first intentional mission expansion toward the "ends of the earth" was initiated by the Antioch church and their sending of Paul and Barnabas (Acts 13:1-3). Antioch thus became a main mission hub and was later joined in that role by the church at Ephesus (Acts 18-19). With the development of new centers, the centrifugal movement of mission of the NT era became decentralized and diffused (Ott and Strauss 2010:28). Multiple centers organized, sent, and supported missionaries instead of only the Jerusalem church.

While the Jerusalem church was mostly Jewish, most members at Antioch and elsewhere were Gentiles living in a pagan community. How would converts from the Gentile culture, called "Christian" in Antioch (Acts 11:26) for the first time, be taught to live? Did they have to follow the cultural patterns of Jewish believers in Jerusalem?

The Jerusalem Council: The Gospel and Contextualization

The mass of Gentile conversions precipitated a theological and missiological crisis in the church. The Jerusalem church could not imagine being true Christians without circumcision and the other rites of Judaism, while the Gentile converts struggled with those requirements. Said in another way, the church

> Was the worship and obedience of God by an uncircumcised Gentile believer of equal value to God as that of a circumcised Jewish believer?

had to define the continuity and discontinuity between Judaism and Christianity. The worship of the one true God of the OT and the obedience of his Law remained unchanged. The issue was over the rituals and ceremonies associated with worshiping and obeying God. The meaning of worship and obedience was unquestioned, but could the forms or practices of worship and obedience change for different people groups? In other words, was the worship and obedience of God by an uncircumcised Gentile believer of equal value to God as that of a circumcised Jewish believer?

The Jerusalem Council inaugurated a new paradigm for handling inter-cultural theological disputes between groups of Christians and for cross-cultural missions. As the Council worked through the theological problem, there were four phases.

The Dissension Phase (Acts 15:1-5)

Did the conditions for becoming part of the messianic community include becoming "naturalized Jews" or "Jewish proselytes" through circumcision and obedience to all the Jewish laws? (Flemming 2005:44). Was circumcision a symbol for all time and all peoples of entering into an authentic relationship with God? The church disagreed strenuously.

The Discussion Phase (15:6-18)

The apostles and elders gathered from far and near for a full discussion. Peter reminded the group that God had chosen him to evangelize Gentiles. When Gentiles were converted the Holy Spirit came upon them, just as upon Jewish converts. Gentiles were saved by grace through faith, just like Jews. Then Paul and Barnabas spoke of the "signs and wonders God had done through them among the Gentiles" (15:12). James concluded the discussion by applying Amos 9:11-12 to the present situation. In James' presentation, "God's present activity among the Gentiles became a hermeneutical key for understanding the biblical text.... Amos, rightly interpreted, gives Scripture's grounding for the theological principle of salvation for the Gentiles by faith apart from circumcision" (Flemming 2005:46).

The Group Consensus Phase (15:19-29)

> It is my judgment, therefore, that we should not make it difficult for the Gentiles who are turning to God. Instead we should write to them, telling them to abstain from food polluted by idols, from sexual immorality, from the meat of strangled animals and from blood. For the law of Moses has been preached in every city from the earliest times and is read in the synagogues on every Sabbath. (Acts 15:19–21)

The consensus, articulated by James, had two main elements: First, the church should not make it needlessly difficult for Gentiles to become Christians by requiring them to do everything that Jewish Christians considered essential; second, both Jewish and Gentile Christians should abstain from certain things. The meaning of the required abstentions or prohibitions is the subject of lengthy discussion that is summarized below (see Schnabel 2004:1015-1020).

One interpretation is that part of the prohibition is universal and part is advisable for the sake of maintaining Gentile-Jewish harmony, though not universal. Thus, the decree against sexual immorality was universal, applying to all Christians, but the other decrees were not universally binding. Paul avoided giving offense to fellow believers over eating meat offered to idols, but did not see that as practicing idolatry for himself. Neither the laws of Kosher nor vegetarianism were enforced in the early church (see 1 Cor 8:13,25; Rom 14:6,21).

Another interpretation is that the decision contained three universal prohibitions, that stand in contrast to circumcision: (1) No idolatry ("food polluted by idols," "meat of strangled animals," and "sexual immorality" as part of pagan temple prostitution); (2) no general "sexual immorality," that might not be part of temple prostitution; and, (3) no murder ("blood") (Schnabel 2004:1017). All three prohibitions were thus understood to be part of the Decalogue, while circumcision was part of the ceremonial law that ended at the Cross.

Following the latter interpretation, the decision would mean that Christians could choose whether or not to be circumcised, but no Christian should be guilty of idolatry, immorality, or murder. Jewish and Gentile Christians could have an equally authentic walk with God, being saved by grace through faith, while practicing their shared faith in different cultural styles. Some matters of the Christian faith are eternal and universal, while others are open to contextualization within different cultures.

The Communication Phase (15:30-33)

The phase of full and open communication occurred as the decision was communicated to Antioch. The Council sent Silas and Judas Barsabbas as special envoys to accompany Paul and Barnabas to Antioch to lend credibility and support. The decision of the Council was articulated fully and "the people read it and were glad for its encouraging message" (Acts 15:31). This final step concludes a process and provides an enduring biblical model for handling intercultural conflict regarding the meaning and application of biblical principles.

Some important principles stand out in the story of the Jerusalem Council (Flemming 2005:48-53):

First, the Council met in response to issues raised by God's visible activity in human hearts and performed a task of theology under the Spirit's direction. When God works in unusual ways, the church must, as a matter of principle, be willing to be flexible.

Second, the process was guided by Scripture and constrained by the commitment to know God's truth in the matter. There was no compromise with eternal, universal principles in the flexibility shown by the Council.

Third, the community and its leadership, from James the brother of Jesus to lesser known leaders, performed their theological work and in the end reported that "it seemed good to the Holy Spirit and to us" (15:28). The leaders led with a combination of firmness and flexibility.

Fourth, the decision advanced God's mission, shaped and redefined the church community, and opened the door of missions to a vast Gentile population.

The Pauline Model of Missions

Next to Jesus Christ, the Apostle Paul is the leading missionary of the NT record. Both Jesus and Paul are cherished as models for contemporary missions. Jesus, the sinless One, modeled missionary service done in human frailty but without human sinfulness. Paul, a fellow sinner save by grace, demonstrated that through the power and wisdom of God, mistake-making Christians can be effective missionaries. Yet, "one should not try to perceive Paul as the master strategist whose methods are normative for the church for all time.... [Rather, Paul models] certain methodological principles from which he did not deviate" and which are valid for all times, peoples, and places (Glasser et al. 2003:294). The Pauline principles of mission include the following:

Conversion as the Basis of Mission

Paul's own dramatic conversion to Jesus Christ was the basis of his missionary service. This is not to suggest that every authentic conversion will be as visibly dramatic as Paul's. His complete reversal from being a persecutor of Christians to being a missionary for Jesus Christ required the drama of the Damascus road. Others turn to Jesus in their childhood or in gradual stages. One cannot effectively cross boundaries of faith, language, culture, and religion on behalf of Jesus without having a changed life that moves consistently and directly toward Christ.

Training as Essential for Mission

Even a dramatic conversion like Paul's did not fully prepare him to be a missionary. His training started under the guidance of Ananias and the community in Damascus (Acts 22:12ff). Paul's activities of the next few years are not all clear, but they included three years in Arabia and fifteen days in Jerusalem with Peter and James the brother of Jesus (Gal 1:17-18), followed by early work in Syria and Cilicia (21). During these early years of obscurity he witnessed in synagogues, studied the OT deeply, received mentoring and guidance from Christian leaders, and learned lessons about mission to the Gentile world. After being a trainee in mission Paul became a trainer and mentor of missionaries. The high quality of the missionary training Paul provided contributed significantly to the work of the early church.

Prayer as Essential for Mission

When Paul discussed God's will that all humans would be saved he started by saying "I urge, then, first of all, that petitions, prayers, intercession and thanksgiving be made for all people" (1 Tim 2:1). To the Ephesians he said, "I have not stopped giving thanks for you, remembering you in my prayers" (1:16). For Paul, prayer was a missiological necessity and method that went beyond his wishes for the well-being of his sisters and brothers in Christ. Prayer was needed to guide missionaries, overcome the powers of evil, and soften hard hearts.

Teamwork as Integral to Mission

Paul followed the rabbi-disciple model of the day, with a small cluster of younger colleagues who travelled and worked with him; however, he did not function as an eastern guru who embodied all knowledge. Rather, he built a missionary team with people like Barnabas, Silas, and Timothy, worked cooperatively with the sending church at Antioch, and established communities of fellowship where he worked. His missionary team included people of different cultures and professions, as this partial list shows: Barnabas was a Levite (Acts

4:36), Timothy was half-Jewish (16:1), Titus was Greek (Gal 2:3), Luke was a Gentile doctor (Col 4:14), Sosthenes was a former synagogue ruler (Acts 18:17), Gaius and Aristarchus were Macedonians (19:29), Tychicus and Trophimus were Asians (20:4), and there was Zenas the lawyer (Titus 3:13). Women featured significantly among Paul's associates. There were Phoebe (Rom 16:1), Priscilla (16:3), Lydia (Acts 16:14), and others (Rom 16:6, 12). Paul generously gave his team members credit for their joint labors with himself, even naming Sosthenes as a co-sender of an epistle (1 Cor 1:1). Paul modelled the unity-in-diversity that is so valuable for today's multi-cultural, twenty-first century missionary teams serving cross-culturally.

Theological Reflection and Contextualization as the Basis for Mission

Paul modeled doing the work of missions in a thoughtful, reflective way. As the most prolific writer of the NT, Paul wrote as he worked his way through the missiological challenges he faced. Much of his writing involved the task of bringing both Jews and Gentiles from many different cultural-religious groups to faith in Christ. The debates over circumcision and food offered to idols show the complexity of

> Paul held fiercely to core biblical principles but was utterly flexible on differing cultural expressions that were consistent with those biblical principles.

the mission task. Different issues arose from communities of believers in widely varying contexts and he worked through the issues theologically and contextually. Which elements of the developing church and its beliefs were absolute and universal and which could be culturally defined? He summarized his approach by saying "I have become all things to all people so that by all possible means I might save some" (1 Cor 9:22). He held fiercely to core biblical principles but was utterly flexible on differing cultural expressions that were consistent with those biblical principles.

Church Fellowship as Central to Mission

The formation of Christian communities was basic for Paul's methodology because it was part of his theology. Individual believers received spiritual gifts which were to be used within the body of Christ for the work of mission (1 Cor 12). Being a member of one of the house church clusters of the day was a normative part of being a believer in Jesus Christ.

Strategic Planning as Essential to Mission

Paul did not develop a complete strategic mission plan in the modern sense but he did work strategically. He sought places where Christ was not known so that his work would not duplicate the pioneering work of other missionaries (Rom 15:20). He planned and plotted his work geographically to expand into unevangelized people groups. He would make the first entry into a particular place, plant a church, and then move on when the church was self-sustaining and able to evangelize its area. When the church was firmly planted he considered that he had "fully preached the Gospel" (Rom 15:19) in that place. Sometimes he made return visits and wrote epistles to follow up his initial work. His approach reveals his confidence in the inherent power of the Gospel and in his Spirit-gifted missionary colleagues.

Suffering as Inevitable in Mission

Part of God's missionary call through Ananias to Paul was that "I will show him how much he must suffer for My name" (Acts 9:16). Paul later summarized the fulfillment of those words by reviewing his sufferings (2 Cor 11:23-33). To the Colossians he wrote, "I fill up in my flesh what is still lacking in regard to Christ's afflictions" (1:24). Paul did not mean that he supplemented Christ's redemptive suffering on the cross. Rather, he meant that his missionary work encountered suffering as a continuation of Christ's suffering as the greatest missionary. That missionary suffering would only end when God's mission had been fully completed.

Paul's suffering included several dimensions: (1) He suffered in the stressful conflict with evil powers; (2) he suffered in the general complexity and tension of crossing boundaries of culture and religion; (3) there was overt hostility from those who resisted or rejected his work; (4) the conflict among multicultural believers who became Christians from different backgrounds was a challenge; (5) there were the physical sufferings, like shipwrecks, beatings, and imprisonments which were significant but possibly less difficult to bear than the others. Near the end of his life he expressed the deepest satisfaction in his work for Christ, saying, "I have fought the good fight, I have finished the race, I have kept the faith" (2 Tim 4:7). However, his missionary career involved suffering all the way from Damascus to his martyrdom in Rome.

Mission After the Apostolic Church

God's mission continued after Apostolic times through the many eras of the church. However, faithful or unfaithful the church may have been, God's project of redemption never ceased. Major developments in the church's mission history are discussed later.

Act 8: A Special End Time Message

Seventh-day Adventists believe that God has called them to proclaim a special end-time message that prepares the world for the Second Coming of Jesus. That message is summarized by the three angels of Revelation 14. The next chapter discusses the Adventist theology of mission in more detail.

Act 9: Consummation of the Kingdom

At the end of sinful human history, the church of Christ is ready for its ultimate union with him because they have accepted the righteousness he provided on the Cross. Jesus returns as conquering king. The righteous dead are resurrected and they ascend with the righteous living to be with Christ. Christ destroys the united forces of evil and binds Satan alone on earth for 1,000 years. After the millennium, Satan's evil forces are resurrected and make war on the Lamb. God then destroys every evil being for eternity in the second death. He then recreates the heavens and earth which have been so damaged by sin and brings the New Jerusalem to Earth with its Tree of Life. (See Stefanovic 2009:551ff. for an ex-position of Rev 19-22.)

Postlude: Cosmic Perfection Restored

When the events described in the book of Revelation have been completed, God's mission for lost humanity will have been completed. God's cosmic Kingdom will be fully restored. God will continue to have a mission in the sense of superintending and sustaining his cosmos, but it will not be a salvific mission because there will be no one needing salvation from sin.

> The whole universe will have become witnesses to the nature and results of sin.... Never will evil again be manifest. Says the word of God: "Affliction shall not rise up the second time." Nahum 1:9. (White GC:504)

> The great controversy is ended. Sin and sinners are no more. The entire universe is clean. One pulse of harmony and gladness beats through the vast creation. From him who created all, flow life and light and gladness, throughout the realms of illimitable space. From the minutest atom to the greatest world, all things, animate and inanimate, in their unshadowed beauty and perfect joy, declare that God is love. (White GC:678)

Chapter

GOD, THE SOURCE OF MISSION

~•~

Introduction

The previous chapters presented a theology of mission in narrative form. This chapter uses a systematic theology approach to address important issues in a theology of mission.

The Justification of Mission

The idea that mission has to be justified may come as a shock to those who have lived and worked with the Great Commission ringing in their ears. However, the validity of Christian mission has been challenged in every age, starting with the NT. In Thessalonica, Paul and Silas faced a hostile mob that protested "These men who have caused trouble all over the world have now come here" (Acts 17:6). Through the centuries, the other world religions have strongly condemned efforts to convert their people to Christianity. Challenges have also arisen within the church about the validity and need for mission.

The contemporary challenges to the validity of mission have come from several interrelated perspectives (Ott and Strauss 2010:55-56).

1. Christian mission has been seen as a partner of Western colonialism and imperialism and thus needs to be questioned. This questioning was particularly strong in the mid-twentieth century as European colonies were becoming independent.

2. Missionaries are sometimes perceived as destroyers of culture because they advocate the change of traditional beliefs and practices that are unbiblical. Indeed, some missionaries have advocated the changes of cultural beliefs and practices that are not truly contrary to the Bible. But even when cultural changes have been clearly required by Scripture, some critics have condemned missions. This criticism frequently parallels the anti-colonial critique.

3. Religious pluralism asserts that every religion offers an equally valid spiritual pathway. In this view, Christian mission is arrogant and bigoted. Followers of other religions should be left alone in their chosen pathway. In the era of postmodernity, this critique finds strong traction.

4. Truth, morality, and ethics are seen as matters of personal and cultural perspective. The concept of universal truth based on the Bible is unacceptable. Postmodern thinking also favors this view.

5. The association of Christianity with war, violence, and genocide in the Crusades, Nazi Germany, Northern Ireland, Rwanda, the Balkans, and elsewhere is sometimes seen as an indication that Christianity has nothing good to offer.

6. Mission is sometimes seen as an advocate of extremist Christian fundamentalism, alongside other forms of religious fundamentalism, like Islamic and Hindu extremism.

7. The global spread of Christianity makes sending missionaries seem unnecessary. Christianity is already the largest world religion. Missionary service is expensive and sometimes unhealthy or dangerous.

The first response to these and other challenges is to repent in humility when and where they are true. The second response is to apply lessons learned from history to our own situations so that we do not repeat the same mistakes. After that, Christian mission can and must be defended in every appropriate way by correcting wrong information and sharing a more complete picture.

Through the decades, Christian mission has been the conduit for amazing humanitarian service around the world. However, the fact is that opposition to Christian mission is a permanent reality coming from the other world religions and from agnostic, atheistic, and secular/postmodern perspectives. The groups that condemn Christians missions have well-developed systems of thought and some have aggressive missions of their own. Furthermore, many of them provide commendable humanitarian services around the world. This means that the main justification for Christian mission is internal—within Christianity. Because the call to mission is received by believers within the church, its ultimate justification is a theological task based on the Scriptures. At the center of the Bible there is the Triune God and his mission to humanity.

> The justification of mission must start with the very person, plan, and character of God himself as revealed in the Scriptures. The Bible begins with God as the Creator of all that is, and all that He creates is good, because God himself is good. (Ott and Strauss 2010:55-56)

At the Fall of humanity, the Creator adopted a second role, that of Redeemer. This Creator-Redeemer embarked on a divine mission for humanity as a direct expression of God's character. In the Mosaic Law, God taught his people how they must relate to him in the first four commandments. God will not tolerate the worship of other gods, allow himself to be represented by images, or tolerate blasphemy, because he alone deserves worship. The last six commandments explain how his creatures should relate to each other to reflect his character (Exod 20). God's divine mission was centered in the life, teaching, and atoning work of God the Son. Upon his resurrection, Jesus invested his church with the responsibility to continue God's mission under the guidance of God the Holy Spirit. This brief overview shows that mission is not about missionaries, but about God. "For this reason Christian mission—insofar as it is in harmony with God's own mission—has universal legitimacy" (Ott and Strauss 2010:58).

Starting in the mid-twentieth century, the Latin phrase *missio Dei* (mission of God) has been used to name the concept that mission comes from the very character of God as revealed in the whole Bible. As valuable as the

> Mission comes from the very character of God.

Great Commission is for justifying mission, the *missio Dei* points to a deeper source in God's own character. The ultimate source of mission is neither in a particular group of missionaries, nor a denomination, a nation, an ethnic group, or an ideology. Missionaries can and do make mistakes and those mistakes must never be denied or ignored. But cross-cultural missionaries, like all of Christ's servants, are "jars of clay" (2 Cor 4:7) who carry the most precious treasure available to humanity, the Gospel of salvation.

A Trinitarian Theology of Mission

God's mission, the *missio Dei*, is shared jointly by the members of the Trinity. A general discussion of the Trinity is beyond the scope of this book (see Whidden, Moon, and Reeve 2002 for a full discussion). What will be discussed here is the role of the members of the Trinity in mission. The section about God the Holy Spirit (Pneumatology) will be longer than the others because the Holy Spirit is less understood than the others and because the Spirit has a special role in the era of the church.

The nature and character of God is the "generative center of our understanding of missions" (Tennent 2010:74). Mission exists because God exists and because God has particular character attributes. The attributes of God—like compassion, graciousness, loving faithfulness, mercy, and justice—comprise God's glory and holiness and make him the only valid subject of human worship. God's holiness is the foundation of the absolute, eternal, universal principles undergirding missions.

When Moses asked God "Now show me your glory" (Exod 33:18), God passed before Moses in a cloud and proclaimed

> "The Lord, the Lord, the compassionate and gracious God, slow to anger, abounding in love and faithfulness, maintaining love to thousands, and forgiving wickedness, rebellion and sin. Yet he does not leave the guilty unpunished; he punishes the children and their children for the sin of the parents to the third and fourth generation." Moses bowed to the ground at once and worshiped. (Exod 34:6-8).

When God appeared to Isaiah in the temple he revealed his holiness and glory. Isaiah responded by repenting of his sinfulness, worshipping God, and accepting God's call to mission. "Here am I. Send me!" (Isa 6:1-8).

The first angel of Revelation 14 calls humanity to "Fear God and give him glory, because the hour of his judgment has come. Worship him who made the heavens, the earth, the sea and the springs of water" (v. 7). False worship of false gods is at the center of human rebellion and restoring true worship of the one true God is the core task of mission.

The Triune God interacts with humanity in different ways during the drama of God's mission, the *missio Dei*. The roles of God in mission should not be understood to reflect a hierarchy, in which one is superior to another. As they existed in the mystery of one-who-is-three and three-who-are-one, the Trinity is perfectly equal and unified in the great project of mission.

The term *missio Dei*, is used to show that mission comes from God. Neither the OT patriarchs, nor Israel, nor the OT prophets, the Apostles, the early church, or any humans or human entities initiated God's mission. In *missio Dei*, the concept of sending is central. The Father sends the Son as the primary missionary and the Father and Son send the Spirit to empower the church. The church participates in God's mission by sending its spiritually gifted members into missions.

Certain possible misunderstandings or misuses of *missio Dei* theology need to be avoided (Ott and Strauss 2010:65). The fact that mission comes from God should not be seen (1) as relieving the church of its responsibility so that it lapses into passivity and (2) the church should not legitimize anything and everything it does by claiming that it is part of God's mission.

God the Father: The Source, Initiator, and Sender of Mission

In salvation history, the Father's role is that of the fully engaged source, sender, and initiator of mission. The Father's mission initiatives extend all the way from the Fall of humanity to the Consummation of all things. During the totality of human history he works dynamically among all peoples through his chosen agencies. The Father sends his Word, angels, prophets, signs, and miracles to accomplish his mission. He called Abram and the people of Israel to be his special mission agents. "In the fullness of time" (Gal 4:4) the Father sent the Son as the ultimate missionary, to play the central role in God's mission. The Father also sent the Spirit to empower the launching of his church (v. 6). The Father's role as divine sender does not indicate superiority over the Son and Spirit.

> For what the law was powerless to do because it was weakened by the flesh, God did by sending his own Son in the likeness of sinful flesh to be a sin offering. And so he condemned sin in the flesh, in order that the righteous requirement of the law might be fully met in us, who do not live according to the flesh but according to the Spirit. (Rom 8:3-4; see also Gal 4:4; 1 John 4:9)

> All this is from God, who reconciled us to himself through Christ and gave us the ministry of reconciliation: that God was reconciling the world to himself in Christ, not counting people's sins against them. And he has committed to us the message of reconciliation. (2 Cor 5:18-19)

The stage upon which the Father works is human history. Before any of the great events of the Bible narrative took place, God was already at work. Through the centuries of human history, when no known records of direct missionary work exist, the Father was always at work. Missionaries do not "bring God" to places or peoples, God brings missionaries to the peoples as he wills. African Bishop Samuel Crowther (1806-1891) said, "The only God, known ... everywhere in the world brought the missionaries at his own convenience and time" (Adeuyan 2011:17). God was always in Africa and everywhere because he is the Creator Redeemer.

Understanding God's role in sending his mission agents helps to put the history of modern missions into perspective. Mission is much bigger than the fallible, mistake-making missionaries of any time and place—God's "earthen vessels." Missionary mistakes of the past, present, or future may weaken their influence, but they do not invalidate Christian mission.

God the Son: The Embodiment of Mission

Jesus Christ embodied God's mission within himself in two ways. First, he provided the objective basis for the salvation of humanity by being "the Lamb slain from the foundation of the world" (Rev 13:8). God's mission was possible because he "presented Christ as a sacrifice of atonement, through the shedding of his blood—to be received by faith" (Rom 3:25; see 1 Cor 15:3; Phil 2:8). The objective actions of human sinfulness needed an objective atonement. Thus, the Cross is the foundation upon which Christian mission rests.

Second, Jesus embodied the principles of the Kingdom in his human person in a way that humans could understand. "Jesus is not merely a messenger of good news but the embodiment of it" (Tennent 2010:82). He embodied and demonstrated the new creation to which God's mission called humanity.

The incarnated Christ "translated" divinity into humanity, like a language can be translated. He became a particular man, Jesus of Nazareth, who was a cultural Jew living at a particular time and place. Jesus spoke Aramaic, but the Gospels were translations of his words into Koine Greek. Every subsequent translation from Greek is a translation of a translation of the actual Aramaic words of Jesus.

The amazing thing is that the eternal, universal principles governing God's Kingdom were able to be translated into the personal nature and cultural characteristics of the Jewish Jesus. When his contemporaries observed his life, words, and deeds, they saw the Kingdom of God in action. Humans were originally created to understand Kingdom principles and live by them, but sin blocked humanity's view. Jesus demonstrated God's new creation that would restore those principles within the lives of repentant, believing sinners saved by grace through faith.

His Gospel can maintain its universal qualities when it is embodied in different sets of cultural particularities.

Just as God the Son maintained his divine character when he became Jesus of Nazareth, so his Gospel can maintain its universal qualities when it is embodied in different sets of cultural particularities. Just as the characteristics of the Kingdom were retained in his incarnated human nature, so the principles of the Kingdom revealed in his Word can be retained through multiple linguistic and cultural translations.

The book of Acts records the first of "a constant succession of new translations" of the Gospel into countless new cultures. "The reason for this lies in the infinite translatability of the Christian faith" (Newbigin 1996:27, 22). The principles of the Kingdom were first translated or embodied in the Jewish Jesus, then embodied in the lives of converted Jewish Christians, then embodied in Gentile converts who were God's new creation, and thence translated into innumerable cultures to the present day.

A qualification needs to be made about the translation of the principles of the Bible into individual human lives within their cultures. Whereas the translation was perfect and sinless into the life of the Jewish Jesus of Nazareth, the translation into other cultural persons is imperfect because of human sinfulness. Yet, fallible humans are able to give reliable witness to eternal principles because of the Word and the Holy Spirit. The discussion of culture continues in a later section.

God the Holy Spirit: The Empowering Guide of Mission

After Jesus had provided the atonement as the objective basis for God's mission, God the Holy Spirit became the empowering guide of the church in mission. This is not to imply that he was inactive before Pentecost, but to say that he had a special role in the era of the church. The "mission of the Spirit is one of the mighty acts of God along with the incarnation, atonement, and resurrection" (Goheen 2014:101). Understanding his continued role in mission is vital.

Even though the early church experienced the wonders of Pentecost and the dramatic works of the Holy Spirit thereafter, several centuries were required for the church to formulate the doctrine of the Holy Spirit (Pneumatology). The challenge of understanding the Holy Spirit continues to the present day and confronts several problems.

1. The Spirit has been understood in impersonal terms—as wind, fire, water, and oil—instead of as a divine Person. These metaphors are biblical, but no metaphor conveys the whole meaning or truth. The Holy Spirit is as much a divine Person as are the Father and Son.

2. The focus has sometimes been more on the excitement given by the Spirit than on the Spirit's concern for truth and mission.

3. Personal spirituality and sanctification have been an exclusive focus for some. A fuller understanding sees the Holy Spirit as being the member of the Trinity superintending God's comprehensive mission for lost humanity from Pentecost until the Second Coming.

Roles of the Spirit in Mission

Scripture describes several main roles which God the Holy Spirit performs in God's mission (Tennent 2010:95-101).

1. The Spirit empowers the church for the proclamation of Jesus Christ. Shortly before his ascension, Jesus instructed his followers: "I am going to send you what my Father has promised; but stay in the city until you have been clothed with power from on high" (Luke 24:49). The believers obeyed his instructions and, after waiting in the Upper Room, the Spirit was poured out upon them (Acts 2:1-4). What followed was the dramatic proclamation by Peter and others of the "mighty deeds of God" in multiple tongues. From that dramatic beginning, the mission of God moved outward from Jerusalem to include much of the Roman Empire. The reason that the Apostles, their missionary colleagues, and the early believers were effective in proclaiming Christ was that the Spirit empowered them.

"The Holy Spirit is a communication specialist" whose primary work in the early church was to inspire spoken and written words about Jesus Christ (Sunquist 2013:240). He helped the speakers to understand the truth about Jesus and to express it in a way that gave the hearers the best possible opportunity to understand and accept the message. Then he worked with the receivers to soften their hearts and understand the message. Whether the gift of tongues enabled the speakers to speak other languages or non-Aramaic hearers to understand Aramaic sermons does not matter because the hearers understood the apostolic preaching "in his own language" (Acts 2:6).

Nothing but the empowerment of the Spirit can explain the growth of the church in the hostile environment of the times. Nothing but the Spirit's empowerment can explain why a secular-postmodern person, a Muslim, Hindu, Buddhist, or an animist turns to Christ. The Spirit is actively involved whenever a soul turns to Christ.

2. The Spirit teaches the church the principles and message to be proclaimed in mission.

I have much more to say to you, more than you can now bear. But when he, the Spirit of truth, comes, he will guide you into all the truth. He will not speak on his own; he will speak only what he hears, and he will tell you what is yet to come. He will glorify me because it is from me that he will receive what he will make known to you. All that belongs to the Father is mine. That is why I said the Spirit will receive from me what he will make known to you. (John 16:12-15)

Several important aspects of the Spirit's mission are made clear in this text. Part of his nature as God is that he is "the Spirit of truth." His empowerment, that did include enthusiasm and drama at Pentecost, should not be understood to be primarily about spectacular manifestations. Underneath the drama of Pentecost was God's abiding concern for truth. The great sermons reported in Acts were without question inspiring, emotional events, but they were also biblically based, truthful sermons. As the church contextualized the Gospel for Gentiles at the Jerusalem Council and elsewhere, the Spirit guided the process so that God's eternal truth was maintained. When the Spirit guides and the church follows his guidance today, truth is always upheld.

The words of Jesus always had a future orientation. Jesus had more to teach the disciples than they were ready for at that time and which the Spirit would complete in the future. God's truth is dynamic and progressive. The Spirit's work is to teach the church God's dynamic truth in a way that addresses the concrete situations of time, place, and culture so that God's eternal, universal truth is relevant to particular contexts. As history progresses and cultures change, the Spirit "will tell you what is yet to come," or to understand the changing times for the sake of mission.

The Holy Spirit's role in mission is not to develop new content or teachings, but to teach and remind (John 14:26) the church about what Jesus said and did. His work is to teach the "meaning and significance of the person and work of Jesus Christ" (Tennent 2010:96). The prominence Jesus gave to the Spirit's teaching role implies that the church must place great emphasis on teaching and discipleship in mission.

3. The Holy Spirit sustains the church in the suffering and persecution experienced in mission. "For Paul, suffering is an ongoing reflection of and participation in the suffering of Christ (Rom 8:1) … wherever the true church is…. Suffering is a normal expectation for Christian witness" (Tennent 2010:98). Jesus promised that when believers were persecuted the Spirit would give them words to speak (Matt 10:18-20). For Christians in the age of Christendom or in countries that are mostly Christian, these are strange words that possibly sound paranoid. However, in many past eras and in contemporary missions among certain peoples, suffering, persecution, and martyrdom are common. Even where overt persecution does not happen, cross-cultural mission adds a level of stress and complexity to the missionary's work. There are also threats to personal safety, diseases, and increasingly polluted spaces and air that cause suffering. Enduring suffering for the sake of God's mission produces perseverance and other Christian virtues (Rom 5:3-5).

4. The Holy Spirit empowers mission as an overflowing of joyful witness. The Great Commission was undoubtedly known by the early church because it appears in different forms in all four Gospels and Acts. However, the Bible writers do not record a repetition of the Commission on the lips of the Apostles from Pentecost onward. The early church did not witness as an act of burdensome obedience to the Commission, but because the Spirit bubbled over and

spilled out with the good news of salvation in Jesus. Two events coalesced to create that joyful bubbling over of good news—the resurrection of Christ and the outpouring of the Holy Spirit. For the early church, mission was "an extension of the Holy Spirit's life and work through the church and into the world" (Tennent 2010:99). That joyful overflowing even made Paul and Silas sing in prison (Acts 16:25). The Holy Spirit fills hearts and makes them overflow today in witness.

5. "The work of the Holy Spirit is to bring the 'not yet' of the Kingdom into the 'already' of our fallen world" (Tennent 2007:179). In the interim between Pentecost and the Second Coming, the Spirit provides a sweet foretaste of the eternal Kingdom. This theme will be developed in the section about the Kingdom of God.

Cessationism and Mission

The missional roles of God the Holy Spirit have not always been well understood. The major Reformers were so preoccupied with the study of the Bible, ecclesiology, soteriology, and Christology that they did not fully develop pneumatology. Because of their inattention to the Spirit, they "inadvertently created a functional subordinationism in their doctrine of the Holy Spirit" (Tennent 2007:174-5). In other words, they unintentionally placed the Spirit in a subservient, or inferior role to the Father and the Son.

In the centuries following the Reformation

> several major theological traditions developed that either denied completely or extremely limited the active role of the Holy Spirit in performing miracles, divine healing, demonic deliverance, prophecy, tongue speaking, and other elements that later became central features in the Pentecostal doctrine of the Holy Spirit. (Tennent 2007:171)

The view that the Holy Spirit has ceased his work in some way is called "cessationism." Total cessationists believe that the works of the Spirit ceased completely, either when the Apostles died or when the NT canon was closed. For total cessationists, the supernatural works of the Spirit are neither observed in action nor expected to be a part of the church's life and mission today.

Partial cessationists believe that certain of the Spirit's works (e.g., prophecy or tongues) have ceased, while other works (e.g., healing or personal spiritual guidance) continue to the present day. They differ about which gifts continue.

Functional cessationists affirm the biblical works and gifts of the Spirit in theory, but do not expect or experience them in real life, here and now.

Why are there cessationists of any kind when the works and gifts of the Spirit are so clear in Scripture? There may be many reasons, but here are a few possibilities.

1. The inspired biblical record includes many of the great works of the Spirit, but not at the same length as it describes the persons and works of the Father and Son. The biblical picture of the Son is the most complete because of his incarnation.

2. The doctrine of the Holy Spirit developed slowly and incompletely in Christian history.

3. The work of the Spirit has at times been smothered by dry formalism and dead orthodoxy that leaves no room for the Spirit's energy and creativity.

4. The sensationalism and lack of theological grounding sometimes characteristic of modern Pentecostalism have caused some to be skeptical about the genuine works and gifts of the Spirit.

5. Functional cessationism may be part of a mistake identified by missiologist Paul Hiebert (1994:196). The "Flaw of the Excluded Middle" is a concept that describes why Christians who belong to the culture of Western modernity struggle to understand and deal with events, powers, and spirits that are beyond scientific study. For them, any manifestation of spiritual actions or powers is a "mere superstition" and the only solution is to stop believing that the manifestations are real. Instead of claiming the power of God over evil spirits through the ministry of the Holy Spirit, they deny that evil spirits and powers exist. They do not believe evil spirits are real and thus do not truly believe the Holy Spirit is real. This means that believers who may affirm the works and gifts of the Holy Spirit are, in fact, functional cessationists.

6. Functional cessationism may also be caused by a misunderstanding of the biblical teaching of the latter rain of the Holy Spirit. Several biblical passages refer to an "early rain" and "latter rain" (Joel 2:23; Hosea 6:3; Zech 10:1; Jas 5:7). The two metaphors were drawn from the agricultural cycle of rains in Palestine. The early rain is understood to refer to the coming of the Holy Spirit at Pentecost while the latter rain refers to a special end-time, eschatological bestowal of the Spirit that prepares the way for Christ's Second Coming.

The agricultural metaphor, like all metaphors, does not tell the full story. The metaphor could imply a dry season between the early and latter rains when the Spirit ceases his work. Here the metaphor breaks down. In between the early rain of Pentecost and latter rain at the end of time the Holy Spirit has been and continues to be constantly at work. If that were not the case, no one would have been converted and the church would have ceased to exist. The hardness of human hearts that may cause the work of the Spirit to be less effective in different times and places does not mean the Spirit has ceased his work. God the Holy Spirit is always fully engaged in his mission and Christians should claim his presence and power in the same ways the early church depended upon him. Whether the special, eschatological, bestowal of the Spirit will be more intense in the future is in his sovereign hands. Christians can trust that the Spirit will use them today and every day in whatever way he wishes.

The Holy Spirit in Adventist History

A brief review of church history helps to explain how Adventists understand the current role of the Holy Spirit in mission. The major Reformation did not produce a well-developed pneumatology, as we have seen. Among the leaders of the Radical Reformation there was a greater emphasis on the Spirit, especially among the Anabaptist and Holiness movements. Wesley and the Methodists had roots in the Radical Reformation and Adventists have roots in Methodism.

John Wesley (1703-1791) and the Methodists provided "a pneumatological corrective to the theology of the magisterial Reformers" (Luther and Calvin) by promoting a return to the original apostolic roots of Christianity (Tennent 2007:174). Wesley taught that the Christian experienced salvation in two phases. The first phase was conversion and the gift of salvation called justification. The second phase, that could be either an instantaneous or gradual experience, sanctified and purified the believer. He believed that the Spirit continued to work but that "the supernatural gifts of the Spirit were not active in the churches of his day ... because of spiritual deadness, not God's plan." Wesley did not develop a systematic doctrine of the Holy Spirit, because Methodism was largely a religion of ordinary less-educated people and their meetings emphasized personal experience.

Adventists locate their early roots in Wesleyan Methodism, the Great Second Advent Awakening, and the Millerite Movement. Among Millerites, there were many manifestations of enthusiasm, like prostration, swooning, shouting, visions, tongues, dreams, and healings. The Adventist founders, including Ellen White, experienced spiritual manifestations and exuberance in church, at camp meetings, and on other occasions

> The worldview of those early Sabbatarian Adventists included a conscious awareness of supernatural forces. Believers were "attacked" by Satan, but often left meetings "victorious" or "triumphant" over the powers of evil. Even disease was brought upon them by the power of Satan or evil spirits, and could be removed through prayer and the rebuke of these evil spirits. (Fortin and Moon 2013:791)

Adventists pioneers had to contend with fanaticism and extremism that developed in the group. When Ellen Harmon had her first visions she hesitated to share them because she feared being identified with extremists. Yet, all of the gifts and works of the Spirit were affirmed by early Adventists and the spiritual gift of prophecy was affirmed in the ministry of Ellen White.

Ellen White received a vision in 1850 that was pivotal in shaping the developing church and its view of spiritual gifts. Instead of looking to "unhealthy and unnecessary excitement," the focus should be on the Word of God. She insisted that "even the work of the Holy Spirit should be tested by the Word of God" (Fortin and Moon 2013:792). The individual's experience needed to be tested by the Bible to avoid fanaticism.

Early Adventists rejected certain things sometimes associated with a belief in the Spirit's work. They did not accept the Holiness Movement belief of a "second blessing" of the Spirit that gives instantaneous, total, sinless perfection. In 1899-1900 there was a "holy flesh" movement in Indiana teaching that the Spirit would replace earthly flesh with "translation flesh." The "translation flesh" movement was fanatical and died out with guidance from Ellen White.

Adventists believe that the Spirit empowers the believer in a lifelong "growing up" process of sanctification and that glorification provides sinless perfection (Fortin and Moon 2013:873).

The gift of tongues at Pentecost was identified by early Adventists as a continuing gift of the Spirit. "There were four recorded incidents of speaking in tongues among early Sabbatarian Adventists. Some of these incidents were considered genuine and others spurious" (Fortin and Moon 2013:792). The fear and experience of fanaticism and the focus on the Bible as the only reliable base for faith and practice have led most Adventists to understand the tongues of Pentecost as known human languages. (The full discussion of unknown tongues is beyond the scope of this book.) Many examples, including recent ones, of the gift of tongues as known languages support the Spirit's continued work in this way for the sake of mission. In the context of mission and evangelization, the speaker typically uses one language and the hearer understands in another language. Whether the gift is one of speaking or hearing is not always clear. However, the Adventist experience is that the gift of tongues is for missions.

Pentecostalism and Mission

Pentecostalism came onto the scene in the early twentieth century, giving the works and gifts of the Spirit special priority. In 1900, a Holiness preacher named Charles Parham began to preach about the Holy Spirit and the gift of tongues in Topeka, Kansas. Starting in 1906, William Seymour led a multi-cultural group in Los Angeles in the Azusa Street Revival. From those small beginnings, Pentecostalism has spread around the globe and into many forms of Christianity to become the fastest growing of all Christian groups (Johnson and Ross 2009:100).

Pentecostalism can be rightfully critiqued when it lacks a firm theological foundation, departs from biblical doctrine, and reduces Christianity to a sensational, subjective, personal experience. However, the Pentecostal movement has given renewed focus on the faith and practice of the early church, challenged the error of cessationism, highlighted the dangers of dry, theoretical Christianity, and linked "the work of the Holy Spirit to mission in an unprecedented fashion" (Moreau 2004:148). Adventists would do well to avoid becoming functional cessationists in reaction against Pentecostalism.

Spiritual Gifts and Mission

Understanding the role of the gifts of the Holy Spirit in the present-day work of missions is vital. The church need not wait for a dramatic latter rain experience that mirrors the drama of the early rain at Pentecost to be certain that the Holy Spirit is empowering the church for mission. He empowers the church through the spiritual gifts and fruit he gives to its members. The main spiritual gifts passages are in Romans 12, 1 Corinthians 12, and Ephesians 4. The fruit of the Spirit is discussed in Gal 5:22-23.

Peter Wagner offers the following definition: "A spiritual gift is a special attribute given by the Holy Spirit to every member of the Body of Christ according to God's grace for use within the context of the Body" (1974:42).

Spiritual gifts are often related to but not identical to natural temperaments and abilities. All human skills and abilities are gifts from God, even if one does not know or worship God. Prior to the Damascus road, Paul had a set of God-given abilities he actually used against God. When Christ became the center of his life and he became a member of the body of Christ, Paul's abilities became refocused and reorganized for Christ's mission (Turner 1998:278). In the same way, someone with a good singing voice or the ability to relate skillfully with other people does not have a spiritual gift unless those abilities are transformed and used by the Spirit. Some spiritual gifts enable a believer to serve effectively in ways beyond their natural temperament and preferences.

There is a close connection between gifts of the Spirit and fruit or virtues of the Spirit. "But the fruit of the Spirit is love, joy, peace, forbearance, kindness, goodness, faithfulness, gentleness and self-control" (Gal 5:22-23). The virtues or attitudes described as fruits of the Spirit are also gifts from the Spirit that characterize followers of Jesus Christ. The difference is that all Christians "should share in and strive for all such fruit," while believers do not typically have all of the spiritual gifts (Turner 1998:279). Paul's intention was to emphasize the wide variety of ways the Spirit works to enable different believers to contribute to the mission of the church.

The term "spiritual gift" implies a "gift theology" that compliments a "consecration theology" (Wagner 1974:34-35). Consecration theology implies that to understand God's will and fulfill his mission, believers should seek to have a deeper walk with God. Consecration suggests an imperative of the Christian life—"we should be more consecrated to fulfill the mission of the church." Gift theology suggests an indicative of the Christian life—"because we have accepted Christ, the Spirit has already given us spiritual gifts for the mission of the church." In other words, believers can be assured that, because God has a role for them to play in his mission, he has given them the spiritual-missional abilities to play that role.

Spiritual gift theology follows salvation theology, where there are both indicatives (what God has already done) and imperatives (how humans should respond). Before God gave his ten imperative commandments, he said, "I am the Lord your God, who brought you out of Egypt, out of the land of slavery" (Exod 20:2)—therefore, you should obey these commandments. Obedience is the joyful response to the salvation already provided in Jesus Christ.

> Collectively, the church can feel confident that the Spirit has given to its members what they need to fulfill God's mission.

Spiritual gifts come from God the Holy Spirit just as salvation comes from God the Son. Collectively, the church can feel confident that the Spirit has given to its members what they need to fulfill God's mission. The church should respond to what the Spirit has done by identifying, nurturing, empowering, and facilitating the giftedness of its members.

The individual believer must respond to the spiritual gifts the Spirit has bestowed in several ways: (1) grow in a life-long process of sanctification to become better able to use the Spirit's gifts in mission; (2) identify, understand, and develop their own spiritual gifts; (3) actively use the gifts for mission within the congregation; and (4) "do not think of yourself more highly than you ought, but rather think of yourself with sober judgment, in accordance with the faith [or gifts] God has distributed to each of you." Yet, there is a place for godly confidence because "God has allotted to each a measure of faith" (Rom 12:3).

God the Spirit, Sovereign over Mission

God has chosen to use the church as his primary human mission agency. Understanding that God the Holy Spirit empowers the church explains where its resources and power for mission come from. However, God remains sovereign over his mission and God the Holy Spirit works directly upon the hearts and minds of all humans.

> [The church]…is not in control of the mission…. Because the Spirit is himself sovereign over the mission, the church can only be the attentive servant. In sober truth the Spirit is himself the witness who goes before the church in its missionary journey. The church's witness is secondary and derivative. The church is witness insofar as it follows obediently where the Spirit leads…. This picture of the mission is as remote as possible from the picture of the church as a powerful body putting forth its strength and wisdom to master the strength and wisdom of the world. The case is exactly the opposite. The church is weak. It is under trial. It does not know what to say…the mission of the church is not conducted, nor is its success measured, after the manner of a military operation or a sales campaign. The witness that confutes the world is not ours; it is that of one greater than ourselves who goes before us. Our task is to simply follow faithfully. (Newbigin 1995:61-62)

David Garrison (2014) and others have documented contemporary accounts of the Holy Spirit's direct ministry to Muslims around the world. In case after case, Muslims receive dreams and visions showing Jesus Christ and telling the Muslim to go to a certain place to meet a certain person who will tell them about Jesus. When the human encounter occurs, the Muslim learns more and moves toward Christ. God has chosen to use human agents in his mission, but the mission always belongs to God. God's mission will be victorious because of who God is, not because of the very best mission strategies.

The Purpose and Nature of Mission

The purpose and nature of missions have already been introduced briefly in the definitions of mission-related terms. This section probes more deeply (Ott and Strauss 2010:79-105).

Glorifying God, the Purpose of Mission

The first angel's message calls humanity to "Fear God and give him glory, because the hour of his judgment has come, and worship him who made heaven and earth, the sea and the springs of water" (Rev 14:7). This message aims to correct the lies told about God's character when the serpent said "You shall not surely die" (Gen 3:4). God is the ultimate ground of being for the entire universe and when his character is maligned the universe becomes insecure. Thus, the primary purpose of God's mission is that the universe would glorify God in perfect harmony. The ultimate goal for humans is that they would declare that God is Lord of all.

Redemption, the Foundation of Mission

That which best glorifies God and is the foundation of his mission is his work of redemption. The Bible presents the story of redemption starting with the promise of Genesis 3:15. The sacrificial system gave God's method of redemption a practical design that people could understand. The prophets of Israel continued to expound the plan of salvation. God's work of redemption reached its apex in Christ. Today, Christ's work of mediation in the heavenly sanctuary continues (Heb 7:25). "The purpose of mission must always be tethered to the Cross of Christ." Christ was and is many things but he is "first and foremost Savior" (Ott and Strauss 2010:86). "Christ Jesus came into the world to save sinners" (1 Tim 1:15).

The Kingdom and Eschatology, the Hope of Mission

When Lucifer rebelled, he challenged God's reign over the cosmos. When Adam and Eve sinned, Lucifer became the partial, temporary ruler of this world. He was the partial ruler because God retained the overall sovereignty of the cosmos and temporary ruler because his days were numbered. The *missio Dei* was planned to restore God's Kingdom reign to the whole cosmos and save lost humanity.

When Jesus began his ministry, his message was simple. "The time has come," he said, "the Kingdom of God has come near. Repent and believe the good news!" (Mark 1:15). At the end of his ministry, during the forty days before his ascension, Jesus continued to teach the disciples about the Kingdom of God (Acts 1:3). When the disciples asked: "'Lord, are you at this time going to restore the kingdom to Israel?' He said to them: 'It is not for you to know the times or dates the Father has set by his own authority'" (Acts 1:6-7). The Kingdom had come in one sense when Jesus started preaching, but in another sense the Kingdom was still in the future even when he ascended.

The concept that the Kingdom was both present and yet future was made clear in his other teachings. When Jesus interpreted the parable of the sower and soils to his disciples he said that the "secret" or "mystery" of the Kingdom had been given to them (Mark 4:11). The mystery was that the Kingdom was both a present reality and a future hope.

> The mystery of the Kingdom is the coming of the Kingdom into history in advance of its apocalyptic manifestation. It is, in short, "fulfillment without consummation." This is the single truth illustrated in the several parables of Mark 4 and Matthew 13. (Ladd 1993:91)

In other words, the OT promises of the Kingdom were fulfilled by Christ's first coming. His teachings, miracles, exorcisms, and lifestyle demonstrated the presence of the Kingdom. The supreme manifestation of the Kingdom was in the self-sacrificing love of the Cross. But still something of the Kingdom remained in the future. Jesus had fulfilled the promises of the Kingdom but the Kingdom would yet be fully consummated by his Second Coming.

The NT speaks frequently about "this age," "this present age," "this evil age," and "the age to come," or the "future age" (Matt 12:32; 13:49; Luke 18:30; 1 Cor 2:6-8; 1 Tim 6:19). "This evil age" will be replaced by "the age to come" with great apocalyptic events—the Second Coming, resurrection of the dead, and the other events described in Revelation. In the age to come, sin, evil, and death will be replaced by righteousness, goodness, and eternal life in the whole cosmos.

The church, planted at Pentecost, exists in the "overlap of the ages," in the "already but not yet" era between the First Coming of Christ and the Second Coming when "this evil age" will be replaced by "the age to come." Some of the features of the "age to come" are now present. To use some contemporary metaphors, the Kingdom is like a "time warp" that reaches "back from the future," bringing the present into the "magnetic field" of the future.

Understanding the "already but not yet" character of God's Kingdom is vital for understanding the church's mission.

The "overlap of the ages" gives the church a special "window of opportunity"...

The meaning of this "overlap of the ages" in which we live, the time between the coming of Christ and His coming again, is that it is the time given for the witness of the apostolic Church to the ends of the earth. The end of all things, which has been revealed in Christ, is so to say held back until witness has been borne to the whole world concerning the judgment and salvation revealed in Christ. The implication of a true eschatological perspective will be missionary obedience, and the eschatology which does not issue in such obedience is a false eschatology. (Newbigin 1954:153-154)

The "overlap of the ages" gives the church a special "window of opportunity" for mission to prepare the world for the Second Coming as the winds of strife are held back (Rev 7:1). During this time, all peoples are to be warned of judgment and told of salvation offered in Jesus Christ. Mission, properly understood, focuses urgently on the opportunity now available—"now is the 'acceptable time,' behold, now is the 'day of salvation'" (2 Cor 6:2).

The Kingdom, God's mission, and the church are closely related in several ways (Ladd 1993:109-117).

1. "The church is the people of the Kingdom, never the Kingdom itself" (110-111). This is because the church is "an empirical body of human beings" while the Kingdom is the invisible sphere of God's rule. Believers will only enter the Kingdom at the eschatological consummation. The church is a means of mission, not the end or goal of mission.

2. The proclamation of the Kingdom brings responsive humans into a new kind of fellowship as members of the body of Christ, the church. As illustrated by the parables of the wheat and tares (Matt 13:24-30) and the dragnet (vv. 47, 52), not everyone in the church is a true child of the Kingdom. The dual character of the church as part of this age and the age to come should make the church very humble about itself. But the church is more than a mere human institution because it functions in the "magnetic field" of the Kingdom. Therefore, the church can fulfill its mission in humble confidence.

3. The church's mission is "to witness to the Kingdom" (111) among all peoples. The church gives witness of the Kingdom through relationships that are humble, forgiving, selfless, and loving because it reflects the character of the Kingdom.

4. The church "is the instrument of the Kingdom" (114) to do the same works that Christ delegated to the Twelve and the seventy disciples. Jesus said, "As you go, proclaim this message: 'The Kingdom of heaven has come near.' Heal the sick, raise the dead, cleanse those who have leprosy, drive out demons" (Matt 10:7-8). In authentic mission, the church addresses human suffering and need and confronts the powers of this evil age.

5. The church "is the custodian of the Kingdom" (114). The message of the Kingdom which the church proclaims is decisive for humanity. "The final destinies of individuals will be determined by the way they react to these representatives of God" (117). This does not imply that the church controls or dispenses salvation or that people must respond in a specific time or place. However, the revealed truth the church carries within itself as the custodian of a sacred trust is decisive for all humanity. Mission is about eternal destinies.

Mission anticipates the day of consummation when the overlap of the ages merges into the age of the eternal Kingdom of righteousness. "The gathering of all peoples into one is the eschatological deed of God" (Goheen 2014:51) that is proclaimed by the church until the Second Coming.

All Peoples, the Scope of Mission

Understanding the scope of mission is a decidedly theological matter. Peter's theology was incomplete until he recognized that Cornelius and other Gentiles were part of his mission assignment. The NT uses many different words to make the point that people of all categories and groupings are included in God's mission. The term "people group" is used to express the widely diverse groupings of people needing the Gospel. The theological basis for the conviction that God's mission includes all people groups is that they all descend from Adam and Eve, Christ made atonement for them all, and God has a heavenly home awaiting for them all. The task of mission is to reach them with the Gospel in a way they can comprehend within their linguistic, cultural contexts. The NT uses various words related to people groups.

Figure 4.1
NT Words Related to People Groups

ethné	Nations, ethnic groups	Matt 24:14; 28:19
phulé	Ethnic group, tribe	Rev 5:9; 7:9
glôssés	Tongue, language group	Rev 5:9; 7:9
laos	People, nation, crowd	Rev 5:9; 7:9
ethnos	Nation, people, Gentiles	Rev 5:9; 7:9

The scope of mission clearly has a geographic dimension, as "to the ends of the earth" (Acts 1:8) indicates. As William Carey and the others launched the modern missionary movement in the early-nineteenth century, geography was appropriately at the forefront. Whole continents and nations needed to be reached and travel was very difficult. As global Christianity has grown and modern travel has shrunk the world, geography is no longer the most prominent dimension of mission.

The people group model clarifies the scope of mission in the globalized world. Almost every local church has a wide diversity of people groups within its reach. The problem is that some of the people groups are "hidden" from sight. For example, an Indian, Hindu, Gujarati-speaking people group can easily function within its own social-religious circle in a town with many churches. If they do not intentionally identify people groups in their area, the churches may remain totally unaware of the Indian group. Once the Indian group is identified, the next step is to make a strategy to reach it with the Gospel. The local church should assume that certain strategies which are effective with Methodists or Baptists will probably not work with Hindus.

The geographic dimension of mission remains a challenge even when a local church faithfully identifies and reaches the people groups in its area. Vast areas of the world, with billions of people, remain unreached by the Gospel. Crossing geographic boundaries usually involves crossing cultural, linguistic, and religious boundaries also. Only cross-cultural, long-term missionaries, supported by the world church can reach those billions of people.

Reconciliation, the Fruit of Mission

Glorifying God and receiving his salvation establishes vertical reconciliation with God. However, horizontal reconciliation with humanity is also an essential dimension of mission. Human sinfulness is expressed through acts of violence, exploitation, and hostility in every type of human relationship. The fruit of being reconciled with God is experiencing and promoting reconciliation in all human relationships. The peace of God establishes a "new humanity [that] is no longer divided by race, ethnicity, social standing, or gender (Gal 3:28).... We have been adopted into a new family of God (Eph 1:5), and our primary citizenship is now in heaven (Phil 3:20)" (Ott and Strauss 2010:97).

Incarnation, the Character of Mission

The incarnational ministry of Jesus provides a model for cross-cultural missionaries. In the words of Paul writing to the Philippians:

> Have this mind among yourselves, which is yours in Christ Jesus, who, though he was in the form of God, did not count equality with God a thing to be grasped, but emptied himself, by taking the form of a servant, being born in the likeness of men. And being found in human form, he humbled himself by becoming obedient to the point of death, even death on a Cross. (Phil 2:5-8)

Some aspects of Christ's incarnation apply to missionaries and some do not. The divine Christ voluntarily experienced a radical change in his person when he became a man that missionaries cannot experience. The human Jesus of Nazareth was an ethnic Jew living in first century Palestine but without the sinful propensities of humanity. Human missionaries retain their ethnicity and birth-culture wherever they may serve; however, they can closely identify with another people group as they learn its language and culture.

The heart of the incarnational model of mission is found in Paul's call to "have this mind among yourselves, which is yours in Christ Jesus." Having the mind of Christ means being humble and selfless and "and surrendering one's rights for the sake of others" (Ott and Strauss 2015:103).

Christ's model applies to every Christian, but it has special relevance for cross-cultural missionaries. Leaving the comfort zone of the home culture to serve in a totally different cultural environment requires adults to learn things that even small children know in the host culture. Living life on the terms of some else's culture is a very selfless act, even if it is enjoyable in many respects. Many people assume their right to live freely by personal cultural styles and preferences will be respected wherever they are, but missionaries must be prepared to surrender that right. In some places, missionaries endure resistance, hostility, abuse, violence, or persecution. Basic human rights may or may not be respected. Some contemporary Christian missionaries and believers risk martyrdom and some die for their faith and work.

The Church and Mission

~•↰

The Tasks of Mission

Believers through the centuries have understood that the church fulfills the purposes of God's mission in various ways. There is a great deal to be learned from the history of missions, both from its mistakes and victories. This chapter discusses selected phases in the history of mission and uses them in thinking theologically about the tasks of mission today. Comprehensive discussions are available to expand this brief overview (see Bosch 1991; Bevans and Schroder 2004; Ott and Strauss 2010).

The discussion of mission in the NT in chapter 3 has shown that the overall mission task is to make disciples who are fully embedded in a local church community. Disciples make other disciples who make others until Jesus returns. A number of other tasks function under the umbrella of discipleship.

Proclamation and Discipleship

The scope of mission for Martin Luther and the other major Reformers did not extend much beyond Christian Europe. The task of mission was to preach the Gospel to lost sinners and reform the church, but not to plant new churches. Europe already had enough churches of which everyone was a nominal member.

The Pietist and Moravian missionaries of the seventeenth and eighteenth centuries, the earliest Protestant missionaries to have a broader global vision, retained the Lutheran view of the mission task except for broadening it beyond Europe. They saw the task of mission as leading lost sinners to salvation in Christ, not to the planting of churches. Unconverted souls were destined for eternal damnation and the urgent task of mission was to lead individuals to accept Christ. There was no clarity about what would be done with the newly converted. Discipleship training was neglected. The European context, where everyone was a nominal member of a state church, probably was responsible for this missiological blind spot that hampered missions in other lands where there was no history of Christianity.

The one-sided emphasis on initial, individual conversion over disciple making has persisted through other historical eras. One popular motto of the nineteenth century was, "No one should hear the Gospel twice until everyone has heard it once" (Ott and Strauss 2010:110). Others felt the urgency of reaching the unevangelized so intensely that to linger after the first proclamation for in-depth disciple making seemed unjust to those who had not yet heard the Gospel at all.

That the proclamation of the Gospel with a call to decision is a central task of biblical mission is beyond debate (Acts 4:12; Rom 10:13-14). There are amazing anecdotes about total life changes resulting from a single Gospel contact. However, many of those anecdotes are about people who already had a Christian background, not about Muslims, Hindus, or Buddhists. An exclusive emphasis on proclamation is unwise for several reasons.

1. The Great Commission is only partly fulfilled without extended discipleship training and church planting.

2. Shallow conversion, nominalism, syncretism, and lack of lifestyle change are frequent outcomes of hearing the Gospel superficially. Truly hearing the Gospel requires sustained and repeated teaching, especially for those without a Christian background. "Even Paul and Barnabas faced the challenge of being misunderstood by their hearers (Acts 14:8-18)" (Ott and Strauss 2010:111). True conversion involves a 180-degree change in direction and a single allegiance to the Lordship of Christ with a continuing journey toward Christ.

3. The biblical emphasis on the local church as the community of fellowship and faith and the primary locus of mission is undercut by a one-sided emphasis on proclamation.

4. The Adventist challenge may be to blend zeal to proclaim the Gospel quickly to every person with solid realism about what it means for a person to really hear and obey the Gospel.

Church Planting

As already noted, the early Pietist and Moravian missionaries did not make intentional church planting and disciple making central in their missiology. They did establish churches, but those churches were more like necessary holding containers than well-planned communities. The missionary task was thought to be complete when people accepted Christ. This left new converts in a position of spiritual vulnerability.

Thankfully, the mission community moved toward church planting. William Carey called for churches to be planted. Rufus Anderson (1796-1880) and Henry Venn (1796-1873), both leading mission board administrators, called for churches to be planted that were self-governing, self-propagating, and self-supporting (the "three-self theory"). Donald McGavran and many others defined mission as "the proclamation of the message to all mankind and gathering them into the church" (Ott and Strauss 2010:116).

Several reminders and clarifications about church planting are in order:

1. The disconnection of individual faith and practice from church fellowship is unknown in the NT. Converts automatically became members of the body of Christ as a matter of spiritual and missional necessity. They needed the church and the church needed them.

2. There is not a direct command to plant churches in the Great Commission or elsewhere, but there are indirect commands. Jesus said, "I will build up my church" (Matt 16:18; Titus 2:14). Baptism signifies not only "repentance, forgiveness, and a new life (Rom 6:3-4), but also of enfolding into the body of Christ (1 Cor 12:13) and identification with the community of faith" (Ott and Strass 2010:119). For Paul and his colleagues, planting churches was always linked with proclamation.

3. Adventists have a well-established pattern of establishing "companies" that develop into formally organized local churches. Where conferences/fields have many small churches that struggle for their existence, the goal of continued church planting may slip out of sight, but it needs to be kept ever in focus.

4. The challenge of planting churches in creative-access or restricted-access contexts where public worship is difficult or forbidden requires creativity and flexibility. In the Communist era, many Adventists worshipped in secret or underground congregations. In such settings, the importance of Christian fellowship was greatly multiplied.

Civilizing or Culture Transplanting

During the colonial era (see figure 5.1), virtually all missionaries were Europeans or Americans and many of them believed that one of their tasks was to "civilize" as well as evangelize the peoples with whom they worked. The people they served were frequently illiterate, scantily clad, practitioners of animistic religions. Converts typically embraced the education, medical care, and general development that the missionaries brought.

Missionaries of the colonial era were often unable to make a separation in their own minds between their own cultures and Christianity. Thus, being British, German, or American and being Christian seemed like the same thing to them. Neither could they separate the African or Asian or South American cultures of their converts from certain unbiblical traditional beliefs and practices. Widow-burning in India, cannibalism in the Pacific Islands, and voodoo in Africa had to be eliminated from the lives of Christian converts. Traditional peoples did not make a neat separation between their religion and their culture and missionaries were not trained to intentionally identify good things to be retained. The task, as many missionaries saw it, was to perform a *tabula rasa*, to wipe the slate clean of every cultural element and replace it with "Christian culture." The

"Christian culture" usually resembled the missionary's own cultural way of being a Christian. Lacking the insights available today from cultural anthropology and missiological training, they tried to both evangelize and civilize, or to lead converts in Africa or Asia or Latin America to live just like Christians in England or Germany or Australia. Obviously they failed because many ancient cultural traditions remain to the present day.

Figure 5.1
Defining Colonialism

"Colonialism" refers to the imposition of control by a political power upon a territory outside its own boundaries. Examples of colonialism are found in the oldest records of antiquity, including the Bible. Modern colonialism is dated between the sixteenth century with Spain and Portugal colonizing Latin America and the mid-twentieth century when most colonies became independent. The era of "high colonialism" started in 1885 with the Berlin Conference, where the European powers carved up the world map between themselves. The First World War started the decline of colonialism and after the Second World War its demise was only a matter of time. The modern missionary movement (c.1750-1950) was initially opposed by Western colonial governments who feared missionizing would upset colonialized populations. When the colonial powers began to be criticized, they attempted to use missions to justify their colonialization. The colonial expansion of transportation and communication aided missions in many ways but the relationship of missions with the colonial powers was ambivalent and ambiguous.

When the colonies became independent there were predictions that Christianity would die out because of the bitterness caused by the "civilizing" approach. Amazingly, that did not happen. In the last half-century, Christianity has become an ever more globalized religion. One of the reasons is that the modern missionary movement, though influenced by European colonialism, remained independent from it in important ways.

While historical mistakes must be humbly acknowledged and corrected, the harsh critique of missions in the colonial era is sometimes unjust and inaccurate. Dana Robert has researched the relationship of missions and colonialism in depth. Robert notes that missionaries have been either demonized or idealized, depending on the ideologies of the historians who write about them. Those who have written to promote missions have idealized them while critics of colonialism have demonized them. "In the 1990s ... the icy grip of the 'colonialism paradigm' over mission history began to thaw" (2008:2) and a more accurate and nuanced research developed that paid attention to what missionaries had actually done. "Contrary to popular critiques, missionaries were often the first to fight for the rights of indigenous people in opposition to colonial policy" (Ott and Strauss 2010:123).

Robert also demonstrates that, far from being a one-way flow of influence, the modern missionary movement precipitated a powerful two-way flow that heavily influenced Christianity on the missionary sending side (2008:6). In other words, the Christianity that exists today in Europe and America is powerfully shaped by its missionary encounters with the rest of the world.

Yet, there is no defense for the cultural imposition of the "civilizing" model. Under different historical circumstances, the same imposition of a "Christian culture," that is actually the missionary's culture, can still happen unless the Gospel is faithfully contextualized. Missionaries from anywhere can make the same mistake when they try to transport their preferred style of Christianity into another society.

What factors have accounted for the rejection of the "civilizing" model of mission?

1. Demographic changes and the success of missions. In the time of Martin Luther, 92% of Christians resided in the global north (Europe and North America). When William Carey went to India in 1793, the number was 86%. Today, only about 35% of Christians reside in the global north (Johnson and Ross 2009:53). The demographic shift has been caused partly by secularism in the global north, but mostly by the success of Christian mission and the receptivity of people in the global south. In spite of its shortcomings, the modern missionary movement was a phenomenal success story.

2. Globalization. Closely related to the demographic changes, globalization has put many or most people into constant and regular contact with people who are culturally and religiously very different from themselves. Within the church, members fellowship regularly with people who practice their faith in different cultural styles. This makes the church more aware that it can practice the faith in different cultural styles while faithfully following biblical principles.

3. The culture concept. The culture concept was developed in the late-1800s and began to have a strong influence on missionary training by the mid-1900s. Without understanding the culture concept, people cannot distinguish between their faith and their culture. Thus, for many early missionaries, being Christian was inseparable from being European or American. They lacked the conceptual tools to distinguish between things that were culturally different but biblically innocent and those that were biblically unacceptable for all cultures. Those distinctions can now be made because of the culture concept.

4. Contributions of missiology. The discipline of missiology rejects colonialism and racism and seeks to learn and apply the historical lessons of both historical successes and failures in mission. In recent decades, the theory and practice of faithful contextualization have received great emphasis. The mistake of "civilizing" is repeated when a missionary from anywhere to anywhere fails to distinguish between their own culture and the Gospel and tries to transplant their culture. This "helicopter" method attempts to lift a "prefabricated church" from America or Korea or Jamaica or anywhere else and insert it into any other society. Missionary training is now very explicit about how to carry the authentic Gospel across cultural boundaries in a way that respects local cultures.

Humanitarian Service

The proper relationship of evangelization and humanitarian service in mission has produced a long and heated debate. In this discussion, "humanitarian service" refers to ministries that relieve human problems like poverty, hunger, illness, suffering, or calamity. "Wholistic mission" (sometimes spelled "holistic") refers to a missiology that includes both evangelization and humanitarian service.

The divide among Protestants has been between conciliar, mainline, Protestant denominations who are more theologically liberal and evangelical denominations who are more conservative (see Ott and Strauss 2010: 128-162). Figure 5.2 summarizes the major points that have divided mainline and evangelical Christians. The distinctions are stated very sharply and do not necessarily apply to every group. The mainline positions were held by the World Council of Churches through the 1970s. In recent decades, mainline groups have worked to recover and strengthen the role of evangelism. However, they continue to lean more toward religious pluralism than evangelicals.

Figure 5.2
Evangelization and Humanitarian Service

Mainline Protestants	Evangelical Protestants
• God's Kingdom is to be established in human history and structures. • The church is just one of multiple agencies working to establish the Kingdom. • The world sets the agenda for the church. • Salvation comes through socio-political means. • Conversion from other religions to Jesus Christ may not be a goal of mission.	• God's Kingdom was initiated in the church but will be fully established beyond this world. • Other agencies do good works but the church is the exclusive agency of salvation and the Kingdom. • The Bible sets the agenda for the church. • Salvation comes through spiritual means. • Conversion of all people to Jesus Christ is a primary goal.

One of the consequences of mainline Protestant missiology has been a dramatic decline in the number of missionaries sent by mainline denominations. Between 1900 and 2000 the number sent by mainline groups declined from 80% to just 6% of all Protestant missionaries (Ott and Strauss 2010:134). The great majority of Protestant missionaries now come from evangelical groups.

The relationship between evangelization and humanitarian service continues to be discussed as a matter of clarification and definition within the evangelical camp. There are some who say that mission is only evangelism. To be fair, most evangelicals who take this view are engaged in humanitarian service in some way. However, these good works are "considered subordinate to evangelism and church planting" (Ott and Strauss 2010:138). In this view, there is a dichotomy between ministry for the physical and spiritual needs of humanity. This missiological dichotomy arises from a dualistic doctrine of humanity that separates the spiritual nature from the physical nature. The goal of mission from that perspective is saving the human soul from eternal hell fire. The physical, psychological, and social needs of humanity call for Christian kindness and charity, but do not really constitute mission.

The Adventist wholistic doctrine of humanity implies a missiology that sees evangelization and humanitarian service as interwoven and overlapping.

> The moment one regards mission as consisting of two separate components one has, in principle, conceded that each of the two has a life of its own...if one suggests that one component is primary and the other secondary, one implies that the one is essential and the other optional. (Bosch 1991:405).

For those who believe that both evangelism and humanitarian service belong together in mission, there is an on-going discussion about how they relate to each other. Donald McGavran is famous for the concept of "social lift" that follows conversion. He meant that people's lives improve automatically when they abandon harmful practices and adopt biblically guided lifestyles. When churches are planted and memberships grow in non-Christian surroundings, whole communities will be uplifted by the changed lives of the Christians. McGavran was critiqued by advocates of wholistic mission who were unwilling for humanitarian relief to be a mere by-product of conversion. Humanitarian service must be an intentional part of mission, along with proclamation and conversion (Ott and Strauss 2010:142).

Adventists have long noted that when converts stop wasting money on tobacco, liquor, drugs, and other harmful things, their whole lives improve. However, some who do make those lifestyle changes and walk closely with the Lord continue to live in dire humanitarian need. Others in dire need remain completely unresponsive to evangelism, with or without humanitarian aid. Christian mission needs to be intentional about humanitarian service, rather that expecting it to happen automatically.

The accusation that converts are mere "rice Christians" has a long history going back to nineteenth century Christian missions is Asia. Sometimes material aid has been given both to attract potential converts and to meet their real needs. The opponents of Christian mission are quick to level the charge that humanitarian service is provided as a bribe without a true concern for the wellbeing of humanity.

Describing the relationship of evangelism and humanitarian service takes careful thought. Some have spoken of evangelization as having "priority" or "primacy," with humanitarian service being subordinate. Humanitarian service can also be seen as a "bridge" to evangelism. Evangelism and humanitarian service can also be seen as "partners in a marriage."

Ott and Strauss prefer the word "ultimacy" to describe evangelism (2010:147). They mean that evangelization offers the ultimate solution of the Gospel for humanity's greatest need. In the words of Jesus, "Do not fear those who kill the body but cannot kill the soul. Rather fear him who can destroy both soul and body in hell" (Matt 10:28). "What does it profit a man to gain the whole world and forfeit his soul?" (Mark 8:36).

John Stott speaks of the "centrality" of the Gospel (Stott and Wright 2015:50). He thinks that evangelism and social service are so intrinsically linked that speaking of primacy is not the best option because it still implies human dualism.

The following points outline an Adventist perspective of the relationship between evangelization and humanitarian service:

1. The relationship of humanitarian service and evangelism must start with a wholistic doctrine of humanity (anthropology), salvation (soteriology), and missiology. Humans were created as an indivisible unity of spiritual, physical, psychological, and social elements. Salvation encompasses all elements of the human being, including the physical body, which will be recreated at the Second Coming. Mission must, therefore, address humans comprehensively. No separation can be made between the physical and spiritual needs in a truly biblical missiology.

2. The relief of human suffering is a temporary and palliative ministry because of the persistence of suffering and death until the Second Coming. The scope of human suffering and the limitation of church resources for humanitarian service mean that the most earnest attempts will not solve the problem. Yet, the church is called to minister to human need with a whole heart and to the full extent of its capacity.

3. People whose hearts are open to God's grace can and will receive the ultimate solution, eternal life in Christ. The "pearl of great price" (Matt 13:46) is the news of God's Kingdom coming in fullness through Jesus Christ. The "pearl" is the best gift Christian mission can offer. Humanitarian service may attract people to the Gospel as a demonstration of authentic, Godly love. However, it must never be used in a manipulative way or as a bribe to attract needy people. The evangelist or missionary must closely examine their motivation when providing material gifts that might attract people to the church. The material needs of people should be met without consideration of their response to evangelism. Unresponsive people in material need should also receive available assistance.

The Church and Mission

The church and mission have a deeply theological relationship, not merely a pragmatic one. In other words, mission is not just a mechanism for adding members or planting churches (Newbigin 1995:59) and the church is not merely a vehicle for mission projects. Mission is rather an expression of the church's very nature. "The church does not exist for its own sake. It is called to mission" (Staples 1999:24). Believers do mission to be church.

Russell Staples finds "more than 100 terms, metaphors, images, and analogies of the church in the New Testament" (17). He believes that the two images which best express Adventist self-understanding are the church as the family of God (Eph 2:19) and as the ark or lifeboat of salvation (Heb 11:7).

> The church does not exist for its own sake. It is called to mission.

"A family is a primary institution" that provides the members' primary identity, meaning, and purpose. The lifeboat metaphor is directly tied to Adventist premillennial eschatology and expresses the core of Adventist mission—calling people to safety in Christ in preparation for his Second Coming. The two metaphors fit together well. People who board the lifeboat of salvation become members of the family of God (18-19).

The Pauline metaphor of the church as the body of Christ conveys the same basic meaning as the family of God metaphor. The body of Christ metaphor is especially important for missions because it is linked with spiritual gifts that empower mission (Rom 12; 1 Cor 12; Eph 4). The body metaphor also highlights the validity of church structures that facilitate and give coherence to mission.

Another important church metaphor for Adventists is the church as a remnant. Fundamental Belief No. 13 states that "the universal church is composed of all who truly believe in Christ, but in the last days, a time of widespread apostasy, a remnant has been called out to keep the commandments of God and the faith of Jesus" (www.adventist.org/en/beliefs). The remnant metaphor is linked in Adventist missiology with the Three Angels' Message (Rev 14), which is the special message to be proclaimed.

Staples emphasizes that metaphors only express aspects of complex realities and that some possible interpretations should be avoided. The whole range of biblical images and metaphors needs to be studied to develop a fuller understanding of the church (1999:17). Adventists need to avoid feelings of exclusivity or smug self-confidence that may be produced if the family of God, lifeboat/ark, or remnant metaphors of the church are applied simplistically. Such erroneous conclusions could work against the mission of the church.

Church history testifies that the mere fact of institutional existence is not enough to assure the church that it is fully or properly engaged in its God-given missions. Just as Peter had to be converted to mission in the story of Cornelius, so the church has to be converted and re-converted to its mission. As the church's inner life changes with time and as the world around it changes, the church is constantly in danger of losing its multi-focal mission vision. The church can easily become myopic, keeping only part of the moving panorama of mission alive in its vision. The church is always tempted to do good things that distract it from a part or all of God's mission. Therefore, the challenge is to be constantly guided by the Spirit in discerning, defining, re-defining, and fulfilling its mission assignment under God.

The church is the community where God's Kingdom is revealed as a foretaste of its full revelation to come at the Second Coming. Because of the church's faults and failures, the Kingdom's presence in the church is always partially hidden from sight. However, by the grace and power of God, the Kingdom is also present in the church in a visible form when its members exhibit God through gifts and graces of the Spirit.

History of Church and Mission

As we have seen, the church of the Protestant Reformers lacked both the vision and the intentional structures necessary for global mission. The Pietists made significant moves in world mission, but not until William Carey went to India in 1793 did Protestants become significantly engaged in global mission.

William Carey established the Baptist Mission Society to promote mission and support his team in India; however, the Baptist Mission Society was a mission agency separate from any church or denominational structure. Individuals became supporting members of the mission society apart from their church membership.

The mission society model remains the most common model among Protestants until the present day. Many Protestant groups have a congregational, non-centralized organizational style. Thus, typical mission societies are supported by individuals or clusters of congregationalist churches that send and support missionaries who plant more congregationalist churches. Roman Catholic missions are conducted by missionary orders, like Maryknoll and the Society of the Divine Word.

By the twentieth century, a problem with the mission society model became apparent. The "church" (as congregation or denomination) and "mission" (located in the mission agency) were separate but parallel entities that included some of the same people but having different purposes. The church was for "over here" at home in nominally Christian nations and the mission agency was for "over there" among non-Christian peoples. This led to "churches without missions and to missionary organizations that are not churches," to mission "work outside of ecclesial structures," and to mission as "an activity carried out [only] in non-Western cultures" (Goheen 2014:75). The local church planted on the mission field amounted to little more than a "container into which missions might place their converts" (Goheen 2014:74) rather than a missional community for its own area made up of both local members and expatriate missionaries.

As the twentieth century progressed, a consensus developed among most Christian groups that the church is missionary at its core. A church does not merely do missions as a part of its ministry package and those involved in doing missions are not to be separated from the churches they plant and serve. Being missionary comes from the essential nature of the church. This position is both a missional ecclesiology and an ecclesial missiology.

Adventist Church and Mission

While the Adventist Church has shared many of the same challenges as other Protestant groups, the church was blessed to have had a missional ecclesiology from the beginning. Early cross-cultural missionaries were sent by the Mission Board of the General Conference. The General Conference Secretariat continues to direct the service of cross-cultural missions from within the structure of the church.

I witnessed the consequences of having a structural separation between a mission society and the local church of another denomination when I worked in Malawi. Missionaries were sent and administered by their American mission agency to plant churches in Malawi. The governance of missionary work within Malawi was directed by a board that had no Malawian members. The local church boards had no missionary members. They all worshipped in the same churches on Sunday but did not have a structural relationship. The body of Christ metaphor is not fulfilled when church and mission function in this way.

A cross-cultural Adventist missionary sent by the General Conference ideally has structured relationships with several church entities: (1) The local church and conference from which they leave for missionary service; (2) the General Conference Secretariat that selects, trains, and sends them; (3) the calling administrative entity that supervises their work on the field; and, (4) the local church where they work. The Adventist Church is a global church and it's missionaries need all of these relationships to fulfill the body of Christ metaphor of the church.

The Adventist system avoids the problems on a non-ecclesial missiology, or a system that disconnects mission agencies from the church. However, the missionary's relationship with the sending local church and conference needs to be strengthened. To illustrate, when I served in Malawi the structural relationships identified above were in place except for the first one. I had no structured relationship with a local church, conference, union, or division in my homeland, the United States. This lack of structure diminished the flow of news and information from where I served to the church of my homeland. Ideally, the sending local church and conference should have a sense of ownership and participation in the service of "our missionary."

The Motivation for Mission

Part of being sinful humans is having mixed motivations for almost everything. In subtle and subconscious ways, human selfishness slips in to mix with the very best of motives. Personal motives, both good and bad, influence the motivation for missions. The faulty motives of other individuals and of other generations of missionaries are frequently easier to identify than our own faulty motives. Missionary methods and practices of the past can be critiqued, but their true motivation is known only by God. Jonah is a biblical example of a missionary whom God used effectively in spite of seriously mixed motives. The path of sanctification includes the purification of motives for all of life. Being effective in mission requires allowing God to identify and purify wrong motives for engaging in any aspect of God's mission.

There are some clearly wrong motives for mission, such as: (1) condescending pity for the needy that can produce a messiah complex, (2) the appeal of adventure that can lead one to be more of a mission tourist that a servant missionary, (3) an individualistic goal of self-fulfillment, or even spiritual growth that can produce an unhealthy inward focus in place of an outward focus on others, (4) the desire to add "missionary" on one's service record for the sake of career advancement, and (5) the desire for material gain. Most missionaries can name blessings and benefits that come from their service; however, receiving those blessings should be a secondary motive to the good motives described below.

Good motives for mission include:

1. Glorifying God. When people turn from false gods to worship the one true God as the result of missions, he is glorified.

2. The love of Christ. Paul said, "Christ's love compels us" (2 Cor 5:14). Christ loves the world (John 3:16), Christ loves me, I love Christ, therefore I want to share Christ with the world.

3. Compassion for the needy. Jesus had compassion for the multitudes because they were like sheep without a shepherd (Matt 9:36). Their neediness was comprehensive, including both material and spiritual needs.

4. Obedience. The Great Commission is as much a command as is the Decalogue.

5. A sense of calling. Along with the spiritual gifts, God gives believers particular calls and gifts to perform various aspects of his mission.

6. Eschatological urgency. Biblical prophecy points to an imminent Second Coming and billions of people need to hear the Gospel.

An Adventist Theology of Mission

Adventists hold many beliefs in common with other Christians, especially those of the Wesleyan-Armenian school of theology. These commonalities include believing in the Bible, the Trinity, the Fall, salvation in Christ, and others.

With regard to mission, we believe that all Christians share the task of world mission. The policy statement that follows is part of the de facto Adventist theology of mission.

> To avoid creating misunderstanding or friction in our relationships with other Christian churches and religious organizations, the following guidelines have been set forth:
>
> 1. We recognize those agencies that lift up Christ before men as a part of the divine plan for evangelization of the world, and we hold in high esteem Christian men and women in other communions who are engaged in winning souls to Christ.,...
>
> 6. The Seventh-day Adventist Church is unable to confine its mission to restricted geographical areas because of its understanding of the Gospel commission's mandate...Any restriction which limits witness to specified geographical areas therefore becomes an abridgment of the Gospel commission. The Seventh-day Adventist Church also acknowledges the rights of other religious persuasions to operate without geographical restrictions. (*Relationships with Other Christian Churches and Religious Organizations*, General Conference Working Policy, 2013-14: O 110)

The rationale for recognizing the work of other Christian groups has three elements:

1. The Great Commission applies to all Christians. When they obey the Commission they are fulfilling "a part of the divine plan for the evangelization of the world."

2. A non-Christian who accepts Christ and joins any Christian fellowship has taken the most essential step. A Buddhist who becomes a Baptist, for example, has come under the saving power of the Cross.

3. The practical challenge of reaching the unevangelized peoples of Earth overwhelms the human and material resources of our own church and calls for the participation of all Christians.

While recognizing the valid work of other Christian groups, Adventists also believe they have a unique, end-time missional role, as George Knight explains:

> Seventh-day Adventists currently support one of the most ambitious mission programs in the history of Christianity....They have planted their [churches], schools, medical institutions, and publishing houses in all parts of the earth, impelled by the driving force of a belief that holds that the Second Coming of Christ will not happen until "this Gospel of the Kingdom shall be preached in all the world for a witness unto all nations" (Matt 24:14).
>
> The extensiveness of Adventist mission outreach is the product of a prophetic consciousness based on Christ's "Great Commission" of Matthew 28:19-20. While accepting that commission as a mandate to Christians in general, Seventh-day Adventists have been driven by a more specific mission to preach the message of the three angels of Revelation 14 (the "everlasting Gospel" linked with the distinctive Adventist doctrines) "to every nation, and kindred, and tongue and people" (Rev 14:6-12).

> The three angels messages of Revelation 14 constitute the special end-time message that Adventists believe is their missional duty to proclaim.

According to Adventist understanding, the end of the earth's history will not come until the voice of the three angels has been heard throughout the earth. That view has undergirded and pushed forward the Adventist drive for world mission....[They] have not seen themselves as one denomination among many, but as a people with God's end time message (Rev 12:17; 14:12). That line of prophetic interpretation has dominated Adventism. (2005:vi)

The three angels' messages of Revelation 14 constitute the special end-time message that Adventists believe is their missional duty to proclaim. The first angel proclaims the "eternal Gospel," which is the same Gospel preached by Jesus and the Apostles, but with a particular end-time focus. The first angel fulfills Christ's promise that "this Gospel of the kingdom will be preached in all the world as a witness to all the nations, and then the end will come" (Matt 24:14). The angelic call is to "fear," "give ... glory," and "worship" the Creator God of the Bible. The false gods of non-Christian religions are to be excluded from worship. The false understandings of God are to be corrected. Fearing and glorifying God means giving him the place he deserves in one's life through repentance and being converted to enter a right relationship with him. Worshipping God as Creator means affirming the biblical Creation and is an allusion to the Sabbath commandment (Exod 20:11), which is a memorial of creation. Thus, the Sabbath will be a major issue in the final crisis of human history. The first angel also proclaims that "the hour of his judgment has come."

> The judgment referred to here is the first phase of the judgment (the pre-advent judgment) taking place in heaven before the Second Coming....This judging takes place at the same time that the final proclamation of the Gospel goes throughout the earth. Both have the same purpose; they draw a clear line of demarcation between those who are on God's side and those who are against him. (Stefanović 2009:454)

The second angel declares the fall of Babylon, which has deceived and seduced the nations. "Babylon is an end-time worldwide religious confederacy ... arrayed against God and his faithful people....Whereas the Gospel is everlasting, Babylon is short-lived ... [and] 'fallen'" (Stefanović 2009:458).

The third angel declares that those who follow the unified, apostate religious system of the end times (the "beast") will be destroyed. God's righteous wrath, the "reaction of God's holiness" (2009:461), will consume the wicked.

The "distinctive Adventist doctrines" (Knight 2005:vi), that many other Christians do not hold, and are linked with the proclamation of the three angels' messages, include:

1. Adventists proclaim the nearness of Christ's Second Coming with a special intensity and emphasis derived from the study of biblical prophecy. Belief in the Second Coming is shared by virtually all Christians, but the intensity of expectation and the historicist interpretation of prophecy are quite rare.

2. Adventists have a wholistic doctrine of humanity that sees all aspects of human nature as part of an integrated unity. The physical, mental, emotional, relational, and spiritual dimensions are seen as part of one unified whole. This perspective implies the duty to care for one's wholistic wellbeing through diet, lifestyle, and relationship building as a good steward of God's creation. The doctrine of wholism has helped Adventists to avoid much of the contentious conservative-liberal debate about evangelism and humanitarian ministries in mission. Healthcare, lifestyle training, education, relief, and development have worked in natural partnership with evangelism and church planting in Adventist mission. The Adventist uniqueness with regard to wholistic mission is a matter of degree and emphasis because some others do share the same basic perspective.

The wholistic, non-dualistic doctrine of humanity also leads to the doctrine of unconsciousness in death. Souls do not leave bodies at death to become ancestors, saints, ghosts, or spirits of some kind. This understanding provides a clear biblical approach for mission among peoples involved in worship or veneration of ancestors or saints and the many forms of spiritism. The majority of Christian groups disagree with the Adventist view of death and thus are much more challenged when confronting animistic spiritism. Adventists have a unique missional opportunity and responsibility in teaching the biblical view of death.

3. Adventists teach the perpetuity of all Ten Commandments, with emphasis on the Sabbath commandment. By asserting its perpetuity, Adventists do not mean that the Law is a means of earning salvation. That would be a perversion of the "eternal Gospel" of salvation by grace through faith. Neither does the church claim that Adventists (or any others) obey the Law perfectly. It is meant that the Decalogue is the unchanging standard for human life and behavior. This position gives Adventist mission a firm position in relation to the perspectivalism, relativism, and pragmatism that is common in postmodern Western culture, Eastern religions, and animistic folk religions. The seventh-day Sabbath presents varying challenges and opportunities for Adventist mission. Some non-Christians accept the Sabbath more easily than some Sunday-keeping Christians. Adventists are not wholly unique regarding the perpetuity of the Law and the Sabbath, as there are others who agree with the church's position.

4. Adventists believe that "the testimony of Jesus" (Rev 12:17; 19:10), which "is the spirit of prophecy" (Rev 19:10), empowers and informs the end-time mission of the remnant.

> Revelation 12:17 states clearly that God's end-time remnant is characterized by a special possession of the testimony of Jesus given through those who have been called by God to be his prophets. In the end-time, the church will once more be in possession of the prophetic ministry as it was in the time of John. (Stefanović 2009:560-561)

The Adventist church believes the spirit of prophecy functioned in the work of Ellen G. White, whose writings were authentically inspired, though non-canonical in their function. Her role as one of the primary Adventist founders and her work in early Adventist mission remains a valuable guide for contemporary missions. In holding this position, Adventists are wholly unique.

Adventists see themselves as having a special end-time remnant message that combines the commonalities of the Christian message with the unique features described above. The dynamism seen in Adventist mission can be attributed in large measure to the unique points in its theology of mission.

Chapter

Mission and a Theology of Religions

~•~

Introduction

The theology of religions, or how Christians view non-Christian religions, is a topic needing thoughtful attention for several reasons: (1) While other theological matters usually receive healthy emphasis, the theology of religions is often neglected; (2) Christian mission among the world religions is a massive challenge requiring much better understanding; (3) religious pluralism, with its assumption that all religions are equally valid spiritual pathways leading to the same destination, needs to be addressed; (4) the destiny of the unevangelized or the never-evangelized is a particular issue in missiology that needs attention.

Secularism and Religion

Today's world is often seen as becoming an ever more secular, irreligious place. Many predications have been made of the complete demise or elimination of religion as a part of the process of modernization and human development. Communism made a serious attempt to completely eliminate religion.

The *Oxford English Dictionary* definition of "secular" includes these elements:

> Of or belonging to the present or visible world as distinguished from the eternal or spiritual world; temporal, worldly. Belonging to the world and its affairs as distinguished from the church and religion…. Chiefly used as a negative term, with the meaning non-ecclesiastical, non-religious, or non-sacred. (www.oed.com/)

Significant forces at work have promoted secularity. The culture of Western modernity, with its scientific method, "finds little if any place for the supernatural and the transcendent…. Religious beliefs, values, and institutions are increasingly marginalized and lose their plausibility and power" (Moreau et al. 2000:865).

Secularization has weakened the general perception of the Bible as a source of truth. Except for funerals and weddings, many modern people rarely enter a church. People who do affirm a belief in God are sometimes agonistics or functional atheists who live their daily lives as if God does not exist. Others are deists, believing that God exists but is detached and uninvolved with human life.

The proportion of humanity that has become secular in the sense of having no faith or spirituality or religion of any kind in their lives is debatable. Even in China and the former Soviet Union, many people retained underground religious beliefs and practices throughout the Communist era. What has clearly happened is that many people in Europe, North America, Australia, and New Zealand have decreased their participation in traditional Christian practices and institutions. In place of traditional Christianity, many people have turned to non-traditional Christianity, New Age movements, neo-paganism, Eastern religions, or other activities that appeal to the supernatural and transcendent in some way. Sometimes the label "secular" is applied to people who are not religious in a traditional way, but it may not describe them accurately. "Secular" is also sometimes used as a synonym for false religion, but that use of the word is inaccurate.

All around the world there are people, often wealthy and highly educated, whose relationships with the beliefs, practices, and institutions of their respective world religions are non-traditional and non-orthodox. Like nominal Christians, there are nominal or non-practicing Muslims, Hindus, and Buddhists whose beliefs and practices are considered non-orthodox; however, nominal practitioners of all religions generally continue to self-identify with the religions of their history.

The discussion of secularism sometimes implies a coming world without religion but Scripture does not point in that direction. Biblical prophecy portrays a final end-time conflict between true and false worship. The dragon (Rev 12:17) and the great harlot (17:1) of prophecy symbolize the united forces of false worship that make war on the pure woman and her Son (12:1, 5). The final eschatological war (as depicted in Rev 13 and 19) is not between worship and no worship, or religion and no religion, but between true and false religion and worship. The final demarcation between true and false religion will be made at the end of time. This biblical perspective implies that Christian missions will always need to engage adherents of other religions.

Figure 6.1
Basic Kinds of Religion

World Religions
• Global religions with written scriptures, formal theologies, specialized clergy, and structured institutions.
• All have orthodox traditions and syncretized sub-traditions that often have characteristics of animistic folk religions.
• Examples: Christianity, Islam, Hinduism, and Buddhism are the largest.

Traditional, Folk, Primal, or Ethnoreligions
• Localized religions associated with traditional, tribal, or indigenous peoples, animistic in character.
• Typically lacking written scriptures, formal theologies, specialized clergy, and structured institutions.
• Examples: Native American, African Traditional Religion, and Australian Aboriginal religions.

World Religions as a Mission Priority

Before discussing the major world religions, a special mention regarding mission among Jews is necessary. In 1910, the world Jewish population stood at 13.1 million, or 0.7% of the population. By 2010, the Jewish population had grown to 14.6 million, which comprised only 0.2% of the population (Johnson and Ross 2009:7). Adventist mission among Jews remains a theological, missiological priority even though the numerical challenge is comparatively small.

The non-Christian world religions need to be a high priority in global mission for several reasons: First, because the majority of humanity self-identifies with one of them. All of the major world religions have grown dramatically in the past century. Rather than becoming less religious, significant segments of the world religions have become even more fundamentalist and radically religious. Mission must go where the people are.

Table 6.2
Growth of Religious Groups, 1910-2010

Group	1910 Number (millions)	1910 World Pop %	2010 Number (millions)	2010 World Pop %	Change % Pop
Christians	612	34.8%	2,292	33.2%	-1.6%
Muslims	221	12.6%	1,549	22.4%	9.8%
Hindus	224	12.7%	948	13.7%	1.0%
Buddhists	139	7.8%	468	6.8%	-1.0%
Agnostics/Atheists	0.36	0.0%	777	2.0%	2.0%
Chinese Folk	392	22.3%	458	6.6%	-15.7%
Ethnoreligionists	135	7.7%	261	3.8%	-3.9%
New Religionists	7	0.4%	64	0.9%	0.5%
Others	29	1.7%	89	10.6%	8.9%
Total	**1,759**		**6,906**		

Source: Data from Johnson and Ross 2009:7.

As table 6.2 shows, all groups experienced growth, but their share of the world population changed in different ways. The biggest loss of share was among Chinese Folk religionists (15.7%) because of the suppression of religion under Communism; Ethnoreligions, like African Traditional Religions, lost 3.9% of their share, often because of conversion to Islam or Christianity; the share of Agnostics and Atheists grew from almost nothing to 2%, still a relatively small share of humanity; Islam increased its share the most, by 9.8%; the combined share of Islam, Hinduism, and Buddhism grew 9.8%, from 33.1% to 42.9% of humanity; Christianity continues to hover at about one-third.

The second reason to make the world religions a priority in mission is that in spite of their great numbers, "in those places where people have embraced an enduring world religion other than Christianity, we have had and are having little mission success" (Muck and Adeney 2009:8). This lack of mission success is caused both by factors within the religions themselves and by ineffective mission methods.

Third, mission among the world religions should be done in a way specifically designed for non-Christian people, rather than the traditional Christian-to-Christian model that Adventists have used. Established evangelistic approaches have Baptists and Methodists in mind, but the same approaches have been used among Buddhists and Muslims. Those non-Christian peoples who have responded well to Adventist missions have been traditional, tribal, animistic peoples. An approach is needed for each non-Christian group that brings the Gospel to bear upon their questions and contexts.

Fourth, the non-Christian world religions are centered in what is called the "10/40 Window," that starts 10 degrees north and ends at 40 degrees north of the equator. However, globalization and migration have scattered adherents of all the religions across the globe, bringing them within reach of almost every local church. The mission agenda of almost every congregation should include local populations of Muslims, Hindus, Buddhists, and others.

Saying that the world religions need to be a mission priority does not imply a withdrawal from mission among other Christian groups or from people who are truly irreligious and secular. Rather, the challenge is to remedy an imbalance that leaves a huge portion of humanity virtually untouched. A well-articulated theology of religions is a necessary part of becoming more effective among the world religions.

Defining "Religion"

"Religion" and "culture," and their relationship with each other, are such complex parts of human life that neat, all-inclusive definitions are impossible to make. Yet, working definitions are necessary and helpful. There are several approaches made in defining religion (Partridge 2013:20-22).

"Essentialist" definitions focus on the inner essence, core, faith, or first-hand experience of a religion. For example, the essence of Christianity is salvation by grace through faith in Jesus Christ.

The "functionalist" approach seeks "to determine the social, psychological, or political role played by the things we call 'religious'" (21). For Islam, one function of religion is that it provides fellowship in the *umma*, a community similar in function to the Christian church.

The "family resemblance" approach defines a religion by a set of traits, like Smart's seven dimensions of religion. For example, the ritual dimension is very important for Hindus.

Putting these approaches together, religion can be defined as a "classifier" used to establish self-identities and the identities of others. Thus, an Adventist is one who believes in the Bible rather than the Qur'an, worships on Saturday instead of Sunday, and lives a healthy lifestyle that includes certain things and excludes other things.

The working definition of "religion" for this book draws on Partridge (2013:20-22), Corduan (1998:21), and Smart (1998:13-22). Notice that the definition blends dimensions, essence, functions, and classification.

A religion is a system of rituals, experiences, narratives, doctrines, ethics, organizational structures, and ritual objects that together provide values, meaning, and coherence to individuals within a social group that help them cope with and rise above the issues of daily life and gives them self-identity. Religions venerate or worship objects, powers, persons, or beings.

Dimensions of Religion

The study of religion is complex and certain models are helpful in the endeavor. Ninian Smart presents a model that identifies seven dimensions present in every religion. Figure 6.3 is adapted from his model (1998:13-22).

Figure 6.3
Smart's Dimensions of Religion

1. Practical, ritual dimension	• regular worship, preaching, prayers, rituals, practices, liturgies, festivals, pilgrimages, sacrifices
2. Experiential, emotional dimension	• feelings of awe, peace, love, hope, gratitude, penitence, ecstasy, conversion, release, joy, mourning
3. Narrative, mythic dimension	• stories of human origin, origin of death and suffering, founding of religions, religious heroes, origin of rituals
4. Doctrinal, philosophical dimension	• systematic, intellectual organization of narratives, belief systems, shaping a worldview, creeds
5. Ethical, legal dimension	• application of narrative and doctrinal dimensions to life, rules that express principles, moral-ethical codes
6. Social, institutional dimension	• organizations, structures, leadership, hierarchy, finances
7. Material dimension	• buildings, art work, ritual clothing, shrines, sacred places, statues, icons, altars, tombs

Source: Adapted from Smart 1998:13-22.

Smart's typology identifies dimension or features that are used to describe every religion. The different religions give varying emphasis to the seven dimensions. For example, the doctrinal, philosophical dimension is not emphasized in the traditional religions of non-literate, traditional people groups but highly emphasized by Christians. Islam lacks a structured hierarchy corresponding to Roman Catholicism, and Hinduism lacks a well-defined ethical system.

The implication for Christian mission is that all religious dimensions have to be engaged when proclaiming and contextualizing the Gospel for any particular group. A religious group that lacks its own well-defined doctrinal system will be adding a totally new religious dimension when they learn and accept Christian doctrines. Those with highly ritualized public festivals will feel a sense of loss when joining the typical Adventist church, where public religious festivals are not emphasized. There are traditional religious styles that can be borrowed from local culture, while following biblical principles. Some styles cannot be adopted but every dimension of religion needs to be intentionally addressed in the process of faithful contextualization.

Sources of Human Religiosity

Why are humans religious? Did the tendency to be religious originate within humans or with God? Two approaches have been popular in modern times.

Subjective Origins Theory

The subjective approach locates the origin of religion within the deep, subconscious needs, feelings, and thoughts of humanity. The emotional experience of love and hate, happiness and sorrow, comfort and pain together create a human need to reach beyond human experience to something that is called a "spirit" or a "god." Because all children suffer in some way from their families and parents, they form idealized mental images of perfect parents and call those images "gods." According to the subjective approach, all of Smart's dimensions of religion are human creations developed in response to inner human needs.

The subjective explanation of the origin of religion cannot withstand a careful critique. There are, without question, human needs and emotions that reach for a solution beyond humanity. However, the feelings of inner need may also be a gift from God, not merely a human internal response. The feelings of joy, comfort, peace, and awe that are part of religious experience may be part of a real encounter with God rather than mere subjective imaginations. When God walked in the Garden and called out to Adam and Eve, "Where are you?" (Gen 3:9), their inner emotional responses were the result of a real encounter with God. Christians believe they continue to have authentic encounters with God that originate outside of themselves. The Fall damaged but did not entirely remove the image of God. A "moral consciousness" remained through which God could communicate (Rodriguez 2013:436).

Evolutionary Origins Theory

The second explanation for human religiosity is the approach that pairs religious evolution with biological evolution. In this theory, primitive humans evolved from "lower" kinds of religion to "higher" forms and will eventually have no religion at all.

The first stage of religious evolution is the *magic* and *mana* stage at which people are aware of impersonal spiritual powers. *Mana* is a Melanesian word that refers to impersonal power that is localized in physical objects called fetishes. Through magic, the *mana* is manipulated by the use of fetishes to bring evil upon others or goodness upon self, family, and community.

The second stage is *animism*, which adds personality to the spiritual powers of the *mana*/magic stage. There are nature spirits that occupy all parts of nature and ancestor spirits that maintain interactive relationships with living humans. The spirits can bring either good or evil and must therefore be manipulated. Shamans are experts who know how to manipulate the spirits. The spirits have limited knowledge and power and can operate only in specific areas of influence.

In the third stage, *polytheism*, the spirits become gods and goddesses of superior power and knowledge. They are not easily manipulated, but must be worshipped and petitioned. However, the possibility of manipulating the gods through correct worship still exists.

In the fourth stage, *henotheism*, multiple gods are recognized, but one god is selected as the object of worship. The selection of a god is made by individual, family, tribal, or occupational preference, or because of geographic location.

Israel's unfaithfulness to Yahweh during OT times may have been an expression of henotheism.

The fifth step is *monotheism*. As people evolved, they eventually realized that there must be a single, all-powerful, all-knowing, everywhere-present God above all others. Some supernatural beings like angels, spirits, or saints were understood to exist, but as inferior beings to God. Judaism, Christianity, and Islam are the main monotheistic religions.

The final stage of the evolutionary model is *beyond gods*. At the highest level, humans become wholly rational without a need for supernatural beings, which after all, were figments of imagination and mere superstition.

The critique of the evolutionary model is that it has never been shown to function in real life. Different peoples do practice every form of religion described in figure 6.4, in many different variations, and they do change their religious practices and beliefs over time. However, the linear, evolutionary progression from *magic/mana* to being *beyond gods* has never been documented through field research. Understanding the different religious types shown in the figure is valuable because they are readily visible among different people groups around the world.

Figure 6.4
Basic Religious Types

Monotheism	• Single, all-powerful, all-knowing, everywhere-present God must be worshipped with submission, cannot be manipulated.
Henotheism	• One god is selected from among the pantheon of gods by family, tribe, or professional group.
Polytheism	• Multiple gods form a pantheon, are more powerful than spirits but not all-powerful, less open to manipulation than animist spirits.
Animism	• Personalized nature and ancestor spirits have limited power and scope of influence, are manipulated by expert practitioners for evil or good.
Magic	• Impersonal power is localized in fetishes, manipulated to bring good or evil to others and goodness to self, family, and community.

Original Monotheism

The Bible narrative describes the origin of religion as what scholars have called "original monotheism" (Corduan 1998:32). The Creation story tells of God who existed "In the beginning" (Gen 1:1), before humanity or anything else existed on Earth. When Adam and Eve were created, God made them aware of himself and established a relationship with them. He gave them standards of good and evil by which to live (2:16-17). When they sinned and were alienated from God, he took the initiative and came walking in the garden to find them and describe to them the consequences of their fall (3:8-24). He also spoke of the "seed of the woman" who would destroy the serpent and provide salvation (3:15).

Although the details in Genesis are minimal, God provided a system of sacrifice pointing forward to the Messiah that Abel followed but Cain scorned (4:1-8). When Eve gave birth to Seth and Seth became the father of Enosh, the Bible reports: "Then men began to call upon the name of the LORD" (4:26). The phrase "call upon the name of the LORD" (Yahweh) is used repeatedly to describe worship at an altar of sacrifice during the OT patriarchal period (12:8; 13:4; 21:33; 26:25). The sacrificial worship of God by the OT patriarchs was a prototypical form of the system that was greatly elaborated by Moses in the wilderness sanctuary and practiced in the Jerusalem temple to prefigure Jesus the Messiah. Another view is that "call" refers to "the missionary activity of pro-claiming the name of the Lord to other people" (Doukhan 2016:125). Patriarchal worship was an act of witnessing to the one true God among all who observed. "Calling upon the name of the LORD," was an early element of God's mission.

The Bible does not portray the Fall as producing a mildly sinful state. Rather, sinfulness came upon humanity in full-blossom as Adam and Eve were cast out of the garden and as Cain murdered his own brother, Abel. After the Fall there was a movement toward many ungodly forms of religion. The multiplicity of today's religions evolved from spiritual ancestors along humanity's religious pathway that departed from original monotheism in different ways and varying degrees. The biblical picture is not of religious evolution, but rather of religious devolu-tion, from original monotheism to a myriad of other ungodly religious forms. Corduan describes the move way from original monotheism (1998:34-35).

First, people turned away from worshipping the one Creator God. As they faced the daily problems of sickness, hunger, violence, and death, humans turned to idols, spirits, gods, and even themselves as objects of worship. As Satan had deceived Adam and Eve, so he and his demons continued to deceive humanity by offering alternatives to faithful monotheism. People worshipped creation instead of the Creator (Rom 1:18-22).

Second, original monotheism was replaced by magic, animism, polythe-ism, and henotheism in many different patterns. The overall direction is that as "monotheism is left behind, ritual and magic increase" (34). Along with the dominance of ritual and magic in religion came the assumption that spiritual manipulation techniques can earn divine favor, avert divine anger, and fulfill human needs. Worship became an act of manipulation rather than submission.

Third, as religious change occurred, tension developed between those who held to original monotheism and those who departed. There were reformers, like Noah, Moses, and the prophets, who called people back to true worship. However, ancient Israel remained stubbornly henotheistic, worshipping Yahweh and other so-called gods. Not until the Babylonian Exile did Judaism become firmly monotheistic. Even among those who were nominal monotheists there was slippage from the ideal as people conformed to influences around them. The prophetic call for a remnant (Jer 23:3; Rom 9:29) was a call to worship God "in spirit and in truth" (John 4:23).

The religious development traced above is a faith statement based on confidence in the revealed Word of God. However, there is anthropological evidence for "primitive" or "original" monotheism based on the research of Wilhelm Schmidt (1868-1954). Schmidt's extensive research was done among traditional peoples of Africa, America, Australia, Asia, and Europe. Among some of the most ancient cultures, he found evidence of exclusive worship of the Creator God, with little or no magic or animism. Even where Schmidt found magic and animism, his data "show universal and ancient remnants of belief in an original God" whose characteristics are in close alignment with the God of the Bible (Corduan 1998:34). Schmidt's "remnants" or fragments of divine truth may explain why all of the world religions retain different elements that are similar or identical with the biblical narrative.

Elias Brasil de Souza discusses the relationship of the religion of the OT with the Ancient Near Eastern religions.

> We may reasonably suggest that God directed human history in ways that certain truths would never be lost. Moreover, God may have guided certain institutions as they appeared in human history so that they could later be turned into effective means of communicating God's saving purposes for the world.... Some parallels [between themes in Scripture and Ancient Near Eastern literature can be best] explained by positing a common origin, especially certain thematic and structural correspondences such as ideas of a conflict between good and evil, the end of evil, and the resurrection. Certain core truths known to Adam and Eve and the patriarchs were passed on from generation to generation of God's people until they were eventually recorded in Scripture.... It seems clear that some core truths were known to the human race since the garden of Eden. And even those who rejected God's sovereignty also preserved some glimpses of truth, though distorted by polytheism and idolatry.... The religion of Israel and that of neighboring [pagan] nations have a common origin, which goes back to the garden of Eden and the patriarchs. (2015:135-136)

Christian Views of the Other World Religions

There is a wide spectrum of belief among Christians about the other religions. Some think they all came from the devil, while others think they all came from God. Saying it another way, some see total discontinuity, others see complete continuity, and still others see a mix of continuity and discontinuity between Christianity and the other religions.

The view on continuity has moved in two different directions in recent times. Some postmodern thinkers believe that the religions have no common ground because they are founded on radically different presuppositions, ask completely different questions about life and reality, and reach very different conclusions. On the other hand, some Christians who encounter the other religions regularly notice that they share some of the same basic features of religion with Christianity. These observations lead them to become religious pluralists who equate the similar features of all religions and find great commonalty.

A closer look, however, shows that Christians attach very different meanings to some of the same outward dimensions. For example, most religions practice prayer, but Christians understand the meaning of prayer in a different way from other religions. Most religions have a god or multiple gods, but the God of the Bible is understood differently from the other deities. The continuity is more at the external level than at the deep, internal level that addresses the deepest questions. The nature of God, the nature of humanity, the nature of the human predicament, and the nature of the solution to the human predicament are understood very differently.

Figure 6.5 illustrates the continuity and discontinuity Christianity has with the four largest non-Christian world religions. The world religions are far too complex to summarize in one table and each religion has many variations. The purpose of the figure is only to illustrate continuity and discontinuity in broad strokes.

Figure 6.5
Christianity and the Other World Religions

	Continuity	Discontinuity
Islam	Promotes a God-centered life of submission and reverent worship.	**Islam**: God is One. **Christianity**: God is Triune.
Hinduism	Seeks oneness with the ultimate, spiritual reality.	**Hinduism**: Ultimate reality is in Brahman who is impersonal. **Christianity**: Ultimate reality is in God, who is relational and personal.
Buddhism	Shows sympathy and compassion for human suffering.	**Buddhism**: Humans seek to escape suffering. **Christianity**: Humans seek divine strength within suffering.
Confucianism	Has a universal system of moral order that guides human conduct.	**Confucianism**: Moral order is impersonal and socially structured. **Christianity**: Moral order is based on God's character, involves relationship with both God and fellow humans.
All	Have Smart's seven dimensions of religion with varied combinations and emphases (1998:13-22).	**Others**: Fulfilling the dimensions creates merit to solve the human predicament. **Christianity**: Fulfilling the dimensions is a non-meritorious response to salvation in Christ.

Source: Adapted from Goheen 2014:359.

The Destiny of the Unevangelized or Never-Evangelized

What happens to those who, through no fault of their own, die without hearing the good news of salvation in Jesus Christ so that they can accept or reject it? What does it mean to be evangelized or reached with the Gospel? In this discussion, the words "evangelize" and "reach" are used as synonyms that refer to giving a person an opportunity to accept Christ.

Figure 6.6
Evangelizing or Reaching

Evangelizing or reaching a person means teaching the Gospel in a way that
- is faithful to the Bible
- is appropriately contextualized for their culture
- occurs over an adequate time period, with repetitions if necessary
- uses appropriate language, methods, and media in communication

The elements in figure 6.6 describe the human side of an encounter between the church and a non-believer. The church's role is to facilitate a person's encounter with the living God, through the Holy Spirit. When evangelization is with people of the same cultural group, many of the factors are automatically present. In cross-cultural evangelization, the process is much more complicated, requiring contextualization of the Gospel message for people whose language, culture, and religion are different. Because of the Spirit's amazing power, people can come to Christ in spite of unskilled evangelization, but they can also be turned away by shoddy methods. The church's duty is to use the best possible approaches for every people group.

Many people have never been evangelized or have been poorly evangelized. How large is the unevangelized portion of humanity through the ages?

In OT and Intertestamental times, the knowledge and worship of God were taught and shared by his people. How many people had an opportunity to learn from God's OT people is impossible to know. Israel was at the crossroads between Africa, Europe, and Asia, but regions like the Americas, Oceania, and Australia were isolated by distance and travel technology. It seems safe to say that many people of OT times did not have the opportunity to learn from God's OT covenant people.

The early church spread the teachings of the Apostles about Jesus Christ and planted churches far and wide through its centrifugal, going-out style of missions. Transportation was better because of the Roman Empire's road system and improvements in sailing. However, major world regions were still isolated.

Starting in the Middle Ages, Christianity became increasingly a European religion. Not until the modern missionary movement did the church's missionary vision and the technologies for transportation make global evangelization possible. Today, Christianity is truly a global religion, but even so, many millions remain unevangelized.

One popular mission slogan in modern times has been to preach the Gospel to every person "in this generation." However, it is doubtful that any generation in the Christian era has ever fulfilled that worthy goal. Jesus promised that "this

Gospel of the Kingdom shall be preached in the whole world as a testimony to all nations, and then the end will come" (Matt 24:14) referring to the final generation before the Second Coming.

Figure 6.7
Texts Suggesting Narrow Access to Salvation

- For wide is the gate and broad is the road that leads to destruction, and many enter through it. But small is the gate and narrow the road that leads to life, and only a few find it. (Matt 7:13-14)

- Whoever believes in the Son has eternal life, but whoever rejects the Son will not see life. (John 3:36; see 1 John 5:12)

- I am the way and the truth and the life. No one comes to the Father except through me. (John 14:6)

- Salvation is found in no one else, for there is no other name under heaven given to mankind by which we must be saved. (Acts 4:12)

- For there is one God and one mediator between God and mankind, the man Christ Jesus. (1 Tim 2:5)

- Whoever has the Son has life; whoever does not have the Son of God does not have life. (1 John 5:12)

What, then, is the eternal destiny of the billions of people who have never been evangelized or who were evangelized poorly so that they did not really have a good chance to make an informed choice? To rephrase the question, are the unique, saving merits of Christ's atonement available to those who do not know about his work on the Cross and thus cannot explicitly accept them? Are the missionary people of God, Israel and the church held responsible by God for their failure to fully evangelize humanity in each generation? Is God, himself, responsible for not empowering Israel and the church to evangelize every living soul in every generation?

These questions are particularly poignant for missionaries who have worked diligently among the world religions with little positive response. Christians whose ancestral peoples lived and died without a knowledge of the Gospel have a personal stake; however, the main issue is not the sorrow or concern Christians may feel for unresponsive people they have worked with or for their own ancestors. Trying to construct a theology that opens a wider door of salvation for the unevangelized because of personal concern is not appropriate. God alone is the Judge of all humanity and speculation about the eternal destiny of any particular person or people group is futile, be they apparently active Christians, Christians who have drifted away, or the unevangelized. The destiny of the unevangelized is important because it is interwoven with basic Christian teachings and raises important theological issues than need to be addressed, not because one is trying to ascertain the future of particular people.

Figure 6.8
Texts Suggesting Wide Access to Salvation

- And I, when I am lifted up from the earth, will draw all people to myself. (John 12:32)

- Consequently, just as one trespass resulted in condemnation for all people, so also one righteous act resulted in justification and life for all people. For just as through the disobedience of the one man the many were made sinners, so also through the obedience of the one man the many will be made righteous. (Rom 5:18-19; see 1 Cor 15:22)

- God was reconciling the world to himself in Christ, not counting people's sins against them. (2 Cor 5:19)

- This is good, and pleases God our Savior, who wants all people to be saved and to come to a knowledge of the truth. (1 Tim 2:3-5)

- That is why we labor and strive, because we have put our hope in the living God, who is the Savior of all people, and especially of those who believe. (1 Tim 4:10)

- For the grace of God has appeared that offers salvation to all people. (Titus 2:11)

The theology of the unevangelized has its own complex history, categories, and terminology. This chapter does not attempt to trace the history of each position, to identify the main advocates of each position, or to engage every one of the interwoven issues. (For further study: Rodriguez 2013:429-442; Dybdahl 1999:54-62; Goheen 2014:331-369; Moreau et al. 2000:761-762, 951-953; Ott and Strauss 2010:292-316; Skreslet 2012:97-134; Tennent 2010:191-226.)

I will discuss the destiny of the never-evangelized by using three simple propositions: (1) none of the unevangelized can be saved through Christ, (2) all of the unevangelized can be saved in different ways, (3) some of the unevangelized can be saved through Christ.

Several theological assumptions and themes are intertwined with the question of the destiny of the unevangelized.

The Great Controversy Theme

The destiny of the unevangelized involves the Great Controversy, or cosmic conflict theme, which is an organizing principle of Adventist theology. "The heart of this conflict has been Satan's charges that God is unfair, severe, unforgiving, arbitrary, revengeful, supremely selfish—'a being whose chief attribute is stern justice' (SC 11)" (Fortin and Moon 2013:850). The ultimate goal of the Great Controversy is to demonstrate to the entire cosmos that God's character is loving and just.

In the context of the great cosmic controversy between good and evil, Satan accuses God of being biased in his relationship with humanity. For this reason God has to demonstrate before the universe his impartiality and justice in allowing some humans to be eternally destroyed and others to receive eternal life (Job 1:6-12; 2:1-6; Rev 12:7-12). (Fortin and Moon 20013:903)

God's character is potentially challenged either by asserting that all the unevangelized will be lost or that all will be saved. On the other hand, God's character is vindicated when he is understood as accurately assessing the innermost lives of every human to determine their responses to his influences upon them, other than through direct evangelization.

Special and General Revelation

The life, teachings, and works of Christ are the ultimate divine acts of special revelation. The Bible, authored by inspired writers, is the written vehicle of special revelation. The Bible reports true prophets, who conveyed special revelation with a local, limited scope (like Samuel, Nathan, and Gad in 1 Chr 29:29). Adventists consider the writings of Ellen White to be a non-canonical special revelation that came through the spiritual gift of prophecy.

The unevangelized suffer from lack of access to God's special revelation. However, God's general revelation is accessible to all humans through several main avenues: (1) The created order reveals the "great intellect, wisdom, creativity, and ability ... and 'eternal power and divine nature'" of God (Ps 19; Rom 1:19-20; Moreau et al. 2000:829); (2) God's providential care for his creation shows his love and goodness for every creature (Acts 14:17); (3) the inner voice of conscience, of right or wrong, testifies of God's moral character (Rom 2:14-16); and (4) the inner human awareness of and longing for God (Ps 42:2).

While general revelation is available to all, not all of humanity benefits from it equally because of human limitations and sinfulness. The evidences of general revelation are distorted by sin at work in the world and misunderstood by humans because of their responses as free moral agents. Some people are more receptive to God's influence through general revelation than others. Yet, God does reveal himself in significant ways through general revelation.

Paul indicates that general revelation holds people "without excuse."

For since the creation of the world God's invisible qualities—his eternal power and divine nature—have been clearly seen, being understood from what has been made, so that people are without excuse. (Rom 1:18)

Paul also writes of people lacking access to special revelation who "have the requirements ... written on their hearts."

For it is not those who [merely] hear the law [receive special revelation] who are righteous in God's sight, but it is those who obey the law who will be declared righteous. Indeed, when Gentiles, [Muslims, Hindus, Buddhists, etc.] who do not have the law, do by nature things required by the law, they are a law for themselves, even though they do not have the law. They show that the requirements of the law are written on their hearts, their consciences also bearing witness, and their thoughts sometimes accusing them and at other times even defending them. This will take place on the day when God judges people's secrets through Jesus Christ, as my gospel declares. (Rom 2:13-16)

There are biblical examples of people, like Melchizedek, who apparently found "full acceptance by God apart from the knowledge provided by special revelation or the Gospel. However, Scripture is silent concerning how such individuals came to faith so we must exercise caution about drawing conclusions from such exceptions" (Moreau et al. 2000:829).

In spite of the limitations of general revelation, those who lack access to the Bible are able to respond positively to God. Being unreached by Israel or the church does not necessarily mean being unreached by God, who uses general revelation.

The Role of the Holy Spirit

"The wind blows wherever it pleases. You hear its sound, but you cannot tell where it comes from or where it is going. So it is with everyone born of the Spirit" (John 3:8).

God the Spirit empowers the church for the mission of God and through the church leads humanity toward the Gospel of Jesus as recorded in Scripture. But the Spirit can never be limited to what the human institution of the church does. In some eras, the church has left whole continents beyond the reach of mission, just as millions are unreached by the church today. Whatever the church does or does not do, the Spirit retains direct, individual, universal contact with every human being. The broad scope of the Spirit is seen in the fact that he is the one who inspired the writers of the Bible which, in turn, is the main vehicle of special revelation. The only limitation of the Spirit's work is the degree of openness within the human heart and mind. This is not to diminish the role of the church in mission because God is the one who chose to work through the church. However, the church should never think that it controls God's mission.

Amos Yong discusses a "pneumatological theology of religions" (2003:43). He says that the particularity of God's revelation through the "Word made flesh" (John 1:14) needs to be balanced with the universality of God's revelation through the Spirit poured out on all people (Joel 2:28; Acts 2:17). In other words, God's particular revelation through Jesus is known specifically to those who have access to the Bible. However, the Spirit's universal work extends to all peoples, including those who do not explicitly know about Jesus Christ. The

Spirit's work for unevangelized people is to soften their hearts, guide their lives using good influences available in their contexts, and make the truth available through general revelation ever more clear. This approach may be a plausible explanation for Melchizedek and other biblical characters who had no recorded access to special revelation.

There is contemporary evidence of divine initiatives by God the Holy Spirit, who augments the guidance of general revelation. Contemporary followers of other religions, notably Muslims, are receiving dreams and visions that point them to Christ (Garrison 2014). Many of the visions and dreams pass the test of truth because they direct the person toward Jesus and the Bible. When individuals obey the guidance of the dreams, they are often led to conversion to Jesus Christ.

Some cautionary points need to be made about visions and dreams: (1) people from Western cultures tend to be suspicious about visions and dreams and may need to be more open to extraordinary methods used by God, while others may be uncritically open to them and need to exercise caution; (2) every vision and dream must be tested by the Bible; (3) saying that someone has a vision or dream from God should not be understood to suggest that they have the gift of prophecy. Such manifestations should be understood as supernatural interventions for people who lack normal access to the Gospel.

Predestination or Freewill

A dividing line in the discussion of the unevangelized involves the contrasting positions of predestination and freewill theology. Adventists have a freewill theology, following in the tradition of Arminius, John Wesley, and the Methodists.

John Calvin (1509-1564) was the father of the Calvinist or Reformed branch of Christianity. The Calvinist doctrine of unconditional election, or predestination, states that God chooses who will be saved. The doctrine of double-predestination states that God chooses some for salvation and others for damnation. From this perspective, the never-evangelized would be understood as being among those who are not chosen by God for salvation.

Jacobus Arminius (1560-1609) was a Dutch theologian who opposed Calvin's teachings. In opposition to Calvin, Arminius taught that God gives humans freedom either to choose or reject salvation in Christ.

> The key distinctive doctrine in Arminianism is *prevenient grace*. It may not be a biblical term, but it is a biblical concept assumed everywhere in Scripture. It is a powerful but resistible drawing of God that Jesus spoke about in John 6:44. ["No one can come to Me unless the Father who sent Me draws him."]....Arminians believe that if a person is saved, it is because God initiated the relationship and enabled the person to respond freely with repentance and faith....Anyone who shows the first inkling or inclination of a good will toward God is already being influenced by grace. (Olson 2006:159-161)

"Prevenient" grace can also be called "preceding," or "enabling," or "going before" grace. Prevenient grace is the work of God upon the hearts of all human beings to draw them unto himself. Without the enabling power of grace, humans are so lost in sinfulness that they cannot accept God's offer of salvation, even when they are evangelized. With prevenient grace, they are given the capacity to accept God's invitation, but God never forces or coerces them because he respects the human freewill to either accept or reject the invitation.

John Wesley (1703–1791), the founder of Methodism, embraced Arminian theology and was its most prominent champion. He believed every human being was given sufficient prevenient grace to make a freewill decision, for or against God.

Said Wesley, "Yea, I am persuaded every child of God has had, at some time, 'life and death set before him,' eternal life and eternal death; and has in himself the casting voice" ("The General Spread of the Gospel," Sermon 63. www.umcmission.org).

His belief that all humans have life and death set before them to make a choice included the "heathens." Wesley declared that morality and good behavior outside of Christ have no value, either for Christians or non-Christians. Then he asserted that no one has the right to condemn "all the heathen and Mahometan [Islamic] world to damnation."

> Let it be observed, I purposely add, "to those that are under the Christian dispensation," because I have no authority from the Word of God "to judge those that are without." Nor do I conceive that any man living has a right to sentence all the heathen and Mahometan world to damnation. It is far better to leave them to him that made them, and who is "the Father of the spirits of all flesh;' who is the God of the Heathens as well as the Christians, and who hateth nothing that he hath made. ("Without God in the World," Sermon 125. www.umcmission.org)

Wesley's sermons did not directly address the destiny of the unevangelized; however, the assumption that he understood the "heathens" to be unevangelized seems safe to make. He refused to judge them, affirmed them as God's children, and trusted that they were under God's care.

Wesley's refusal to condemn non-Christian peoples did not imply that Christians should be passive or unengaged with them in mission. On the contrary, he felt that Christian missions were vital for calling non-Christians to Christ. This position produces a tension regarding the motivation for mission.

> There was a tension in Wesley between the idea that all people have a chance to know God and the need for human agents to take the message out to save the world. Wesley's freewill theology demanded the former [that even the unevangelized have a choice] while his missional understanding of Scripture required the latter [that the church has a missional obligation]. (Tompkins 2016:4)

More will be said about the vital topic of the motivation for mission and the unavoidable tension it involves.

Eternally Conscious Hellfire or Unconscious Extinction

Two contrasting theologies of death shape views of the destiny of the une-vangelized. The doctrine of eternal hellfire is held by some who also hold that salvation is not available to the unevangelized. This combination means that those who never had an opportunity to explicitly accept Christ suffer eternally alongside those who explicitly rejected Christ. Some try to solve the problem by suggesting that Christ will evangelize the lost in purgatory, giving them a "second chance." On the other hand, the doctrine of eternal hellfire would seem to promote the position of universalism, where everyone can be saved and no one goes to hellfire.

The Adventist doctrine of death states that the lost will pass into eternal, unconscious extinction to "be as if they had never been" (Obad 1:16; cf. Mal 4:1; Ps 37:20). Those whom the church never evangelizes, whom God reaches through general revelation and the influence of the Spirit, but who reject his initiatives, will experience unconscious extinction or annihilation. God's love, justice, and glory are better vindicated by unconscious extinction than by placing the lost into eternally conscious suffering in hellfire.

Ellen White and the Unevangelized

Ellen White grew up in a devout Methodist home and her theology of salvation belonged to the Wesleyan-Arminian branch of Christian theology. She believed that human nature was weakened by sin, though not totally depraved (White SC:17). In that weakened state, humans lack the ability to respond to God's gracious offer of salvation. Only by God's grace can they take the first steps to Christ.

Although she did not use the term "prevenient grace," "White refers to God's intervention in human life in ways similar to Wesley's concept of prevenient grace. Prevenient grace is God's universal work of grace upon all humankind to draw them to him" (Fortin and Moon 2013:250-251). Prevenient grace gives the sinner the ability to take the first step toward God. Having been blessed by prevenient grace and perceiving the loving offer of salvation, the human has a freewill choice to make. Prevenient grace is persuasive but not coercive. Most important for this discussion is the concept that God's prevenient grace reaches every human being to give them an opportunity to respond positively to God.

Adventists started sending missionaries overseas in 1874, but the work of missions remained in its infancy during White's lifetime. Her own cross-cultural service was limited to immigrant groups in North America and to service in

Europe and Australia. She did not interact with Muslims, Hindus, Buddhists, or tribal animists. Thus, she did not confront the issue of the unevangelized as starkly as contemporary Adventists must do. However, she did present themes that outline a theology of the unevangelized that is consistent with her Wesleyan-Arminian heritage.

Andrew Tompkins has written insightfully about Ellen White and the possibility that the heathen (her term), who have never heard the Gospel, could be saved (2016). He notes that certain favorite statements on the topic have been frequently repeated without setting the context and he offers the beginnings of the contextual study that has been missing. Others are studying the background and full meaning of her statements.

Three chapters offer a concentrated discussion of the unevangelized: (1) "Hope for the Heathen," *Prophets and Kings*; (2) "The Least of These My Brethren," *Desire of Ages*; (3) "Who Is My Neighbor," *Christ's Object Lessons*. Relevant portions of the three chapters appear below.

"Hope for the Heathen"

Throughout his ministry Isaiah bore a plain testimony concerning God's purpose for the heathen. Other prophets had made mention of the divine plan, but their language was not always understood. To Isaiah it was given to make very plain to Judah the truth that among the Israel of God were to be numbered many who were not descendants of Abraham after the flesh. This teaching was not in harmony with the theology of his age, yet he fearlessly proclaimed the messages given him of God and brought hope to many a longing heart reaching out after the spiritual blessings promised to the seed of Abraham.

The apostle to the Gentiles, in his letter to the believers in Rome, calls attention to this characteristic of Isaiah's teaching. "Isaiah is very bold," Paul declares, "and saith, I was found of them that sought Me not; I was made manifest unto them that asked not after Me." Romans 10:2. (White 2013:PK:367)

At times those who have no knowledge of God aside from that which they have received under the operations of divine grace have been kind to his servants, protecting them at the risk of their own lives. The Holy Spirit is implanting the grace of Christ in the heart of many a noble seeker after truth, quickening his sympathies contrary to his nature, contrary to his former education. The "Light, which lighteth every man that cometh into the world" (John 1:9), is shining in his soul; and this Light, if heeded, will guide his feet to the kingdom of God. The prophet Micah said: "When I sit in darkness, the Lord shall be a light unto me... He will bring me forth to the light, and I shall behold his righteousness." Micah 7:8, 9.

Heaven's plan of salvation is broad enough to embrace the whole world. God longs to breathe into prostrate humanity the breath of life. And he will not permit any soul to be disappointed who is sincere in his longing for something higher and nobler than anything the world can offer. Constantly he is sending his angels to those who, while surrounded by circumstances the most discouraging, pray in faith for some power higher than themselves to take possession of them and bring deliverance and peace. In various ways God will reveal himself to them and will place them in touch with providences that will establish their confidence in the One who has given himself a ransom for all, "that they might set their hope in God, and not forget the works of God, but keep his commandments." Psalm 78:7. (White PK:376-377)

This chapter focuses on the universal character of God's mission, with special emphasis on Isaiah's prophecies. White points out Paul's insight that "Isaiah is very bold" in emphasizing God's concern for the Gentiles. Israel's exclusivism had blinded its mission vision, placing "the theology of his age" out of harmony with God's will and Isaiah's message. But God's universal mission would move forward and modern missionaries are a fulfillment of OT prophecies.

Then she makes three points: (1) No one who is "sincere in his longing for something higher and nobler" will be "disappointed," because God uses that desire to draw the unevangelized to himself (Fortin 2018); (2) God constantly sends angels to bring deliverance to people in bad circumstances and to place them in touch with a higher power; (3) God reveals himself in many ways and uses providence to lead people to place their trust in him.

In summary, the chapter emphasizes God's miraculous preparation on the hearts of non-Christian peoples to receive missionaries when they come. However, the three main points can be appropriately applied to those never evangelized. God is actively fulfilling his mission among all of humanity, sending angels, and revealing himself in many and various ways.

"The Least of These My Brethren"

Those whom Christ commends in the judgment may have known little of theology, but they have cherished his principles. Through the influence of the divine Spirit they have been a blessing to those about them. Even among the heathen are those who have cherished the spirit of kindness; before the words of life had fallen upon their ears, they have befriended the missionaries, even ministering to them at the peril of their own lives. Among the heathen are those who worship God ignorantly, those to whom the light is never brought by human instrumentality, yet they will not perish. Though ignorant of the written law of God, they have heard his voice speaking to them in nature, and have done the things that the law required. Their works are evidence that the Holy Spirit has touched their hearts, and they are recognized as the children of God. (White DA:638)

This *Desire of Ages* chapter is an exposition of the apocalyptic judgment scene of Matt 25:31-46 which follows the parables of the Ten Virgins and the Talents. The chapter follows the "Synoptic Apocalypse" of Matthew 24. Knowing that his betrayal and death were approaching, Jesus gave his followers a wide-angle view of the future to which John the Revelator would add much detail.

When the Son of Man comes in his glory, and all the angels with him, he will sit on his glorious throne. All the nations [*panta ta ethnē*] will be gathered before him, and he will separate the people one from another as a shepherd separates the sheep from the goats…. Then the King will say to those on his right, "Come, you who are blessed by my Father; take your inheritance, the kingdom prepared for you since the creation of the world. For I was hungry and you gave me something to eat, I was thirsty and you gave me something to drink, I was a stranger and you invited me in, I needed clothes and you clothed me, I was sick and you looked after me, I was in prison and you came to visit me." (Matt 25:31-32, 34-36)

The "sheep" are saved because of deeds of love and righteousness to "the least of these by brethren" that reflect God's transformation of the hearts. *Ta ethnē*, meaning "all peoples," is an inclusive term that embraces all of humanity (Matt 24:9; 28:19; Mark 11:17; Luke 21:24; Rom 15:11) (Brown 1975:2:793). "All peoples" is a preferable English translation that avoids the modern nation-state implication of "all nations." The scene describes the criteria for God's judgment that apply to all of humanity, not only to Israel or the church. By implication, the unevangelized are judged by these criteria and have the potential of being among the "sheep."

White's statement that "their works are evidence that the Holy Spirit has touched their hearts, and they are recognized as the children of God" is "perhaps the most obvious where White states that the heathen may be saved without a full knowledge of Jesus as Savior and by living up to the light they have received" (Fortin 2018).

White's exposition of the biblical passage can be summarized as follows: (1) Through general revelation, (2) God's prevenient grace, and (3) the drawing of the Holy Spirit, (4) people who never receive the explicit knowledge available through special revelation, (5) can know and follow the principles of God's Kingdom, and (6) be saved.

"Who Is My Neighbor?"

Wherever there is an impulse of love and sympathy, wherever the heart reaches out to bless and uplift others, there is revealed the working of God's Holy Spirit. In the depths of heathenism, men who have had no knowledge of the written law of God, who have never even heard the name of Christ, have been kind to his servants, protecting them at the risk of their own lives. Their acts show the working of a divine power. The Holy Spirit has implanted the grace of Christ in the heart of the savage, quickening his sympathies contrary to his nature, contrary to his education. The "Light which lighteth every man that cometh into the world" (John 1:9), is shining in his soul; and this light, if heeded, will guide his feet to the kingdom of God.

No distinction on account of nationality, race, or caste, is recognized by God. He is the Maker of all mankind. All men are of one family by creation, and all are one through redemption. Christ came to demolish every wall of partition, to throw open every compartment of the temple, that every soul may have free access to God. His love is so broad, so deep, so full, that it penetrates everywhere. It lifts out of Satan's circle the poor souls who have been deluded by his deceptions. It places them within reach of the throne of God, the throne encircled by the rainbow of promise. In Christ there is neither Jew nor Greek, bond nor free. All are brought nigh by his precious blood. (Galatians 3:28; Ephesians 2:13). (White COL:385-386)

This chapter is an exposition of the parable of the good Samaritan (Luke 10:25-37). A lawyer came to Jesus and asked a much disputed question—"Who is my neighbor?" The Jews assumed that Samaritans and heathens were not their neighbors but they debated who within Judaism was their neighbor. Jesus broke the paradigm by teaching through the parable that "our neighbor is every person who needs our help. Our neighbor is every soul who is wounded and bruised by the adversary. Our neighbor is everyone who is the property of God" (376). The Samaritan was closer to God than the highly religious priest and Levite because he treated the wounded man in a Godly manner.

The statements that the light "will guide his feet to the kingdom of God" and that "all are brought nigh by his precious blood" leave room for interpretation; however, White's explanation of the text is that people who have no explicit knowledge of God can fulfill the essence of his will for humanity. The Spirit illuminates their minds and God's prevenient grace draws them to himself.

The Church's Continued Missional Task and Motivation

The potential availability of salvation for the unevangelized did not weaken the church's obligation, privilege, and motivation for mission in White's thinking. The following passage is representative of her strong, much repeated emphasis on the church's missional obligation to fulfill the Great Commission.

Multitudes perish for want of Christian teaching. Beside our own doors and in foreign lands the heathen are untaught and unsaved. While God has laden the earth with his bounties and filled its storehouses with the comforts of life, while he has so freely given to us a saving knowledge of his truth, what excuse can we offer for permitting the cries of the widow and the fatherless, the sick and the suffering, the untaught and the unsaved, to ascend to heaven? In the day of God, when brought face to face with him who gave his life for these needy ones, what excuse will those offer who are spending their time and money upon indulgences that God has forbidden? (White MH:288)

Placing statements like "Multitudes perish for want of Christian teaching" next to the statement that "Among the heathen are those who worship God ignorantly, those to whom the light is never brought by human instrumentality, yet they will not perish" (DA:638) produces a missiological tension. Perhaps the resolution is found in several affirmations: (1) Mission has eternal consequences for people who are now living; (2) the church's responsibility is to do the work of missions, not to judge any individual people group; (3) the theological commitments already discussed require that the church not try to escape this missiological tension.

Major Concepts

In his remarks about Ellen White's view of salvation for the unevangelized, Gerhard Pfandl comments that

> God's usual way of saving the heathen is through the preaching of the gospel, but occasionally for reasons known only to him, God reaches out to people who have never heard and never will hear the gospel and brings salvation to them. Such occasions, however, are not the rule but the exception. Some will object to this teaching and argue that God's justice requires that every person receive an opportunity for salvation. While this seems perfectly logical, it is nevertheless unscriptural. (2012)

Without a doubt, the ideal is that God's people would have evangelized every human being who ever lived. However, it seems easy to demonstrate that many millions or billions have not been blessed in this way. To argue that God only "occasionally" or as an "exception" saves some of the unevangelized masses is speculating about something known only to God. Speculating that large numbers will be saved is equally unwarranted. To affirm that the Spirit can and does reach human hearts directly but then to assert that the concept that every human should have "an opportunity for salvation" is unscriptural raises a major question. Why would a God of justice ever withhold the direct voice of the Spirit that provides the opportunity?

In summary, four themes or concepts regarding the unevangelized emerge from a study of these and other passages in the writings of Ellen White: (1) Honest-hearted truth-seekers in other religions have an authentic spiritual hunger given to them by God; (2) God gives every human adequate light upon which to make an intelligent decision, for or against himself; (3) God's judgment of each person is based upon their response to the knowledge and opportunity they have had; (4) some who have never had access to explicit knowledge about God and salvation through Jesus Christ will be saved because they respond to the Spirit's influence upon them; (5) nevertheless, many are being lost and the church has the urgent missional task of bringing the Gospel to them.

There is a clear tension between the concepts that (1) some will be lost if the church does not evangelize them and (2) that God provides adequate light about the plan of salvation to all human beings. Ellen White did not try to resolve that tension and neither should we.

Having discussed theological issues related to the unevangelized, the time has come to examine the three propositions and show how they relate to the theological issues.

Proposition 1:
None of the Unevangelized Can Be Saved Through Christ

The traditional view held by both Protestants and Catholics has been called restrictivist, exclusivist, or particularist. It states that no one can be saved without knowing and explicitly accepting salvation by grace through faith in Jesus. The unevangelized are not able to know and accept Christ and are, therefore, lost. Salvation is simply not available to the unevangelized.

One of the strongest points of the restrictivist view is the motivation it provides for mission. William Carey, Hudson Taylor, and the others who ignited the modern missionary movement were driven by the conviction that millions would die eternally if no one proclaimed the Gospel to them.

The restrictivist position makes the most sense from a double-predestinarian position. The unevangelized are understood to be predestined for damnation. If God had predestined them for salvation, he would have ensured that they would receive the Gospel. As for the unevangelized living, there seems to be no motivation for mission because God will decide their eternal destiny. Yet, to be fair, Calvinists have a distinguished history in world missions that is hard to understand from an Arminian perspective.

Wesleyan-Arminian theology emphasizes God's love, justice, and the human freewill, as well as his sovereignty. As an expression of his sovereignty, God created humanity with the freedom of choice to accept or reject the Gospel. The freedom of all to choose implies that they must have a reasonable opportunity to make a choice. Thus, the restrictivist position is not a good option for Adventists.

Proposition 2:
All the Unevangelized Can Be Saved in Different Ways

The second proposition is that all of humanity, including the unevangelized, can be saved through many different avenues. Every religion defines the human predicament in specific ways and offers different but equally valid solutions in this view. In the twentieth century, a major swing occurred away from the traditional restrictivist view toward this universalist position.

Several factors have favored the growing support for the universalist position:
1. Globalization brought many more Christians into regular contact with non-Christians; they observed adherents of other religions who were good, moral, ethical people with whom they could have friendship; Christians observed the deep commitment of non-Christians to religious activities similar to their own (see figure 6.3); declaring that some or all of those good, sincere people would be lost made Christians very uncomfortable.
2. Observers noticed that culture and religion are often so closely intertwined that becoming a Christian sometimes seems virtually impossible.
3. The fight against colonialism, racism, and ethnocentrism made Christian evangelization seem colonial and racist, to some, suggesting that attempting to convert people of other religions to Christ is actually wrong.

Universalists see all religions as being equally valid pathways to the same destination. All religious texts, like the Qu'ran for Muslims and Vedas for Hindus, are given equal value with the Bible. Salvation is seen as equally available through all religions. The only requirement for salvation is sincerity and devotion to one's chosen religious pathway. Adherents of other religions should be left alone to follow their chosen spiritual pathways. Christian mission may exist from the universalist perspective, but only for the performance of humanitarian service.

Proposition 3:
Some of the Unevangelized Can Be Saved Through Christ

Another way of stating Proposition 3 is to say that salvation is potentially available to all humans, including those who, through no fault of their own, lack specific knowledge of Christ and are thus unable to explicitly accept the Gospel. My term for this position is "potential inclusion," meaning that those who die without ever being evangelized are potentially included in salvation. Potential inclusion does not suggest the universal inclusion of every human being because the Bible is quite clear that many will be lost (Matt 7:13-14; Luke 13:23-24).

Proposition 3 assumes that (1) Christ is "the apex of revelation and the norm by which all other beliefs must be critiqued"; (2) the historical incarnation, death, resurrection, and ascension of Jesus Christ are "the decisive events in human history"; (3) the atonement of Christ is the sole means by which a person can be saved (Tennent 2010:197).

The reasoning in support of the potential inclusion position is as follows: (1) God created humanity with a free will and allows eternal destinies to be linked with human choice; (2) because of Adam's choice to disobey God, all humans are in a lost position by default; (3) God reveals his plan of salvation explicitly through special revelation, but special revelation has not been available to all people; (4) in God's love and justice, he reveals himself through general revelation to all humans, including those who lack access to special revelation; (5) the Holy Spirit moves powerfully upon the hearts and minds of every human being drawing them to God; (6) God's prevenient grace, using every available means, works persuasively, though not coercively, to draw every individual to God and to give them the capacity to respond positively. The "some of the unevangelized who can be saved through Christ" are those who respond positively to God's initiatives toward them.

The theology of *missio Dei* provides a unifying theme for the potential inclusion position. God is the instigator of his mission to lost humanity. Even though God has worked primarily through Israel and the church, he has reached directly to every human being who has ever lived. Both Israel and the church have failed, at different times and among different people groups, to share God's special revelation; but the failures of God's people do not ultimately block God's wish to give every human an opportunity for salvation.

The potential inclusion position does not validate speculation about who or how many among the never-evangelized will be saved. The huge numbers of the unevangelized and the broadness of God's mercy, combined with the power of the Holy Spirit, could suggest that large numbers will be saved. On the other hand, the small number of visible, positive responses to the Gospel among some people groups when they are evangelized could suggest that very few will be saved. As with those who are well evangelized, only God knows who among the never-evangelized will actually be saved.

The Motivation for Mission

The restrictivist view that only people who explicitly know and accept Jesus Christ can be saved is highly motivating for missions. What happens to the motivation for mission if salvation is understood to be potentially available to the unevangelized? Why should the church invest its money and send its members into mission, especially in difficult places, if God can save people whom the church never reaches? The church can be highly motivated for mission for a number of reasons.

1. Because mission is part of the unfinished Great Controversy between Christ and Satan. Christians have the sacred honor of investing their brief lives in the grand narrative of God's mission that began with Lucifer's rebellion and continues until God makes all things new again.

2. Because being lost is the default condition of humanity since the Fall. God's mission through the church is to proclaim Christ's atoning solution at the Cross.

3. Because fulfilling God's mission brings glory to God.

4. Because God made the church missionary in both its essence and function. Without mission, the church denies its core nature and fails to be God's primary human agency.

5. Because God commands his believers to be missionaries. Jesus gave the Great Commission and it is as binding as the Decalogue. Obeying all of the commands of God is not an onerous obligation but a glorious privilege.

6. Because of people's desperate need. Jesus spoke of lost people who were like "sheep without a shepherd" (Matt 9:36). Today's world has more lost sheep who desperately need the Gospel than ever before in human history.

7. Because non-Christian people whose hearts are open to God will be drawn much closer to him when their faith becomes explicitly focused on Jesus Christ. Christians cannot be satisfied with leaving non-Christians with less than the full light of the Gospel. Whatever God does directly in the lives of nonbelievers only gives the believer more reasons to glorify God.

8. Because bringing a person into of the body of Christ provides the spiritual fellowship that they need.

9. Because the existence of spiritually receptive non-Christians gives great hope to evangelists and missionaries, even in the most difficult mission contexts.

10. Because being part of God's mission is a great blessing to the church and its members.

11. Because the task of evangelizing or re-evangelizing people who already know of Christ and the Bible is massive by itself.

Chapter

An Overview of Mission History

~•ᔕ

Introduction

The history of Christian mission is a rich and detailed tapestry of the church's interaction with exceedingly diverse people groups over two millennia. This brief chapter approaches the impossible task of surveying mountains of information about missions by discussing large scale periods, paradigms, and philosophies of mission.

The Expansion and Contraction of Christianity

The history of how Christianity spread into different world regions tells the story of missions in a helpful way. Famed historians Kenneth Latourette (1970) and Stephen Neill (1986) outlined the geographic expansion of Christianity as shown in figure 7.1.

**Figure 7.1
Geographic Expansion of Christianity**

Through the Roman Empire
As a persecuted religion (100-313)
As state religion (313-500)

Through Europe
Germanic, Frankish, Anglo-Saxon peoples (500-800)
Scandinavian peoples (1000-1200)

To the World
Roman Catholic European missions (1500-1700)
Pietist European missions (1700-1800)
European/North American Protestant missions (1800-1950)

Partnership of World Christianity
Unreached peoples (1950-)

Source: Adapted from Goheen 2014:118.

Even though Latourette and Neil outlined the expansion of the church geographically, they did not view the process as being one of simple, mechanical, territorial expansion. They were also interested in how the Gospel takes root in some cultures but not others and how it expands and recedes in different times and places (Goheen 2014:118).

On a global scale, Christianity started in the global south and gradually evolved into a religion of the global north so that it accounted for about 92% of believers in Luther's day. Then the trend reversed, and today the majority of Christians reside in the global south.

The rhetoric of Christian expansion is sometimes one of constant progression and expansion but the reality is much different, as already noted. Rather than speaking of a constant progression, Andrew Walls recommends the concept that "Christian expansion is serial" (2002:30). In other words, Christianity has experienced a series of advances and recessions. The advances tend to happen at the frontiers and the recessions in the heartlands of the Christian faith. Until the coming of Islam in the seventh century, the Middle East and North Africa were major Christian centers. Thereafter, Europe was the main center of Christianity for many centuries until European Christianity receded into secularity and nominalism.

The reason Christian recession has happened in the heartlands of the faith, notably during the era of Christendom, is that cultural forms become identified with the essence of Christianity. For example, the cultural forms and preferences of being European or American become directly equated with being Christian. That misguided equation removed the necessary element of cultural critique and Christianity slipped into syncretism. The painful irony is that nations that were once centers of the modern missionary movement have slipped into Christian recession.

The cross-cultural transmission of the Gospel on the periphery of the faith, says Walls, is responsible for the series of advances that have produced today's global Christianity. The reason is clear in the Jerusalem Council (Acts 15), where Jewish and Gentile Christians asked themselves which beliefs and practices were essential for all believers. Bringing the Gospel to any new people group always involves the same process, even for those who do not know the terminology of faithful contextualization. The vitality of Christianity is renewed when its essential principles are properly distinguished from the cultural ways of applying those principles to everyday life.

Cultural Periods of Christian History

As Jesus Christ was incarnated into Jewish culture, so his Gospel is able to be incarnated into particular cultural contexts. Walls has divided Christian mission history into six phases. During each phase, a particular cultural form of Christianity has been dominant. "In each phase the expression of the Christian faith has developed features which could only have originated in that culture whose impress it has taken within that phase" (1996:16). As each age merged into the next, new questions were asked growing out of the changing cultures, the Bible was read in different ways, and Christians reached solutions for their relevant issues. As one phase blended into the next, certain features of the old were carried over into the new phase. Thus, Christianity in this century retains features that grew out of each of the major eras of the past. Walls's model is valuable because it is like a large scale historical case study illustrating and informing the cross-cultural transmission of the Gospel today. The titles of each era are adapted from Walls (1996:16-25).

The Jewish Era

The first Christians were Jews who had no idea that they were part of a new religion. Their practice of the faith grew directly out of the cultural context of Judaism, with some influence from the Hellenistic world. Their priorities and questions were Jewish. Shortly before Christ's ascension the disciples asked, "Lord, will You at this time restore the kingdom to Israel?" He replied simply and kindly, "It is not for you to know" (Acts 1:6-7). The question arose from their Jewishness and Christ's answer was contextualized for them. Every era and every culture has different limitations and the Gospel adapts to each, just as Jesus condescended to his disciples' limitations.

When the Christians at Antioch began witnessing to pagan friends, they found that the Jewish word "Messiah" had little meaning for them. Although they may have been unaware of the possibilities of confusion and syncretism, they contextualized their vocabulary by preaching "the Lord [*Kurios*] Jesus" (Acts 11:20). The Greek word *Kurios* was ambiguous and easily misunderstood because of its use to identify pagan officials and gods; however, the church filled the word form with appropriate biblical meaning. The use of *Kurios* is just one example of the Spirit-led cross-cultural transmission taken by the Jewish church. Following the holocausts of AD 70 and AD 135, the Jewish state disappeared and Christianity survived because it moved from the center at Jerusalem to Antioch, Ephesus, Corinth, Rome and other places in the Gentile world.

The Hellenistic-Roman Era

The second dominant cultural expression of Christianity was Hellenistic-Roman. This was the era of the early church fathers, the formation of the biblical canon, and the church councils that defined core Christian doctrines. The questions asked of Scripture were those of Greek philosophy and the answers were stated in philosophical terms.

Jewish identity had been defined by *orthopraxy*, or performing religious practices and duties in the correct way. During the Hellenistic-Roman period, Christianity shifted to emphasize the *orthodoxy* of a "logically expounded belief set in codified form, established through a process of consultation, and maintained through effective organization" (Walls 1996:19). Christians continued to be identified by their religious practices, but the emphasis was placed on Christian doctrines.

Hellenistic-Roman thought had an "inbuilt arrogance" that "maintained that there was one desirable pattern of life, a single 'civilization' in effect, one model of society, one body of law, one universe of ideas" (Walls 1996:18). Humanity was divided into two groups—Greeks, who were civilized and conformed to the cultural pattern, and barbarians or savages who did not.

Major elements of the Hellenistic-Roman era were passed onward as a mixed legacy to other eras, including our own. Doctrine remains so important that wars have been fought and denominations split over doctrinal differences. At times, cultural arrogance has accompanied and weakened Christian missions.

The Barbarian Era

The end of Hellenistic-Roman Christianity was brought about by the collapse of the Western Roman Empire (5th century) before the barbarian tribes and the rise of Islam (7th century) with its control of lands to the east and south. The tribal peoples of Europe were seen as "barbarians" and "savages," destroyers of Hellenistic-Roman culture. Once again, Christianity persisted because of its cross-cultural transmission from the Christian center to the periphery among the tribal peoples.

When the tribal peoples of Europe became Christians, they accepted many of the elements of Hellenistic-Roman Christianity, but also shaped the faith in new ways. The tribal style of Christianity was "a new creation, conditioned less by city-based, literary, intellectual, and technological tradition than by the circumstances of peasant cultivators and their harsh, uncertain lives" (Walls 1996:19-20). The Christian legacy from the Jewish and Hellenistic-Roman eras was passed through their own tribal cultural filter and the faith was reformulated.

The reformulation produced two closely related themes that persist to the present day. First, the communal, tribal societies of the era were naturally drawn toward understanding themselves as a "Christian nation." They easily identified themselves with the nation of Israel and saw parallels between Israel and themselves as a Christian nation. The second development was the emphasis on Christian custom or tradition. As communal peoples, they valued and enforced a single set of customs for the entire community. The church, as a Christian nation, was one community that must follow a single tradition.

The Western European Era

The Age of Discovery, the Renaissance, and the Enlightenment provided the cultural background for a new phase of Christianity in Western Europe, and like its predecessors, drew on the previous phases. Three new features stood out in the new formulation. The first new feature was the use of vernacular Scriptures. For many centuries, the Bible had been available only in its original languages or in Latin. The Protestant translation of the Bible into vernacular languages and the technology of printing reshaped the faith and set the pattern of Bible translation as a prominent part of missions. It is safe to say that the vernacular Scriptures was a wholly positive change, with no negative consequences, unlike some other changes throughout the eras of Christianity.

The second change was a movement away from the tribal, tradition-bound orientation of the previous era to a strong emphasis on the individual believer who made spiritual decisions independent of kinfolk. The Christian faith became a strongly individual matter between oneself and God. The new emphasis on individual faith was a positive corrective step away from domination by the group but also a negative step that produced an individualistic, privatized faith that could undervalue the church as a community.

The third change for Protestants was the rejection of the custom or tradition that was so highly valued during the tribal era. The Reformers taught *sola Scriptura* as the authority of Christian belief and practice and rejected the Roman Catholic reliance on church tradition.

The Era of European Expansion and Recession

During the colonial era, the European presence expanded until much of the globe was ruled by colonial governments. During this period, almost all European peoples, at home or abroad, professed Christianity; however, a serious recession of the faith among European peoples started in sixteenth century and reached major proportions by the eighteenth century. Two Great Awakenings happened in the eighteenth and nineteenth centuries, but by the twentieth century it was clear that many great European cities "had never really been evangelized at all" (Walls 1996:21).

In contrast, the nineteenth and twentieth centuries saw an amazing cross-cultural Christian expansion in the global south. Once again, cross-cultural diffusion was the key to keeping Christianity alive in the world.

The Era of Global Christianity

Walls calls the sixth era the era of "Cross-Cultural Transmission." Perhaps calling it the era of Global Christianity is more descriptive. This era is a work in progress. Characterizing it is difficult because the faith is now passing through many different cultural filters. Centers of Christianity now exist on all of the continents. Global Christianity is developing with multiple cultural forms of the faith existing contemporaneously rather than a single "Christian culture" or "Christian nation" enfolding them all. "The reason for this lies in the infinite translatability of the Christian faith" (Walls 1996:22). Whether or not a particular cultural form of the faith is pleasing to God and faithful to the Bible depends on how diligently believers in each cultural setting bring themselves under the unwavering scrutiny of biblical truth.

Paradigms of Christian Mission

During the two millennia of Christian mission history, the church has conducted mission according to different paradigms. In other words, different frameworks, patterns, philosophies, and theologies have guided the work of missions.

The paradigm approach is important for missiology because it marks a move from general church history into mission history (Goheen 2014:121). A mission paradigm is the way the church of a particular time period understands and conducts missions. Mission paradigms are based on theological assumptions that grow out of how the Bible is interpreted. Paradigms are shaped by political, economic, cultural, and historical environments. How Christians perceive themselves and those to whom they take the Gospel shapes a paradigm. How non-Christians view Christians and Christian missions shapes the work of missions.

As time passes, the whole human environment changes. Nations invade other nations, or are invaded themselves. Nations are colonized or achieve political independence. Economies prosper or collapse. Diseases, epidemics, and plagues kill millions. Amazing new medical treatments are discovered. New technologies, like printing, electricity, telephones, steamships, airplanes, computers, smartphones, and the Internet become part of daily life. The religious environment within Christianity changes, as does the internal environment of the non-Christian religions.

The aggregate of these and other changes produce new environments that require new ways of living. As the lives of Christians change, along with the lives of those needing the Gospel, the collective theory and practice of mission changes and a new mission paradigm emerges. Paradigms develop and change over generations and centuries, although rapid cultural change speeds paradigm shifts. New paradigms do not completely replace older paradigms, but rather build on them while reaching out in new directions. There are macro-paradigms, or large-scale paradigms that generally characterize all of Christians missions of a particular era. Micro-paradigms or small-scale paradigms are characteristic of particular parts of Christianity (Bosch 1991:188).

Major Mission Paradigms

Outlines by Bosch and Myers

Bosch divides Christian mission into six paradigms (1991:181). Bryant Myers also sees six paradigms but uses different dates and paradigm titles (1996:8-9).

Figure 7.2
Mission Paradigms

David Bosch		Bryant Myers	
31-313	Early church	33-200	Apocalyptic, early church
150-1453	Eastern church	200-500	Greek, patristic Orthodox
313-1800	Roman Catholic, medieval	600-1400	Christendom, medieval Catholic
1517-1800	Reformation		
1800-1918	Mission in the wake of the Enlightenment	1500-1750	Reformation, Protestant
		1750-1950	Modern mission era
1918-today	Ecumenical or postmodern	1950-today	Emerging mission paradigm of third millennium

Source: Bosch 1991:181-182; Myers 1996:8-9.

Myers' Paradigm Outline

Myers extends his outline of historical mission paradigms by identifying five characteristics of every mission paradigm. His five points are very broad and generalized, but they provide a snapshot of the different mission eras. He identifies (1) a biblical text that characterizes the mission ethos, (2) the main perceived goal of mission, (3) the people who typically did missions, (4) the central mission focus, and (5) the nature of the church in each paradigm (1996:8-9).

Figure 7.3
Myers' Mission Paradigms

Apocalyptic-Early Church: 33-200	Reformation-Protestant: 1500-1750
• Make disciples (Matt 18:18-19) • Goal of mission is disciples • Apostles and martyrs • Eschatology as central • Church as eschatological community	• Gospel is the power of salvation for all who believe (Rom 1:16) • Goal of mission is renewal and reformation • Preachers and reformers • Centrality of Scripture • Church as a reforming community
Greek-Patristic Orthodox: 200-500	**Modern Mission Era: 1750-1950**
• God so loved the World (John 3:16) • Goal of mission is life • Itinerant evangelists and healers • Theology as central • Church as worshipping community	• Come over and help us (Acts 16:9) • Goal is salvation and a better life • Volunteers and cross-cultural missionaries • Centrality of the mission task • Church as a civilizing, Westernizing community
Christendom-Medieval Catholic: 600-1400	**Emerging Mission Paradigm: 1950-**
• Compel them to come in (Luke 14:23) • Goal of mission is expanding Christendom • Monks and conquistadors • Centrality of church, state, and culture • Church as powerful institution	• They preached, drove out demons, and healed (Mark 6:12) • Goal is to call people to faith and work for spiritual and social transformation • All the people of God in all of life • Wholism of life, deed, and word • Church as a pilgrim community

Source: Adapted from Myers 1996:8-9.

Goheen's Paradigm Outline

Goheen sees the characteristics of missions as falling naturally into four paradigms: early church, Christendom, Enlightenment, and ecumenical (2014:122-185).

The Early Church Mission Paradigm

The early church mission paradigm lasted about three hundred years. Even though the early church obeyed Christ's centrifugal call to mission ("Go ye!"), the local congregation was also an attractive, magnetic, centripetal force that drew people into its fellowship. Believers had a living sense of continuing

Christ's mission until the Second Coming. Coming from many different cultures, they found their primary identity in being members of the Kingdom of God which was present, though not in its fullness.

The Jerusalem Council model of contextualization was part of the mission paradigm. The universal principles of Scripture applied to all, but differing cultural styles were allowed. At the same time, the Gospel placed a gap between believers and their cultures, which caused them to adopt a "prophetic-critical stance within culture" (Goheen 2014:123). Because of this stance, the church was vigilant against the temptations of pagan cultures in multiple cultural forms. Idolatry was vigorously condemned as the confession "Jesus is Lord" replaced the confession "Caesar is Lord" of the emperor cult. Much of the attractive power of the early church was in its counter-cultural style because people of integrity saw the decadence of the popular culture and longed for something better. The early church is thus an excellent example of Andrew Walls' "Indigenizing" and "Pilgrim" principles in action and in tension (1996:7-8).

The early church understood the need to provide in-depth discipleship training for new members. New members went through a three-year catechetical process that included lessons needed to live a Christlike life and be part of Christ's mission. They were taught to live exemplary moral and ethical lives, to practice generosity, to be forgiving, and to live in unity. Within the church, barriers between genders, wealthy and poor, slave and free were broken down.

Deliberate missionary activity was done by itinerant evangelists, but ordinary Christians "chattered the Gospel among the common folk of the empire" (Goheen 2014:126). Martyrdom, miracles, and exorcisms were common.

The church was also unfaithful in some ways as it capitulated to culture and the Greek worldview. The doctrine of the "immortality of the soul in a celestial home" replaced the biblical view of death (127). The church became absorbed with its own inner life rather than with mission. The first moves away from Sabbath to Sunday worship were made as part of the capitulation to the life of the Roman Empire. The change of weekly worship is a prime example from church history of contextualization done the wrong way, giving cultural relevance priority over eternal, universal biblical principles.

The mission paradigm of the early church eventually shifted its focus from mission outside itself to maintenance within itself. "The dynamic and flexible forms of the early church in mission to the world gave way to an institution that was a custodian of orthodox doctrine against heresy" (127-128).

The Christendom Mission Paradigm
Constantine and Mission

The conversion of Constantine in AD 312 commenced the Christendom mission paradigm that, according to Goheen's model, lasted until the seventeenth century Enlightenment.

Constantine's conversion changed Christianity in significant ways that consequently changed the church's understanding of its mission. The church changed from being a weak, illegal community on the cultural periphery to being the official state religion at the center of culture and power. From its new position of privilege, the church saw less reason to challenge its culture and its sense of mission declined.

The church's incorporation into the political-religious hierarchy of Christendom produced a condition that was ambiguous for its mission. In other words, there were both positive and negative dimensions.

The positive dimension for mission was found in the "indigenizing" nature of mission. Following Christ's incarnational model, the church is supposed to immerse itself in its culture. The church participates in culture, is in solidarity with it, and is a place to feel at home. Under Christendom, Christianity related to European culture in these ways and shaped the cultures of Europe in many positive ways. The Christian legacy in European culture includes ethical values, emphasis on human dignity, the value and moral responsibility of the individual, and the obligation to help the needy (Goheen 2014:132). This is not to imply that European culture ever fully reflected biblical values and principles but to say that Christianity shaped Europe for the better.

The negative dimension for mission was the loss of the "pilgrim" understanding of the church and its "prophetic-critical and antithetical" relationship with its own culture. The entire society was assumed to be Christian and the church became "an uncritical arm of state policy rather than an arm of God's redemptive purposes" (132).

These changes in the church's self-understanding inevitably changed its mission and ministry. In place of an outward-facing, missional stance, ministry became an inward-facing service for the populace who were already considered to be Christian. Both inward and outward ministry is appropriate but the latter was lost in the Christendom model. The church was "established," therefore, the missionary task had been completed and the church would minister only to its own community.

Outside the empire or state, the church's mission was subsumed within the purposes of explorers and empire builders. Violence and coercion were used to "compel them to come in" (Luke 14:23). Charlemagne, with his defeat and forced conversion of the Saxons at the point of the sword, is an example of this model in action. Salvation from eternal hellfire through the sacrament of baptism given through coercion was seen as a great blessing to be dispensed by the church.

Monastic Missions

Starting in the fifth century with the formation of the Benedictine order by Benedict (480-543), the main work of missions was done by Catholic orders. From the thirteenth century onward, the Franciscans, Dominicans, and Jesuits were the leading missionary orders. Their work was both within the Christian realm and beyond among the pagan tribes of Europe. During the age of discovery they started going beyond Europe.

Monastic missions were a more gentle part of the Christendom paradigm. Bosch notes that Western monasticism differed from Eastern monasticism by being less individualized and more communal and by being more independent from government (1991:231).

The pattern of mission typically involved a monk bringing the Gospel to a hostile tribe who persecuted or martyred him. In the aftermath of the martyrdom, the tribe reflected on his virtues and message and became more open. More monks arrived, the tribal ruler was converted, and the tribe became Christian. Eventually, a monastery was established that became the religious, commercial, intellectual hub of the community. Because the first conversion was inevitably superficial, the monks conducted long term discipleship training. Over time, the cultures of the European tribes were reshaped by the Gospel (Goheen 2014:134-135).

Bosch suggests four reasons for the success of monastic missions: (1) The monks were held in high esteem by the populace; (2) the monks lived exemplary lives that made a great impact on the community; (3) the monasteries were centers of essential trades, agriculture, culture, and education; and (4) the monks were patient, tenacious, and persevering (1991:231-232).

The formation of the Franciscan and Dominican orders in the thirteenth century marks a renewed emphasis on missions. Raymond Lull (1235-1315) was an exemplary missionary of the Franciscan order, who "articulated by far the most advanced understanding of missions to date" (Goheen 2014:136). He said that missionaries should have a good knowledge of Muslim language and culture, preach the Gospel, and be willing to die a martyr. Lull, himself, died a martyr in North Africa.

Early Colonialism and Missions

The era of Christendom moved into a new stage with the age of discovery. Starting in the seventh century, Europe was fenced in by Islam toward the south and east and it lacked the sailing technology to travel westwards. When Portugal and Spain developed new sailing technologies in the fifteenth century, Europeans could sail to the Americas, around Africa, and onward to Asia. With their new sailing ships and the military might of gunpowder, Europeans commenced a new era of conquest and colonialism.

The mission paradigm was reshaped significantly by the new situation within Europe and its capabilities for global travel. By the fifteenth century, the peoples of Europe had been Christianized by the monastic orders and the church started looking abroad. In 1493, Pope Alexander VI gave the right to rule and evangelize different world regions to Portugal and Spain. As European colonialism expanded, missions followed in its pathway. "The brutal conquest of Central and South America ... saw missionary work and political subjugation go hand in hand" (Goheen 2014:137-138). Thankfully, there were missionaries like Bartolomé de las Casas (1484-1566) who opposed coercive conversion and promoted humane treatment of colonized peoples in Central America.

The Jesuit order, under Ignatius Loyola (1491-1556), was the primary instrument of Roman Catholic mission starting in the sixteenth century. The Congregation for the Evangelization of Peoples was founded by Pope Gregory XV in 1622 to direct missionary work by the various religious institutions.

Protestant Reformation and Missions

The Christendom era continued with the arrival of the Protestant Reformers. The difference was that Europe became fragmented into Catholic and Protestant states instead of being all Catholic. The close relationship of churches and their respective rulers remained.

Protestant missions remained mostly a work within Europe and North America until the Pietists of the eighteenth century. Roman Catholics criticized Protestants for "perverting" Christians instead of converting pagans and Jews. Several factors explain why the Reformers were slow in leading their followers into cross-cultural missions beyond the borders of Europe: (1) They believed the Apostles had already fulfilled the Great Commission, (2) their energies were occupied by conflicts and wars with each other and with Catholics, (3) they rejected the monastic order and did not replace it with an alternative structure for missions, (4) they lacked the government backing which had supported Catholic missions, and (5) their states were not sea-going, colonizing powers (Goheen 2014:139).

> Protestant missions remained mostly a work within Europe and North America until the Pietists of the eighteenth century.

"There were at least two developments that began to break with Christendom assumptions and would gradually transition the church into a new paradigm of mission" (139). The first development was the rediscovery of biblical themes, like *sola Scriptura*, salvation by grace through faith, the priesthood of all believers, and others. Closely related to these biblical themes was a renewed understanding of the individual's relationship with God. European Christianity had developed among the tribal peoples, where the religious commitments of the leaders and the group were paramount. Reformation Christianity had a more individual focus, where the individual believer is directly accountable to God. These theological shifts opened the door for a new paradigm of mission.

The second development that challenged the Christendom model of mission came from the Anabaptists. The Anabaptists "rejected the symbiotic relationship between church and state and defined the church as a pilgrim, missionary, and martyr church" (140). Anabaptists saw Europe as a mission field, not Christian nations, and placed the responsibility for mission on believers instead of on rulers. The Great Commission had not been fulfilled by the Apostles but must be obeyed by every believer.

The first significant Protestant move into global mission came in the late-seventeenth century among the Lutheran Pietists.

The Pietist reaction stressed a crisis conversion experience for the individual and subsequent personal piety to nourish the new birth and growing sanctification. Out of the warmth of this commitment to Christ would flow evangelistic zeal and missionary vision. Thus, each individual Christian was responsible for mission, not the state or the church. Mission was carried out by gathering serious individuals together to support one another in this enterprise. *Conversion of individual people was the goal of mission*, and church planting or transforming society was at best minimally important. The best-known early Pietist groups were the Methodists, the Danish-Halle mission, and the Moravian movement associated with Nikolaus von Zinzendorf. (Goheen 2014:141, emphasis supplied)

The Pietist mission paradigm was a positive one for several reasons: (1) It took the main responsibility for mission away from clergy and rulers and gave it to believers; (2) it broke missions out of the enmeshment of culture and politics that was part of the Christendom paradigm; and (3) it motivated and enabled German Moravians to send more missionaries abroad in just two decades than all Protestants had sent in the previous two centuries.

While the Pietist paradigm was responsible for making the early moves in Protestant missions, it also had some negative implications for mission: (1) By narrowing the goal of mission to individual conversion, Pietists excluded the social, cultural, and political dimensions of mission; (2) by defining the task of missions as belonging to individual believers, Pietists made missions the work of specialists rather than the whole church; (3) the role of the church was, thus, diminished on the sending side of missions; (4) on the receiving side of missions, the importance of church planting was neglected; (5) on the mission field, churches were organized as necessary places for new converts to worship but the biblical role of the body of Christ and convert's need for on-going fellowship and discipleship were not fully understood.

The Christendom paradigm probably gave Pietist missionaries a limited view of the work they did among non-Christian peoples. In Europe, where almost everyone was nominally Christian, evangelization meant bringing revival and a particular style of Christianity to people who were already relatively well informed about the Bible. Leading Hindus or Buddhists to Christ was a much more difficult task that Pietists may have underestimated.

The Enlightenment and Mission

The European Renaissance that started in the fourteenth century culminated in the Enlightenment of the eighteenth century. In addition to its artistic and scientific dimensions, the Enlightenment brought a comprehensive philosophical, theological, and culture shift toward a secular, rationalist, humanist worldview. The medieval view of God's providential rule was replaced by the concept of human "progress toward a paradise constructed of human effort. Salvation was to be found in human ability" (Goheen 2014:142). Through reason, science, and technology, Western peoples would lead the world to a human-produced utopia.

Europe's great advances over life in the medieval period produced a feeling of cultural superiority and confidence.

The cultural shifts of the Enlightenment came after more than a millennium of Christendom in which the church and state, culture and Christianity were virtually fused. Unlike Christians of the early church, Christians of medieval Europe did not critique their own culture. Thus, when the Enlightenment brought yet another mistaken religious-cultural worldview, Christians accepted it uncritically. The scope of the Gospel was reduced and compartmentalized to become a matter of individual piety, ethics, and morality. The modern missionary movement paradigm was shaped both by the positive motivation to share advancements with the world, but also by the negative cultural assumptions of the era.

The Modern Missionary Movement Paradigm

The modern missionary movement (c. 1750-1950) witnessed an "unprecedented outpouring of financial and human resources toward the cross-cultural missionary enterprise" (Goheen 2014:144). When William Carey went to India in 1793, only about 14% of Christians were outside Europe and North America, meaning that Christianity was a White person's religion. By 2000, about 60% of Christians lived outside Europe and North America. While much of that growth has come after the era of independence starting in 1950, it was made possible by pioneering mission work done during the "great century of missions," the nineteenth century.

Yet, ambiguity surrounds the modern missionary movement. Three critiques can be made about missions of the era: First, the continuing sequence of scientific and technological discovery and advance in the West produced an almost unavoidable conviction of cultural superiority. Missionaries typically went from nations that enjoyed modern communication, transportation, and medicine to places where people enjoyed none of those benefits and who welcomed them. Missionaries lacked the insights of cultural anthropology that looks beyond the products of a society to see the many virtues within its culture. An illiterate, semi-clothed society that cannot successfully treat malaria, nevertheless has admirable qualities.

Second, White missionaries did not critique Christianity in their own societies adequately and did not distinguish between their own cultures and their Christian faith. Being British or German and being Christian was part of the same equation. On the mission field, therefore, bringing people to Christ meant teaching them to be Christians in the style of the missionary's home culture. The concept of contextualization that planted a culturally appropriate but biblically faithful church was unknown.

Third, starting at the end of the nineteenth century, Christian missions became more intertwined with European colonialism than previously. The great powers were colonizers for a long time, but the era of high colonialism started in 1884 when large portions of the globe were carved up at the Berlin Conference.

In earlier times, colonial governments often viewed missions as a nuisance. But they began to use missions as a justification for colonialism when questions about the justification of colonialism began to arise.

In David Livingstone's model, colonialism was about the "Three Cs"— Christianity, commerce, and civilization. As a missionary to Africa, he was responsible for much of the early exploration of the continent that opened to door to colonialism. One of his passions was eliminating the slave trade on the continent of Africa.

Christian mission has been an easy target for harsh criticism and occasional demonization because of its association with colonialism. Some opponents of Christianity use colonial-era missions to condemn contemporary missions. A wholesale condemnation of missions alongside colonialism is common in the academic world. Such condemnation often arises from postmodern, agnostic, or atheistic assumptions.

A reasoned, credible defense of colonial-era missions can be made without denying the mistakes of the era. Robert Woodberry analyzed a mass of public data from former colonies in association with the missionary approaches used during the colonial era. His conclusion was that "conversionary Protestant" missions made a demonstrable difference in "the development and spread of religious liberty, mass education, mass printing, newspapers, voluntary organizations, and colonial reforms, thereby creating the conditions that made stable democracy more likely" (2012:244). In other words, many former colonies are better off because of the work of Christian missions.

To say that colonial-era missionaries were in complete alignment with colonials and viewed their own mission project as subordinate to the colonial project is simply inaccurate (Skreslet 2012:63). Dana Robert (2008) documents the way missionaries worked to "convert" colonialism so that it would serve the purposes of mission rather than the other way around. The cultural affinity that a British or American missionary on the field enjoyed with officials of the British colonial government was an asset that was frequently used to benefit missions.

Others emphasize the need for missionaries to win the approval of local chiefs and leaders to gain access and build a long term relationship with local peoples. Conversion during the modern colonial era was voluntary, not by coercion as during the earlier era of Catholic missions in Latin America. Local people had to perceive benefits they would incur by receiving missionaries before their chiefs gave permission for them to start work.

Yet another valuable point is that after the very first missionaries had made the very first converts, those converts became the teachers, evangelists, and pastors who did village-by-village evangelism and church planting. There were not enough missionaries on the ground to do all of the work.

The point here is to defend Christian missions—not colonialism. Postmodern, pluralist thinking rejects the conversion motivation of Christian missions. If the goal of converting non-Christians to Christ is delegitimized, then missions as Adventists understand it is delegitimized, with or without colonialism.

The Mission Society

"One of the most remarkable phenomena of the Enlightenment is the emergence of the missionary societies: some denominational, some interdenominational, some nondenominational, and some even anti-denominational" (Bosch 1991:327). The very first missionary society was William Carey's Particular Baptist Society for Propagating the Gospel among the Heathen established in 1792. The mission society was a free-standing, voluntary organization that appointed its own leaders, raised its own funds, and had a singular focus on world missions.

The mission society remains the dominant model for Protestant missions today. Various factors contributed to the development of mission societies, but the refusal of churches and denominations to fulfill their missionary obligation is probably the most significant. The congregationalist model that is common among Protestants means that local churches often lack the capacity to select, train, support, and administer missionaries. The short-term mission phenomenon of the twenty-first century is a form of engagement that is possible even for small churches. Today's mega-churches are increasingly engaging in long-term missions because they have the organizational and financial ability. The missionary society continues to provide an avenue for individuals and local churches to combine forces for missions.

The validity of the mission society model that places the responsibility for mission outside of both the local church and the denomination has been debated. Advocates point to several factors including (1) the reluctance or inability of churches to engage in the serious, long-term work required to plant churches in new fields; (2) the bureaucratic inertia of churches and denominations that slows and complicates mission; and (3) the creativity and flexibility made possible by the specialization of mission agencies.

The main critique of the mission agency is that it undercuts the foundational theological assumption that the church is missionary at its core. By removing the missionary function from the church organization and placing it elsewhere, an artificial division between church and mission is created that cannot be defended.

> The difficult responsibility of missions must rest upon the church, and whenever the church degenerates to the point that it can no longer serve as an organ of Christ's redeeming love, the task of mission ought not to be assigned to a group of church members, but the church itself ought rather to be reformed, so that it can again become what it ought to be. (Bavinck 1960:61)

From its formation, the Seventh-day Adventist Church placed missions at the core of its organizational structure. As in every institution, this arrangement can produce a degree of inertia at times; however, the strength of the structure is also a major asset in the long-term fulfillment of the church's mission. This is not to suggest that independent Adventist mission agencies of various kinds are inappropriate, but to locate the main responsibility for mission within the church.

An Adventist Mission Paradigm

The world is entering a unique period of its history. The lessons of history are valuable, but many of the patterns of history have completely changed. The human race is much larger than ever before. The world religions are more numerous and more varied than ever before. World economic conditions are extremely diverse, with extreme wealth and extreme poverty creating a growing gap between people. Globalization, with its excellent communication and transportation modes, links humanity more closely than ever before. Human migration is occurring at an unprecedented scale. Urbanization reaches new heights.

Turning to Christianity, the church has never before been the global religion it is today. The Western cultural model of Christianity has lost the dominance it had for many centuries. The church of the West has experienced the weakening forces of secularization and postmodernity. The structures and channels that provided a privileged conduit for missions during the colonial era are gone. Christianity now takes more cultural forms than ever before. Global Christianity has many new centers. Among Adventists, about 92% of members are outside of Europe and North America.

The new era demands an updated mission paradigm for obeying the same Great Commission, to share the same Gospel, based on the same Bible. Perhaps the salient quality of the new paradigm is that it will require more creativity to design and implement more and better methods, for a world with unprecedented diversity. The idolatry of favorite but outdated and ineffective methods will need to be sacrificed. A distinction is needed between the Adventist message, that never changes, and the methods used in mission that must change whenever and however needed. Following are suggested elements of an Adventist mission paradigm for the twenty-first century. The elements are not presented in an order of importance and some of them overlap with each other.

Well-Informed Mission

Developing, constantly updating, and implementing the Adventist mission paradigm will require that the collective missiological literacy of the church be constantly improving. Doing mission on auto-pilot in this complex era is not an acceptable option. The zeal and commitment of the church must be guided by a deep understanding of the topics addressed in this book and many others. If the mistakes of the colonial era can teach the church anything, it is the need to understand the issues, results, and unintended consequences of mission very deeply.

Almost every pastor serves diverse communities and congregations, where one size can never fit all. The complexity faced by church administrators is even more profound.

Church and Mission United

Adventists have a history of keeping church and mission together and that unity must continue. "God is a missionary God ... God's people are a missionary people" and the church is missionary at its core (Bosch 1991:372). This is the reason for having regular local and world mission reports during Sabbath services and for funding world missions from the church's offering plate. This is also why the work of cross-cultural missionaries is administered within the administration of the General Conference, divisions, unions, conferences, and institutions. Adventist theology does not support delegating or outsourcing the missionary work of the church. The independent agencies that have developed in recent decades may be valid expressions of deep and loyal commitment to Adventist missions but they need to be seen as supplementary to and be coordinated with the main work of Adventist global mission. This is not to argue that the official church does everything right, that it is always as creative and agile in missions as it could be, or that making structural adjustments is unnecessary. The point is that the church, in all of its organizational dimensions, is no longer truly the church if its focus is only inward and it stops reaching outward to the world with intentionality.

Another important reaffirmation is the centrality of the local church in mission. Mission is directed from administrative offices, but the contact people have with the Adventist message is through the members and pastors of local churches in their communities. "The church-in-mission is, primarily, the local church everywhere in the world" (378). The local churches make up the global family of the world church in which spiritual and material blessings are shared. This is why Adventist local churches belong to a "sisterhood" of churches. The sisterhood works cooperatively in local and global world mission.

Faithfully Contextualized Mission

Adventist mission reaches out to more people groups and cross-cultural missionaries come from more cultures than ever before. This complex reality has several implications. The church needs a deep understanding of culture and its role, both in the lives of Christians and those to whom they bear witness. Too many Adventists proclaim a Gospel that is "oblivious to culture" (Goheen 2014:185), or they suffer the illusion that they practice a culturally neutral Christianity. They may affirm the need to respect cultural diversity but lack an understanding of how the Gospel and culture come together. Perhaps they lack the ability or willingness to critique their own cultural form of Christianity and to see its imperfections. If they participate in cross-cultural missions, they may practice "helicopter mission," where they attempt to airlift their form of the faith into another people group. Migrant Adventists may try to transport their style of Christianity from their former home to their new home.

The church needs to understand the need for and process of faithful contextualization both for same-cultural and cross-cultural missions. Contextualization is needed for same-culture ministry because every culture evolves and needs to be constantly realigned to the biblical norm. For cross-cultural missions, the task is to lead converts to a cultural style of being faithfully Christian in personal lifestyle, relationships, worship and liturgy styles, and in all aspects of life. To make that possible, contextualized materials and methods are necessary.

Creative Evangelism

Evangelism is part of the core of the mission paradigm; however, mission is the primary or larger category, while evangelism is the secondary category. In other words, "Evangelization is mission, but mission is not merely evangelization" (Bosch 1991:411-412). Discipleship training of members and humanitarian service of various kinds are also elements of mission.

> Evangelism has the distinctive role within mission of being the direct proclamation of the Gospel.

Evangelism has the distinctive role within mission of being the direct proclamation of the Gospel with the intention of calling people to accept salvation through Jesus Christ. The reaction against Western individualism should never cause the church to undervalue the significance of "personal responsibility and personal decision" (416) to become a follower of Jesus.

Authentic evangelism occurs in many different forms, like preaching, personal Bible studies, small groups, print publication, radio and TV, and electronic media. In this century, the public proclamation that was favored in the past is no longer effective among many people groups around the world. Public preaching is not even possible in many Muslim, Hindu, and Buddhist settings. The challenge is to find creative new methods to proclaim the same message.

There are unhealthy forms of evangelism that involve manipulation and empire building. The word "proselytism" is used in missiology to refer to evangelism that abuses individual freedoms and distorts "the Gospel of grace by means of coercion, deception, manipulation, and exploitation" (Moreau et al. 2000:794). Healthy evangelism is persuasive without being manipulative, always respecting the freedom of choice to refuse the Gospel invitation. "The one who evangelizes is a witness, not a judge… I can never be so confident of the purity and authenticity of my witness that I can know that the person who rejects my witness has rejected Christ" (413). Even if one's witness is authentically biblical, the mode of communication may be flawed or the hearer may not yet be spiritually prepared to make a decision.

The Adventist mission paradigm for this century will reaffirm the validity of evangelism that seeks conversion to Jesus Christ. The contemporary trend toward pluralism that affirms every religion as offering equally valid pathways to salvation is not valid. God may decide to save an unevangelized person in his wisdom and mercy but the church's privilege and obligation is to call every person to conversion to Jesus Christ.

Intentional Discipleship

Adventists need to steer away from the "baptism model" of mission toward the "discipleship model." The baptism model uses baptism as the single marker of success, while the discipleship model uses multiple markers, one of which is baptism. The multiple markers are defined by the context. In every context, the goal is to use the combined ministries of the church to nurture spiritual maturity along a path that includes baptism.

Humanitarian Service

Adventists have a wholistic theology of the human being as a unity of physical, emotional, and social dimensions. As a missionary, Jesus Christ offered wholistic healing for all human dimensions, not only for spiritual salvation. "Since one's theology of mission is always dependent on one's theology of salvation ... the scope of how one defines salvation determines the scope of the missionary enterprise" (Bosch:1991:393). This means that Adventist mission does more than offer salvation and eternal life at the Second Coming. Humanitarian ministries are part of mission, not merely bridges or byproducts, but an integral part of mission. Wholistic mission should address every form of alienation, oppression, discrimination, social evil, and injustice. Mission includes a message to transform all personal and social relationships.

Christian Education

Christian education has been part of the Adventist mission paradigm from the beginning. Schools educating indigenous peoples were part of the earliest initiatives in the former colonies. In the last century, multiple generations of national teachers, pastors, health care workers, and administrators have been prepared for service in Adventist schools. Schools have performed the tasks of Adventist mission in all its dimensions.

Seminars and other meetings lasting a few days or weeks have value in providing informal and non-formal education; however, the missional quality and value of formal education provided by Christian teachers over many years can hardly be overstated. The continuing Adventist mission paradigm will give priority to education.

Mission in Global Partnership

In an era of globalized Christianity, all Christians, everywhere, share the responsibility for mission. When Christianity was mostly in the West, the responsibility rested mostly on the church of the West. Today, the responsibility is shared by global Christianity.

When mission was "from the West to the rest," mission was also from the more wealthy and powerful to the less wealthy and powerful. The Adventist church of the West is still relatively wealthy but it is now a minority. The majority church of the global south is rich in human resources and spiritual vitality, though relatively poor in material resources.

A new form of global partnership in mission is needed for the new mission paradigm. The shared missional focus of that partnership needs to be on the least-evangelized peoples concentrated in North Africa, the Middle East, Asia, and Europe. The partnership will break away from the mission-from-wealth-to-poverty model of the modern missionary movement to the mission-from-weakness model of the Apostle Paul. "God has chosen the foolish things of the world to put to shame the wise, and … the weak things of the world to put to shame the things which are mighty" (1 Cor 1:27). "For when I am weak, then I am strong" (2 Cor 12:10). The new model could be called "Gideon's band mission" (Judg 7).

Some difficult truths are implied by the mission-from-weakness model. On the side of the church of the global south, the former pattern of dependency on monies from the West for local ministries needs to be surrendered. Jesus exhorted his disciples, "Freely you have received; freely give" (Matt 10:8). On the side of the church of the global north, certain patterns of "iMission" or "Selfi-Mission," that expend large sums to give a blessing to short-term mission travelers may need to be carefully considered. The theme of mission as sacrifice and self-limitation that characterized the early NT church, the modern missionary movement, and the early Adventist church needs to be rediscovered and emulated.

Strategic Mission

As shown in the chapters on mission strategy, all mission needs to be a carefully planned, strategic endeavor. All branches of the church, with the numerous independent ministries included, need to work in coordination. All forms of volunteer service need to be carefully coordinated with long-term missionary service and local indigenous service. Duplication of effort needs to be avoided and efficiency maximized. More is said in later chapters about mission strategy.

Urban Missions

Mission in this century is primarily an urban ministry instead of a rural ministry in villages and jungles as in the past. In some respects, villages and jungles are preferable to cities, but the population is now in the cities. The cities bring together every variation of culture and religion, requiring the fullest possible range of creativity and contextualization. Every element of the Adventist mission paradigm will need to function at its best in urban contexts.

Mission Among the World Religions

The mission paradigm will give high priority to mission among the non-Christian world religions because their adherents comprise the majority of humanity among whom Adventist mission has had the least successes. The religions will need to be studied deeply and understood well. The theology of religions is a neglected topic that needs more emphasis in theological education. The challenges of religious pluralism must be addressed. Dialogue with the followers of other religions will be considered a normal part of missions. Adventists will need to support each other in trying new and creative methods, some of which will inevitably fail.

Peace-making Mission

In a world consumed by hatred and conflict of every kind, intentional peace-making is a much needed dimension of mission. The church's best starting place is within its own communities that are increasingly diverse. Multi-cultural church boards need enhanced cultural competence. Community outreach will include facilitating peaceful encounters between conflicting groups.

Mission with, for, and by Migrants

Human migration, in its various dimensions, constitutes a major factor in twenty-first century missions: (1) Refugees leave home under duress, traveling toward different destinations, through many different nations, and in need of humanitarian services on the entire journey; (2) voluntary immigrants travel to various destinations, intending to start new lives; (3) both refugee and immigrant groups include adherents of the major world religions who are potentially more open to the Gospel because of their transition; (4) both groups include Adventists who join existing churches or plant new ones in their new homes. Human migrants in all four categories provide unique challenges and opportunities for mission that must be addressed. Adventist migrants of all kinds are actually cross-cultural missionaries who carry the Adventist message with them and need missiological training and skills to maximize their work.

Long-term Missionary Service

Several factors have combined to cause a dramatic decrease in the number of long term Adventist missionaries, as already noted. The scale of the unfinished mission task demands re-commitment to long term service as a permanent part of the Adventist mission paradigm.

Mission among the least-evangelized peoples who constitute the church's unfinished task is the most challenging work in Adventist mission history. Effective work requires deep levels of language, cultural, and religious knowledge that only long-term missionaries can have. Long-termers can provide the coordinating hubs around which short-term volunteers can offer their best service.

Short-term and Volunteer Service

Short-term volunteers of all kinds add a valuable dimension to the Adventist paradigm. Individuals can be personally engaged in missions away from home. Specialized service can be provided for specific tasks, like architectural designing. Institutions abroad, like schools, with limited budgets can be sustained.

Philosophies or Models of Modern Missions

A philosophy of mission is comprised of "the integrated beliefs, assertions, theories, and aims which determine the character, the purpose, the organization, the strategy, and the action of a particular sending body of the Christian world mission" (Terry, Smith, and Anderson 1998:13). Describing missions in this way overlaps with thinking of missions as following different paradigms. The philosophies or models of mission discussed below describe approaches taken in modern times, starting with the modern missionary movement. A variety of philosophies of mission are observable in the past and present practice of world mission (13-15).

Individualism

In this philosophy, mission happens through the spontaneous witness of the individual Christian in the daily affairs of life. There is no intentional "doing" of mission or structures for mission because mission is only the personal witness of the individual believer's life.

Colonialism

Not all missions of the colonial era subscribed to this philosophy. In this approach, mission is supported by state churches who send and support missionaries with tax funds. A prime example is the Danish-Halle Mission to South India, in which the king of Denmark supported the Halle missionaries.

Ecclesiasticism

"This philosophy exists where the mission is a department of a structured, hierarchical church, or an order of a church" (14). The Roman Catholic and Orthodox churches have missionary orders that report to the hierarchy. Some Protestants do missions from within their denominational structures, although they may not be hierarchical like Roman Catholics.

Congregationalism

Many or most Protestant missionaries are sent by congregationalist churches with the intention of planting free-standing congregationalist churches on the mission field.

Associationalism

In this model, committed individuals and churches join associations or agencies to sponsor missions. In some cases, the agency is made up of persons who are members of many different churches or denominations. Other agencies are made up of missionary-minded congregations that join mission associations as whole churches. This is the dominant Protestant, congregational, free-church, and evangelical church model.

Faith Missions

All of the philosophies want to be led by faith and the Spirit but faith missions are noted for not using elaborate fund raising methods or relying on official church offerings. A faith "mission is inspired, supported, and carried out by the direction of the Holy Spirit and by persons and groups compelled by the Spirit's leading to support the mission" (Terry et al. 1998:14). The faith mission model was pioneered by Hudson Taylor and the China Inland Mission.

Supportivism

A mission following the supportive model specializes in supporting other types of mission in different, specialized ways. Examples include Mission Aviation Fellowship, Wycliffe Bible Translators, and Bible societies.

Institutionalism

An agency following this philosophy supports specific institutions, like hospitals, orphanages, or schools. Some agencies support only one institution. There is some overlap between this category and the Supportivism model.

Ecumenicalism

"This philosophy exists where the purpose of the mission is the promotion of Christian unity in one form or another" (14). Some groups work for unity between denominations through the World Council of Churches and similar national bodies.

Pentecostalism

This approach describes missions that depend "on signs, wonders, miracles, healings, exorcisms, and charismatic manifestations to attract large crowds to hear and respond to the Gospel" (15). Those who use this model do not only believe in the validity of healing and exorcism, they use signs and wonders as a primary method of evangelization.

Wholism

Wholistic mission includes all human dimensions, including the spiritual. However, there are agencies that minister primarily to social and physical needs, either because their funding sources forbid direct evangelization or the context makes it impossible. Faith-based, Non-Governmental Organizations (NGOs) like World Vision and Adventist Development and Relief Agency (ADRA) support a wide variety of programs that promote the comprehensive well-being of humanity.

iMissionism or SelfiMissionism

This philosophy exists where the primary goal of mission is to bless the missionary, through spiritual growth, broadening the life experience, or bringing personal maturity. Short-term Mission is sometimes built on this philosophy.

Service to local people is rendered, but the primary goal is to give those making the trip a valuable experience.

An Adventist Philosophy of Mission

Adventist mission is complex, with both official and unofficial dimensions. The official dimensions involve every organizational entity, in every nation and people group where the church works. The unofficial mission agencies are not funded or administered by the church. They include a diverse spectrum of Adventists with varying convictions, ranging from strongly loyal "supporting ministries" to some nearer the fringes of the church. The face that Adventists present to the world is a composite of both the unofficial and official missions of the church. The philosophy of mission described below best describes the official dimensions of Adventist mission because of the very wide diversity found in the unofficial groups.

In agreement with the philosophy of individualism, Adventists believe that a Christian's personal life carries an essential unspoken witness but we also believe mission requires overt, intentional witnessing in harmony with a believer's spiritual gifts. Members should not feel compelled to do all of the same things as others and there are appropriate times to do nothing except to build relationships. However, it is important to both "walk the talk" and "talk the walk." We believe that "I would rather see a sermon than hear a sermon" but also that "I need to hear the sermon so that I can understand what I am seeing even better."

The Adventist emphasis on the separation of church and state means that they have never practiced mission as a component of either colonial government or independent government activities. During the colonial era there was some cooperation with government healthcare and education functions and that cooperation continues today in some nations.

The Adventist emphasis on the separation of church and state means that we have never practiced mission as a component of either colonial government or independent government activities. During the colonial era there was some cooperation with government healthcare and education functions and that cooperation continues today in some nations.

Adventist polity is not congregationalist, therefore we do not establish free-standing local churches on the mission field. Local churches are organized into the sisterhood of Adventist churches and served by pastors paid and administered by fields or conferences.

Adventists do not have official mission agencies that are separate from the church structure, but there are some unofficial agencies. Adventist Frontier Mission (AFM) and some others use the association model to support Adventist missionaries.

Some unofficial Adventist agencies or institutions use the faith missions model that depends on prayer without fund raising publications or programs.

There are unofficial Adventist agencies that follow the supportivism and institutionalism models. For example, Adventist World Aviation provides aircraft and professional pilots where other forms of transportation are difficult. Adventist Health International (AHI) is a Loma Linda University based agency that offers support and guidance for hospitals that request its help. The Adventist Layman's Services and Industries (ASI) sponsors numerous initiatives and services around the world. Maranatha Volunteers International specializes in sending volunteers to building projects around the world.

Ecumenicalism and Pentecostalism are not part of the Adventist philosophy of mission. The church does work to have good relationships with other denominations, but without seeking ecumenical unity. Adventists do believe in the powerful works of the Spirit, but exorcism and healing are not used as primary outreach methods, as they are with some Pentecostal groups.

The Adventist philosophy of mission is very wholistic because we believe that salvation embraces the whole person. Many official and unofficial Adventist entities serve the whole person. Evangelization includes the development of a healthy lifestyle as part of being a follower of Christ.

Both short-term and long-term mission service brings blessings to those serving. However, iMissionism or SelfiMissionism is not part of a well understood philosophy of Adventist mission. The primary goals of mission focus on the recipients of mission initiatives. The blessings of service in any capacity, from the pulpit, to the Sabbath School, to church maintenance, to cross-cultural missionary work are accepted with gratitude, but as secondary to the purpose of being a blessing to others.

Chapter

Phases of Adventist Mission

~ • ⌒

Introduction

The Seventh-day Adventist vision for global mission did not arrive fully developed when the church was born in the years following the disappointment of 1844. Time was needed for the church to develop a full system of beliefs that would be proclaimed around the world, to have an organizational structure to administer world missions, and to have sufficient members and monies to support global missions.

George Knight has outlined five phases in the development of Adventist mission (2005:v-xxvi). This chapter follows Knight's basic outline but with a few adjustments. The dates marking the phases are not intended to be rigid. Only the major movements in Adventist mission are discussed. In every sector of the church there have been smaller scale movements, strategies, and initiatives.

Overview of Membership Growth Patterns

Before considering the phases of Adventist mission, a brief overview of membership growth patterns will be helpful. Tables 8.1 and 8.2 summarize growth patterns starting in 1910 when Adventist world mission was well under way. In 1910, the world membership stood at 90,808 and by 2016 it had grown to over 20 million. In 1910, the North American membership accounted for 67% of the total and in 2016 it made up just 6.2%. Clearly, the church's commitment to carrying the Adventist message outside the nation of its birth has become a reality. However, the church's engagement in world mission took time to develop.

Table 8.1
Adventist Membership by World Region

Region	1910	1930	1950	1970	1990	2016
Africa	981	48,182	95,807	439,345	2,064,324	7,975,080
Asia	724	41,802	85,474	319,929	1,118,930	3,723,465
Europe	16,995	106,193	162,716	206,978	239,376	377,063
Latin America	6,793	42,708	133,120	552,454	2,270,549	6,205,873
North America	60,873	124,581	250,939	439,726	760,148	1,237,004
Oceania	4,442	19,277	28,656	93,432	241,553	490,294
Total	**90,808**	**382,743**	**756,712**	**2,051,864**	**6,694,880**	**20,008,779**

Source: General Conference Annual Statistical Reports

Table 8.2
Adventist Membership Distribution by World Region

Region	1910	1930	1950	1970	1990	2016
Africa	1.1%	12.6%	12.7%	21.4%	30.8%	39.9%
Asia	0.8%	10.9%	11.3%	15.6%	16.7%	18.6%
Europe	18.7%	27.7%	21.5%	10.1%	3.6%	1.9%
Latin America	7.5%	11.2%	17.6%	26.9%	33.9%	31.0%
North America	67.0%	32.5%	33.2%	21.4%	11.4%	6.2%
Oceania	4.9%	5.0%	3.8%	4.6%	3.6%	2.5%

Source: General Conference Annual Statistical Reports

Phase I: The Shut-Door Mission Era (1844-1852)

Following the Great Disappointment of October 22, 1844, William Miller, Ellen Harmon (later White), James White, and the other Adventist pioneers believed that their only mission was to help those who had been disappointed to maintain their hope in the Second Advent. They believed that the door of salvation was shut to those who had not accepted the Second Advent message and passed though the Great Disappointment experience. During this first phase, the infant church was developing both the doctrinal and membership base that was needed to even consider a broader mission. Gradually the shut-door position eroded and in 1848 Ellen White encouraged her husband to print a paper that, though "small at first," would eventually go "clear around the world" (White:LS:125). By the early 1850s a somewhat more open-door missiology had developed based on the third angel's message of Rev 14:9-12.

Phase II: A Partially Open Door (1852-1874)

Between the initial openness and J. N. Andrews' departure for Switzerland in 1874 as the first official missionary, the missional door swung further open in stages. Some believed that the Great Commission could be fulfilled within the United States where there were immigrants representing every nation. Then in 1855 Joseph Bates advocated sending literature around the world. In 1856 James White advocated mission to "corrupt Christianity," though not to "the heathen" (Knight 2005:x). A significant initiative came from European immigrants in America who sent literature to their relatives and friends in Europe. When Adventists became aware of small groups of believers in Europe, Australia, and South Africa their vision expanded further. James White declared in 1863 that "ours is a world-wide message" (Knight 2005:xi). In 1871, Ellen White called for young people to learn foreign languages and to go to the whole world. "Adventists were still reluctant missionaries at best" when Andrews went to Switzerland because "they still had an inadequate vision of worldwide mission," but their vision was broadening (Knight 2005:xv). In this phase, Adventists strengthened the organizational structures and a power base needed to support world mission.

Phase III: An Expanding Vision for Mission (1874-1901)

The sending of J. N. Andrews to Switzerland in 1874 marked the official entry into Adventist world mission. Some unofficial, self-supporting missionaries had already gone to several nations, but Andrews was the first to be sent officially.

The late-nineteenth and early-twentieth centuries saw a major expansion of Protestant global mission and Adventists were part of that trend. Many new mission agencies were organized. The Student Volunteer Movement, with the motto, "The evangelization of the world in this generation," was influential on university campuses.

Church leaders, including Ellen White, travelled to visit groups of Adventists in Europe. A worker's conference was conducted in Europe in 1882. Official missionaries went to Australia and New Zealand in 1885 and South Africa in 1887. S. N. Haskell and P. T. Magan made a two-year world tour to survey opportunities for mission in 1889-1891 and published their reports in the *Youth's Instructor*. Publications in different languages were started.

At first the focus of missions was on Protestants, but gradually the church's mission vision broadened to include Catholics and non-Christian peoples. In 1930, retiring General Conference president, W. A. Spicer, spoke in retrospect about the 1890s.

When I came back from Europe in 1892, to be secretary of the Foreign Mission Board, I tell you truly we didn't have much of an idea of going to the heathen. We didn't expect to go in any really strong way. We never expected to go to the Catholic countries. We thought: We will get a few along the edges, and the

Lord will come; but the Lord all the time had in mind this purpose, of calling the heathen, of calling through all the Catholic lands for His people to come. (Spicer 1930:3)

Spicer's statement that "We thought: We will get a few along the edges, and the Lord will come" shows how far the church's mission vision had expanded. By 1930, the church was deeply committed to mission among all groups and its actual global engagement with all groups was on the rise.

The GC Session of 1879 created a Missionary Board to oversee foreign missionaries under the GC Committee. Between 1879 and the reorganization of 1901/1903, the board was led by different people, including W. C. White. Evaluating its actual impact on Adventist mission is difficult because its role and status in the church were in constant flux (Trim 2017b:3). The same need for reorganization felt by other organizations in the church was felt by the church's foreign missions program.

At the end of this phase, the foundations were laid and missionaries were sent from North America, Europe, Australia, New Zealand, and South Africa to the rest of the world.

By the end of the 1890s Adventism had been established on every continent and on many islands of the sea. In this.... period of Adventist mission the denomination aimed to reach the "heathen" and Catholics as well as the world's Protestants, though Adventists usually began their work even in non-Christian countries among pockets of Protestants in those lands. (Knight 2005:xix-xx)

Phase IV: Mission to All the World (1901-1960s)

The reorganization of the church in 1901/1903 marked the beginning of the next phase in Adventist mission. The reorganization gave to the union conferences the responsibility for administration within their territories that the GC had previously attempted to exercise from headquarters. The responsibility for foreign missions and missionaries formerly held by the somewhat poorly defined Mission Board was given to the GC Committee. In subsequent years, the title of Mission Board was sometimes used but "the GC Committee *was* the Mission Board" (Trim 2017b:7).

The administrative tasks of recruiting, training, sending, and supporting missionaries were assigned to the GC Secretary and his staff, who together made up the GC Secretariat. The overarching task of the Secretariat was to lead the world church in the evangelization of unreached peoples in unentered territories. The world church's members and its monies were to be directed in a coordinated mission program. The non-Christian peoples of China, India, and Africa received high priority.

Two leaders in this phase provided exceptional leadership in world mission for almost thirty years. Arthur G. Daniells (1858-1935) served as General

Conference president from 1901 to 1922. William A. Spicer (1865-1952) was secretary from 1903 to 1922. Spicer replaced Daniells as president in 1922 and served until 1930, while Daniells was secretary from 1922 to 1926.

An important development for mission in this phase was the formation of church departments in 1904. A variety of organizations involving literature and other types of outreach had functioned as independent entities until then. In 1904 the separate entities were gathered into departments of the church with directors who served under the direction of general administrators.

The early developments in healthcare and education started at Battle Creek blossomed and spread worldwide during Phase IV. The typical model of wholistic Adventist mission throughout the world field included evangelization, church planting, education, publishing, and healthcare. Broadcasting was added as the technology developed.

Two world wars and the great depression slowed world travel and decreased church income but did not dampen fervor for world mission. By the mid-twenties the church had become truly international, with more members outside than within North America. Adventists in Europe, Australia, New Zealand, and South Africa joined North America as active senders of missionaries.

A frequently used organizational unit on the field was the mission station. As the church presence in a particular nation or region became strong enough, fields, unions, and divisions were organized. Territorial assignments were adjusted between the organizational units as the church grew. Mission stations often became school campuses when administrative offices were established in towns or cities.

Almost all missionaries in Phase IV were sent "from the West to the rest," from the relatively wealthy parts of the church to where there were few members and where local economies were weaker. Most church administrators in the world field were expatriates from the West. However, educational institutions were steadily training indigenous peoples who would serve as leaders in the next phase.

When the Second World War ended, several factors developed that would shape world mission: First, strong mission zeal was unleashed in the West that had been constrained by the events of history; and committed young adults, including my own parents, who had grown up during the great depression and survived or endured the war, came forth eager to serve in world mission. Second, the post-war economic recovery brought increased resources to the church for the support of missions. Third, energies promoting nationalism and independence that had been restrained by the war were released and anti-colonial movements blossomed in the European colonies. These movements shaped mission and produced the next phase.

Phase V: Post-Colonial Mission (1960s-1990)

Although the other phases were shaped largely by factors within the church, Phase V received much of its character from historical factors outside the church.

The wave of condemnation that fell upon European colonialism after the Second World War produced a wave of national independence in the 1960s. Part of the critique of colonialism was a critique of Christian missions. In many minds, "mission" and "the missionary" belonged to a by-gone era that had been repudiated alongside colonialism. The "missionary go home" sentiment was common in some places. Ecumenical groups in several places went so far as to declare a complete moratorium on receiving missionaries and funding from abroad. The moratorium was never implemented but it showed the thinking of the time. Whether quickly or gradually, the trend was to replace Adventist missionaries with local workers. Even in the West, many believed that the era of cross-cultural missionaries had ended. That perception continues to influence thinking about mission.

There had been some predictions that when the colonies became independent the religion of the European colonizers would be rejected. Those predictions did not come true because Christianity in the former colonies continued to grow after independence. In Africa, for example, the Christian portion of the population grew from 9.4% to 47.9% between 1910 and 2010 (Johnson and Ross 2009:9). The Adventist church of Africa in 1970 was about 450 times larger than in 1910 and the church of 2010 was about 14 times larger than that of 1970. Yet, the post-colonial era was definitely a new and different era for Christian missions.

The more liberal or conciliar Christian groups, including the World Council of Churches, tended toward a more negative narrative that equated colonialism and Christian mission. More conservative, evangelical mission thinkers joined the condemnation of colonialism but remained more positive toward global mission. The 1974 International Congress on World Evangelization at Lausanne, Switzerland met at a time when the future of Christian missions was uncertain. The Lausanne Covenant reaffirmed the validity of mission as coming from the will of God, not from that of fallible humans and churches.

> We affirm our belief in the one-eternal God, Creator and Lord of the world, Father, Son and Holy Spirit, who governs all things according to the purpose of his will. He has been calling out from the world a people for himself, and sending his people back into the world to be his servants and his witnesses, for the extension of his kingdom, the building up of Christ's body, and the glory of his name. (Stott 2012:12)

The rejection of slavery, colonialism, and racism did not need to imply a rejection of Christian mission and cross-cultural missionary service because Christian mission was grounded in the will and character of God. Millions of non-Christian people lived beyond the reach of a local church and could be reached only by cross-cultural missionaries. The church must unite to send missionaries from everywhere to everywhere to evangelize non-Christians. The appointment of indigenous church leaders in the former colonies did not eliminate the need for continued partnerships and coordination in mission between all the different parts of the global Christian church.

During Phase V, there was a major switch to indigenous Adventist leaders all around the world. By 1980, most administrative positions from field/conference, to union, to division levels were held by indigenous people. The elected and appointed staff of the General Conference headquarters increasingly reflected the diversity of the global church.

Adventists did not stop sending cross-cultural missionaries, but some shifts occurred. First, the jobs to which they were called changed. Instead of serving in church planting or general leadership positions, missionaries were called to fill more technical positions in hospitals, colleges, development, and other technical work.

The second shift was that the old "from the West to the rest" missionary pattern started to change. An increasing number of missionaries were called from the global south. A process started that disconnected the popular image of "the missionary" from "a White woman or man" so that "the missionary" became "any kind of man or woman." In 2018, about 70% of official Adventist missionaries are from outside North America. Those that come from the global north are very multiethnic. The GC missionary workforce comes from about 70 nations and serves in about 90 nations.

A major forward step for Adventists was taken when, in 1966, the Department of World Mission and the General Conference Institute of World Mission were established at the Theological Seminary at Andrews University. This addition brought the formal study of missiology into theological curricula and the training of cross-cultural missionaries.

The Adventist Development and Relief Agency (ADRA) became a major part of comprehensive Adventist mission strategy during this phase. ADRA was founded in 1956, but its impact came to be felt somewhat later. Although ADRA does not engage in direct evangelization and church planting, it follows the example of Jesus by responding to human need, suffering, disaster, and poverty.

During the 1960s, the Student Missionary program started on Adventist campuses. College students would take a year off from their studies to work abroad, typically as elementary or secondary school teachers or as English language teachers.

The earlier phases of Adventist mission involved the church reaching into an entire world unreached by the Adventist message. As time passed, the most responsive peoples were in Sub-Saharan Africa, Latin America, Oceania, and parts of Asia. A pattern of membership growth was established that produced a substantial imbalance in the distribution of the membership. By 2016, six of the church's divisions, along with the Middle East North Africa Union and Israel Field, in which 74% of the world population was located, would have only 23% of the membership. The other seven divisions, with only 26% of the world population, would have 77% of the membership.

One of the reasons for the uneven distribution of members is found in the people groups in particular regions. Christ's parable of the sower or soils (Matt 13) teaches that people respond to the Gospel in different ways; however, a poor response can also be caused by inattention or poor strategy and methods by the church.

Starting in Phase V, the church experienced "mission drift" and entered a period of mission "on autopilot" (Trim 2017b:15-16) with several characteristics: (1) Instead of focusing on the least-evangelized peoples, emphasis was given to the best-evangelized regions, where the church was already best established, through programs like "1000 Days of Reaping," "Harvest 90," and the "Net" programs of the 1990s; (2) no systematic reallocation of resources and relocation of personnel was made from areas where the church was already well established to areas where it was not established; and (3) the number of cross-cultural missionaries sent by the GC fell, even as the unevangelized world population grew dramatically.

No church leader or committee made a decision to ignore the least-evangelized. Apparently, the church simply lost a part of its collective mission vision and developed tunnel vision that looked for easy successes, instead of using its rapidly growing membership to enter challenging areas.

Phase VI: Intentional Mission for the Least-Evangelized (1990-Present)

In the 40 years after the World War II the Adventist membership grew dramatically in Latin America, Sub-Saharan Africa, Oceania, and the Philippines. By the late-1980s, church leaders became concerned about the relatively poor church growth in much of Europe, Asia, the Middle East, and North Africa, as already noted. By one report, over 90% of church monies were being spent for existing church activities and mission among other Christians (Watts 1989:913). Only a small fraction was being allocated for mission among the least-evangelized peoples of the world who were mostly among the non-Christian world religions.

General Conference president, Neal Wilson, led a serious move to reach out in new directions. Gottfried Oosterwal and Russell Staples, missiologists at Andrews University, served as valued consultants for Wilson and his colleagues. The *Adventist Review* published a six-part series in July-August 1987, featuring the unfinished task of mission in the major parts of the world.

In 1989 and 1990, the General Conference went through several stages of strategy development. Charles Taylor and Mike Ryan were involved in the early steps of the new initiative. The 1990 General Conference Session launched the Global Mission Initiative. The Office of Global Mission, that would later become the Office of Adventist Mission, was established. In the intervening years, the new initiatives have shaped Adventist mission in some important ways (McEdward 2012:25-41).

Shifting Toward the Least-Evangelized

Starting in the 1990s, a process was started to shift mission resources and personnel toward the least-evangelized peoples. Cross-cultural missionary budgets were moved away from areas where Adventists were well established to areas without an effective presence. The transfer of budgets is complicated by the fact that the regions of the church that have grown most rapidly are often the most economically challenged. Thus, shifting a budget from a hospital or university in a developing nation to a 10/40 Window location creates a potential setback for the hospital or university that loses valuable workers.

When the transfer of budgets brings new workers to unevangelized areas, they become truly frontline missionaries who reflect the comprehensive nature of Adventist mission. Some are church planters, while others are pastors, teachers, healthcare workers, relief and development workers, or administrators. The body of Christ has many different parts, all of which are needed for smooth functioning. The kind of expatriate workers needed depends on factors in the local membership and the local population. The overall goal is to build missional capacity so that local members eventually assume the leadership of all aspects of mission work.

Part of the intentional move toward unevangelized people groups has been initiating or giving new emphasis to different kinds of service.

1. The new category of Global Mission Pioneer was added to enlist indigenous Adventists for work among their own cultural-linguistic groups. The challenge has been to provide adequate training and supervision for people who work among the most challenging people groups.
2. Special training and networking has been provided for Total Employment missionaries who follow Paul's tentmaking model. Tentmakers support themselves in a wide variety of professions and often have access where official missionaries cannot go.
3. College students have been encouraged to become "Waldensian students" who enroll in universities to witness as they are able.
4. Centers of Influence are being established to offer comprehensive, community-focused ministries that are appropriate for the context.

The transfer of missionary budgets away from well-established areas does not suggest an abandonment of long-term cross-cultural missionary service by the church. On the contrary, cross-cultural missionary service has continuing validity for three main reasons:

1. Cross-cultural missionaries are the necessary first agents of mission to populations where the church is not established or poorly established.
2. The world church has a wealth of skills and professions within its membership that it can share to fill specific needs. For example, an Adventist university in Asia needs a professor of biology but has none among its indigenous membership. A call is placed to the General Conference and a professor comes from Europe, Africa, or America.

3. Cross-cultural missionary service promotes diversity in the church that is beneficial in a globalized but polarized world. That biology professor from Europe, Africa, or America serving in Asia brings valuable diversity when she works at the Asian university.

Improving Methods Among the Least-Evangelized

A concerted attempt has been made to increase the church's awareness of the unfinished task and enhance its mission methods among the least-evangelized peoples. Global Mission Centers have been established for Judaism, Islam, Hinduism, Buddhism, Postmodern-secular, Urban, and Orthodox peoples. Among other duties, the centers produce contextualized materials, experiment with new methods, raise awareness in the church, offer training programs, mentor church members and leaders, and promote mission among the world religions.

As new approaches to the world religions have been tried, new issues have emerged. The General Conference Global Mission Issues Committee was established in 1997. The committee brings together General Conference and division leaders and missiologists at an annual meeting to discuss mission issues arising from the field. In nations dominated by the non-Christian world religions, Christian mission encounters a wide range of restrictions. One persistent issue is knowing what to do with new converts in restrictive places to provide on-going spiritual nurture. How can missions best proceed where public conversion, baptism, and membership in public churches is forbidden? These and other issues were addressed in a document entitled *Roadmap for Mission* voted by the General Conference Annual Council of 2009.

Enhancing Academic Missiology

The academic study of mission has been strengthened in recent years as the church has seen its value. The Department of World Mission of the Theological Seminary at Andrews University began teaching missiology in the mid-1960s. Masters and doctoral degree programs have been offered there for a long time that have produced a steady flow of graduates; however, a new era began in 2015 with the start of a Doctor of Missiology program that makes doctoral level mission studies accessible to more people.

Masters and doctoral mission studies programs are being offered by an increasing number of Adventist universities. The Adventist International Institute of Advanced Studies in the Philippines and the Adventist University of Africa in Kenya, both General Conference institutions, offer masters and doctoral programs in missiology. The combined programs provide a greatly increased pool of mission teachers to serve the world church.

Improving and Broadening Cross-Cultural Missionary Service

A concerted attempt has been made to enhance the effectiveness of cross-cultural missionary service among the least-evangelized peoples. The GC now refers to its cross-cultural missionaries as International Service Employees (ISEs). The GC Institute of World Mission provides three-week Mission Institutes for out-going ISEs and one-week Welcome Home sessions when they return from their place of service.

New Adventist organizations have become active in sending and supporting cross-cultural missionaries. Until recent times, the General Conference has sent and supported most official missionaries. The South Pacific Division is a long-time sender of missionaries to the Pacific islands. Today, the Northern Asia Pacific Division and South American Division send and support a significant number of missionaries to places like Mongolia, China, and the Middle East-North Africa. Other divisions are showing interest in joining the trend.

Since 2010, several structural changes have been made at General Conference headquarters that have made an impact on world mission. An official Mission Board has been reestablished to oversee world mission initiatives. The parts of Treasury and Secretariat involved with selecting, sending, training, and administering missionaries have been merged into the office of International Personnel Resources and Services (IPRS) that is lodged within Secretariat. The Institute of World Mission was moved from Andrews University to be at world headquarters.

In a concerted effort to rise above a preoccupation with essential bureaucratic responsibilities for the sake of leading the world church in mission among the least-evangelized, the GC Secretariat has been reorganized into a "Mission Family." The family includes the Secretary, Under Secretary, Assistant Secretary, and Associate Secretaries; the Office of Adventist Mission, which supervises the world religion centers; Adventist Volunteer Services, that oversees short-term volunteers; Institute of Adventist Mission, which trains long-term missionaries; International Personnel Resources and Services, that administers long-term missionaries; the Office of Archives, Statistics and Research, that publishes statistical reports and conducts mission-related research; and the Office of Membership Services, which operates a global membership software system (see www.adventistmission.org).

Other Changes and Trends

During the 1990s, Short Term Mission (STM) became a growing mode of Adventist mission service. People of all ages, from elementary school to the retirement years, travel abroad for a few days or weeks. STM travelers typically conduct evangelistic meetings, offer healthcare clinics, or perform a variety of construction and maintenance tasks.

In recent years, a large but unknown number of Adventists have become immigrant missionaries from everywhere to everywhere. Adventists from many African and Asian nations have a significant presence in the local churches of Europe, North America, and the Middle East. Collectively, these immigrants have changed the face of the Adventist church in their new places of residence. The immigrants have brought much vitality and commitment to Adventist mission. Immigrant churches sometimes face a significant challenge in witnessing effectively to the traditional, native peoples of their local church communities.

Conclusion

Phase VI is a work in progress. Many steps have been taken by the church in precisely the right directions. Several steps seem necessary as the church moves forward: (1) to implement and fulfill positive directions already taken because good plans and ideas have no value unless fully implemented; (2) to be willing to be guided by the Spirit into new, creative, and sometimes unconventional methods that offer hope for more effective mission among the least-evangelized peoples groups; (3) to fully engage parts of the church in global mission that in previous phases were recipients of monies and missionaries but now are well established; and (4) to increase the personal sacrificial support of world missions by all members of the church.

An Adventist Mission Case Study: Malawi, Africa

The story of Christian mission in Malawi is a story of receptivity and growth. The history of Adventist mission in Malawi provides a good case study of the strategies, trends, and developments starting in Phase IV of Adventist mission.

Malawians take their name from the *Maravi*, an old name of the *Nyanja* people, who are the "people of the lake." The nation's pre-independence name under the British Empire was Nyasaland. Today, the nation calls itself, "The Warm Heart of Africa." Malawi had a population of about 0.9 million in 1900 and 16 million in 2013. The population that was virtually all rural a century ago is now about 15% urban. In land mass, Malawi compares to the nation of North Korea and the American state of Ohio.

Malawians traditionally practiced a local form of African Traditional Religion. Today, the religious distribution is Christian 87%, Muslim 11.7%, other 1%, and none 0.3% (CIA 2018). The Adventist membership had grown to 452,994 in 3,129 churches and companies by 2015. Malawi is part of the Eastern-Africa Indian Ocean Division and the Malawi Union Conference is divided into three local conferences.

David Livingstone trekked through Malawi in 1859 and the first Anglican missionaries arrived in 1861. George James, a Battle Creek College attendee from England, went to Malawi in 1893 as a self-supporting Adventist missionary. He itinerated in the villages around Blantyre, playing his violin, singing, and preaching. Being unable to start and sustain mission work by himself, he departed with the intention of joining missionaries at Solusi Mission in Zimbabwe, but he died along the way (Doss 1993).

Malawi followed South Africa and Zimbabwe as the third recipient of Adventist mission initiatives in Africa. In 1902, the General Conference purchased Plainfield Mission from the Seventh Day Baptists. The mission was later renamed Malamulo (Commandments) Mission. The first Adventist missionaries were Thomas Branch, with his family, and James Booth (*SDA Encyclopedia* 1996:2:12-17;178). At the 1905 General Conference Session, president A. G. Daniells singled out Malawi by calling for the church to "materially strengthen our missionaries in Nyassaland [sic], Rhodesia, China, Korea, Ceylon, Turkey, and Egypt" (Daniells 1905). As time passed, Malamulo gained a reputation among Adventists in North America as an exemplary mission station.

After opening Malamulo Mission station, the church opened others, notably Matandani in 1908, Luwazi in 1928, Mombera (now Lunjika) in 1929, and Lakeview in 1934. All of the mission stations were in rural areas, among the largely rural population. Local churches and pastors, schools and teachers, and clinics and medical assistants were administered from the mission stations.

In 1958, church administrative functions were shifted from mission stations to field offices that were established in Blantyre and Mzimba. Norman Doss, my father, was the first president of the North Nyasa Field in Mzimba. The early mission stations that were once like mini-conferences have evolved into institutional campuses and some smaller mission stations have been downsized to local church locations. During the mission station era, most church planting was in rural areas, where most of the population lived. As the urban population grew, more urban churches were planted and their membership grew dramatically. The urban churches now provide much of the income for the three conferences of the Malawi Union because more of their members are employed.

Adventist mission was decidedly focused on the most receptive peoples in Malawi from the beginning. Not only did Adventists focus on areas where there were already some Christians, but where there were some seventh-day Sabbath keepers. Both Malamulo and Luwazi mission stations were established where Seventh Day Baptists had started but failed to establish lasting work.

As the Christian sector of the population has grown ever larger, Adventist evangelization has been progressively more focused on people who are already Christians. The 13% Muslim population is concentrated among the Yao tribe along the shores of Lake Malawi. These indigenous Muslims have been comparatively receptive to evangelization compared to Muslims in the Middle East because they are essentially animists. Adventists have lacked an effective strategy for Indian and Lebanese Muslims and Indian Hindus, who comprise a significant part of the business community.

The early Adventist leaders did not practice formal comity, where the territory is divided between denominational groups. Yet, clusters of converts to each denominational group often developed in the villages near their large mission stations. Today, the Adventist membership concentration is roughly proportional to the population of the nation's three regions.

In the very earliest years, the missionaries were responsible for doing all of the evangelism and church planting by themselves, but that soon changed. A basic literacy school was started at Malamulo, with Thomas Branch's daughter, Mabel, as the first Adventist school teacher in Malawi. In 1905, a group of seven boys from the school were baptized. One of the early converts was Morrison Malinki, who was Branch's translator. Malinki became a teacher and then a pastor and his sons, James and Joseph, followed in his footsteps. James Malinki went on to become a cross-cultural missionary planting churches in surrounding nations.

Christopher Robinson introduced several features during his 1912-1920 stay at Malamulo. He organized teacher training institutes, started Young People's Societies, began classes for girls and women, and started annual camp meetings. The annual camp meetings continue to be a significant element of mission strategy, both for discipling members and evangelizing non-members. Camp meetings in rural areas draw nearby churches to central locations where they construct temporary elephant grass meeting enclosures and huts. In the cities, large public facilities are rented or people gather outdoors on church properties.

The early camp meetings were linked with local churches in an on-going discipleship strategy. When people responded to evangelistic calls at camp meeting, they were linked with pastors and lay leaders of churches near their homes. Back home they were enrolled in a one-year Bible Class that met each week during Sabbath School. At the next year's camp meeting they graduated to Baptismal Class and went home to study each week for another year. At the next camp meeting they were baptized. The typical journey to full membership thus took at least two years.

Observation and anecdote suggest that this long-practiced discipleship strategy was more effective than the short evangelistic series of recent times. Urban evangelism with celebrity preachers in large public stadiums has been less effective as a discipleship strategy. In these large public efforts, the linkage of the new member with the local church is not as effective as in the camp meeting model and local church evangelism model. The local church with its pastor and leaders seems best suited to be the focus of evangelism and discipleship.

A medical clinic was opened in 1915 by nurse Irene Fourie. Carl Birkenstock became the first physician to work at Malamulo in 1925. Specialized work for leprosy patients started in 1926. As time passed, medical clinics were established at the large mission stations and in some isolated areas. Major medical and dental offices and hospitals have been opened in Blantyre, Limbe, and Lilongwe. From its humble beginnings, Adventist medical ministry has become a significant provider of Malawi's national healthcare services. Those services include some medical specialties, dental care, training of nurses, and laboratory technicians.

Adventist Health International, based at Loma Linda University, now has a highly valued partnership with Malamulo Hospital for providing physician surgical residencies.

A printing press went into operation at Malamulo in 1926 and became Malamulo Publishing House in 1965. Literature sales and distribution has been an enduring part of mission strategy in Malawi. Bible translation and publication has been done by Bible societies, removing the need for Adventists to perform these tasks. A Voice of Prophecy correspondence school has functioned since the 1950s. Radio and TV ministries have been started in recent years.

Teacher training began in 1925 and pastoral training in 1947 at Malamulo. In the early days a pathway was established from teaching to the Gospel ministry that persisted for about 50 years. Teachers who demonstrated aptitude for ministry became pastors and were eventually ordained. The first ordination of five pastors occurred in 1929. Today, the Adventist University of Malawi offers various healthcare courses at its Malamulo campus and several BA level programs, including theology, at its Lakeview campus.

Malawian teachers and pastors carried heavy responsibilities from the earliest years. James Malinki opened Lunjika Mission and James Ngaiyaye worked with Rex Pearson in opening Luwazi Mission. Malawians went as pioneering cross-cultural missionaries to many surrounding African countries. B. B. Nkosi became the first Malawian Field president in 1966 and F. A. Botomani became the first Malawian Union president in 1980.

Although their number has decreased, Malawi has the use of some General Conference ISE budgets for expatriate missionaries. Those who come usually serve in healthcare or with ADRA. A number of Malawians have served the church in other countries as cross-cultural missionaries. Many others are bringing their Malawian cultural style of being Adventist into congregations around the world where they have emigrated.

The story of Adventist mission in Malawi is one of steadily growing missional capacity. The Malawi Union has a wealth of spiritually gifted and committed members who are well able to evangelize their own country and serve outside their country. The nation's need for improved economic growth constitutes a factor that limits the church's missional capacity. The world church can probably best participate with Adventists in the Malawi Union by doing things that enhance its educational institutions so that more of its members will be well educated for service.

Chapter

Cultural Anthropology and Mission

～•ᖚ

Introduction

Cultural anthropology provides conceptual tools and research methods that are very helpful in missions. This is not to say that Christians should adopt all of the presuppositions behind anthropology, or any other social science. In the interest of maintaining the primacy of scriptural principles, anthropology must be used critically and selectively.

This chapter discusses some selected concepts and methods that are useful in cross-cultural missions. For detailed discussions of cultural anthropology from a Christian perspective, see the works of Paul Hiebert (1983; 1985; 1994), Charles Kraft (1996), Brian Howell and Jenell Paris (2011), and others.

Anthropology has five subfields. Physical or biological anthropology studies human origins and is controversial for creationists because of its evolutionary approach. Archeology studies ancient cultures and is useful for understanding the roots of contemporary cultures and the multiple cultures of biblical times. Linguistics studies the use of language in a way that broadens the understanding of cultures and is very helpful for Bible translation. Cultural anthology focuses on all of the dimensions of cultural groups. Finally, applied anthropology specializes in doing field research in the service of specific endeavors, such as Christian missions. In this book, "anthropology" refers to cultural anthropology, rather than to the broad discipline of anthropology with its different branches.

Howell and Paris define cultural anthropology as "the description, interpretation, and analysis of similarities and differences in human cultures" (2011:5). Their succinct definition highlights the value of cultural anthropology for missions. Cultures are so similar and so different, all at the same time, that having a deep understanding of particular cultures greatly assists the tasks of mission.

Anthropology and sociology are closely related social sciences with different perspectives and approaches. Sociologists have historically studied Western societies, favoring quantitative research methods. In other words, they collect data through surveys and analyze them using computer programs to produce numerical results. Anthropologists have historically studied non-Western peoples favoring qualitative methods. In other words, they use interviews, participant observation, and other methods to collect data that are reported in narrative format.

Anthropology is particularly valuable for Christian missions because of its focus on the Other. The other person, gender, culture, social group, ethnic group, language group, economic group, or religious group are all the Others who are our "neighbors," who are to be loved like "Us," and who need the Gospel (Matt 22:39; Luke 10:29). Anthropology can help Christians to focus on and understand the Other better so as to love them as Christ loves them.

> Anthropologists are more likely to study cross-culturally than sociologists.... Christians can rely on anthropology more to understand the relationship between Gospel and culture, at home and abroad.... [Anthropology is] the systematic study of the Other [or Them], whereas all of the other social disciplines are, in one sense or another, studies of the Self [or Us]. (Howell and Paris 2011:14-15)

Contributions of Cultural Anthropology for Mission

A Comprehensive Approach

Paul Hiebert identifies three major contributions of anthropology. The first is that it offers a wholistic, or "comprehensive approach to the study of human beings" (1983:20) in an era that tends to slice and dice humanity into its component parts. Anthropologists study humans of both genders, of all age groups, in every geographic location, of every ethnicity, of every economic and social status, and of every religion. Anthropology is interested in both the great differences between peoples and the universal commonalities shared by humanity. What do all people everywhere think, feel, or do as they live their lives? How does the thinking, feeling, and doing differ between groups? Understanding both the diversity and commonality of peoples is extremely helpful in missions as it conforms to the biblical portrayal of humanity. The Bible names Adam and Eve as the parents of all humanity but also records its wide diversity.

The Culture Concept

The second contribution anthropology makes to missions is the culture concept itself. The biological features of human beings are highly visible but they may be less significant than their cultures. For example, people of Asian, African, or European ancestry who are multi-generation residents of Canada may have more in common with each other than with their respective ancestral peoples. Until the culture concept was developed, skin color and bone structure were thought to be reliable indicators of essential human attributes.

Hiebert defines culture as "the more or less integrated systems of ideas, feelings, and values and their associated patterns of behavior and products shared by a group of people who organize and regulate what they think, feel, and do" (1985:30).

Charles Kraft says that culture consists of

all the things that we learn after we are born into the world that enable us to function effectively as biological beings in the environment. We are each carefully indoctrinated from before birth in the patterns of behavior that adults around us feel to be appropriate. By the time we become aware of what's going on, we have already been pressed into the cultural mold. (1996:6)

Howell and Paris define culture as "the total way of life of a group of people that is learned, adaptive, shared, and integrated" (2011:36).

Metaphors for Culture

Howell and Paris discuss several metaphors that help to understand culture (38-42). Every metaphor fits culture well in some ways but not so well in other ways. Much can be learned about culture by thinking about the metaphors.

Culture as Water or a River

The water metaphor implies that, just as every fish lives in water, every human lives in culture, cannot live without culture, but may be unaware of being a creature of culture. After all, the fish does not know it lives in water. Unless their perspective is broadened, people think their way of life is the only normal, natural, proper way to live. The river metaphor implies that everyone is moving with the cultural current, where some drift near the center and others near the edges, while others swim against the current. The metaphors do not fit culture completely because fish cannot change the water but people can and do change their cultures as they interact with them.

Culture as a Lens

The lens or spectacles metaphor makes it clear that everyone has a particular view of reality that is shaped by their culture. The world looks strange when viewed through another person's spectacles. The metaphor suggests the need for one to consider and value how others perceive reality and not to think that one's own view is necessarily the best. The metaphor is inaccurate in the sense that implies that cultural filters are fixed and unchanging, like spectacle lenses.

Culture as the Rules of a Game or as a Map

The game rules and map metaphors show that culture provides directions and guidelines for life. These metaphors are weak because they suggest that culture is fixed and unchanging rather than dynamic and changing.

Culture as an Onion

The onion metaphor illustrates that culture has many levels, from the shallow to the deep. The shallow levels include behaviors and material products. Going deeper, there are values and beliefs. At the center there is worldview, the deepest assumptions about what is really real and how life works.

Culture as a Conversation

Howell and Paris favor the conversation metaphor. "Understood in this way, culture is not so much a *thing* that people *have* as it is an *activity* they *do*. Culture is a practice" (2011:41). Like a conversation, culture is practiced dynamically by individuals interacting with others, giving and receiving inputs, and adjusting to an unfolding relationship. Individuals shape conversations and outcomes. Just as a conversation is never repeated in exactly the same way even with one's spouse, so individuals do not live within their societies in exactly the same way, all the time.

Characteristics of Culture

A Society Is a Culture in Action

If culture is like the script of a concert or play, a society is the concert or drama where the script is performed. A society is the members of a group living and acting according to how their culture directs them. The group creates the culture and the society is the group (Hiebert 1983:33).

Culture Is a Total Way of Life

The culture concept views culture as embracing every aspect and dimension of life, from cradle to grave. Every human is part of at least one culture and no one is "more cultured" than another. In the anthropological view, an illiterate person who wears no clothing has just as much culture as a highly educated person who plays the violin in a symphony. An outsider may view the illiterate person as having a simple culture when, in fact, it is very complex in its own way.

Culture Is Created and Shared by Members of a Group

Culture, by definition, is something that belongs to a group of people, not to an individual. Individuals within groups have their own preferences and differences from each other, but broadly speaking they conform to the group. Even people who see themselves as cultural non-conformists are easily recognizable to cultural outsiders as members of their respective cultures.

Culture Has a Cognitive, Intellectual Dimension

Every culture has a cognitive dimension, or body of knowledge that is used in life. Traditional peoples who are illiterate store and transmit their information orally. Village elders or shamans are frequently repositories of very detailed, memorized knowledge. Medicine men use detailed knowledge about diseases and cures. Traditional sailors in the Pacific navigate great distances between small islands without modern instruments. Modernity has greatly increased the available knowledge, first through printing and then digital storage. The Internet gives immediate access to an almost infinite body of knowledge. Knowledge includes basic belief and assumptions about what really exists or is really real. Ancestral spirits are "really real" in some cultures but "mere superstitions" in others. Even in an age of printing and the Internet there are many illiterate or semi-literate people living with oral traditions.

Culture Has an Affective, Emotional Dimension

Every human being experiences the same basic emotions, such as love, hatred, joy, sadness, surprise, pain, anger, peace, and fear. However, culture shapes and regulates how the basic human emotions are felt and expressed. There are "cool" cultures who prefer emotions to be expressed with reserve and understatement. "Warm" cultures enjoy strong expressions of emotions and often use hyperbole, or overstatement. In some cultures the bereaved weep quietly at the funeral, while in others they weep loudly. The free expression of anger, though probably not enjoyed by any society, is tolerated in some societies but strongly disapproved in others. Some societies approve kissing and hugging by spouses in public while others do not. In some societies people can allow inner feelings to be shown on their faces, while in others the face must be calm at all times. Communication between people of "cool" and "warm" societies is challenging. The vocabulary used to describe a particular emotion may be so culturally specific that making a precise translation to another language is very difficult. For example, different concepts of marriage produce specific words that give the emotions of marriage culturally specific nuances.

Culture Has an Evaluative, Moral, Ethical Dimension

Every culture evaluates what is true or false, right or wrong, beautiful or ugly. "Each culture has its own moral code and its own culturally defined sins" (Hiebert 1985:33). The highest values, primary allegiances, and main goals of life are defined.

Individuals in every culture have values that express their "preferences and include such things as cleanliness, security, health, and job satisfaction" (C. Doss 2009:81). Cultures also have collective values that express the preferences of the group. As with other cultural elements, there is much variety between cultures. Some cultures highly value community and others individualism, some independence and others interdependence, some relationships and others material possessions. Values are collected into value sets. Thus, Filipinos, Russians, and Congolese may share some of the same values but each society has a unique combination of values that gives it particular cultural characteristics. In a globalized world there is some overlapping between cultural value sets.

The Bible teaches eternal values that offer the best possible life for all cultures. Universal biblical values include love, mercy, justice, purity, truthfulness, fidelity, honesty, modesty, and others. Biblical values are expressed in human lives in different cultural styles.

Every culture has some values that are affirmed by Scripture, while others are not. For example, some societies highly value theft and deceit and teach their children to become skillful thieves. Some societies support biblical values but express them wrongly. For example, almost every society agrees with the Bible that a husband should love his wife. However, when a society approves wife-beating as an expression of love it strays from the biblical ideal.

Culture Is Manifested by Behaviors

Culture defines appropriate behaviors for almost every aspect of human life. There are patterned behaviors for every stage of life, from childhood, to adolescence, to marriage, to child raising, to old age. Every kind of human relationship has prescribed behaviors. Behaviors are defined for greetings, addressing older or younger people, relationships between men and women, or how to express emotions. In formal settings, like weddings or funerals, correct behavior is more carefully defined. In less formal settings, like daily life around home, there is a greater range of permissible behavior. Specific meanings are attached to behaviors. For example, certain hand gestures are rude in some societies but not in others.

Culture Is Manifested by Material Products

The range of objects used at home, work, or play is almost infinite. Traditional societies have relatively few products, while modern industrial societies have a greater number of material products. Architecture and art are cultural products that express the values of a society.

Culture Organizes and Regulates a People Group

Culture tells every individual at every stage of life and in every position in society what and how to think, how to express feelings, and how to behave. Individuals are frequently unaware of the degree of control their culture has on them. Culture assigns particular status (value and authority) to people occupying particular roles (positions and functions). Culture defines penalties for non-compliance. For example, young boys and old men must function in particular ways in the give and take of daily life. Different groupings, such as classes, castes, tribes, clubs, or parliaments, are used to organize society. Culture distributes social power and sets boundaries for its use.

Culture Is both Learned and Created

Even before birth, babies hear speech and music and sense emotions that start the process of cultural formation. At birth, children begin to absorb culture like a sponge from everyone in their environment. The teaching is both planned and unplanned, formal and informal. When children become adults, they continue to learn the new elements of their cultures and sub-cultures through education or on their jobs. If people move to live in a new culture they learn and absorb new patterns. While people learn and absorb their culture passively like a sponge, they also make active individual contributions that steer the group in different directions. The culture of the present is the aggregate of traditions of the past and innovative contributions of the very moment. People who interact with multiple cultures can learn and practice them all in varying degrees. Cross-cultural missionaries intentionally try to learn new cultures so that they can fit into life among the people they serve as much as is biblically faithful.

Culture Is Patterned

The behaviors, ideas, and products of a culture are grouped together into patterns called cultural traits or customs. For example, there is a cluster in every society associated with eating. Cultural insiders in every home of a given society have similar food and food implements, think about food in similar ways, and behave in similar ways when they eat. Individuals can and do depart from cultural patterns but if they depart too much from the pattern they will be viewed as unacceptable.

Culture Is Integrated

"Culture is an 'integrated system,' not a random assortment of quaint customs. Ideas, behavioral patterns, and material products are related to one another as cultural traits, and these are linked to each other in broader patterns called 'cultural configurations'" (Hiebert 1983:30).

To illustrate, picture a woman whose culture places a high value on cleanliness and order. Her value reaches into every aspect of her life. Her relationship with her husband, the way she lives every part of her life, her work and church relationships, and her perceptions of other cultures are all shaped by the value of order and cleanliness. The value of order and cleanliness is linked with other values, like honesty and efficiency, to constitute a cultural configuration or pattern that generally characterizes her society. However, society is only a "more or less" (1983:44) integrated configuration that reflects the values of the culture. There are some people and institutions in her society that are not orderly, clean, honest, or efficient. The woman may live in a neighborhood with some houses and yards that are not as well kept as her own, giving her displeasure.

Cultural integration means that changing one part of culture potentially changes many other parts. The changes are often unpredicted and unintended. The introduction of computers and mobile phones has changed global societies in innumerable and different ways. When the mobile phone arrived it was linked with existing cultural patterns in each society in a way that changed every society in different ways. People in Botswana, Pakistan, Belgium, and Peru all use iPhones but they use them in different ways. Americans generally love the mobile phone but hate the picture of a Thanksgiving dinner table surrounded by family members who are all using their smartphones instead of enjoying family fellowship.

When non-Christians accept Jesus they adopt new values and lifestyle behaviors that are integrated into their existing cultures. Becoming good, Christlike persons who live by biblical principles is good for themselves and their communities. However, the integration of Christian patterns with their cultural patterns sometimes has unanticipated complexities. For example, converts in one group faced unintended consequences when they stopped drinking alcohol. The thick beer they drink provides energy for their work and income for the women who brew it. Beer also symbolizes hospitality and community. When Christians withdrew from all alcohol-related activities they became isolated from their communities and were viewed as anti-social (Howell and Paris 2011:31). Thus, alcohol, nutrition, family income, and social relationships were integrated within a traditional society, but that integration was upset by the coming of Christianity. The newly converted Christians had to develop a new sub-culture and a new pattern of relating to their larger culture.

Culture Is Dynamic and Adaptive

Every culture, on every continent, in every age has faced constant change. The idea of stable, unchanging cultures in the past is a myth. Whether voluntarily or by coercion, societies have always adapted to changing natural, political, military, economic, and technological realties. Migration moves people into very different contexts where they must make dramatic cultural changes. Cultural patterns are not fixed by historical ancestral roots. For example, my own ancestral roots are European and some of my ancestors migrated to America before the American Revolution. Other Europeans migrated to the other continents. Today, people around the globe with European ancestry exhibit a wide variety of cultural patterns that differ both from each other and from contemporary European cultures.

Cultures Are on Different Trajectories

One of the erroneous assumptions of the colonial era was that all cultures move on the same trajectory, toward the same destinations. The Western societies were seen as being further up the same ladder that all other societies were climbing. The task of the West was to help those further down on the ladder to climb up more quickly. A general feeling of cultural superiority resulted from this perspective and cultures were thought of as being "higher" or "lower."

By the early 1900s cultural anthropologists had done enough field research to reject the concept of a single trajectory. They realized that cultural diversity is not "the manifestation of culture at different stages of development, but evidence of fully developed cultures that had taken different paths based on particular historical and environmental contexts" (Howell and Paris 2011:29). Thus, African or Asian societies were not immature versions of Western culture but mature manifestations of cultures moving in different directions. People in colonized lands generally welcomed Western education, technology, medicine, and economic development but integrated these additions into their existing cultural patterns. As globalization has become more pervasive in the post-colonial era, every society has influenced and shaped every other society. Yet, societies retain distinct trajectories.

Cultures Are "Small Core" or "Large Core"

The difference between small and large core cultures is the number of cultural elements required for one to be considered a true cultural insider. In small core cultures, the number of required elements is small. Cultural insiders will accept a person with quite a few foreign characteristics if they demonstrate a small core of essential cultural traits. Western cultures tend to be small core cultures. In large core cultures, the number of cultural traits required for one to be considered an insider is large.

Any newcomer, including a cross-cultural missionary, has a comparatively harder time being accepted into a large core than a small core culture. Many least-evangelized societies have large core cultures. Becoming a Christian in a large core culture marginalizes a person much more dramatically than in a small core culture.

Cultures Are "High Context" or "Low Context"

The high context and low context model describes in broad terms how societies relate and communicate. High context societies have close, long-term relationships and are culturally homogenous. Low context societies are more culturally diverse and relate to more kinds of people in short-term encounters. These differences shape their communication styles.

High context people know each other well and can communicate effectively with few words and details. A single word, a period of silence, or a body motion are understood accurately within the group. Much of effective communication is done implicitly, or beneath the surface. Cultural outsiders have difficulty receiving the intended message even if they know the language because they do not understand the context.

Low context people use many words and explanations to communicate effectively because of their more diverse cultural context. Their communication is very verbal and explicit.

People going from high to low context societies are likely to receive detailed explanations to help them adjust because explicit communication is the norm among their hosts. Those going from low to high context societies need to request more detailed explanations because their high context hosts do not normally communicate explicitly and in detail.

Although there are regional variations, the low context societies are concentrated in Europe and North America and high context societies are concentrated in Asia, Africa, and Latin America. High and low context styles function within a spectrum in any single society. In every society, family members or close friends use a higher context style because they know each other so well. With one word or look, spouses can convey volumes of meaning.

Cross-Cultural Comparison

"The third major contribution of the field of anthropology to the understanding of humankind is its use of the method of 'cross-cultural comparison'" (Hiebert 1983:33). Cultures are best understood in comparison with each other. Figure 9.1 illustrates how anthropologists would study death in different cultures. The characteristics of each culture are studied along both a horizontal and vertical axis. Each culture is studied by itself along the horizontal axis (A1 to A5). Then the elements are compared between cultures (1A to 1C).

Figure 9.1
Cross-Cultural Comparison of Death-Related Perspectives

	1: Cognitive	2: Affective	3: Evaluative	4: Behaviors	5: Products
A: Culture	Beliefs about death	Expressions of grief	Values about death	Funeral rites	Caskets and graves
B: Culture	Beliefs about death	Expressions of grief	Values about death	Funeral rites	Caskets and graves
C: Culture	Beliefs about death	Expressions of grief	Values about death	Funeral rites	Caskets and graves

Comparing cultures in a thoughtful, structured way is very helpful in missions for understanding why particular approaches fail or succeed. New methods can be tried and responses evaluated.

Challenges of Cross-Cultural Comparison

One response to the idea that cultures should be compared is to reject the whole idea of comparison and to let every culture be valued just as it is; however, comparison is both unavoidable and potentially very helpful. To love the Other one has to understand the Other and the best way to understand the other culture is through comparison. That being said, cultural comparison is challenging because (1) the differences between cultures are deep, (2) making accurate comparisons is difficult, and (3) the one making the comparisons tends to use their own culture as the norm. The tendency is to compare the best ideals of my culture with the worst evils of the other culture. For example, the best American values may be compared with Muslim extremist terrorism, or, conversely, the best Muslim values may be compared with the sordid immorality and violence of some American movies. Both comparisons are inaccurate and unjust.

Depth of Cultural Differences

Comparing cultures is difficult because cultural differences are profound because they extend beyond the readily observable to the deep assumptions that shape and govern societies. "People do not simply live in the same world with different labels attached but in *different* worlds" (Hiebert 1983:33). Planet Earth provides a single basic environment within which are variations related to location and weather; however, social-cultural variations are deeper than environmental variations. Societies living next to each other are often profoundly different.

Race, Ethnicity, Culture and Human Identity

Cultural comparison is complicated by the way human cultures define themselves and others. When babies are born, parents give them names that become part of their identity. Groups of people also assign identity markers to themselves and to others. The marker of "race" focuses on inherited, physical characteristics. The marker of "culture" focuses on non-inherited, learned characteristics. The marker of "ethnicity" includes the multiple factors such as ancestry, physical features, culture, language, and nationality (Howell and Paris 2011:77; Eriksen 1996:28-31; Hutchinson and Smith 1996).

In the common usage, "race" and "ethnicity" are often used as synonyms, but this usage is inaccurate. While "race" emphasizes a single identity marker, "ethnicity" includes multiple markers. Historically, too much significance has been given to "race." Members of the "White race" and the "Black race" were assigned certain characteristics on the basis of their skin color. The truth is that people around the world with similar skin color live and act very differently from each other.

Imagine identical triplet boys, born of Anglo-American parents in the United States, who were orphaned at birth. The three boys were adopted as infants by families in Poland, Ghana, and South Korea, where they grew to adulthood. At age 30 they were reunited. How would they perceive each other?

The triplets would have a double surprise. First, they would each be amazed to see two other men who were identical with themselves in basic physical features. But a second surprise would follow quickly. In spite of being identical triplets, they each would be very different from each other because of the profound cultural differences of their adoptive families and homelands. The three men would have the same inherited physical features, but three different sets of learned cultural characteristics, meaning they had three different ethnicities. Their biological relatives in America would experience them all as cultural "foreigners." This example illustrates that culture, the learned characteristics of humanity, is stronger than physical features.

Racism and Ethnocentrism

Humans tend to compare themselves with others unfavorably. When people do not understand aspects of the Other, a vacuum is created in their minds and the vacuum is typically filled with negative attributions.

Racism is a negative comparison based on the Other's race, or physical features and ancestry. A classic example of racism is the attribution of negative characteristics to people with dark skin and positive characteristics to people with light skin.

Ethnocentrism is a negative comparison based on the Other's ethnicity, which includes the multiple factors of ancestry, physical features, culture, language, and nationality. Thus, the concept of ethnocentrism includes racism but goes further in identifying the sins of humanity against the Other.

> *Ethnocentrism* is the use of one's own culture to measure another's, putting one's own culture (*ethno*) at the center (*centrism*) of interpretation and typically devaluing the other culture. Ethnocentrism is inevitable because humans are socialized to see their way of life as normal, natural, and often superior. Nevertheless, it is important to identify ethnocentrism in ourselves and in the world and work toward reducing it. (Howell and Paris 2011:33)

Howell and Paris identify three types of ethnocentrism (2011:33-36):

1. "*Xenophobia* is an intense, irrational dislike of people from other countries or cultures" (33). The Ku Klux Klan asserts that black people are inferior and Nazi Germany tried to eliminate Jewish people. The hatred of other religions, races, ethnicities, or people groups takes many forms around the world.

2. "*Cultural superiority* is the belief that one culture is more enlightened, advanced, civilized, or intelligent than another....Cultural superiority can be found all over the world; no society has a monopoly on cultural arrogance" (35). When missionaries work among people who are illiterate, poorly educated, or living in poverty, they must actively resist a feeling of superiority.

3. "*Tacit ethnocentrism* is the assumption that one's own way of life is just normal, not cultural" (35). Ethnocentric people think their way of life is the "normal, natural, proper" way to live. By inference, other cultures are "abnormal, unnatural, or improper." Only other cultures have speech "accents," eat "ethnic" food, and listen to "ethnic" music. A non-ethnocentric view recognizes that everyone has a speech accent, eats ethnic food, and listens to ethnic music because everyone has ethnicity and lives within a particular cultural context. Thus, my own Anglo-American English speech is accented. When my family eats Thanksgiving dinner with mashed potatoes, veggie-chicken and dressing, and pumpkin pie we are eating ethnic food and enjoying an ethnic celebration because we are an ethnic family. Non-ethnic families do not exist.

Unless it is challenged, ethnocentrism can be present among both rich and poor, powerful and weak people. People who are, themselves, objects of prejudice and ethnocentrism can be ethnocentric. Sadly, Christians can be ethnocentric. Healthy feelings of patriotism and appreciation for one's own nation and culture are acceptable for Christians, just like healthy self-respect; however, the appreciation for oneself and for one's culture can be exaggerated. Ethnocentrism is an exaggerated love for one's ethnic group just as egotism is an exaggerated love for oneself. Christians dare not exempt themselves from either egotism or ethnocentrism. Part of every Christian's spiritual journey of sanctification is away from both egotism and ethnocentrism. The first step is for the Christian to confess, "Lord, I can see that I am ethnocentric. Transform me and give me a Christlike love for all people of all cultures, even when their cultures are not pleasing to me."

Identifying and confronting ethnocentrism within oneself is absolutely essential for participation in Christ's mission to the world. In the course of cross-cultural service, one inevitably encounters people whose culture is unpleasing from the missionary's cultural perspective. Through training and experience, one learns how to relate to those differences in a loving way.

Cultural Stereotypes

A cultural stereotype is a generalization about a group of people that, by nature, tends to be preconceived and oversimplified. Stereotypes can reduce humans to mere caricatures of themselves. At their worst, cultural stereotypes are racist and ethnocentric. Yet, humans naturally make categories and generalizations as a way of organizing their understanding of reality. Generalizations are usually based on some aspects of reality. Yet, generalizations have to be used with caution. As the saying goes, "All generalizations are false, including this one."

Cultural comparison produces generalizations that can be wrong, partly right, or mostly right.

Generalizations have value in providing "quick orientation points to facilitate understanding" (C. Doss 2009:80). Name almost any cultural group and a list of characteristics will pop into your mind. Those characteristics become the starting point from which to interact with that group. Developing good cross-cultural relationships requires constant updating so that wrong impressions are corrected and accurate knowledge is added.

Figure 9.2 arranges some common stereotypes about "Westerners" and "Non-Westerners." Dividing the world into "Western" and "Non-Western" cultures is an illustration of both the usefulness and perils of stereotyping. Putting all of humanity into just two parts is a reductionist oversimplification. Making one group the "Non-West" implies that the "West" is the normative, defining group. Even defining "West" and "Non-West" is difficult. Yet, there is a part of humanity that belongs more to the European-American culture of modernity than the other part of humanity. Many societies function in between the two major cultural sectors.

Figure 9.2 Common Cultural Stereotypes			
Westerners Toward Non-Westerners		Non-Westerners Toward Westerners	
More Negative	More Positive	More Negative	More Positive
Innocent, ignorant	Family oriented	Aggressive	Well educated
Lazy and corrupt	Have group harmony	Harshly pragmatic	Reliable
Inefficient	Very spiritual	Tense, discontented	Strong as individuals
Overly emotional	Content	Lonely	Live good lives
Slow	Have servant attitude	Corrupt and greedy	Free of superstition
Indifferent		Materialistic	Confident
Poor and uneducated		Loud and dominating	Organized
Helpless		Competitive	
Superstitious		Selfish and self-centered	
Weak as individuals		Have superiority attitude	

Source: Adapted from Cheryl Doss 2009:80.

Everyone will identify generalizations about themselves and their own cultures in Figure 9.2 that are completely wrong, partly correct, or mostly correct and they will resent generalizations that are not correct. At their best, cultural stereotypes provide an initial quick focus upon which to start building long-term, positive relationships with accurate mutual understanding.

Cultural Relativism

"Cultural relativism is the view that cultural practices and beliefs are best understood in relation to their entire context" (Howell and Paris 2011:31). Elements of a particular culture may seem illogical or even offensive to those of another culture, but they must be viewed from within their own historical, economic, political, and religious context to be understood. This is not to imply that every element of a culture is proper, right, good, or true for Christians simply because it is "cultural." Giving approval to everything because it is "cultural" would be to adopt moral, ethical, or epistemological relativism. There are absolute biblical principles that apply to every culture. Cultural relativism merely affirms that the many cultures of the world develop an infinite variety of ways to live within their very different contexts.

Some culturally approved elements are transparently wrong—like racism, immorality, or spouse beating. But many cultural elements that are displeasing to outsiders have their own internal history and logic and are not necessarily against Scripture. For example, adult men and women sit on opposite sides of the church in some societies to show solidarity with those who are not yet married, or widowed, or divorced. In other societies, the norm is for parents and children to sit together.

The missionary's task is to withhold judgment to discern that internal history and logic. Through the process of faithful contextualization, the beliefs and practices of a particular culture are brought before the Word of God to be affirmed or modified or abandoned.

Forms, Meanings, and Symbols

Communication does not happen directly from one mind to another. Rather, humans communicate using forms to which they attach meanings. Forms can include vocal sounds, hand gestures, facial expressions, written marks, and many other things. In the English language, the letter "A" is the first of twenty-six letters that make up a set of symbols called an alphabet. Letters are combined into words and particular meanings are assigned to them. In academics, the meaning of "high grade" is attached to the letter "A" to make it a symbol.

The words you are reading now are vehicles that convey particular meanings because English speaking cultures have constructed a system of communication.

> Human behavior and products are not independent parts of a culture; they are closely linked to the ideas, feelings, and values that lie within its people. The association of a specific meaning, emotion, or value with a certain behavior or cultural product is called a symbol.... In North America, for example, sticking out a tongue at someone signifies ridicule and rejection; in Tibet it is a symbol of greeting and friendship.... In one sense a culture is made up of many sets of symbols. For instance, speech, writing, traffic signs, money, postage stamps, [or uniforms worn by] waiters and airline pilots [or police and military officers]. (Hiebert 1985:37)

Stated as a formula, Form + Meaning = Symbol. For example, a culture values the law and wants to give policemen authority to enforce the law (the meaning). Most societies attach the meaning of law to a police uniform, hat, and badge (the forms). A policeman then becomes the symbol of the law as he walks down the street in his uniform, hat, and badge. Trouble makers will say, "Watch out! Here comes the law." The law is also symbolized by a stone carving of the Mosaic Law and the statue of a lady holding up a set of scales. Societies could choose any other forms they wish to symbolize the law and justice.

Figure 9.3
Form and Meaning

Forms	Meanings
Letters: "A" and "Ω" (Alpha and Omega)	First and last, start and finish, best and worst, Greek language
Words: YHWH, *Theos, Allah, Deus, Gott, God, Dieu, Maykapal, Mulungu, Andriamanitra*	Supreme Divine Being, Trinitarian God, mono-person god, Creator, supreme spirit, divinity
Numbers: 1, one, *een, evas, un, um, uno, okan, umodzi, ib tug, jeden, yi*	Best, least, first, alone, starting, humility, pride
Colors: Red	Stop, love, communism, deficit, danger, wedding, immorality, anger, blood of Christ
Soft Handshake	Gentleness, politeness, weak character, dishonesty
Upraised Thumb	Positive approval, victory, agreement, rudeness, insult, obscenity, immoral invitation

The examples of form and meaning in figure 9.3 illustrate several points about symbols.

Forms Are Necessary

Forms of some kind, be they written or spoken words, non-verbal sounds, body gestures, or facial expressions, are needed for human communication. There is no direct, mind-to-mind communication of meaning between humans without the use of forms. Even God uses the forms of human language and visual imagery familiar to the prophets when he inspires them.

Symbols Are Communal

The meaning attached to forms to make them symbols has to be shared by the communicators for good communication to happen. Symbols are useful only within a community that assigns shared meanings. Small children often make nonsense words and gestures that have meaning only to themselves.

Symbols Are Arbitrary

Symbols are typically arbitrary. Had the English language developed differently, we would say "Look *down* at the sky" instead of "Look *up* at the sky." The meanings of "up" and "down" are not inherently attached to the two words.

Symbols Have Multiple Meanings

Symbols can have multiple meanings, even within the same culture. The same color can symbolize many different things. Symbols often convey different and contradictory meanings in different cultures. In America a white dress traditionally symbolizes a pure bride, while in India it traditionally symbolizes a grieving widow.

The Meaning of Symbols Changes

Symbols can convey either the same or different meanings in different time periods. The Cross has had a stable meaning for Christians for two millennia. On the other hand, the English names for the days of the week and the months of the year were named after pagan gods but the pagan meanings have fallen away. The names of days and months have become cultural artifacts that lack the original meanings associated with the words.

Meanings do not adhere magically and forever to forms. Using the word "Wednesday" (originally, "Woden's-day") does not mean that one worships the pagan god Woden (or Odin). Neither is anyone (that I know of) attracted to paganism by using the word "Wednesday." The main focus of attention should be on contemporary meanings conveyed by particular symbols.

Forms that once carried unbiblical meanings can be given new biblical meanings. The Hebrew and Greek alphabets and words of the Bible were originally pagan symbol sets that the Bible writers used as vehicles of divine truth. The great "I AM" (Exod 3:14) inspired the prophets to use originally pagan words like *El*, *Elohim*, and *Elshadai* to identify the Creator-Redeemer. The prophets gave God-inspired meanings to the words that had once conveyed pagan meanings. Martin Luther used the German *Gott* and English speakers use "God," both of which came from Germanic words for pagan gods.

The same process happens with contemporary Bible translation. Indigenous languages are used and biblical meanings are inserted into new symbol sets. Bible translation is a complex task because the deep cultural meaning of words has to be understood to convey biblical meanings. Choosing the best names for God is difficult when the available words convey unbiblical meanings. Translators sometimes face the difficult choice of using a flawed local word for God's name that retains too much unbiblical meaning or using a foreign word (perhaps Hebrew or Greek) that makes Christianity seem like a foreigner's religion.

Some forms cannot be given new meanings because the linkage of form and meaning is too strong. For example, in places where pigs are abundant but sheep are unknown, substituting the phrase "lamb of God" with "pig of God" in a Bible translation would be completely unacceptable. The biblical meanings of "pig" as an unclean animal and "lamb" as the atoning sacrifice are too powerful to be exchanged in a Bible translation.

Form and Meaning Can Be Separated

In some cultures and religions, form and meaning can be separated. For example, the communion bread and wine are seen by some Christians as representing the body and blood of Christ as a memorial. Christ is not understood to be actually present in the symbols. Some religions that use images say that their images only represent and remind them of their gods or saints. The separation of form and meaning is common among modern Western peoples. They have no problem agreeing that using the form "Wednesday" to name a day of the week does not mean worshipping the pagan god Woden.

In other cultures and religions, form and meaning cannot be separated. For example, Christ is understood by some Christians to be actually present in the bread and wine symbols. Religious images are understood to actually be the saints or gods, not to merely represent them. Using the form "Wednesday" to name a day of the week is seen as actually being a worshipper of the pagan god Woden. The view that form and meaning cannot be separated is most common among traditional peoples with an animistic tradition.

Cultural Views of Time

People all around the world use watches to measure time, but the social function of time differs greatly. Hiebert compares the traditional American and Arab views of time (1983:34).

Americans highly value being "on time" and define it as arriving between five minutes before and five minutes after an appointment. Coming more than five minutes early intrudes upon the hosts, who may not be ready. For an arrival up to fifteen minutes after the appointed hour an apology without a detailed excuse is sufficient. A credible excuse is needed if one is more than fifteen minutes late. There are variations between American sub-cultures.

In the Arab world, servants must arrive at the appointed hour to prepare the venue. If servants arrive more than ten minutes after the stated time they are late and disobedient. Colleagues and peers are "on time" if they arrive an hour after the appointed time and "late" fifteen minutes thereafter.

The potential for cultural misunderstanding is clear. An American who comes to an Arab event at the stated time arrives during "servant time" when the venue is not yet prepared. An Arab who arrives one hour after the stated time at an American event is seen as being rude and insulting. To have positive relationships, business people need to understand the other's view of time, and practice reciprocal give-and-take. When the American is in the Middle East, he should expect to adapt, whether he is in the host or guest role. When the Arab is in the United States, the same applies. They should both communicate ahead of time to make sure they arrive at the "right time." While secular business people have the right to expect reciprocal flexibility, missionaries should be willing to do the flexing as they fit into the local cultural patterns.

Cultural concepts of time shape social relationships, as illustrated in the comparison of Arabs and Americans. Neither the American nor the Arab are right or wrong because they are expressing cultural preferences. However, there are worldview issues linked to time that do involve right and wrong. Hiebert discusses five worldviews of time (2011:50-54).

Figure 9.4 Concepts of Time	
Linear Time	• Has a beginning and end • Has sharp boundaries between time segments • Units are uniform, have equal duration and value • Never repeats itself, each time unit tells a unique story • Is the biblical worldview in prophecy, the Great Controversy metanarrative, human life • Is used in modern science, technology, transport, communication • Western culture is the dominant representative • Linear time is either rigid or elastic
Cyclical Time	• Repeats itself in life cycles, seasons, years • Has no beginning or end • Is renewed in rebirth, new beginnings, reincarnations • Common in Eastern religions
Event Time	• Has a beginning and end, like linear time • Has fuzzy boundaries between time segments • Events have different value • Is measured by sequence of events: Meal time, work time, sleep time, church time, etc. • Some Western sub-cultures and many global cultures prefer event time • Societies of biblical times experienced daily life as event time
Pendular Time	• Oscillates forward and backward between opposites, day-night, summer-winter • Moves slower or faster • Sometimes comes to a dead stop
Dream Time	• Involves leaving present time to enter "eternal now" where unborn, living, and dead persons unite • Involves return to present time • Associated with rituals, séances, and altered states of consciousness

Source: Adapted from Hiebert 2008:51.

Linear Time

Uniform linear time is used by modern science and favored by Western societies. Hourly workers and airline schedules follow linear time. Time moves only in one direction, never repeats itself, is measured in uniform blocks, and has sharp boundaries. Biblical time is linear, moving through the stages of the Great Controversy from perfection to perfection, with the Creation, the Fall, the Cross, and the Second Coming in between. Biblical prophecy moves through linear time. In the Bible, human life is linear, from birth to death, with no second chances to receive salvation.

The main alternative to linear time for Christians is event time. Saying that biblical time is linear does not imply that event time is wrong. The societies of biblical times probably experienced daily life as event time, even though the movement of the Bible narrative is linear. In today's world, people who want the sermon to end "on time" at the published hour have a cultural preference for linear time.

Another way of comparing contemporary views of time among Christians is to say they all have linear time but some have "elastic linear time" and others "rigid linear time." People who want the sermon to end on the published hour are "rigid" and those who are happy to let the sermon balloon out into other events are "elastic."

Cyclical Time

Cyclical time is observable in the natural seasons of the weather, the agricultural seasons, and the rotation of the planets and stars. Eastern religions have a cyclical view of time, with unending reincarnations. According to Eastern religions, humans will always have another chance in another life to earn merit for a redemption. The biblical view of linear time and salvation by grace contradicts the eastern religion view.

Event Time

Event time traces its passage by distinct events. For a dairy farmer there is milking time, breakfast time, work time, lunch time, rest time, work time, dinner time, milking time, and bed time. The number of minutes each event requires is not as significant as that the event happens. Time boundaries between events are fuzzy.

The Bible narrative includes events that combine linear and event time. The days of Creation were linear but Creation was a cosmic event with significance beyond its linear character. The Sabbath is a linear event that occurs on a weekly cycle but with deep significance as an event. The stages of Christ's life and work were cosmic events that made time insignificant, even though his coming was prophesied in linear time. The sermon, or the encounter with God in Bible reading, or prayer, can be special events whose significance exceeds the passage of time. Preachers and worshippers whose culture prefers event time do not care if the sermon goes beyond the published hour, assuming the sermon is good.

Pendular Time

Pendular time oscillates or swings back and forth between polar opposites, like day and night, life and death. At the experiential level, time sometimes feels like it is racing forward uncontrollably, creeping forward intolerably, or repeating itself unbearably. In a moment of crisis, time seems to stand still. The biblical narrative records Israel oscillating between periods of obedience and disobedience. However, the biblical view of time, itself, is not pendular.

Dream Time

Dream time is part of everyone's experience, but some cultures interpret it as having cosmic dimensions. In some societies every dream is seen as a communication from the spirit world. People in many cultures have dreams about their deceased parents or relatives, but some believe that the dreams are authentic encounters and communications with the dead. Many people have near-death experiences that include amazing dreams. Some people believe near-death dreams are authentic encounters with the afterlife followed by a return to this life. Dreams and visions are part of the prophetic calling, part of the end time gifts of the Spirit (Joel 2:28), and dreaming is a natural part of being human. However, biblical principles are to be applied in evaluating dream time.

Multiple Concepts of Time

All societies use multiple concepts of time and understand which is appropriate for which activity. Linear time people who fulfill (or try to fulfill) every appointment at the stated time also practice event time at birthday parties or football games, when they relax and enjoy the event. Event time people whose day has fuzzy time markers also know how to get to the airport before the plane takes off. People who interact effectively with other cultures learn which pattern is appropriate for which events, in which culture.

Having intercultural competence means relating well with different concepts of time. The first necessary step is to separate cultural preference from right and wrong. The linear time person needs to acknowledge that the fuzzy time boundaries of the event time person are neither right nor wrong. The event time person needs to acknowledge that the linear time person who wants events to start and end at announced times is also neither right nor wrong. Unless care is taken, ethnocentrism can come into play with regard to time.

The right or wrong occurs in a multicultural church when believers are able or unable to accommodate each other in love. There are ways members with contrasting time preferences can complement each other if they overcome the ethnocentric insistence on doing things their own way. Probably every church needs some "let's get things started" people and some "just let things flow" people who make a creative tension between themselves. As for the cross-cultural missionary who serves among a people whose dominant time preference is opposite to their own, the task is to accept and live gracefully within local preferences. The pastoral or lay leadership roles in any society probably require one to adopt the "let's get things started" posture within its preferred style of relating to time.

Cultural Views of Space

Cultures define and experience personal space and social space differently. A social zone or zone of interaction surrounds every person and varies in size. In Malawi, two friends meeting on a footpath will often start a conversation when they first see each other, shake hands when they meet, and continue talking until out of earshot. In other societies, the two friends would restrict their conversation to a smaller zone.

The personal zone for North Americans surrounds a person at about 4 to 5 feet. To have a conversation people stand within the personal zone. Because no one wants to smell the other's breath, they may stand at right angles instead of facing each other. The personal zone is smaller in Latin America and southern Europe. People in those societies feel they are only making authentic contact when they stand very close to each other. When people from these contrasting societies interact, they sometimes make each other uncomfortable. As one moves closer the other moves back, then closer, then back again. One feels invaded and the other feels rejected.

Intimate space for most cultures is at about one foot. In some cultures, only very close friends, family members, spouses, or lovers enter the intimate space. Some people hug complete strangers, while for others a hug from a stranger is an invasion of privacy or a potential assault. One pastor who serves three churches with contrasting cultural views of intimate space told me how his greeting patterns must change during the course of a single Sabbath. The first church expects the pastor to hug the women and kiss them on the cheek. The second church wants just an arm around the shoulder and a touch of cheeks. If he does otherwise, both churches will think him unfriendly and distant. The third church expects the pastor only to shake hands with the women. His reputation would be put at risk of he hugged and kissed the women because even married couples do not hug or kiss each other in public.

Social Statuses, Roles, and Relationships

Statuses

In common usage, status refers "to a person's general position in a society" in regard to rank, esteem, wealth, or power. A more technical definition of status is "a position in a social system occupied by designated individuals" (Hiebert 1983:141). For example, teachers, policemen, and doctors occupy specific places in society. Individuals within a society occupy more than one status. For example, a woman may be a daughter, wife, mother, grandmother, professor, Sabbath School teacher, and local church elder.

Ascribed and Achieved Status

Individuals receive status from society in two different ways—by ascription or achievement. Ascribed status is usually received at birth or through kinship. The children of royalty or of caste systems receive their status simply because of who their parents or relatives are. Children of royalty remain royalty even if they live bad lives and those born into low castes stay there no matter how good their lives may be. Those trying to rise higher than their ascribed status are blocked by society in various ways.

Other societies assign status on the basis of achievement. Children born into poverty on the "wrong side of town" are permitted to rise to the highest status through intelligence and hard work. Those born into good circumstances do not receive high status unless they prove themselves through achievement. Achievement societies have "rags to riches" stories that give high respect to achievers.

Many societies blend ascribed and achieved status in different ways. Generally speaking, achieved status is dominant in Western societies. But the United Kingdom and some other Western democracies have monarchies and royal families that function by ascription.

Roles

A role is an expectation or set of expectations placed on a particular status. Society defines how a person is to fulfill their role in an exemplary way. For example, a policeman is allowed to use deadly force to fight crime, but only within a set of strict parameters.

Every social status has a number of roles associated with it. Church school teachers have role relationships with students, parents of students, fellow teachers, parent-teacher associations, principals, pastors, local churches, school alumni, and others. This cluster of role relationships comprises the teacher's role set. As every teacher knows, there is potential role conflict between their multiple role relationships because each role has differing expectations. What parents expect is sometimes different from what school boards and church boards expect.

Cultures define roles differently and construct role sets differently. For example, in some societies teachers receive high respect from parents and are rarely challenged. In other societies, teachers are constantly challenged by parents about issues like student discipline. Some societies do not have parent-teacher associations or alumni associations, but there may be other relationships in the teacher's role set.

Sex and Gender Roles

Anthropologists view sex and gender as different but closely related realities.

Sex refers to the biological natures of males and females. Gender is about "what it means to be male or female in a particular culture" (Howell and Paris 2011:88).

The basic sexual biology of humanity is the same across all cultures. The Bible prescribes one basic standard for sexual relationships that applies to all humans—one woman, with one man, within a faithful marriage, for as long as they both live. There are many complex contemporary issues related to sex, gender, and marriage that are beyond the scope of this book.

At the moment of birth, every society starts shaping the baby to fulfill cultural gender expectations for boys or girls. Clothing identifies the baby's gender. Adults talk to infant girls and boys differently. From childhood until old age, cultures define a set of expectations for how females and males will function.

> Gender is socially constructed; it does not flow automatically from biological sex.... A gender status is a position a person can occupy in a social order that is directly related to maleness and femaleness .... Each gender status is connected to a gender role, a set of expectations regarding proper behavior and appearance for a particular gender. (Howell and Paris 2011:89)

Cultures of the past have defined gender statuses and roles very differently. The Bible narrative portrays God-fearing people of many generations, in many cultural contexts, applying God's principles for gender relationships in many different ways.

Societies renegotiate and redefine gender roles as circumstances change. During World War II, millions of men went abroad, leaving their homelands in short supply of workers. To fill the gap, thousands of women stepped forward to perform jobs previously thought of as belonging exclusively to men. In America, "Rosie the Riveter" and many of her "sisters" built thousands of aircraft and produced untold varieties of war equipment. The women dressed differently when they built war equipment than before the war. When the war ended and the men came home, many women married and became housewives. If they continued working, their jobs were often traditional "women's" jobs where advancement was slow and wages were low. In contemporary society, more women are breaking "glass ceilings" and moving to jobs traditionally held only by men.

Societies differ about whether or not gender roles should be firmly separated. Some societies do not want men and women to step into each other's roles at all. Other societies are willing for men and women to step back and forth between traditional male or female roles. The issue is not over the roles themselves, but over exchanging roles. For example, many societies assign the role of cooking to women and car repair to men. Some societies insist that men must never cook and women must never repair cars. Other societies allow both men and women to cook or repair cars, according to their preferences.

Cross-cultural missionaries often work where gender roles are different from their own cultural patterns. One missionary wife was accustomed to handling banking and travel agent matters for her family. In their place of service, her husband had to take over those functions because women were not allowed into banks or travel agencies. Their change of roles meant renegotiating their marriage relationship by redefining which roles each would perform.

Vertical and Horizontal Roles

All societies have role pairs, like employer-employee, teacher-student, parent-child, and husband-wife. In hierarchical societies, one person in the role pair is socially superior to the other. In egalitarian societies, the two individuals are socially equal to each other. In other words, hierarchical societies favor vertical roles while egalitarian societies favor horizontal roles.

To illustrate, students in hierarchical societies show respect by standing when teachers enter, always calling them "sir" or "madam," and never challenging their opinions. In egalitarian societies, students show respect less overtly, relate to teachers more as social equals, and feel free to challenge their opinions. Teachers and students who move from either kind of society to the other may feel uncomfortable and have to make adjustments.

Patron-Client Relationships

Some societies have a painful history of political patrons who rule over their underlings (clients) as despotic "godfathers." However, there are also more positive patron-client relationships in many societies. In the West the mentor-mentee relationship is one form of patron-client. A pastor or teacher can be a patron who is a lifelong spiritual adviser and professional supporter for a church member, student, or younger colleague. Patrons can be either male or female.

In collectivist societies, the patron-client relationship can embrace many aspects of life and can be very positive. Patrons function like parents who assumes broad responsibility for the well-being of their clients. Clients receive many material benefits and special help in difficult times of illness, death, or emergency. They also receive security, dignity, and prestige from their association with the patron. Clients respond by giving their labor and loyalty to the patron. Just as patrons respond to special material needs, so clients support their patrons in the community in times of conflict. "The relationship is one of mutual interdependence" (Hiebert 1983:152), but without strict contractual agreements. At its best, the system is a sustaining mutual support and safety net.

Establishing good patron-client relationships can be challenging for missionaries coming from societies where they are not common or where they function differently. They are challenging when there is significant disparity between missionary income and local income and where missionaries typically want to alleviate local poverty as much as they can. Understanding patron-client relationships can help to prevent the mistakes that often happen in situations of disparity. Missionaries have to avoid playing the "big bwana" role that can be paternalistic. Locals need to avoid taking the "poor beggar" role that can be manipulative.

One important key is to give full value to the non-material benefits given by the client to the patron. Locals can and do support missionaries by guarding their reputations in the community, giving advice that helps them avoid or correct social blunders, guiding their interaction with local authorities, helping with language learning, and in many other ways. Locals are often fellow Christians who work in loving partnership alongside the missionary. Their services are often critical for missionary success and could not possibly be purchased.

Another key is to dispense material benefits in ways that maintain mutual respect. Goods and services should be exchanged equitably based on local standards because the patron-client relationship can be manipulated and exploited by either party. An example may be helpful.

One missionary started dispensing items like soap, salt, and food at the back door every day to whoever came from the local town. The recipients (clients) gave nothing in exchange and thus lost their self-respect because they were in "poor beggar" mode. With good intentions, the missionary (patron) was in "big bwana" mode and felt exploited. The number of people coming for daily handouts was unmanageable and relationships were damaged.

A different missionary received similar requests at the door but always gave an equitable work assignment in exchange for the item requested. The exchange was made in a way that maintained the dignity of both parties. Those unwilling to work stayed away and the process was manageable for the missionary. One old man, who was too weak to work, came regularly for a small gift of money. His friendship and prayers are still treasured.

Missionaries have client relationships with patrons like local authorities who must grant visas, building permits, or permissions for special events. Missionaries also relate as clients to indigenous church leaders who supervise their work. Sometimes they have dual client and patron relationships with some of the same local leaders. For example, the missionary college president reports to an indigenous board chairman while also raising funds to develop the campus.

People raised in patron-client societies sometimes move to places where that type of relationship is less common. In their new social settings they may feel that their personal, relational safety net has disappeared. An example would be students from developing nations who go to Europe or America for higher education.

Patron-client relationships should not be idealized, as if they embody some kind of utopia. Neither should they be seen as inherently exploitive for the client. They can be very good for both patron and client when guided by Christian principles.

Culture Shock and Fatigue

People who encounter another culture can experience cultural disorientation or culture shock. The familiar cultural markers that map out life are shifted or absent in the new context. People who are highly functional in their home societies feel inadequate and incompetent. Even young children know the language and function better in the local culture than visiting adults.

The experience of culture shock is an individual matter that varies greatly in intensity. Some people experience it strongly on a brief trip of just a few weeks. For those who live in another culture over an extended period, there is a typical cycle they pass through. The first weeks or months are frequently a "honeymoon" period that corresponds to a tourist's experience. During the honeymoon, the local people are idealized and seemingly can do no wrong. The early bliss is replaced by the culture shock period when the local people seemingly can do no right. During the low period, the missionary's cry is "What is wrong with these people? Get me out of here." Gradually, the missionary makes peace with the local culture by recognizing its strong points, accepting its flaws, and remembering that their own culture also has many flaws. Many people find resolution to culture shock after about a year.

Over time, the missionary becomes a well-adjusted "bicultural person" (Hiebert 1983:41), who lives effectively in between their home culture and their service culture. The culture shock cycle is a recognized reality and understanding it helps the missionary to cope when it happens. The painful cycle may reoccur when difficult conflict situations occur.

Sometimes the term "culture fatigue" is more accurate than "culture shock." Even a well-adjusted missionary may expend such great amounts of energy relating well with the local culture that they become culturally fatigued. Taking time away from the local people to recharge their relational batteries is a positive coping strategy.

There are negative coping strategies that missionaries need to avoid. Some international workers form cultural ghettos wherever they go. Except for the bare minimum required to do their work, they associate only with people from their home culture. The cultural ghetto strategy may be understandable for diplomatic, military, or business expatriates who are moved frequently from place to place; however, it is not an acceptable option for Christian missionaries. Enjoying fellowship with people from one's home is normal and healthy; however, following Christ's incarnational model means that a missionary will participate wholeheartedly in fellowship with local people.

Ethnographic Research

Good cross-cultural missionary service requires that the missionary have a research mindset. Actually, a researcher's mindset is also helpful for ministry among one's own cultural people. Effective strategy rests on intentional, continual, deepening research of the other culture. Many aspects of the other culture, like dress, food, housing, music, public festivals, and greeting styles, are immediately visible and easily knowable. As the missionary studies a culture, its deeper elements become known only gradually. The deeper aspects of a culture are the ones most essential for leading people to become mature disciples. Because memory alone cannot be trusted in developing a deep understanding of another culture, systematic notes and records need to be kept for continued analysis. (Many valuable guides or templates for doing cultural research are available at www.mislinks.org/understanding.)

Although most missionaries are not professional anthropologists, they can borrow some of the methods anthropologists use. The basic research method used is "ethnography," which means writing (*graphy*) about people (*ethno*). Howell and Paris say that

> cultural anthropologists engage in ethnography by studying multiple aspects of life in a particular place or among a group of people to create a picture of how those people understand and live in the world. Anthropologists write up their research in accounts called *ethnographies*, rich descriptions and analyses that include the anthropologist's experience of "being there."... Participant observation is the primary method associated with ethnographic research. (2011:10-11)

Participant observation means moving between being an outsider (observer) and an insider (participant). As a foreigner, the cross-cultural missionary will never be a complete insider; however, they can join in with cultural events to the extent that Christian principles permit. The outsider position is also valuable because it permits detached analysis and comparison. Ethnographic methods include general observation, personal interviews, focus groups, and surveys.

A good starting point for research is to make a geographical study. Commercial maps give a head-start in mapping rivers, lakes, forests, road systems, and major landmarks. Handmade maps can locate significant features of small villages or towns.

The Internet is a good source for demographic research. Statistics can be gathered about age, marital status, income levels, educational levels, literacy rates, occupations, population size and growth rates, crime rates, religious affiliation, and ethnicity groupings.

The researcher also studies the people-group's inner life. The inner life includes attitudes, values, interests, emotions, marriage, family, childrearing patterns, attitudes toward material possessions, attitudes toward work and education, and much more.

Because the mission task is primarily a spiritual-religious one, the religiosity of the local people is of great significance. What is the place of religion in daily life? What are the main emotions associated with local religiosity? What are their traditions and rituals? What religions and branches of religions are present? How do local people define a truly good person? What is their attitude toward other religions? How do locals view Christian missions? What other Christian denominations are active and how are they viewed? How are Adventists viewed by Christians and non-Christians? What do the local people know about the Gospel and what is their attitude toward it? What is their history with Christians and missionaries? Many misconceptions exist among non-Christians about what

Christians believe. For example, local Muslims think that Christians believe that God and Mary were the parents of Jesus in a human way. Does being a "Christian" mean being like an immoral Hollywood movie star in the general view? What are the obstacles to be overcome? How should a Christian live and behave in the local setting to be viewed as a truly good, ethical person?

The general history, political history, and economic history of a people provide a broader framework in which to understand them. What is their current state with regard to their political and economic institutions? How do they define good government? Is the economy barter based, cash based, or cashless? Do they use banking systems? How do they define wealth and poverty? What is the general relationship between community members who are wealthy and poor?

Knowing the local language opens a door into the heart of the culture and understanding the local worldview. Every living person hears the Gospel best when it comes in their mother-tongue, even if they know other languages. This makes language study essential for understanding people and building relationships.

The information gleaned by various means needs to be compiled in a people-group profile. A people-group profile is "a profile of the way the people within a specific culture live, act, think, work, and relate. It is a 'map' of the culture's social, religious, economic, and political views and relationships" (Terry and Payne 2013:158).

Cross-Cultural Communication

The guiding principle for cross-cultural communication of the Gospel is that it must be receptor-oriented. In other words, the human sender (preacher, teacher, missionary) of the Gospel message must use methods of communication that will best allow the receiver of the message to understand the message accurately and accept it. Communicator-oriented communication focuses on the message-sender's preferences instead of the message-receiver's needs. That orientation needs to be reversed.

Every Christian communicator has a set of preferred and habituated methods of communicating that are shaped by their age, gender, personal temperament, family, culture, education, and experience. Without conscious adaptation, they will communicate in exactly the same way almost anywhere in the world. To some extent, that is unavoidable and acceptable. We each are who we are, wherever we are. However, understanding the necessity of receptor orientation can make us willing to change habituated methods for the sake of the Gospel.

Adventists have collective denominational communication preferences. We favor public evangelistic preaching and personal Bible studies covering a series of essential doctrinal topics. The sequence of topics and the emphasis given to each is quite standardized. The argumentation is supported by the use of a series of proof texts found in different books of the Bible. These methods are appropriately receptor-oriented for Christians who are already familiar with the Bible, the basic Christian doctrines, and the public preaching and Bible study modes of communication.

The classic Adventist methods are not receptor-oriented for many other people groups, especially the least-evangelized peoples. The wrong question to ask is: How do I feel comfortable communicating the Gospel to Muslims, Hindus, Buddhists, and postmoderns? The right question is: How do I need to communicate the Gospel to give Muslims, Hindus, Buddhists, and postmoderns the best opportunity to understand it accurately and accept it fully?

Receptor orientation maximizes the congruence between the intended and the received messages. The intended message and the actual received message are often quite different, even in a marriage. An example from real life may help. During a family dinner Gorden says to Cheryl, "Please pass the ketchup." Cheryl replies, "You don't like my lentil roast!" Gorden replies, "You misunderstand me. I love your lentil roast but I love it even more with ketchup." Somewhat begrudgingly, Cheryl responds, "Oh, all right." We agree to disagree about whether Cheryl's good lentil roast is even better with ketchup. That conversation gets repeated at our table, generally with good humor.

If communication in a happy marriage is challenging, crossing barriers of language, culture, and religion makes effective communication infinitely more challenging. Just imagine the complexity of discussing food preferences with hosts in a very culturally dissimilar setting.

The Elements of Communication

Communication is a process that has four elements—sending, receiving, responding, and confirming. These elements are repeated many times as people are in dialogue. All steps are needed for complete communication.

Step 1: Sending

The sender chooses, encodes, and sends the message using verbal and non-verbal codes. The non-verbal codes (body gestures, tone of voice, facial expressions) are mostly unconscious, but they carry the emotional elements of the message. The verbal codes (words) carry the cognitive elements of the message. The sender's gender, age, temperament, family, culture, and religion shape both the message and how it is encoded. The verbal and non-verbal codes can carry conflicting meanings. In the personal example, this is when I say to Cheryl, "Please pass the ketchup." The words, by themselves, convey a neutral cognitive message but the body language makes the message either positive or negative.

Step 2: Receiving

The receiver decodes (interprets) the message using the filters of gender, age, temperament, family, culture, and religion. The receiver usually decodes the words more consciously and the non-verbal elements less consciously. Decoding is more accurate when verbals and non-verbals agree. If the verbal and non-verbal elements are in conflict, the receiver's interpretation usually favors the non-verbals. In the example, Cheryl interprets my message ("Please pass the ketchup") as, "I don't like your lentil roast!" That interpretation did not come from my words, but it could have come from the non-verbals. Or, it could have come from the filters through which she filtered the message.

Step 3: Responding
The receiver encodes and sends a response using all of the processes described in Step 1. Cheryl responds, "You don't like my lentil roast!" At this point we have miscommunicated. Decoding her words and the disappointment on her face, I quickly respond, "You misunderstand me. I love your lentil roast but I love it even more with ketchup."

Step 4: Confirming
The original sender receives the response and decodes it using all of the processes described in Step 2 and then replies. The dialogue may end or continue. When both agree about what the original sender intended to communicate, the communication process is complete. That does not mean they have to agree about the issue involved. In the example, Cheryl replies, "Oh, all right." She may still wish I did not ask for ketchup, but she understands that I really like her lentil roast.

Communication Static

In radio or TV broadcasting, there is atmospheric interference that disrupts the reception. Static of different kinds is an inevitable part of face-to-face communication. Some static is physical, like noises that intrude or public address systems that are too loud or not loud enough. Other static comes from the gender, age, temperament, family, culture, and religion factors that filter communication.

Inaccurate perceptions of any kind about Christian beliefs and practices function as serious static that impedes full communication. Speaking the receptor's language poorly, or not at all, or relying on a translator with less than ideal abilities creates serious static. Sometimes missionaries have no choice but to rely on a translator whose technical language skills are acceptable but who is not a Christian. The inevitably mixed-messages sent by such a translator seriously inhibit communication of the Gospel. Missionaries create communication static when they do and say things that are acceptable for Christians in their home cultures but are interpreted as bad in their host cultures. The classic Adventist methods can create static so that some receptors are unable to receive the Adventist message accurately.

> **Figure 9.5**
> **Moishe and the Pope**
>
> About a century or two ago, the Pope decided that all the Jewish people had to leave Rome. Naturally, there was a big uproar from the Jewish community. Therefore, the Pope made a deal. He would have a religious debate with a member of the Jewish community. If the representative won, the Jews could stay. If the Pope won, the Jews would leave. The Jews realized that they had no choice. They looked around for a champion who could defend their faith, but no one wanted to volunteer. It was too risky. In desperation, they finally picked an old man named Moishe, the street sweeper, to represent them. Being old and poor, he had nothing to lose, so he agreed. He made only one condition. Not being used to saying very much, he asked that neither side be allowed to speak. The Pope agreed.
>
> The day of the great debate came. Moishe and the Pope sat opposite each other for a full minute before the Pope raised his hand and showed three fingers. Moishe looked back at him and raised his index finger. The Pope waved his hand in a circle around his head. Moishe pointed to the ground where he sat. The Pope pulled out a communion wafer and a glass of wine. Moishe pulled out an apple. The Pope stood up and announced, "I give up. This man is too good. The Jews may stay."
>
> An hour later, the cardinals asked the Pope what had happened. The Pope said, "First, I held up three fingers to represent the Trinity. He responded by holding up one finger to remind me that there was still one God common to both our religions. Then, I waved my hand around me to show him that God was all around us. He responded by pointing to the ground, showing that God was also right here with us. I offered the wine and the wafer to show that God absolves us from our sins. He pulled out an apple to remind me of original sin. He had an answer for everything. What could I do?"
>
> Meanwhile, the Jewish community crowded around Moishe, amazed that this old, somewhat feeble man had done what all their scholars had insisted was impossible. "What happened?" they asked. "Well," said Moishe, "first he said to me that the Jews had three days to get out of the city. I told him that not one of us was leaving. Then he told me that this whole city must be cleared of Jews. I let him know that we were staying right here. And then he took out his lunch, so I took out mine."

Source: http://scripting.com/98/04/stories/moisheAndThePope.html

Trialogue: Communicator, Bible, Recipient

Cross-cultural mission communication involves a "trialogue" between three cultures—the missionary, Bible, and recipient cultures. The missionary starts by being aware that she is a person of one culture among many human cultures. She understands that when she reads the Bible she understands it through cultural lenses.

Next, the missionary understands that the Bible writers were people of culture writing to various cultures. Moses, David, Malachi, and Paul lived in very different cultures. The better the cultures of the Bible are understood, the better its message can be understood and applied to the missionary's own culture. Using the Bible as the norm, she seeks to understand its meaning for herself, within her own culture.

Then the missionary seeks to understand the recipient culture. Initially, the message moves from the cultural context of the Bible, through the lenses of the missionary culture, and into the cultural world of the recipient. The well-trained missionary does her best to separate her own cultural preferences from biblical principles. Eventually, recipients make their own engagement with the Bible. Having access to a mother-tongue Bible, either as a reader or as a hearer, allows recipients to make direct engagement with the Bible. The principles of the Bible come to life in a cultural context that is different from both the Bible's and the missionary's cultural contexts.

To illustrate, Presbyterian missionaries came to Lake Malawi in 1875. Gradually, the missionaries learned the Chinyanja language, put it into writing, and taught basic literacy. An early translation into Chinyanja (now called Chichewa) of the New Testament was published in 1886 and the whole Bible in 1922. In the first stages, Malawians were dependent upon the missionaries for understanding the Bible. But quickly the number of believers grew and Malawians became teachers, evangelists, and pastors. Except at the earliest stages, most converts came to Christ through the work of fellow Malawians who used the Chichewa Bible.

For effective cross-cultural communication to occur, careful attention to cultural body language, and non-verbals is needed. Missionary communication with local people happens all the time, not just from the pulpit or in other formal settings. Some hand gestures that are innocent in one culture are obscene in others. Putting the hands in one's trouser pockets, sometimes even when preaching, is innocent in some cultures and rude in others. Greeting styles vary a great deal between cultures. There are firm or floppy handshakes, bowing in different degrees, and kissing one cheek or both cheeks or touching cheeks and kissing the air. Touching of any kind between unmarried or unrelated men and women is totally forbidden in some cultures. Any public display of affection between spouses is perceived as performing marital intimacies in some cultures. The distance of comfortable dialogue varies from standing nose-to-nose to standing at arms' length from each other.

One of the often ignored components of communication is emotional intensity. Cultural preferences range from very low to very high emotional intensity in communication. Some cultures do not take public speakers seriously unless they speak with high volume and great emotional intensity. Others prefer quiet, reasoned, low emotional intensity speech and discount highly emotive communication. Communication is enhanced by adapting to the preferred emotional intensity level of the receivers.

The various adaptations needed to maximize effective cross-cultural communication are part of what Paul referred to when he said, "I have become all things to all people, that by all means I might save some" (1 Cor 9:22). The goal is not to become a cultural chameleon whose own identity disappears. In fact, cultural identity runs so deep that it cannot really be changed like a chameleon's colors. Missionaries who try to mimic and copy everything may be seen as making a mockery of the local culture. Yet, effective communication requires a heartfelt, genuine adjustment so that one lives life on the terms of the local culture as much as is reasonably possible.

Factors for Effective Communication

In the complex enterprise of cross-cultural communication there are a number of factors to be blended into an effective strategy for any context.

Mother-tongue communication opens special doors into the human heart. Many people in the world are multilingual, but no language is sweeter than the mother's language. This reality places a high priority on language learning for cross-cultural missionaries.

Age and gender have to be considered. Some cultures value age so highly that they struggle to give credibility to the witness of a younger person. Paul addressed the age factor when he said to Timothy "Let no one despise you for your youth, but set the believers an example in speech, in conduct, in love, in faith, in purity" (1 Tim 4:12). Younger missionaries have the advantages of being able to learn languages more quickly and the strength of youth to withstand hardships. The key is to be aware of the age factor, to give special respect to the elders, and to use the assets of youth (like language learning) to their full value.

Among many of the least-evangelized peoples, male and female roles are defined in ways that challenge missionary communication. In many contexts, men and women do not meet outside of family relationships and very close family friendships. Thus, only male-to-male and female-to-female communication is generally approved.

Culturally appropriate modes of communication need to be used. Public preaching is impossible or ineffective among many peoples. Jesus did not use the mode of formal pulpit preaching very often. In Nazareth, Jesus read the Bible and sat down to teach its meaning (Luke 4:20). In a wide variety of settings, Jesus used parables drawn from the context to teach the deepest lessons (Matt 13). By one estimate, 75% of the Bible is in narrative form (Terry and Payne 2013:172). The stories of the Bible offer an excellent alternative to the proof-text method. Poetry and drama are effective vehicles of the Gospel. Marches and festivals can communicate and depict aspects of the Gospel in contextual ways.

An estimated 60% of the world's population prefers listening to reading (Terry and Payne 2013:171). Included in these "orality" peoples are many who are literate or semi-literate. They can read, but they process and learn primarily through their ears rather than their eyes. Teaching biblical literacy, translating the Bible, and using printed materials will always be valid and important for Christian mission; however, adapting to orality peoples means making generous use of spoken communication. Bible stories are appropriately told in styles appropriate for both children and adults. Bible readings and recordings can be shared using digital technology better than ever before. Creative formats, like human life dramas, can be used.

The mass media have great potential. One of the challenges is to provide materials that are not merely translated, but written for specific peoples. For example, the best broadcasts for Muslims in Indonesia are those written and presented by Indonesians whose logic system and presentation style are authentically Indonesian.

Finally, the Internet has huge potential as a vehicle for many of the other modes. Additionally, the Internet allows real-time dialogue either by texting or conversing with Skype and other programs. Bible lessons can be completed and returned. YouTube can carry whole series of presentations.

Chapter

Worldview and Mission

~•~

Introduction

"Worldview" is a popular word used in many ways to indicate different geographical, theological, philosophical, and cultural perspectives. Many popular uses of the word refer to the surface-level cultural perspectives of different people groups. Theologians often use the word to refer to basic theological assumptions. Missiology, with its emphasis on faithful contextualization, draws theological assumptions together with cultural assumptions to develop a missiological understanding of worldview. The worldview concept has a long history that is well discussed from a missiological perspective by Kraft (1996:51-68) and Hiebert (2008).

Worldview and Missions

At the heart of the missiological task is the call to bring the light of the Gospel to bear upon the deepest cultural presuppositions so that they can be transformed. The goal is authentic biblical Christianity that is practiced in many different cultural styles.

The worldview concept is helpful in missions because it supports the development of cross-cultural competence. Inter-cultural interaction reveals very different perspectives, thought processes, and convictions in spite of mutual friendship and respect, shared beliefs and goals, and similar education. Members of multicultural committees and church boards find themselves asking why the other cultural groups they work with think so differently. Every committee or board has members with different individual opinions, but members from the same cultural group often have shared ways of reaching decisions, solving conflict, and interpreting the Bible. The worldview concept names the factor that gives cultural groups their different perspectives and serves as a conceptual tool for developing inter-cultural competence.

The worldview concept aids disciple making by pointing to deep factors that need to be addressed by the Gospel. The need for conversion and discipleship at a deep worldview level becomes clear when one observes certain beliefs and practices of people in every society who are already believers. Because human sinfulness is both an individual and group reality, the presuppositions of every culture distort the Christian life in certain ways. If being a Christian is only a matter of external behavior and if cultural presuppositions are not challenged by the Gospel, converts retain their allegiances to unbiblical assumptions, even when they establish an allegiance to Jesus Christ. They are thus dual-allegiance believers, or Christo-pagans. For example, believers may continue to have allegiances to materialism and consumerism or to practice ancestor worship and other aspects of animism and spiritism. The worldview concept identifies the deep level of culture where competing allegiances need to be challenged and transformed, bringing single-allegiance and undivided commitment to Jesus Christ.

> Christians must take the worldviews of other people seriously, not because they agree with them, but because they want to understand the people they serve in order to effectively share with them the good news of the gospel. Worldviews are not merely imaginary pictures created by a community to unite its members and keep them in line. Most people maintain that their beliefs are more than useful fictions. For them their worldviews declare the way things really are and are true in an ultimate sense.... It is important to study worldviews to transform them. Too often conversion takes place at the surface levels of behavior and beliefs; but if worldviews are not transformed, the gospel is interpreted in terms of pagan worldviews, and the result is Christo-paganism. (Hiebert 2008:6)

Worldview, the Deep Part of Culture and Religion

The starting point is to understand that cultures and religions have shallow or surface level features that are easy to see and deep features below the surface that are difficult to see. The surface levels include behaviors, clothing, food, music, architecture, and other elements. These features can be easily observed by cultural outsiders and explained by cultural insiders. Studying cultures and religions at the surface level is like swimming on the surface of a lake or swimming pool. Understanding the surface levels of a culture or religion is important but not adequate for missions.

Worldviews are deep level features of cultures and religions. Outsiders cannot observe or understand them easily. Even cultural insiders live much of their lives at the surface level of their own cultures and often cannot describe the deeper levels, even though their lives are patterned by the deep levels. Studying the deep levels of a culture or religion is like using scuba equipment to dive deep under the water.

Some helpful metaphors are used for worldview. A worldview is like (1) spectacles or glasses through which people view everything, but of which they are usually unaware; (2) an internal road map or GPS system, with directions for all of life; (3) a grammar that structures a language, whether or not people can name parts of speech like nouns and verbs; (4) a computer operating system that most computer users are not aware of; (5) an iceberg, with only a small part extending above water and the rest hidden under the water.

Seeking to understand both surface levels and deep levels of culture and religion facilitates more effective cross-cultural relationships and transformational discipleship. Long-term relationships are needed for deep level understanding to be possible.

Figure 10.1
Definitions of "Worldview"

- The fundamental cognitive, affective, and evaluative presuppositions a group of people make about the nature of things, and which they use to order their lives. (Hiebert 2008:15)
- The culturally structured assumptions, values, and commitments/allegiances, underlying a peoples' perception of reality and their responses to those perceptions. (Kraft 1996:52)
- A worldview is a commitment, a fundamental orientation of the heart, that can be expressed as a story or in a set of presuppositions (assumptions that may be true, partially true, or entirely false) which we hold (consciously or subconsciously, consistently or inconsistently) about the basic constitution of reality, and that provides the foundation on which we live and move and have our being. (Sire 2004:17)

Characteristics of a Worldview

The three definitions of worldview in figure 10.1 are complementary and overlapping. The elements and functions of worldview discussed below are not presented in an order of priority.

A Worldview Is a Commitment

A worldview is a largely unconscious commitment at the deepest level of one's self, in one's "heart." The biblical concept of the "heart" "includes the notions of wisdom (Prov 2:10), emotion (Exod 4:14; John 14:1), desire and will, (1 Chron 29:18), spirituality (Acts 8:21) and intellect (Rom 1:21) (Sire 2004:18). Because culture is a group phenomenon, a cultural worldview is a deep level commitment shared by a people group. A commitment has the strength of a pledge, vow, promise, or obligation that has intellectual, emotional, and moral-ethical dimensions.

A Worldview Has a Cognitive or Intellectual Dimension

A worldview is a way of thinking about all of life. Every worldview is supported by a collection of concepts, philosophies, facts, and information. Traditional peoples often keep and communicate their information orally, while modern peoples use print or electronic methods. Modern, scientific societies have an over supply of information, but more traditional peoples have their own significant bodies of intellectual knowledge. Some have tended to overemphasize the intellectual dimension of worldview at the expense of the emotional and moral-ethical dimensions (Hiebert 2008:15), but the cognitive dimension remains essential. Christians hold deep intellectual assumptions about the ultimate nature of reality based on the Bible.

A Worldview Has an Affective or Emotional Dimension

A worldview is an emotion, or ethos, or state of consciousness about all of life. The worldview of a particular people group causes people to interact with and respond to life's happenings in an emotionally characteristic way. One might say that people "feel their way through life" in different ways. Life just "feels good" or "feels right" when it corresponds to one's worldview. Emotions are deeply internalized and are thus extremely powerful. Cognitive beliefs and moral-ethical convictions are leveraged by deeply emotional commitments. Christians assume that God's love for his creatures is a part of ultimate reality and that love for God and fellow humans is an essential emotion in the Christian life.

A Worldview Has an Evaluative, Moral-Ethical Dimension

A worldview is a way of making moral-ethical assessments about all of life. Every society has values and codes of conduct, rooted in strong convictions, that in ultimate reality "this or that IS right" and "this or that IS wrong." Moral-ethical convictions are much deeper than the need to obey a speed limit that could have been set either at 30 or 40 m.p.h. Right is right and wrong is wrong because they pertain to the nature of reality, itself. Some cultural values and codes of conduct are in harmony with Scripture but others are not. For example, some societies value and approve of theft, deceit, murder, and promiscuity while others value honesty, respect for human life, and sexual fidelity. Christians assume that the Ten Commandments express moral-ethical principles that correspond to ultimate reality.

A Worldview Is Expressed as a Set of Assumptions or Presuppositions

The assumptions and presuppositions that undergird a worldview can be expressed as propositional statements. For example, "the Triune God is the Creator of Heaven and Earth and humans were created in his image." Such statements are the building blocks that link with others to make up a complete view of the nature of reality.

A Worldview Is Expressed as a Grand-Narrative or Metanarrative

A grand-narrative, like the Adventist great controversy story, expresses a view of the nature of reality in story form. Stories that express worldviews are called "myths," not in the sense of imaginary fiction, but in the sense of stories with deep meaning about origins and destinies. These foundational stories go far beyond propositional statements to engage the emotions and reveal truth at a deep level.

> At the core of worldviews are foundational, or root myths, stories that shape the way we see and interpret our lives. Myths are paradigmatic stories, master narratives that bring cosmic order, coherence, and sense to the seemingly senseless experiences, emotions, ideas, and judgments of everyday life by telling people what is real, eternal, and enduring. (Hiebert 2008:66)

The Bible tells the great, inspired, truthful story of the great controversy that provides the foundation for the biblically-shaped worldview of a Christian in every culture. The other world religions have their own grand-narratives that tell different stories of humanity and the whole cosmos.

A Worldview Is Partly Conscious and Partly Subconscious

The elements of worldview contained in the great narratives of the different religions are well known to their followers. Christians know the stories of the Creation, the Fall, the Flood, the Exodus, and the Cross. But other important elements function at a subconscious level where they are difficult to perceive and analyze. The "ideas with the most profound consequences are frequently taken for granted....[They] lie just beyond conscious thought, providing a kind of foundation for the deliberations of everyday life....[They] are often the most difficult to weigh and reflect upon" (Gay 1998:1).

A Worldview Is a Hybrid Cluster

In this era of globalization, most worldviews are hybrid clusters of assumptions and commitments drawn from different sources. Modern science and education bring elements of scientific naturalism to almost all people groups. All of the world religions and their grand narratives are spread by migration and propagation. Secularism and postmodernity are global phenomena. Traditional animism is spread by migration and favored by new religious forms in the West.

All of these movements produce an increasing variety of hybrid positions within all of the major world religions and people groups. This cross-fertilization produces a considerable amount of inconsistency. For example, some Christians affirm the worldview of modern science while retaining their belief in the divine inspiration of the Bible, the Genesis account of human origins, the virgin birth, and the resurrection, while others do not hold these traditional views.

The challenge faced by Christian mission is the development of syncretism and dual allegiance that comes from blending conflicting assumptions from multiple sources. The opportunity for Christian mission is that all worldview clusters are in transition and flux, making people potentially open to the Bible and its grand narrative.

Functions of Worldview

A Worldview Defines Ultimate Reality

Sire discusses eight ways to define ultimate reality (2004). *Christian theism* assumes that the ground of all reality is the Triune Creator God who "is infinite and personal (triune), transcendent and immanent, sovereign and good" (26). *Scientific naturalism* assumes that "matter exists eternally and is all there is. God does not exist" (61). *Eastern pantheist monism* assumes that ultimate reality is composed of millions of gods who are one with every human being, animal, and plant (144). Obviously, these three alternative worldviews perceive reality in very contradictory ways.

Christianity assumes that human history partakes of ultimate reality to such an extent that a Supreme Being entered it to live as a human and to redeem humanity through a sacrificial death. Salvation in Christ brings eternal life in fellowship with the ultimate God. In contrast, eastern religions view life as an illusion from which humans seek release and escape in various ways.

Traditional and modern scientific societies tend to define ultimate reality in contrasting ways.

1. *Wholistic vs. segmented.* Traditional peoples understand elements of re-ality to be part of a wholistic design, while modern peoples divide realty into segments. Thus, traditional healers may combine herbalism, spiritism, marriage counselling, and surgery while modern practitioners specialize in segmented parts of the human being.

2. *Organic and relational vs. mechanistic.* Traditional peoples define reality in terms of the relationship between aspects of reality and human beings. Moderns define reality in a mechanical model of cause and effect.

3. *Capricious universe vs. orderly universe.* For traditional peoples, the whole universe is capricious. Natural events and the interventions of gods, spirits, or powers are completely unpredictable. Modern science studies the laws of nature, can predict natural events with a high degree of accuracy, and is not interested in gods or spirits.

4. *Supernatural vs. natural.* Traditional worldviews assume that ultimate reality extends beyond what can be known empirically, while modern sci-ence assume anything unknowable by science is a mere superstition.

5. *Limited human capacity vs. virtually unlimited capacity.* Traditional peo-ples tend to view humans as being controlled by other persons, beings, and powers beyond their control, while moderns believe they are in control of their own lives and destinies.

6. *Limited good vs. unlimited good.* The traditional view is that the total sup-ply of material and human resources in the universe is limited and that one

person's gain is inevitably another person's loss. The modern, capitalist view is that the available supply of resources is virtually unlimited, so long as economic systems are allowed to function.

A Worldview Defines Truth and How to Discover It

Every worldview defines a pathway toward truth and what that truth is. Christianity assumes ultimate truth resides in God, who has revealed it in Jesus Christ and in the Bible. Modern science assumes that truth is found in the scientific method and expressed in its formulations. Eastern religions look to self as the source and expression of truth. Postmodernity denies the existence of universal truth.

A Worldview Provides a Pathway for All of Life

Worldview provides a comprehensive life-pathway along which members of a society must travel at every stage of life, from birth to death. The "proper" way to live as a child, adult, parent, leader, or elderly person "is like this." The proper life-pathway is a part of ultimate reality, not merely a set of superficial rules that could have been made one way or another way.

A Worldview Defines Self and Others

Worldviews answer some very basic questions: (1) Who, what, and why am I? (2) Who, what, and why are Others? (3) How do I relate to We? (4) How do We relate to Them?

A worldview defines how one should view the Self and relate to the Other. Some societies have an independent, individual Self who exists and stands apart from Others. "I am because I am." Other societies have a communal, relational Self, who exists only in relationship with Others. "I am because We are."

Some societies assume that the Other is outside group ethics and morality and is even to be hated (Matt 5:43). Jesus taught in the golden rule that the Other should be loved as the Self and the Us (Matt 19:19; Mark 12:31).

In egalitarian societies, relationships between people "feel good and proper" when everyone is more or less equal in social authority. Hierarchical societies favor relationships in which social authority is ranked unequally, with members of society occupying different levels.

A Worldview Defines Causality

Worldviews answer the question, Why do things happen? What causes the weather, sickness or health, fertility or infertility, happiness or sorrow, car crashes, wars, or famines? Common answers to the question include: (1) God; (2) multiple powerful gods; (3) good and evil personal spirits, including Satan; (4) impersonal powers; (5) impersonal fate; (6) human actions, including self and others; (7) the impersonal laws of nature; (8) random occurrence.

Some societies favor multiple causes but others name a single cause for almost everything. Some think that events like car accidents "just happen" and usually have natural explanations. Others think there is no such thing as an accident because every event has a specific cause beyond the natural world that must be identified to prevent a repetition. To illustrate, some blame a car accident on a nail that punctured a bald tire and say that the real cause was poor maintenance of the car. Others seek to identify the person who placed a curse that caused the nail to puncture that particular tire.

Western secular societies favor causation by human action and natural laws. Eastern religions favor fate or karma. Animistic peoples favor gods, spirits, and impersonal powers. Christians generally agree that God is a dominant cause in the cosmos. However, some Christians see God as the comprehensive cause of all that happens, while others identify other causes. The great controversy metanarrative identifies Satan as the ultimate cause of all evil and God as the ultimate cause of all that is good.

A Worldview Defines Time and Space

Worldviews define time in particular ways (see Hiebert 2008:50ff). The biblical great controversy narrative presents time as linear and non-repetitive. Time moves from pre-sin perfection, to the fall of Lucifer, to the creation of Earth, to the fall of Adam and Eve, to the Cross, to the Second Coming, and to the destruction of evil and the restoration of sinless perfection. Human life moves from birth to death and one's eternal destiny depends on one's response to the offer of salvation in Christ in between birth and death. In contrast, Eastern religions have a cyclical concept of time that repeats. Human life is repeated through multiple reincarnations, with multiple opportunities to do better next time around.

Humans have mental maps of the space that surrounds them. Secular peoples perceive the land around them as being completely secular. Some traditional peoples, like Native Americans, see plains, mountains, and rivers as sacred. Muslims hold that Mecca is a uniquely holy space and Christians speak of Israel and Jerusalem as the "holy land."

A Worldview Defines the Origin and Destiny of Human Beings

The scientific naturalist worldview dominates the modern world, with its view that humans evolved from lesser forms of life and have no destiny after death. Scripture places the origin of humanity at Creation and the destiny of humans either in eternal afterlife or unconscious oblivion, depending on their response to Jesus Christ. Not all Christians agree with this Adventist interpretation of the Bible. Other religions have a wide variety of assumptions about human origins and destinies, including the Buddhist destiny of nirvana, or nothingness beyond either happiness or unhappiness.

A Worldview Defines the Human Predicament and Its Solution

All societies understand that humanity is caught in a predicament and all religions offer a solution of some kind (Halverson 1996:15). Christians call the predicament "sin" and the solution "salvation." Others say the human predicament was caused by childish error, lack of knowledge, ignorance of one's divinity, or irrational thinking. The Christian solution is accepting salvation through Jesus Christ. The almost universal prescription of other religions is the performance of good deeds of various kinds that earn merit. The biblical teaching that good deeds are a response of gratitude for salvation in Christ rather than the cause of salvation constitutes a major paradigm shift that all too many Christians do not experience.

A Worldview Provides a Logic System

The Bible teaches that all humans were created in the image of God and are rational beings, capable of performing the same basic mental tasks. However, people groups exercise their rationality in different ways. There is abstract, scientific logic, the logic of analogy, relational logic, and the logic of wisdom and proverbs (see Hiebert 2008:39ff). No logic system is inherently more rational than any other because all are rational within themselves.

A Worldview Provides Plausible Answers to Ultimate Questions

Against the backdrop of its numerous assumptions and using its own logic systems, every worldview asks questions and provides answers to those questions that are plausible or believable within its society. Sire suggests a list of ultimate questions shown in figure 10.2.

Figure 10.2
James Sire's Worldview Questions

1. What is prime reality—the really real?
2. What is the nature of external reality, that is, the world around us?
3. What is a human being?
4. What happens to a person at death?
5. Why is it possible to know anything at all?
6. How can we know what is right and wrong?
7. What is the meaning of human history?

Source: Sire 2004:17-18.

A Worldview Provides Emotional Security in Vulnerable Times

Great insecurity is experienced during the major transition points of life, like childbirth, puberty, marriage, old age, and death. Times of crisis, like war, famine, violence, or illness produce deep vulnerability. During stressful times, people are guided by their deepest assumptions to find solutions, answers, explanations, and comfort.

People with different worldviews will respond to stress and crisis with different statements like: (1) that is just how life is; (2) it was God's will; (3) I know that the illness happened because my enemy put a curse on me, but I am returning a stronger curse to him; (4) the shaman had weak medicine, but I will find a better shaman to make better medicine; (5) the doctor failed, but modern medicine will eventually find a cure; (6) all I can do is tough it out; (7) God will see me through; (8) that was her fate and destiny; (9) it does not really matter. People are often not satisfied by the answers given by those having a different worldview. For example, the remarks that comfort some mourners at a funeral are disturbing to others.

A Worldview is the Most Powerful and Influential Part of Culture

The characteristics and functions of worldviews combine to make them the most powerful and influential parts of cultures and religions. Worldviews are almost irresistibly persuasive, even in the face of contradictory evidence. In times of conflict or catastrophe, people intuitively revert to worldview positions as their default responses. Thus, a Christian may do things he believes to be explicitly against Scripture because he feels he cannot do otherwise.

Worldview provides the theoretical framework, albeit partly unconscious, that validates a culture and integrates the dimensions of culture. During the never-ending changes that all cultures experience, worldviews validate the changes by reinterpreting and reapplying traditional perspectives. Thus, when one South American group was taught to boil their drinking water to prevent disease, they concluded that boiling the water prevents disease because it kills the evil spirits (Hiebert 2008:30). As this example demonstrates, worldviews are highly resistant to change, even when the surface level aspects of culture change.

Worldview, Culture, and the Bible

The Bible was written over a period of about 1500 years, during which the peoples of the Ancient Near East passed through constant cultural flux and change as empires came and went. The authors, from Moses to John the Revelator, were people of great cultural diversity. The people groups who first read their writings were very different from each other. Thus, one cannot accurately speak of a single "biblical culture" held and practiced by all the diverse peoples of the Bible. Modern Christians are called to apply the principles of the Bible to their cultural contexts, not to adopt the cultural styles of any biblical period.

**Figure 10.3
Cultures in the Bible**

Old Testament Writers

Moses: Multi-cultural, highly educated, elements from enslaved Israelites, Egyptian nobility, desert Yahweh worshippers, Israelite nomads.
Authors of Historical Books: Jewish court historians, priests, scribes.
David and Solomon: Wealthy, powerful Jewish kings.
Prophets: Varying educational levels, from different historical periods, some multi-cultural input from Egypt, Babylon and elsewhere.

New Testament Writers

Paul: Highly educated Jew with strong Greek influence.
Luke: Gentile physician with strong Jewish influence.
Matthew-Levi: Jewish tax collector.
Mark, John, Peter, James: Lesser educated Jews.

Although the writers and recipients of the Bible books had different cultural worldviews, the Bible presents an internally consistent set of worldview assumptions. These worldview assumptions are based on the character of God, the two most basic of which are God's love and justice.

In this discussion, the phrase "biblical worldview" should be understood as the collection of assumptions that apply to all Christians. The phrase "cultural worldview" refers to the cluster of assumptions held by a particular culture or sub-culture. The phrases "biblically shaped worldview" or "biblical-cultural worldview" refer to a worldview in which the universal assumptions of the Bible are put into action by believers within a particular culture.

Human cultures are the vehicles in which biblical assumptions are applied and put into action. A biblical theology of culture states that the right and capacity to create different cultures is part of God's cultural mandate from Creation (Gen 1:28-30). As the Creator completed his work, "all the features of culture are present in Eden in seed form, including language, symbols, communication, relationality, domestication, and meaningful work" (Tennent 2010:176). This means that all people who serve God are people of culture and that there is no non-cultural believer.

The term "biblical worldview" is problematic if it (1) implies that culture is, can be, or should be excluded from theological thought, faith, and practice; (2) suggests a necessarily uniform pattern of theological thought, faith, and practice among the diverse peoples of the Bible and in the modern church; (3) minimizes the missional task of faithful contextualization among exceedingly diverse cultural-religious people groups and implies the need for a uniformity that Scripture does not require. The danger "is that we equate a biblical worldview with our conscious theological formulations rather than with the categories, logics, and assumptions we unconsciously use in creating these formulations" (Hiebert 2008:266).

Figure 10.4
Some Biblically Unacceptable Worldview Assumptions

- Reality is limited to the scientifically observable.
- Time is cyclical, with endless reincarnation.
- Human life is an illusion.
- Good and evil are one (monism).
- Humanity is inherently good.
- Humanity exists because of evolution.
- There is no God, or there are millions of gods, or God is distant and detached.
- There is no absolute right and wrong.
- The human predicament was caused by a childish error, lack of knowledge, ignorance of one's own divinity, or irrational thinking.
- Human good deeds create merit that solves the human predicament.
- The human is an immortal, spirit-flesh duality.

There is only one completely true and accurate worldview in the universe—the worldview of God himself. Every other worldview is distorted by individual and corporate fallibility and sin. The Bible records the history of God's efforts to teach his people to see themselves, others, the world, and the universe as he sees it. Neither the writers of the Bible nor the people of Bible times fully comprehended God's worldview or embodied it in their own lives. The wisdom of God is far beyond what humans can capture in their thoughts, speech, or writing. Only Jesus of Nazareth fully embodied the worldview of God expressed in human cultural form.

The goal of mission and discipleship is the development of a dynamic "biblically shaped worldview" or a "biblical-culture worldview" that includes personal growth into the fullness of Christ and on-going faithful contextualization within the cultural context. The eternal, universal principles and assumptions about ultimate reality revealed in the Bible provide a dynamic norm for every cultural group. At the same time, biblically innocent cultural assumptions remain.

> The church in each locale, as a community of faith, must define what it means to be Christian in its particular sociocultural and historical setting. It must take responsibility for defining and keeping biblical orthodoxy, and it must do so by defining how Christianity is different from its pagan surroundings. This is the faithfulness side of mission. The process of maintaining true faith in this world and age is ongoing, for each generation must learn to think biblically about being Christian in its particular context. (Hiebert 2008:12)

Worldview Transformation

Worldview transformation is only accomplished by the work of the Holy Spirit, but the church needs to understand the magnitude of the necessary change and the factors that best facilitate it (see Kraft 1996:358-457 and Hiebert 2008:307-333).

The weakness of some approaches to evangelism is that they remain at the more superficial levels of behavior and belief without probing more deeply to the level of foundational assumptions. For example, a shallow message is not adequate among people who assume that the human predicament was caused by childish error, lack of knowledge, ignorance of one's own divinity, or irrational thinking. To understand the biblical teaching of salvation in Christ requires understanding and internalizing the biblical teaching about sin. At first exposure, the Christian doctrine of human sinfulness is irrational bad news for non-Christians. They may respond, "I am not a sinner. I have never committed murder, adultery, or theft." Sin is also bad news for Christians but they are not shocked and offended by the teaching because it is already a part of their worldview. Changing a non-Christian explanation for the human predicament requires world-view transformation at a deep level.

An illustration may be helpful to demonstrate the challenge of worldview transformation. Adventists believe in "conditional immortality," meaning that only those who accept salvation in Jesus Christ will experience eternal life. After death, people enter an "unconscious state" of being where they know nothing. Preparations for becoming an Adventist include studying and affirming the "state of the dead" doctrine and the baptismal vows affirm that doctrine. Yet, there are some who continue various practices involving ancestors and the spirit world in contradiction to their doctrinal affirmations. Their worldview transformation is incomplete and they live with dual allegiance. They have a heartfelt love and commitment for Jesus Christ, but have yet to change certain worldview assumptions that remain irresistibly persuasive.

Conversion as Worldview Transformation

Adventists and many other Protestants have emphasized the transformation of beliefs and behaviors. However, "Conversion to Christ must encompass all three levels of culture: behavior and rituals, beliefs, and worldview…[because] if the worldview is not transformed, in the long run the gospel is subverted and becomes captive to local culture" (Hiebert 2008:315). Every person who comes to Christ must experience transformation at the worldview level; however, those who come with a cluster of worldview assumptions that differs significantly from the biblical assumptions have a major transition to make.

Figure 10.5 **Levels of Transformation**	
Conversion Process	**Surface Culture**
• initial contact and interest • prayer, Bible study • lifestyle changes	• behaviors and rituals
• belief and faith in Jesus • repentance and confession • acceptance of doctrines • baptism	• beliefs
• deep cultural assumptions transformed	• worldview **Deep Culture**

Source: Adapted from Hiebert 2008:316.

As already noted, the traditional Adventist method has used a Christian-to-Christian approach that assumes many biblical convictions. Even purely nominal Christians, who do not practice their faith, already hold many Christian world-view assumptions, such as the Bible as the source of truth, the nature of God, the sinfulness of humanity, and Jesus as the Savior of humanity. In contrast, many of today's unevangelized millions hold unbiblical world assumptions illustrated in figure 10.4. The Holy Spirit can transform every worldview, but the challenge for the church is to understand the scale of the transformation needed among all people groups and to use the best available methods.

Incremental Worldview Shifts

Natural, incremental worldview changes "are precipitated by surface contradictions, life's dilemmas, and new experiences that cannot be resolved by simply acquiring more information, enhancing problem-solving skills, or adding to one's competencies. Resolution of these dilemmas requires a change in our worldviews" (Hiebert 2008:316). These gradual worldview changes occur in response to constant, normal cultural change. They can be compared to remodeling a house to add new appliances or keep pace with changes in the neighborhood. In the long term, gradual shifts filter down to make changes at the deep, worldview level.

Radical Worldview Paradigm Shifts

Paradigm shifts, or radical cultural reorganization occurs when a society encounters new data that cannot be accommodated or explained by traditional structures of meaning. For example, the Copernican revolution transformed the traditional map of the universe as a response to new data that came from the use of telescopes. Previously the earth was seen as the center of the universe, but the new science reinterpreted, it as a minor planet circling the sun. Paradigm shifts can be compared to rebuilding a house with some of the old parts, but using a totally new plan.

Conversion and Worldview Transformation

Worldview transformation occurs both incrementally and as a radical shift. Incremental "change occurs when changes on the level of conscious beliefs and practices over time infiltrate and bring about change at the worldview level" (Hiebert 2008:319). Radical "shifts take place when there is a radical reorganization in the internal configurations of the worldview itself to reduce the tensions between surface culture and the worldview. In their own turn, these paradigm shifts reshape the surface culture" (319).

> Normally when we think of conversion, we think of radical paradigm shifts. Conversion replaces an old set of beliefs and practices with new ones. It involves turning from an old path and beginning on a new one. At the worldview level it changes the fundamental ways in which we configure our view of reality. But most worldview transformations are an ongoing process in all individuals and societies.... We must see worldview transformation as a *point, conversion*, and as a *process, ongoing deep discipling.* (319, emphasis supplied)

To illustrate, gradual or incremental worldview transformation occurs when a non-Christian enjoys a good relationship with a Christian and observes a new way of life that touches her. The Christian shares and models a life patterned after Jesus Christ. Over time, what the person sees and learns filters down to make gradual adjustments in her worldview.

A radical shift could occur when a non-Christian sees the problems of humanity in a shocking new way. Instead of seeing the human predicament as a relatively minor problem, the person has their eyes opened to perceive deep depravity in themselves and others. This new insight causes them to rearrange the human data they had observed for a lifetime into a new pattern. That new understanding of humanity drives them to Jesus Christ as their only hope.

The use of Bible stories is an effective way to facilitate worldview transformation. A religion is undergirded by elaborate collections of stories. The Bible is Christianity's story book. One missionary working in an area that was traditionally animistic had weekly meetings with the wives of ministerial students. She learned that in the evening the women were telling and re-telling stories from their traditional animistic mythology. Those stories contained deep worldview assumptions about God, spirits, the origin of humanity, the cause and solution of the human predicament, and the nature of death that were in opposition to the Bible account. The missionary started telling a Bible story each week and asking her class members to repeat the story to their children. The children loved the stories and asked for many repetitions. Many of the Bible stories were new, both to the mothers and to their children.

Facilitating Worldview Transformation

Studying and probing another culture at the worldview level facilitates deeper disciple making. Understanding a worldview different from one's own requires thoughtful, intentional study. The research methods of cultural anthropology are very helpful. When cultural outsiders study other cultural worldviews, their very best work is a mere approximation. Cultural insiders have an advantage, but they have to understand the nature of worldview assumptions so that they can probe their own cultures deeply. The partnership of cultural insiders and outsiders in understanding worldviews has great potential. One who studies another culture must never have "assertive self-confidence" but must maintain a "cognitive nervousness" and humility, along with a healthy respect (Hiebert 2008:91).

Leading another person toward a worldview transformation that potentially turns their world upside down is a responsibility to be taken seriously.

> We must also realize that new converts often experience "conversion shock." Their initial reaction is often one of euphoria and joy. When this wears off, they begin the difficult task of learning to think and live as Christians. They must learn a new language, behave in new ways, and form new relationships. In short, they must be enculturated into a new culture and socialized into a new community. (2008:331)

The newly-found "joy of the Lord" (Neh 8:10) and the "peace that passes understanding" (Phil 4:7) are very real for new converts, but their transitional stress can also be very real. The Christian worker must beware of unintended, unanticipated consequences in the lives of people making major spiritual transitions. The stress of transition is in proportion to the scale of worldview change a convert must made. For example, a Buddhist who becomes an Adventist makes a much greater transition than a Baptist who becomes an Adventist. This implies that the very best processes of faithful contextualization and disciple-making are needed, with a long-term commitment and follow through.

Chapter

Culture and Contextualization

~•〜

C ultural anthropology provides perspectives and conceptual tools that are very helpful in the many tasks of Christian mission; however, culture must be understood theologically for the anthropological perspectives to be applied biblically and effectively.

Niebuhr's *Christ and Culture* Model

One of the best-known books that has shaped Christian thinking about culture is Richard Niebuhr's *Christ and Culture* (1951). Niebuhr discusses five ways Christianity and culture relate to each other. Bear in mind, this discussion is about culture in general, not any particular culture. Niebuhr's points follow in summary form.

1. *Christ against culture.* Sin resides mostly in culture; the church and the believer must establish a sub-culture with a firm boundary against the larger culture. Culture is an enemy of the church.
2. *The Christ of culture.* The church lives at the center of cultural life, having no tension with culture. Culture is a friend of the church.
3. *Christ above culture.* The church approves the good in culture and rejects the bad. The church holds the culture at arm's length, but approves its good features.
4. *Christ and culture in paradox.* Culture is neutral and the line between good and evil must be drawn by individual believers. The church experiences culture as a series of challenges.
5. *Christ the transformer of culture.* Culture is basically good, but it must be permeated and transformed by the Gospel. Culture is like a troubled friend whom the church can help.

Niebuhr's model has been helpful for describing different attitudes toward culture that Christians have taken and continue to take; however, his approach is no longer considered to be an adequate way of understanding culture in an era of globalization. Tennent finds four difficulties with Niebuhr's model.

1. The model is based on a secular understanding of culture, "without theological interpretation," as Niebuhr himself acknowledged (1951:30). Niebuhr "posits Christ and culture as two wholly separate entities or forces" (Tennent 2010:163). This secular view contradicts the view of God as the Creator of the human capacity to develop culture and Christ's incarnation into culture.
2. The model "assumes a Christendom framework" (164), constructed in the era of Western dominance before the fragmentation of Western culture and the emergence of global Christianity.
3. The model assumes a monocultural perspective that is very different from today's global multicultural world. Niebuhr was a famous American theologian and his model described how different American Christians of his day viewed American culture. He was not a missiologist who pondered the cross-cultural task of global mission.
4. The model assumes "an eschatological framework that sees the future as already breaking into the present order" (Tennent 2010:166). Niebuhr comes too close to suggesting that God's Kingdom has already been fully established on earth.

A Trinitarian Theology of Culture

Several theological assumptions support a well-developed theology of culture.

1. God is the Creator and sustainer of both the physical and cultural life of humanity. He continues to influence humans as individuals and as members of cultural communities.
2. Sin has been an objective reality both for individuals and cultures since the Fall. The influence of sin moves from individuals to their cultures and also from cultures to individuals. Some goodness remains within humanity because of God's continued providential activity.
3. God's revelation through the Bible originated outside of all cultures but used the particular languages and cultural forms of the Bible writers.
4. God's Kingdom or "eschatological culture, known as the New Creation, already has broken into the present" (Tennent 2010:174) in partial fulfillment of the coming Kingdom. The new cultural order has already started because the Christian's "citizenship is in heaven" (Phil 3:20). The character of the New Creation transforms believers' relationships with their present cultures. Like Christ, they do not flee human cultural life but seek to be agents for good.

The general Trinitarian theology of mission already discussed is complimented by a Trinitarian theology of culture. God the Father is "the Source, Redeemer, and Final Goal of culture" (176). As the Creator completed his work all the features of culture are present in Eden in seed form, including language, symbols, communication, relationality, domestication, and meaningful work. Later developments such as urbanization, industrialization, state formation, and even globalization are all complex extensions of this original culture. (Tennent 2010:176)

God is the author of human culture and is continuously involved with it, as with all of his creation. "From one man he made all the nations, that they should inhabit the whole earth; and he marked out their appointed times in history and the boundaries of their lands (Acts 17:26). "The earth is the Lord's, and everything in it, the world, and all who live in it" (Ps 24:1). God redeems humanity, not only as individuals, but as members of particular people groups. The culmination of God's work is to draw "a great multitude that no one could count, from every nation, tribe, people and language" (Rev 7:9) into his eschatological Kingdom.

God the Son was incarnated into a particular human culture as Jesus of Nazareth. This reality "guarantees a high view of creation and human culture. It also reminds us of the theological significance of Jesus' entire life, not just His birth and passion" (Tennent 2010:178). In the years before his formal ministry, Jesus participated fully in the cultural life of his family and village, without joining its sinfulness. When his ministry commenced, one of his first acts was to attend the wedding at Cana (John 2:1), a celebration at the heart of culture. "The Incarnation ... represents God's embrace of human culture" (181).

The life of Jesus models for all cultures what it means to fully realize our true humanity. The Incarnation is, therefore, not only a revelation of *God* to humanity but also a revelation of humanity to humanity. In Jesus Christ we learn what it means to be *fully human*. (180, emphasis by author)

The Incarnation also expressed God's critique of culture. Christ's relationship with culture revealed its corruption. He challenged cultural power structures that oppressed the poor and weak. His example shows how people should relate to culture.

God the Holy Spirit is the agent of the New Creation that has broken into human culture as a foretaste of the full and glorious New Creation. "Therefore, if anyone is in Christ, the new creation has come: The old has gone, the new is here!" (2 Cor 5:17; Gal 5:15). The Spirit empowers members of the body of Christ to live within their respective cultures as he lived within his Jewish culture and to partially "live out the realities of the New Creation in the present" age (187). This means that believers retain their cultural identities, but find their ultimate identity in the culture of the New Creation.

A New Creation Model of Cross-Cultural Mission

Cross-cultural mission encounters have theological dimensions that make them different from secular cross-cultural encounters (Tennent 2010:184ff.). In secular cross-cultural encounters no value judgments are tolerated because they are seen as racist or ethnocentric. In contrast, Christ's model both affirmed and critiqued human culture. One of the sorrows of mission history is that the affirmation of culture that is part of Christ's model has not always been practiced. At times, missionaries made wholesale condemnations of cultural features that seemed unbiblical to them.

The post-colonial critique highlighted the cultural superiority and triumphalism of missions in the colonial era. In response, many Christians of Europe and North America developed a guilt complex or failure of nerve that questioned the validity of all cross-cultural missions. This reaction to the post-colonial critique overlooks Christ's dual relationship with culture—affirmation and critique. In other words, if Jesus the missionary to Nazareth would become Jesus the missionary to London, Lagos, Lima, Manila, or any other city, he would both affirm and critique the cultures there. Affirmation and critique remain permanent, dual dimensions of the biblical relationship with culture.

Two principles describe the dual relationship God has with human cultures (Walls 1996:7-9). The "indigenizing" principle says that because God affirms culture he wants his church everywhere to be "a place to feel at home." When people become new creations, they do not have to enter a cultural vacuum because the faith of Christ can become embedded in the particularities of their own cultures. With this understanding, a missionary affirms other cultures for deeply theological reasons, not because they assume "anything goes if it is cultural."

The "pilgrim" principle states that every culture falls short of God's ideal and needs to be transformed by the Gospel. From his early years, Jesus stood against the evil he perceived in his adopted Jewish culture and throughout his ministry "he was an agent of radical transformation....The inbreaking of the New Creation into the present is inevitably a *countercultural* force" (Tennent 2010:188). Thus, the missionary who follows Christ's model is a countercultural force calling people to become cultural pilgrims. The pilgrim believer lives by the universal principles of the Bible that apply to all cultures of all times.

The indigenizing and pilgrim principles are always in tension with each other. The believer is perpetually at home, but not at home within her own culture. "We are full participants in the culture(s) of our birth and we are, increasingly, experiencing and becoming partakers in the realities of the New Creation" (189). The cross-cultural missionary leads people of another culture to the same experience.

The Concept of Contextualization

The word "contextualization" raises questions and fears in some minds. Specifically, some fear that it necessarily means abandoning the primacy of the Bible for the sake of being culturally relevant. Or, some fear it means watering down the Gospel or making conversion easy for the sake of big conversion numbers. Others are resistant or fearful to even bringing culture into a discussion of how to study and share the Bible. While these fears are understandable, they are not necessary when contextualization is understood and practiced in a biblically faithful way. Actually, faithful contextualization deepens a believer's conversion and walk with God.

Culture in the Bible

The starting point in a discussion of contextualization is to reaffirm that the Word of God is the absolute, universal, unchanging standard of faith and practice for humans in every culture. The scriptural design for human life, summarized in the Decalogue and encapsulated in Christ's command to "Love the Lord your God with all your heart and with all your soul and with all your mind" and "Love your neighbor as yourself" (Matt 22:37-39), applies to all.

The next point is to understand the scriptural perspective of culture. At Creation God made Adam and Eve as both individual and corporate beings. Their individual natures sometimes receive more attention than their corporate natures. Their corporate nature began with their relationship with God, with whom they lived in community. God regularly communed and had fellowship with them (Gen 3:3). Their corporate nature was also expressed in their marital and family relationships. As they had children, the first family grew and eventually became a cluster of families with multiple generations.

Adam and Eve were given dominion over all of creation (Gen 1:28-29). This dominion gave them freedom to decide how to use all the resources of nature—except the Tree of Knowledge. In their exercise of dominion, they developed life patterns based on godly ideas, feelings, and values that were linked with behaviors and material objects in the Garden. If one was privileged to view the first family in the Garden before the Fall, one would observe a perfectly sinless culture in operation.

The Fall perverted both the individual and corporate dimensions of humanity. The image of God in both the individual and cultural nature of humanity was damaged, although not totally effaced. To the extent that individuals and groups responded to God's gracious interventions, they reflected his character. When God scattered humanity at the Tower of Babel (Gen 11), people groups developed different cultures as they migrated around the globe and interacted with different natural environments.

God's love and respect for both the individual and cultural dimensions of humanity continues to be clear in the Bible after Babel. The authors of the Bible wrote from within their own cultures, using local languages and thought patterns. Even the names for God were borrowed from local languages. Between Genesis and Revelation, a wide range of cultural variation is exhibited in the biblical narrative of true believers serving God faithfully in different cultural ways.

Contextualization in the Bible

The most profound instance of God's contextualization is the Incarnation.

The Creator became Jesus of Nazareth, who was not a generic human being, but a member of a particular cultural group, living in a small village, in a specific time period. As the Apostles inaugurated the early church and as the believers in Antioch launched intentional cross-cultural missions with Paul and Barnabas in the forefront (Acts 13), the Gospel of Christ was incarnated into multiple cultures. The eternal, unchanging Gospel of Jesus reached beyond the cultural specificities of Nazareth and Jerusalem to those of Corinth, Philippi, and Rome. A Roman believer need not adopt the cultural style of believers in Jerusalem that included circumcision (Acts 15). If they followed the principles of the OT, the emerging writings of the NT, and the oral teachings of the Apostles—all under the guidance of the Holy Spirit—Jews and Gentiles could be equally authentic Christians. Their beliefs and practices were faithfully contextualized because they were biblically faithful and culturally appropriate.

"Although the term contextualization was quite recently minted, the activity of expressing and embodying the Gospel in context-sensitive ways has characterized the Christian mission from the very beginning" (Flemming 2005:15). The NT books, especially the Gospels, demonstrate the shaping of the message for specific audiences. The Book of Acts and the Epistles demonstrate contextualization in constant action as the Gospel of Jesus engaged diverse cultures.

When he wrote to churches in what is modern Turkey, Peter advocated a "differentiated acceptance and rejection of first-century culture" (Jobes 2005:4). A Christian should "live by the good values of society that are consistent with Christian values and reject those that are not, thereby maintaining one's distinctive Christian identity" (2005:171).

John the Revelator contextualized his messages to the seven churches (Rev 2-3). The commendations and exhortations for each were written using the geographic, demographic, and economic characteristics of each church. For example, the exhortation to Laodicea that they should not be spiritually "lukewarm" (3:15-16) was drawn from the lukewarm water supply that fed the city.

The Need for Contextualization Today

Today, as in biblical times, every reader-hearer-recipient of the Gospel message applies it in some way to their individual lives within their cultural-religious context. Cultures are like lenses or filters that shape and select what people understand. How accurately they receive and apply the message is a vital concern in mission. Books could be written about the misunderstandings people have had about the teachings of missionaries.

Almost every preacher, teacher, evangelist, or missionary instinctively tries to make the message credible and relevant for their audience. The "almost" in the previous sentence is there to cover people like the hellfire-brimstone American street corner preacher I heard in Chiang Mai, Thailand. Very few people in his audience knew English, but there he was haranguing the crowds in a kind of English even I could barely understand. The street preacher apparently had no comprehension of the linguistic-cultural-religious gap separating him from his audience.

The issue really is not whether to do contextualization, but how to do it effectively. The greater the religious, cultural, or linguist barriers to be crossed, the more difficult and challenging is the task. For example, if the spiritual journey of an American Methodist into a mature practice of the Adventist faith was located to be 1 on a scale of 10 (10 being long and difficult), the same journey for most Muslims, Hindus, or Buddhists would have to be located at 10. However accurate and Spirit-empowered the "sent-message" may be for people in the speaker's birth culture, people on the other side of those religious, cultural, or linguist barriers may perceive a completely different "received-message." A wrong received-message may cause receivers to reject the message completely or to accept it in a partial or warped way that produces syncretism. Being intentional about contextualization elevates the quality of evangelization and diminishes syncretism.

The Culture Concept

The development of the culture concept in the nineteenth century influenced Christian missions and eventually led to the concept of contextualization. As the reports of explorers and civil servants filtered back to Europe and America from far flung colonies, the discipline of cultural anthropology was developed to study newly observed human phenomena. At first the focus was on physical variations, like hair, skin color, skull sizes, and skeletal patterns. But anthropologists soon realized that people differed in more than biological ways. These non-biological features were called "culture."

Paul Hiebert defines "culture" as "systems of ideas, feelings, and values and their associated patterns of behavior and products shared by a group of people who organize and regulate what they think, feel and do" (1985:30). Underlying culture is a set of deep assumptions about the nature of reality that is called "worldview." To be effective, cross-cultural mission must go well beyond the surface level elements of culture, like food, dress, or music to the worldview level.

The culture concept explains why individuals are strongly shaped by the people groups in which they live. People with ancestors from Asia, Africa, or Europe can live together in America, but have more in common with each other than with their respective ancestral groups. Understanding culture means that mission methodology must be shaped to address cultural, people group characteristics.

A candid analysis shows that too little attention was paid to the cultures of recipient peoples during the colonial era. Missionaries too often tried to simply transplant their own way of being Christian and doing church to other peoples. The insight that the church could not merely be airlifted from mission-sender communities to mission-receivers resulted in a number of terms that attempted to describe the correct method. Various words were used, including "accommodation," "adaption," "inculturation," "indigenization" and "nativization." Each of these words has negative implications and carries certain negative baggage.

In 1972, Skoki Coe, of Taiwan, suggested the term "contextualization" as an alternative that has proven to be more acceptable among evangelical Protestants than the previous terms. In this discussion, the concept is the issue, not the term. Neither the words "culture" nor "contextualization" are found in the Bible. However, both concepts are clearly present in Scripture and must be part of Christian missions.

The word "contextualization" is used differently. Charles Kraft uses the term *Appropriate Christianity* (2005). This term may not be the best because it could imply that culture is privileged over the Bible. Hiebert's suggestion is "Critical Contextualization" (1985:171). He intends "critical" to mean the intentional, selective, disciplined, thoughtful incarnation of the normative Gospel into particular cultures. However, because "critical contextualization" brings to mind "higher criticism" (which Hiebert never supported), the use of this terminology may be problematic for some.

In view of these considerations, the term "Faithful Contextualization" may be best. This term builds on Hiebert's intended meaning that being faithful to the Bible must always be primary and adapting to culture must be secondary, although essential. Several definitions of contextualization are helpful. Flemming says it is "the dynamic and comprehensive process by which the Gospel is incarnated within a concrete historical or cultural situation." (2005:19). Moreau notes that "contextualization is at the 'mixing point' of Gospel and culture" (2012:19). The Gospel and culture will always mix and must mix. There is no such thing as a "culturally generic" or "non-cultural" Christian, any more than there is a "non-individual" Christian.

The Gospel mixes with or engages both one's individuality and culture. This mixing is what Jesus meant by his "in the world but not of the world" (John 17) statement. Following Christ's command produces a Christian community that is "defined by Scripture but shaped by culture" (Moreau 2012:35). The biblical norm is given cultural shaping. Contextualization is

> the process whereby Christians adapt the forms, content, and praxis of the Christian faith so as to communicate it to the minds and hearts of people with other cultural backgrounds. The goal is to make the Christian faith as a whole— not only the message but also the means of living out of our faith in the local setting—understandable. (36)

A look into my own so-called "Christian culture" in America quickly reveals that there are pitfalls to avoid at the "mixing point" of the Bible and culture. The principles of the Bible are very imperfectly embodied in my own native culture, even with its Christian heritage of centuries. If that is the case, the work of leading peoples who have no Christian heritage to mature Christian discipleship must be seen as a long and demanding process.

There are some mistakes to avoid along the path of faithful contextualization. One mistake to avoid is the fiction of "non-contextualization." With good intentions, some say "I read/interpret/teach the Bible just as exactly as it reads." That statement is good if it means that I do not add to or subtract from the Bible or interpret the Bible allegorically or make it mean whatever I want. However, the statement can imply overlooking or ignoring the cultures of the Bible writers and their recipients, the contemporary preacher/teacher/missionary, or the contemporary recipients. When a modern day Korean (or Brazilian or Indian) teaches Mongolians (or Egyptians or Chinese or Indonesians) about the writings of the Jewish Apostle Paul, a deep understanding of all three cultures is required—Paul's, the missionary's, and the recipient's.

Another mistake to avoid is placing the "context over the text," or making culture primary and the Bible secondary. Yet another error is reading the "text out of context," or ignoring the cultural setting of the Bible writers. The goal is to read the "text within context."

Faithful Contextualization

Faithful contextualization is both a process and outcome. As a process, it starts with critiquing my own practice of Christianity in all its dimensions so that it remains biblically faithful and culturally appropriate in my own, ever-evolving culture. Confronting the way I live within my own culture is absolutely essential for cross-cultural mission.

As a process, faithful contextualization aims to lead people to a biblically faithful practice of Christianity in all its dimensions that is appropriate for their culture. The greater the cultural-linguistic-religious distance between the Gospel messenger and the recipient, the greater and more patient the effort will need to be. When doing mission among peoples like Muslims, Hindus, and Buddhists, there is no substitute for long-term service that includes knowing the language, culture, and religion.

The Process of Faithful Contextualization

1. Study of the Culture

The culture is studied carefully using the concepts of cultural anthropology and the participant-observer approach. Questions of right and wrong regarding issues that the missionary does not yet understand are temporarily bracketed, or put on hold. This is learning time, not teaching time. If the missionary rushes forward, they may get it all wrong. The goal is to understand the deeper issues, assumptions, and questions of the culture. The serious study of culture is what sets the process of faithful contextualization apart from traditional, standard evangelism.

2. Fresh Bible Study

The missionary engages in a fresh study of the Bible with the local culture in mind, asking "What does the Word say to this particular people group?"

3. Communal Discussions

The missionary engages the local community of believers in a thoughtful, unhurried discussion about the local culture and the Bible. As specific cultural issues are discussed, the group asks three questions:

- What is approved by the Bible? Every culture has elements that express biblical principles.
- What is biblically neutral? Some elements are only matters of cultural style and preference.
- What is forbidden by the Bible?

The goal is to reach decisions by a communal consensus because (1) the local people understand their own culture best and because (2) they will have to live by whatever decisions are made. The missionary does have a leadership role, but they cannot be confident that a unilateral decision will be accurate. Without the community, the cross-cultural missionary risks supporting things that should be changed or abandoned or trying to change things that are biblically acceptable when understood deeply.

4. Functional Substitutes

The next step is to identify functional substitutes to replace practices that are to be changed or abandoned. When people stop doing something, a disturbing vacuum is created that must be filled with something better.

5. Transformational Ministries

Transformational discipling ministries are needed for supporting the changes to be implemented. Redemptive church discipline is sometimes needed. When changes are made involving practices and beliefs in place for centuries and generations, time and support is required.

The Process Illustrated

In real life, the process of faithful contextualization might look like this. The missionary observes aspects of the local funeral rites that seem unbiblical. He does not rush in demanding changes, but starts observing and discussing the funeral. At a time when people are not mourning a death, he asks believers to explain the meaning of each part of the funeral rite. He focuses on the meanings, not the forms, because he knows that flowers on the grave may have a different local meaning than in his homeland. With the group, he identifies the meaning of each element as biblically acceptable or unacceptable. When the unacceptable elements are identified, the group chooses functional substitutes for each element. For example, if flowers on the grave have an active connection with witchcraft practices, a functional substitute is selected. The group explains the changes to the whole church community, implements them at the next funeral, and evaluates the modified funeral rites afterwards. On-going adjustments can be made so that funeral rites are both biblically faithful and culturally appropriate.

The process is necessary for both pioneering contexts and places where the church is well established. Cultures evolve continually and often retain or add cultural elements with unbiblical meanings. Multi-generation Christians need to continually place their way of practicing the faith under the scrutiny of the Bible.

The Outcome of Faithful Contextualization

As an outcome, faithful contextualization means having a culturally appropriate way of life that is patterned after the normative Word of God in every dimension. The individual is experiencing growth in sanctification that includes personal lifestyle, family relationships, and personal spirituality in a culturally appropriate way. The believer lives as a cultural insider insofar as the Word permits and as a cultural outsider as the Word requires. The believer has a culturally appropriate Christian presence and witness in their community.

The outcome is also a Christian community that shows both the pilgrim and indigenizing principles in action. Like the believers to whom Peter wrote, they are "aliens and outcasts" (1 Pet 1:1; 2:11). They live "by different priorities, values, and allegiances than their pagan neighbors" (Jobes 2005:4).

The degree to which a believer must be a cultural pilgrim or alien varies a great deal in the contemporary world, depending on the degree of religious freedom. However, Christ's "salt and light" principle (Matt 5:13) teaches that believers should not adopt a more culturally alienated position than is imposed by their society or required to be faithful to Scripture. In other words, Christians in highly restrictive societies may have to live as secret believers but those living where there is religious freedom should not adopt an alienated, hermit's lifestyle.

The faithfully contextualized church also shows the indigenous principle in action. Church members remain members of their society. Local people feel at home at church with familiar architecture, music, dress, liturgy, and communication styles that are in harmony with the Bible.

For example, an Indian Hindu who steps into a faithfully contextualized Adventist church in India does not feel that they have joined a traditional Hindu ritual, even though the architecture and many cultural features are Indian. On the other hand, they do not feel that they have left India completely and gone to a Western nation because much of the contextualized service is culturally familiar to them, though biblically faithful.

Conclusion

The goal of faithful contextualization is that the absolute, universal, normative Word of God will dwell within particular cultural groups as authentically as Jesus Christ dwelled among His own Jewish kinfolk in Nazareth. When this happens in the twenty-first century, believers will be authentically Christian and authentically members of their birth cultures, immigrant cultures, or chosen cultures. They will be both Christian and Japanese, Christian and Arab, Christian and Chinese, Christian and American, or European, or African, or Latin-American, all around God's great world.

Chapter

The Global Context Of World Mission

~·~

Introduction

Anumber of overlapping, interlocking global factors and trends make up the environment in which Christian missions functions in the twenty-first century. The global factors differ between continents, nations, and people groups as they are shaped of local factors. Thus, mission must have both a global and local focus at all times. The word "glocal" (global + local) is used to describe a missional perspective that keeps both global and local dimensions in focus.

This chapter discusses factors and trends shaping mission at two levels—the whole world and the six inhabited continents. The time frame for many of the tables is 1910-2010. The reason for using this particular hundred-year span is that it marks two milestones in Christian missions. The 1910 Edinburgh Missionary Conference was the greatest interdenominational mission conference to that date. A century later, the 2010 Edinburgh Missionary Conference centennial convened. Three Adventist delegates attended each of the conferences.

Todd Johnson and Kenneth Ross edited the *Atlas of Global Christianity 1910-2010* for the 2010 Centennial (2009). Their massive work organizes data for the six inhabited continents, which are then subdivided into the 21 regions defined by the United Nations (UN). The data for the UN regions are a gold mine for mission research and strategic planning. The raw numbers have changed since 2010, but the proportions, percentages, and trends remain valid aids for developing missiological perspectives.

The 1910-2010 century is appropriate for Adventist mission studies. In 1910, A. G. Daniells and W. A. Spicer were leading the General Conference in a dynamic expansion of world mission. The Adventist Church had 90,808 members worldwide, 67% of whom were in North America. By 2010, Adventists were truly a worldwide church, with almost 17 million members, about 93% of whom were outside North America. In 2018, the total reported membership exceeds 20 million.

Population Growth

Global Population Growth

Table 12.1 World Population Growth					
Year	**Population**	**Year**	**Population**	**Year**	**Population**
AD 1	200	1800	1,000	1980	4,440
1000	400	1900	1,650	1990	5,310
1500	458	1950	2,525	2000	6,127
1600	580	1960	3,018	2010	6,930
1700	682	1970	3,682	2015	7,349

Source: Wikipedia.org/wiki/World_population. Population in millions.

Mission is about people, therefore, population statistics define the challenge of mission at the most basic level. When Jesus spoke the Great Commission, he was saying, in effect, "Take my Gospel to about 200 million people." Obeying the Great Commission in 1900 meant taking the Gospel to about 1.65 billion and today it means witnessing to 7 billion plus people. Until 1900, the world population growth rate increased only gradually, but the twentieth century witnessed a great surge of growth.

Demographers estimate future population growth in different ways. Using a high estimate, the world population will reach about 20 billion by 2100, 25 billion by 2200, and 35 billion by 2300. A low estimate predicts the population peaking at about 9 billion in 2050 and declining to under 5 billion by 2300. A medium estimate predicts a peak of about 9 billion in 2050 and no growth thereafter. Johnstone thinks that humanity could not continue to exist with the high prediction and suggests the medium estimate as the realistic one. However, caring for the needs of 9 billion people will severely overtax the resources of the Earth (Johnstone 2011:1).

The projected population growth using any option challenges the church by its sheer numbers. As you read these words, many people are dying without being given an opportunity to accept the Gospel and many more are being born. The very best informed and well implemented strategies will be needed for both evangelization and humanitarian mission service.

Population Growth by Continent

Table 12.2 Population Growth by Continent				
Continent	**Population 1910**	**Population 2010**	**Population Growth**	**% Growth**
Africa	124.2	1,032.0	907.8	730.9%
Asia	1,028.2	4,166.3	3,138.1	305.2%
Europe	427.1	730.4	303.3	71.0%
Latin America	78.3	593.7	515.4	658.2%
North America	94.7	348.6	253.9	268.1%
Oceania	7.2	35.5	28.3	393.1%
TOTAL	**1,759.7**	**6,906.5**	**5,146.8**	**292.5%**

Source: Johnson and Ross 2009:9. Population in millions.

Population growth has been unevenly distributed on the continents. Between 1910 and 2010, the world population grew 292.5%. Europe had the lowest growth at 71% and Africa the highest at 730.9%. "By 2000, the populations of most developed countries were in decline," unless they had high immigration rates from less developed nations (Johnstone 2011:3). In the coming century, population growth will be concentrated in the developing nations and the highest growth will be among Muslims in Africa and Asia.

The overall challenge of numeric growth will be complicated by political, cultural, religious, economic, and regional conflict. The continents will differ with each other and within themselves. Richer nations with low population growth rates and poorer nations with high growth rates will be in conflict for resources and opportunities. The well-meaning initiatives of wholistic mission to relieve human need and suffering will be complicated by the fast growth of poor populations and donor fatigue in wealthier nations.

Population Growth by Religious Groups

Population by Major Religious Groups

Table 12.3 Religious Groups by Percentage of Population, 1910-2010			
Group	**1910**	**2010**	**Change**
Christians	34.8%	33.2%	-1.6%
Muslims	12.6%	22.4%	9.8%
Hindus	12.7%	13.7%	1.0%
Buddhists	7.8%	6.8%	-1.0%
Agnostics/Atheists	0.0%	2.0%	2.0%
Chinese Folk	22.3%	6.6%	-15.7%
Ethnoreligionsists	7.7%	3.8%	-3.9%
New Religionists	0.4%	0.9%	0.5%
Others	1.7%	10.6%	8.9%

Source: Johnson and Ross 2009:7.

Statistics for the religions include all who self-identify as followers or members of particular religions. Every religion, including Christianity, has adherents who are considered proper or orthodox and others who are marginal, deviant, or non-orthodox. Every religion also has many branches or denominations that differ from each other and require different missional approaches.

In the last century, the four largest world religions (Christianity, Islam, Hinduism, Buddhism) have all experienced major growth. However, their share of the world population has changed in very different ways. Islam gained the most at 9.8%, because of both high birth rates and active *dawah*, or Islamic evangelism. Hinduism gained 1%, while Buddhism lost 1%, and Christianity lost 1.6% of its share of the population. In 2010, 2.96 billion people, or 43% of humanity, were Muslims, Hindus, or Buddhists.

Chinese Folk religion declined the most at 15.7%, because of communism and the cultural revolution. Ethno-religions, like Native American, Australian Aboriginal, and African Traditional Religion, lost 3.9%. The conversion of Africans to Islam or Christianity accounts for much of the loss among ethno-religions. Although the ethno-religions declined 3.9%, their animistic characteristics are often integrated into the religions they adopt, like Islam or Christianity.

Agnostics and atheists, who are not actually religious groups, grew 2% because of communism and Western secularism. The growth of agnostics, atheists, and new religions brought a particular challenge to mission, especially in the West where many are located.

Population by Christians and Non-Christians

Table 12.4 Population Growth by Christians and Non-Christians				
Year	Population	% of Pop Christian	Christians	Non-Christians
100	200	1.0%	2	198
500	200	20.0%	40	160
1000	400	17.1%	68.4	331.6
1500	458	18.0%	82.4	375.6
1600	580	19.4%	112.5	467.5
1700	682	21.0%	143.2	538.8
1800	1,000	22.7%	227.0	773.0
1900	1,650	34.5%	569.3	1,080.8
1950	2,525	34.0%	858.5	1,666.5
2000	6,127	32.8%	2,009.7	4,117.3
2015	7,349	32.5%	2,388.4	4,960.6

Source: Johnstone 2011:41-61. Population in millions.

The Christian share of the world population has taken two major leaps. Between AD 100 and 500 the Christian share grew from about 1% to 20%, where it stayed with slight decreases and increases until the nineteenth century. Between 1800 and 1900, in the "great century of mission," Christianity surged from 22.7% to 34%. In the last century, there was a small loss but the share remains steady at about one-third.

In 2015, the 4.9 billion non-Christians comprised a challenge for missions that was 3 times the entire world population and 4.5 times the non-Christian population of 1900. Those who know the least about the Bible and the Gospel of Jesus Christ are thus the first priority for Christian missions.

Christian Center of Gravity Shifts

Table 12.5 Shift of Global Christianity				
Continent	**1800**	**1900**	**2000**	**2025**
Africa	2.1%	1.7%	18.4%	24.6%
Asia	4.1%	4.0%	15.4%	18.6%
Europe	83.8%	70.6%	29.0%	21.1%
Latin America	7.3%	11.5%	25.2%	24.9%
North America	2.7%	11.4%	11.0%	9.6%
Oceania	0.05%	0.8%	1.1%	1.0%
Europe + N/America	**86.5%**	**82.0%**	**39.9%**	**30.7%**

Source: Barrett, Johnstone, and Crossing 2008:30. Figures for 2025 projected.

Christianity started in Palestine and then moved into Europe, Asia, and North Africa. During the early centuries, important Christian centers existed in Syria, India, and China. Until the Muslim conquest of the seventh century, North Africa was a major Christian center.

The Christian center of gravity moved gradually northward until about AD 900 when the majority of Christians were in Europe. When Martin Luther started the Reformation, about 92% of Christians lived in Europe. When William Carey went to India in 1793, about 86% of Christians lived in Europe and North America. However, by 2000, North America and Europe accounted for only 39.9% of Christians and by 2025, only about 30.7% will be there.

At the beginning of the Modern Missionary Movement (c. 1750-1950), Christianity was indeed a White person's religion. Theologically speaking, the religion of Jesus Christ has always been a religion for all peoples, but statistically it was not so. As modern missions got under way, it was about taking the Gospel from predominantly Christian Europe and America to the non-Christian world elsewhere. In the last two centuries, the Christian church has once again become a truly global religion. Mission is no longer "from the West to the rest" but "from everywhere to everywhere." Much of today's mission is initiated in the global south and extends to the whole world.

Religion Groups by Continent

Christianity by Continent

Table 12.6
Christians by Continent, 1910-2010

Continent	1910			2010			Change
	Popu-lation	Christ-ians	% of Pop	Popu-lation	Christ-ians	% of Pop	% of Pop
Africa	124.2	11.7	9.4%	1,032.0	494.6	47.9%	38.5%
Asia	1,028.2	25.1	2.4%	4,166.3	352.2	8.5%	6.1%
Europe	427.1	403.7	94.5%	730.4	585.7	80.2%	-14.3%
L/America	78.3	74.5	95.2%	593.7	548.9	92.5%	-2.7%
N/America	94.7	91.4	96.6%	348.6	283.0	81.2%	-15.4%
Oceania	7.2	5.6	78.6%	35.5	27.8	78.5%	-0.1%
Total	**1,759.7**	**612.0**	**34.8%**	**6,906.5**	**2,292.2**	**33.2%**	**-1.6%**

Source: Johnson and Ross 2009:9. Population in millions.

Christianity is the world's largest religion, with 33.2% of the population in 2010. Between 1910 and 2010, global Christianity grew from 612 million to 2.2 billion. Its population share fell from 34.8% to 33.2%, a loss of 1.6%. Christianity is the majority religion on all the continents, except for Africa and Asia.

None of the world religions, on any of the continents, experienced growth that equals the growth of Christianity in Africa. From a mere 11.7 million in 1910, the Christian population in Africa grew to 494.6 million in 2010. Its continental share grew 38.5%, from 9.4% to 47.9%. The Christian growth was mostly in sub-Saharan Africa, North Africa being predominantly Muslim.

Asian Christianity grew from 25.1 million to 352.2 million, a growth of population share from 2.4% to 8.5%. The 6.1% gain of continent share was good but Asia remains the continent with the smallest Christian share and thus the continent presenting the greatest numerical challenge for missions.

Whereas Europe lost 14.3% and North America lost 15.4%, Latin American Christianity lost only 2.7% of its share. Latin America remains the continent with the largest Christian share, at 92.5%. Oceania has a relatively small population, but 78.5% self-identify as Christians.

Islam by Continent

Table 12.7
Muslims by Continent, 1910-2010

Continent	1910			2010			Change
	Popu-lation	Mus-lims	% of Pop	Popu-lation	Mus-lims	% of Pop	% of Pop
Africa	124.2	39.6	32.0%	1,032.0	417.6	40.5%	8.5%
Asia	1,028.2	171.0	16.6%	4,166.3	1,082.5	26.0%	9.3%
Europe	427.1	10.1	2.3%	730.4	41.1	5.6%	3.3%
L/America	78.3	0.08	0.1%	593.7	1.9	0.3%	0.2%
N/America	94.7	0.01	0.0%	348.6	5.7	1.6%	1.6%
Oceania	7.2	0.02	0.2%	35.5	0.6	1.6%	1.4%
Total	**1,759.7**	**220.8**	**12.6%**	**6,906.5**	**1,549.4**	**22.4%**	**9.9%**

Source: Johnson and Ross 2009:11. Population in millions.

Islam is the world's second largest religion with 22.4% of the population in 2010. Between 1910 and 2010, Islam grew from 220.8 million to 1.54 billion. Its share of world population grew from 12.6% to 22.4%, an increase of 9.9%.

Islam in Africa grew from 39.6 million to 417.6 million. Its continent share grew from 32% to 40.5%, an increase of 8.5%. Africa is the continent with the largest Muslim share of the population, 40.5%. Most of that large share is in North Africa.

More Muslims live in Asia than in any other continent. In 1910, Asia had 171 million Muslims and by 2010, a total of 1.08 billion. The Muslim population share in Asia increased 9.3%, from 16.6% to 26%.

Islam in Europe grew from 10.1 million to 41.1 million, or 3.3% in population share. Population gains on the other continents were relatively small, but they have significant Muslim communities. North America had 5.7 million, Latin America 1.9 million, and Oceania 0.6 million Muslims in 2010.

Hinduism by Continents

Table 12.8
Hindus by Continent, 1910-2010

Continent	1910			2010			Change
	Popu-lation	Hindus	% of Pop	Popu-lation	Hindus	% of Pop	% of Pop
Africa	124.2	0.30	0.2%	1,032.0	2.90	0.3%	0.04%
Asia	1,028.2	222.90	21.7%	4,166.3	941.50	22.6%	0.92%
Europe	427.1	0.001	0.001%	730.4	1.00	0.1%	0.14%
L/America	78.3	0.10	0.2%	593.7	0.78	0.1%	-0.11%
N/America	94.7	0.01	0.001%	348.6	1.80	0.5%	0.52%
Oceania	7.2	0.16	0.2%	35.5	0.52	1.5%	1.25%
Total	1,759.7	223.47	12.7%	6,906.5	948.50	13.7%	1.00%

Source: Johnson and Ross 2009:13. Population in millions.

Hinduism is the world's third largest religion, with 13.7% of the population in 2010. Between 1910 and 2010, Hinduism grew from 223.4 million to 948.5 million. It's share of world population grew from 12.7% to 13.7%, an increase of 1%.

Hindus are concentrated in Asia, where they grew from 222.9 million to 941.5 million. The Asian Hindu population share grew slightly, from 21.7% to 22.6%.

Africa had 2.9 million, North America 1.8 million, Europe 1 million, Latin America 0.78 million, and Oceania had 0.52 million Hindus in 2010.

Buddhism by Continent

Table 12.9
Buddhists by Continent, 1910-2010

Continent	1910			2010			Change
	Popu-lation	Budd-hists	% of Pop	Popu-lation	Budd-hists	% of Pop	% of Pop
Africa	124.2	0.03	0.003%	1,032.0	0.30	0.03%	0.03%
Asia	1,028.2	137.1	13.38%	4,166.3	461.40	11.08%	-2.30%
Europe	427.1	0.4	0.10%	730.4	1.83	0.25%	0.15%
L/America	78.3	0.07	0.01%	593.7	0.80	0.13%	0.13%
N/America	94.7	0.4	0.05%	348.6	3.70	1.07%	1.02%
Oceania	7.2	0.07	0.11%	35.5	0.67	1.77%	1.66%
Total	1,759.7	138.07	7.84%	6,906.5	468.70	6.79%	-1.06%

Source: Johnson and Ross 2009:13. Population in millions.

Buddhism is the world's fourth largest religion, with 6.79% of the population in 2010. Between 1910 and 2010, Buddhism grew from 138 million to 468.7 million. Its share of world population fell 1.06%, from 7.84% to 6.79%. Buddhism remains largely a religion of Japan, Thailand, Myanmar, Taiwan, and other Asian nations. North America had 3.7 million and Europe 1.83 million Buddhists in 2010.

Islam, Hinduism, and Buddhism by Continent

Table 12.10
Muslims + Hindus + Buddhists by Continent, 2010

Continent	Population	Muslims	Hindus	Buddhists	Total	% of Pop
Africa	1,032.0	417.6	2.90	0.30	420.80	40.8%
Asia	4,166.3	1,082.5	941.50	461.40	2,485.40	59.7%
Europe	730.4	41.1	1.00	1.83	43.93	6.0%
L/America	593.7	1.9	0.78	0.80	3.48	0.6%
N/America	348.6	5.7	1.80	3.70	11.20	3.2%
Oceania	35.5	0.6	0.52	0.67	1.79	5.0%
Total	**6,906.5**	**1,549.4**	**948.50**	**468.70**	**2,966.60**	**43.0%**

Source: Johnson and Ross 2009:7, 9. Population in millions.

The big three non-Christian world religions, Islam, Hinduism, and Buddhism, may have relatively small portions of their adherents outside their main regions, yet those numbers are significant and growing. They comprise a significant mission challenge and opportunity for the Adventist world family everywhere.

In 2010, the population of Africa included 40.8% who follow one of the big three, with Islam leading at 40.5%. In Asia, 59.7% were of the big three, 26% being Muslim, 22.6% being Hindu, and 11.08% being Buddhist. Europe had 6%, Oceania 5%, and North America 3.2% who were of the big three. Latin America, being the continent with the highest Christian share (92.5%), had only 0.6% of its population who identify as Muslims, Hindus, or Buddhists.

Adventists by Continent

Table 12.11 Adventists by Continent, 1910-2010					
Continent	1910	%	2010	%	% of Change
Africa	981	1.1%	6,219,457	36.8%	35.7%
Asia	724	0.8%	3,407,833	20.1%	19.3%
Europe	16,995	18.7%	273,084	1.6%	-17.1%
L/America	6,793	7.5%	5,468,461	32.3%	24.8%
N/America	60,873	67.0%	1,126,815	6.7%	-60.4%
Oceania	4,442	4.9%	427,589	2.5%	-2.4%
Total	90,808		16,923,239		

Source: GC Annual Statistical Reports.

Between 1910 and 2016, the Adventist Church went from having 85.8% of its members in North America and Europe to having 91.9% on the other continents. Africa had the largest change in membership share, 38.8%; followed by Latin America, 23.5%; and then Asia, 17.8%. The shift of membership shares is a true success story that documents the fulfillment of Adventist world mission. The world church now looks to continents with large Adventist concentrations to fully engage their missional capacity in mission among the world's least evangelized peoples.

Globalization

The factor of globalization is closely related to population growth. Advances in communication and transportation have brought a free interchange of ideas, news, worldviews, products, money, and entertainment in a process called globalization. The Internet and social media bring people into routine contact with others far away. Live news broadcasts allow people to observe distant happenings as they unfold.

Globalization can be defined as "a social process in which the constraints of geography on social and cultural arrangements recede and in which people become increasingly aware that they are receding" (Waters 1995:3).

In the globalized world, people feel that they are members of both a local community and the global community. The merger between local and global in the human experience has produced a new word—"glocal." Being a glocal person produces inner conflict because one feels torn between loyalty to the local and attraction to the global. For example, wearing the same clothing (like Nike shoes) and using the same technology (like iPhones) is appealing. On the other hand, people rebel when they feel that foreign cultures and values are invading their own society. Political conflict erupts in the globalized world as nations weigh the benefits of international alliances and free trade as opposed to isolationist policies and high trade tariffs.

Mission benefits from globalization in many ways. Travel for mission is no longer the expensive, arduous task it once was. Routine contact with different cultures and religions provides contact for building relationships. Modern media offer new conduits for spreading the Gospel.

At the same time, globalization is a challenge for mission. Reactions by the local against the global sometimes produce anti-immigrant and anti-foreigner sentiments that block the relationship building so essential for effective mission among those most in need of the Gospel.

Urbanization

For the first time in history, more people live in urban than in rural areas. "In 1800 only 3% of humankind lived in cities," by 2007, the proportion was about 50%, and by 2100, about 90% will be urbanites. "By 2050, slum-dwellers will constitute 23% of the world's population, or nearly 2 billion people." The number of "meta-cities" (20 million-plus) will grow from 1 in the year 2000, to 9 in 2025, to 23 by 2050. "Most of the meta-cities will be vast, poorly governed and chaotic, with a huge proportion of their population living in slums in dire poverty" (Johnstone 2011:6-7).

The challenges of wholistic mission, that weds humanitarian service, evangelization, and disciple-making, are immense in the massive cities of our times. Missionary service is complicated by the violence, traffic congestion, and environmental pollution of cities. Yet, Christ's model of incarnational service makes accepting the difficulties associated with urban mission a normal part of Christian service. Christians can make unique contributions to humanity in troubled urban areas.

War and Terrorism

War and terrorism have assumed new proportions since the attacks on the World Trade Centers of September 11, 2001. The various wars of the Middle East and North Africa have produced floods of refugees in neighboring countries and Europe. ISIS and Al Qaeda have spread terror all around. Millions have died violent deaths. Into this living catastrophe comes the message of Jesus Christ and his peace that passes understanding. Peace making is more valid that ever as part of Christian mission.

Human Migration

Migration has been part of the human narrative since pre-historic times. But the scale of migration in the twenty-first century is unprecedented. The full range of human migration is too varied to describe in a brief section, but understanding the implications for mission is essential.

The *Oxford English Dictionary* defines migrant-related words as follows: *Refugee*, "A person who has been forced to leave his or her home and seek refuge elsewhere, especially in a foreign country, from war, religious persecution, political troubles, the effects of a natural disaster, etc.; a displaced person;" *Emigrant*, "One who removes from his own land to settle (permanently) in another;" *Immigrant*, "One who ... immigrates; a person who migrates into a country as a settler" (www.oed.com).

The United Nations reports that between 2000 and 2015, the number of international migrants of all kinds increased 41% to reach 244 million (www.un.org). The United Nations High Commission for Refugees (UNHCR) reports:

> We are now witnessing the highest levels of displacement on record. An unprecedented 65.6 million people around the world have been forced from home. Among them are nearly 22.5 million refugees, over half of whom are under the age of 18. There are also 10 million stateless people who have been denied a nationality and access to basic rights such as education, healthcare, employment and freedom of movement....Nearly 20 people are forcibly displaced every minute as a result of conflict or persecution. (www.unhcr.org)

Governments are responding to migration in different ways. Attitudes and perspectives about migration vary greatly between nations and political philosophies. But what are the major implications of human migration for Christian missions in this century?

First, Christians living in nations that receive many migrants need to be certain that they view migrants in a Christlike way. In their hearts, at church, and in their communities, Christians must view migrants as fellow humans, created in the image of God, who need the love of God. Governments are responsible to make and enforce laws and Christians can enter the political process at the ballot box or in other appropriate ways. But migrants who arrive in their communities are to be treated as Christ would treat them.

Second, refugees have a wide range of needs and problems calling for a wholistic missional response. Adventist mission has included a full range of ministries to human need around the world. Properly understood, Adventist mission also includes wholistic service for migrants when they arrive in one's home country from abroad.

Third, many Adventists are among the migrants who reach the United States, Canada, and Europe. They bring both challenges and potential for mission to the communities and churches where they settle. Some of the challenges come from their own need to develop an appropriate hybrid identity that blends their old with their new adopted cultures. The cultural style of being an Adventist has to be negotiated. Which elements of the culture of origin will they retain and which of the adopted culture will they adopt? Second and third generation immigrants face specific challenges that present a missional challenge for the church. Immigrants have great missional potential as they bring their gifts and commitment into new contexts. Immigrant churches are challenged to become more than Caribbean, Asian, or African enclaves in Europe, the United States, or Canada. Their missional task is to witness in a culturally contextualized way to the communities surrounding their churches.

Fourth, migration brings Muslims, Hindus, Buddhists, and others who used to live "over there" to live "over here," which may place them next door to an Adventist church on almost every continent. These transplanted peoples constitute an amazing opening for mission.

Epidemics and Disease

The list of diseases and epidemics that threaten humanity is long—AIDS, Ebola, SARS, Zika, Nipah, MRSA, and many more. Malaria and dysentery kill millions and obesity shortens lives. Alcohol, tobacco, and drug addiction destroy and devastate human lives. The comprehensive Adventist health message has never been a more important part of Adventist mission than it is today.

Climate Change and Resources Crisis

The ecological damage of the earth's land, sea, and atmosphere is well documented. The global crisis in food, energy, and water resources is closely related to climate change. As committed creationists, Adventists have a strong theological mandate to make the stewardship of Earth and its resources part of our mission to humanity. Humanitarian service includes ministering to the overwhelming needs of humanity.

Wealth Distribution and Corruption

Until the Industrial Revolution, wealth was distributed more-or-less equally around the globe. Today, the world's richest 2% own 50%, while the world's poorest 50% own only 1% of the global wealth. The uneven distribution of wealth is augmented by official corruption defined as "the misuse of entrusted power for private gain." Corrupt officials accepted bribes equaling about 10-20% of the Global Domestic Product, or about US$ 1 trillion in 2005. Corrupt bankers bend the rules to benefit themselves and collect excessive fees. Officials in developing nations divert oil revenues and rob sovereign wealth accounts (Johnstone 2011:12-13).

These realities greatly increase the number of people hopelessly caught in poverty and suffering and needing humanitarian services. Other implications for missions include the need to be highly ethical in the management of church and mission funds. Money wrongly taken from humanitarian funds denies relief to the most distressed. Also, people who are among the wealthier part of humanity need to have an unwavering commitment to relieve human suffering and support global mission. God gave the more wealthy what they have not because they are more worthy, but because he wants them to be partners in his mission.

Political, Civil, and Religious Liberties

The United Nations "Universal Declaration of Human Rights" of 1948 and the "International Bill of Human Rights" of 1989 were signed by most member nations, but are often disregarded today. Christian mission is concerned about all human rights and freedoms. Wholistic mission includes advocacy for the rights of women and girls, widows and orphans, street children, homeless people, prisoners of conscience, persecuted minorities, and many others.

The lack of freedom to worship touches missions directly. Religious freedom is restricted in many different degrees. Those restrictions range from social disapproval to rules limiting religious activity to church property, to total denial of the right to worship in any place, and to the threat of death for conversion. Some nations with dominant Muslim, Hindu, Buddhist, or communist populations enact laws prohibiting expatriate missionaries and criminalizing conversion to Christianity.

The variations of religious freedom create a patchwork of different conditions to be navigated by Christian missions. The term "restricted access nations" is used for those that deny access in typical ways for Christian missions. A great portion of humanity lives in regions or nations where access for missions is challenging.

Chapter 13

Introduction to Mission Strategy

~•∽

Introduction

Strategic planning is a phrase heard frequently in the secular business world. Mission strategy is not unlike business strategy in some respects but the motives are different. Mission strategy aims to bring humans of every people group, in every geographic location, into an encounter with the Gospel of Jesus Christ. The goal of that encounter is that they would receive eternal life and salvation through Christ. The language of strategic planning that follows can sound secular but the presupposition of this chapter and the whole book is that planning for mission is a very spiritual task, immersed in prayer, and guided by God the Holy Spirit.

There are different attitudes toward mission strategy (Terry and Payne 2013:6-10). The traditional or standard view is that what worked in the past will continue to work in the present and future. After all, neither God nor the Gospel change, therefore, why should mission strategy change? Many readers will quickly challenge this assumption. Cultures are dynamic and constantly changing. The printed tract that was once so effective now has to be augmented by video, Internet, and social media. Societies differ greatly from each other. Public meetings are attractive among some peoples but not others. Some peoples are highly literate while others have oral traditions of communication.

Another option is the stay-out-of-God's-way attitude. Because the Holy Spirit is like a wind that blows constantly where no one knows (John 3:8), the church should not get in His way by doing any planning. This perspective is not acceptable because it removes the element of intentionality, assessment, and accountability from missions. Individually, missionaries are relieved of accountability because they can claim success for whatever happens. Stewardship of human and material resources demands that methods be constantly assessed for the sake of improvement. The Spirit does produce the successes of mission, but human agents must do their very best.

A third option can be called the get-the-ball-rolling-and-step-away or the diffusion approach. Good plans are made and started but the "process and results" are left to God. An example would be conducting evangelistic meetings in a new area without making plans to lead converts to mature discipleship after the meetings are finished. While the Spirit does lead in unanticipated ways that make His servants sometimes feel like mere observers, a responsible mission strategy focuses on the entire discipleship process.

The responsible, contextualized approach assumes that peoples are very different from each other in different times and places. For example, what worked in 1915 Australia may not work in 2015 Australia. What works today in Mexico probably will not work today in Indonesia. Methods that have served well among Methodists, Presbyterians, and Catholics do not work well among Muslims, Hindus, and Buddhists. Traditional public preaching continues to be effective in some places, but not among large sectors of humanity. Methods that have worked in the past may be effective and, if so, they should be used. But the church has a sacred obligation to assess and evaluate the effectiveness of its methods for the sake of potential recipients of the Adventist message and for the stewardship of its limited resources. Adventist mission is about conveying the Adventist message effectively by whatever biblically faithful methods work best.

Defining Mission Strategy

Strategic planning is a very important yet sometimes neglected dimension of Christian mission on the field. In modern times, strategic planning is a highly developed and specialized activity in many fields of human endeavor, including missiology (see Terry and Payne 2013; Malphurs 2005; Dayton and Fraser 1990). Aubrey Malphurs defines strategic planning as

> the envisioning process that a point leader uses with a team of leaders on a regular basis to think and act so as to design and redesign a specific ministry model that accomplishes the Great Commission in their unique ministry context. (2005:26)

Strategic planning is not a single event but a continual process that casts a vision of where to go and how to get there. Once a vision for the future is articulated, the process works backward to the present to plan the steps needed to get there. The first step taken is the first move into the future. When the plan is made it must be implemented or else the whole process is in vain.

The leader works through the process with a team of valued, spiritually gifted colleagues. Planning is a very thoughtful activity, both theologically and practically. A shared theology of mission undergirds good strategic planning. Because every situation is different, the team avoids generic planning, but always makes plans for particular contexts.

In wholistic Adventist mission, strategic planning is a process that develops a comprehensive ministry plan to fulfill the Great Commission in specific contexts. Strategic mission plans are implemented by methods and tactics that are appropriate for specific contexts and people groups.

Mission Strategy and Mission Tactics

The mission strategy process starts by asking a series of questions:

1. Who are we? How do we understand ourselves and our mission theologically? What is our history in mission? What do we bring with us collectively to an engagement for mission? What cultural traits do we bring with us personally?

2. Who is to be encountered in mission? Which people group(s)? What are their cultural traits and religious beliefs and practices? What is their perception of us?

3. What is the setting and context of the missional encounter? What is the history, economics, and social context of the people group? What is the history of their relationship with Christians and with the nation(s) we come from?

4. What are our goals? The broad goal is to conduct wholistic mission aimed at establishing worshiping fellowships of disciples who become disciple-makers and to address human needs. With a particular people group, what will be the best sequence of steps toward that goal?

5. When people accept Jesus Christ, how shall we continue to serve and minister to them? If there is already a local church, how shall we integrate them into the community? How shall they be led to mature discipleship in that church? If there is no local church, how shall we establish a worshiping community? If a public place of worship is permissible, how shall it be designed? If a public place of worship is not permissible, where will a private place of worship be? What long-term plans shall we make to disciple the converts?

6. Who are the people who will do the work, what are their gifts, what is their preparation for ministry? What training and support do we need to give them? How shall we deploy them?

7. What material resources do we have and what do we need? Given that the money in hand is always less than we could wish, what priorities shall we have? How can we increase funding?

The answers to these strategic questions (and many others) become a set of mission tactics. Money is spent in certain ways and people are assigned to specific tasks in specific places. Mission goals are achieved by individual Christians using their spiritual gifts faithfully in teamwork. Some are lay people and pastors in local churches working in their communities. Others are pioneering cross-cultural missionaries planting churches where none exist. The very best mission strategies come to nothing without good mission tactics performed by faithful Christians working as a team. Conversely, the best mission tactics are diminished if not guided by well-planned strategy.

The Paradoxes of Mission Strategy

Strategic planning for mission includes paradoxical and seemingly contradictory elements (Terry and Payne 2005:19-23).

The first paradox is that the sovereign God has always worked his mission through human plans. Biblical characters like Abraham, Moses, David, Peter, and Paul made plans for fulfilling God's mission. Modern missionaries and mission committees must necessarily make and implement human plans. The humbling challenge is to remember that the planning is for God's mission even though human means and methods are used. No person or committee owns God's mission.

"Strategic planning is both a linear and nonlinear process" and "both an art and a science" (19, 21). Strategy makers think through a sequence of action steps rationally and logically. Demographic and financial numbers are analyzed. Some of the plan unfolds sequentially, step by step, from start to finish. However, the planning process also uses more subjective human experiences, insights, and impressions. On the field, some parts of the plan unfold simultaneously or out of any particular sequence.

Strategic planning and implementation must be both flexible and inflexible. Long-term plans are held firmly but day-by-day action steps are addressed with flexibility as problems are encountered. "Strategic development is both a *determined* process and an *emerging* process, involving both certainty and uncertainty" (20). Unanticipated developments usually make the process somewhat messy and disorderly. This means that the plan needs to remain a servant rather than a master of mission. Yet, well developed plans should not be tossed aside when the first obstacles emerge.

Strategic planning involves both learning the lessons of known history and reaching into the unknown future. The history of mission is a great teacher. Knowing the history of mission prevents planners from constantly "reinventing the wheel" and helps them avoid repeating the mistakes of the past. At the same time, making plans for mission involves reaching into the uncharted and unknowable future. No one has yet done mission twenty or fifty years in the future. Some aspects of mission are common to every time period and among every people group. Other aspects have to be customized for every time period and people group. Understanding which is one of the great challenges of strategic planning for mission.

Strategic mission planning is a simple process that is difficult to implement. Mistake-making humans are the ones implementing the plans and they do have failures. Because real life is messy, things happen out of sequence, at the same time, or at wrong times and the best plans get upset. Knowing when to hold firmly to the plan or when to make adjustments is challenging. Learning the right lessons from the past and reaching forward into the unknown future is a constant challenge.

The inevitable challenges of implementing the very best strategic plans could lead one to abandon the process entirely; however, the church's material resources and member giftedness can also be used pragmatically in the best possible way. Without strategic planning, truly committed members invest themselves and their resources in uncoordinated, overlapping endeavors and their combined accomplishments are diminished.

Ultimately, what empowers the church to persist in carefully planned and well-implemented mission is a firm conviction that God is the sovereign Lord of mission. His mission will succeed because of his Spirit and in spite of the human fallibility of his servants. As the Lord said to Paul, "'My grace is sufficient for you, for my power is made perfect in weakness.' Therefore, I will boast all the more gladly of my weaknesses, so that the power of Christ may rest upon me" (2 Cor 12:9).

Strategic Planning in the Church

Strategic planning starts with the local church—the hub of mission. In simplified terms, the local church makes strategic plans by identifying the people groups within its territory, making plans to reach each group in ways that are best suited to the group, and then implementing the plans. The local conference or field works through the local churches it its territory by empowering, facilitating, augmenting, and coordinating their strategic planning and implementation. The unions and divisions coordinate strategic planning and implementation for increasingly larger territories and the General Conference provides coordination for the world church.

All of the administrative bodies of the church focus or should focus on the local church and its spiritually gifted members. For the unevangelized millions of Lagos, or London, or Lahore, the local Adventist congregations represents the entire world church and its message. The world church will have accomplished its mission, for church members living everywhere have become committed, growing members of a local church; therefore, the combined strategic focus of the global church must be to plant and facilitate local churches everywhere. In territories and among people groups where Adventists have no presence or an inadequate presence for effective mission, the administrative bodies of the church take initiatives to plant and develop effectively witnessing local churches.

Strategic planning has become increasingly important in Adventist mission because of the church's much larger size and changed economic patterns. In 1910, the North American Division (NAD) had 67% of the membership and received 70% of the church's tithe. By 2015, the NAD had only about 6.5% of the membership and received 43% of world church tithe. The 93.5% of the membership outside the NAD is located in 214 other nations, many of which are comparatively poor. As the next chapter will show in detail, the world membership is distributed unevenly, with only about one-quarter of the members living among three-quarters of the world population. Having a much larger membership who can work together in God's mission to humanity is a great blessing; however, intentional strategic planning is needed to maximize the effectiveness of the church's work (*GC Annual Statistical Reports*).

In addition to its official organizations, the church now has a multitude of unofficial "self-supporting," "independent," or "supporting ministry" mission agencies. In some cases, official and unofficial organizations work without much strategic coordination, causing inefficiency, duplication, and diminished effectiveness. However good the mission methods employed may be, they lose overall impact by not being part of a unified mission strategy. The challenge of integrating official and unofficial Adventist mission endeavors into a shared, effective strategy for mission has become urgent.

Mission Strategy in History

The history of mission contains many valuable lessons regarding mission strategy. The lessons start with the early church's greatest missionary—the Apostle Paul.

The Apostle Paul's Mission Strategy

Paul did not have a mission strategy in the modern sense of a formal master plan based on statistical, cultural, political, economic, and religious analysis. "However, it is clear that over time Paul developed a pattern of ministry that could be described as a strategy. In other words, he developed a set of principles that characterized His ministry" (Terry and Payne 2013:55). Overall, his strategy can be characterized as flexible and dynamic as he responded to the peoples he worked among with the guidance of the Holy Spirit. Paul and the other apostles worked in a historical period so very different from ours that we cannot expect to find a check list of methods in the NT that we can simply repeat. However, there are principles in Paul's work to follow.

Paul's effective work in the Roman Empire was facilitated by several factors. Rome had established peace among its diverse peoples (*Pax Romana*) and unified its territories with a good road system. Most people spoke Greek and their culture was shaped by Greek philosophy. Jews of the Diaspora had planted synagogues all over the empire, in which both Jews and Gentile converts worshiped. The Jewish belief in the one true God who is personally engaged with humans had penetrated the pagan environment ahead of the apostles. All of these factors made the first century "the fullness of time" (Gal 4:4), both for Jesus and his apostolic missionaries.

Paul's basic strategy was to preach the Gospel orally, unite converts in local house churches, and appoint leaders. He then worked to lead the newly planted churches to mature discipleship that included their planting more churches. Paul wrote many epistles, some of which are in the NT canon, as part of the discipling process. He did not "hover" over his churches, but he stayed with them long enough to get them well established and then made repeat visits.

Several principles are discernible in Paul's work: (1) Paul always stayed in touch with Antioch, the church that commissioned him and Barnabas (Acts 13); (2) he restricted his work to territory that was small enough to allow continued supervision of the newly planted churches; (3) Paul planted churches in urban centers that could serve as centers for witnessing to surrounding towns and villages; (4) he usually started in new places with Jewish synagogues where both Jews and Gentile converts already knew the Hebrew Bible and worshiped God; (5) because Paul was usually the first to enter a new area, he focused on the most receptive people; (6) his feeling of responsibility for new converts caused him to spend extended time with them, to make repeated visits when possible, and to send written epistles; (7) Paul demonstrated the value of team ministry and the constant mentoring of junior missionaries; (8) he became "all things to all people" (1 Cor 9:19-23), using every method and adapting to every cultural style and preference that was consistent with biblical truth; and (9) miraculous signs and wonders were a regular part of the missionary practice of Paul and the other apostolic missionaries.

Several factors contributed to Paul's amazing success as the earliest church's leading missionary: (1) Paul was deeply convinced that God had called him to be a missionary to the Gentiles (Rom 1:1; 1 Cor 1:1; Gal 1:15), (2) his whole life was dedicated to doing the will of God (Phil 1:21-23), and (3) he relied totally on the power of the Holy Spirit in his missionary work (1 Cor 2:4-5).

Strategy in the Early Church: AD 100-400

The apostolic era ended when John died in Ephesus (c. AD 95-100). The Twelve Apostles, with Paul, Barnabas, Timothy, and the other leading missionaries, had spread the Gospel far and wide by that time. When Jerusalem was destroyed in AD 70, its population had been scattered and gradually the church had become more Greek and less Jewish. As the apostolic era ended, there were an estimated 7,500 Christians who met in urban house churches in Palestine, Asia Minor, Greece, Cyprus, Crete, and Rome (Terry and Payne 2013:63).

The same factors that facilitated mission in the apostolic era generally prevailed, except for a change in the official status of the church. Christianity was at first viewed by as a sect of Judaism and thus a legal religion. After AD 100, Christianity lost its legal status and was viewed as a secret society that threatened the empire. Christians suffered localized, sporadic persecutions until AD 249, when Decius ordered a massive campaign of persecution for those who refused to worship the emperor. Diocletian ordered empire-wide persecution in 303 that led to some 1,500 martyrdoms. Eventually, Constantine issued the Edict of Milan in AD 313 that legalized Christianity and ended the persecution.

In spite of the persecution, the church grew in all directions in this period. By AD 200, Christianity was well established in all parts of the Roman Empire. Believers were present in all levels of Roman society. During the third century, Christianity grew in rural areas in response to political and economic stress in the cities. In the time of Constantine there were an estimated three to five million Christians, but they were spread very unevenly.

The religion proclaimed by the Apostles retained its missionary character as time progressed. The Pauline model of the full-time, itinerant missionary continued to be used. Bishops, like Irenaeus (130-200) and Origen (185-254), led pagans to Christ. However, most converts were won by lay people who witnessed for Christ during their daily activities. People like traders and soldiers carried the Gospel wherever they went. Women played an important role as leaders of house churches in their own homes and by witnessing in their communities.

Public preaching continued as a method, but teaching (catechesis) also played a major role. Catechetical schools trained presbyters (pastors) and sent them on missions. House churches were places of hospitality used for training. Literature evangelism became an effective means of conveying handwritten "apologies, letters, polemics, and ... Scriptures" (Terry and Payne 2013:70). Although the Apostles had circulated their epistles, the routine distribution of literature was an innovation of the early centuries. Social ministries on behalf of the poor, widows, orphans, and the sick functioned alongside evangelism. Mission was the work of local churches and there were no formal mission agencies. The blood of the martyrs was a powerful witness.

Several factors accounted for the church's growth from under 10,000 to perhaps 5 million between AD 100 and 500:

1. Only the power and blessing of God the Holy Spirit on the efforts of the church can account for the growth. The social, economic, and political factors that favored Christianity cannot be credited by themselves for the phenomenal growth.
2. The believers were zealous, committed, and self-sacrificing in their work for God.
3. The message of love, forgiveness, and eternal life was greatly appealing in the pagan environment.
4. "The organization and discipline of the church aided its growth" (Terry and Payne 2013:71).
5. Christianity was a universal, inclusive religion that valued both genders equally and embraced every social, economic, and ethnic group.
6. Although they were not people of sinless perfection, the moral-ethical lives of Christians were a great contrast to typical lives in the pagan environment.

Strategy in Roman Catholic Missions: AD 500-1600

Pope Gregory I (d. 604) set the pattern of Roman Catholic mission in the Middle Ages. The theological basis for mission was sacramentalism, which sees the church as the reservoir and dispenser of divine grace. The sacraments, notably baptism and the Lord's Supper, are means by which sinners receive grace and salvation. Therefore, the main goal of missions was to make the sacraments available to non-Christians to save them from eternal hellfire.

Pope Gregory I used a four-part strategy to Christianize Europe: (1) Monastic orders established churches and ministered the sacraments; (2) he required rulers and kings to evangelize their subjects; (3) bishops were required to evangelize their territories; and (4) he established the method of making accommodations to local cultures as the way to introduce Christianity.

The Catholic monk was the leading missionary of the Middle Ages. When a new area was to be entered, a "mother" monastery would send a band of monks to plant a church and establish a new monastery. When the new monastery was strong enough it would repeat the process. Monasteries were the main centers of worship, pastoral care, education, commerce, and health care in medieval Europe.

The Crusades were definitely not mission strategies, but they did make Christians aware of the mission challenges among Muslims. Raymond Lull (1235-1315), a Franciscan who worked among Muslims in North Africa, developed an excellent mission strategy based on four principles: (1) Missionaries to Muslims must have good training that included knowing the Arabic language, the culture, and the Qur'an; (2) missionaries need to understand apologetics to interact well with Muslim beliefs and practices; (3) missionaries should know how to preach and teach effectively among Muslims; and, (4) if necessary, missionaries must be willing to die as martyrs.

The association of mission and colonialization started in the fifteenth century. In 1493 Pope Alexander VI divided the newly discovered lands of the world between Spain and Portugal. In exchange, they agreed to Christianize their colonies. The agents of mission were priests and monks working with soldiers and civil servants. Conversion was by persuasion if possible but by coercion if necessary. Catholic sacramental theology said that people could be saved from hell through the sacraments, even if they were administered against their will. Through the strategy of accommodation, converts were allowed to retain much of their pre-conversion religions and cultures, in the belief that many generations were needed to make them real Catholics.

The strategy of *tabula rasa* (clean slate) also guided colonial missions of the era. The *tabula rasa* theory assumed that every aspect of pre-Christian culture is evil and must be swept aside and replaced. The Portuguese and Spanish cultures, seen as "Christian cultures," would replace the local cultures in the *tabula rasa* mission theory.

The ironic combination of the accommodation (allowing many non-Christian religious elements to remain) and *tabula rasa* (replacing local cultures) mission strategies produced syncretism on a grand scale that is still visible in the former Spanish and Portuguese colonies of Latin America. Many voodoo characters became Catholic saints and pagan festivals became church festivals. The discussion of contextualization engages issues related to the accommodation and *tabula rasa* strategies.

Matteo Ricci (1552-1610) was a Jesuit missionary who is famous for his work in China. Ricci mastered the Chinese language and culture and had access to the imperial court. Applying the strategy of accommodation, he used Confucian terms for biblical words and concepts and allowed converts to continue venerating their ancestors. His approach was not accepted by Franciscan and Dominican monks and, as a result, the Chinese Rites Controversy followed. The issue was whether ancestor veneration and other Confucian rituals were merely a cultural form (Ricci's position) or whether the forms retained their original unchristian meaning and were thus syncretism. Some Franciscans and Dominicans came to support the Jesuit position, but Pope Clement XI ruled against the rituals and the work of Ricci.

Protestants must remember that until the Reformation, the Catholic Church was the only Christian church, except for some very small groups. Catholic missionaries of the medieval era should be credited for much good work. Without their work, no foundation would have existed upon which Protestantism could do the work of the Reformation and eventually Protestant world missions.

Strategy of Early Protestant Missions

The Protestant Reformers perceived their mission as reforming the Catholic Church in Europe. In 1500, Christians made up only about 18% of the world population, but about 92% of all Christians were in Europe (Johnstone 2011:51). Three centuries would pass before Protestants would put significant strategies and structures into place for global mission. There were, however, some pioneering Protestants who took early steps in world missions.

John Eliot (1604-1690) was a Puritan in the British American colony of Massachusetts who worked with the Algonquin tribe. He translated the Bible and started "Praying Towns" populated by new converts. Eliot trained Algonquins as evangelists and altogether about 4,000 were converted. His "Praying Town" strategy is an example of the "extraction" strategy, where converts are moved away from their people groups into Christian enclaves. Most of Eliot's converts died in King Philip's War of 1675, either in the fighting or in internment camps.

Philipp Spener (1635-1705) and Nikolaus von Zinzendorf (1700-1760) were leaders of the Moravian Pietist missionary movement headquartered in Herrnhut, Germany. "Between 1732 and 1760 this church of 600 members dispatched 226 missionaries" to the Caribbean, Greenland, Ghana, South Africa, and the American colonies (2013:84). The Pietist missionaries comprised the first significant Protestant missionary movement. They were self-supporting laypersons who followed Paul's tentmaker model. They were required to learn the language and culture and translate the Bible. Christ-centered schools and personal Bible teaching were the preferred methods of evangelism. Self-governing churches were planted as soon as possible. Their strategy is unique because they gave first priority to the most difficult places instead of starting where people were most receptive.

William Carey (1761-1834) is called the father of the modern missionary movement that made the nineteenth century the "great century of Protestant missions." In 1792, Carey published *An Enquiry into the Obligations of Christians to Use Means for the Conversion of the Heathens*.

The *Enquiry* was a pioneering document. First, Carey pioneered the field of missiometrics, which is the use of demographics for the purpose of planning mission strategy. Using the best statistics available to him, Carey analyzed the populations of the continents and outlined the challenges of global mission.

Second, Carey called upon Christians to use "means" for missions. This meant raising money and using administrative structures for intentional missions to the world. His Baptist Missionary Society was an independent organization that worked only to serve world missions and became the dominant pattern for Protestant missions to the present day. His Missionary Society was Baptist, but was not structurally connected to either a Baptist denomination or local church.

Carey went to India in 1793, where he worked with William Ward and Joshua Marshman near Calcutta. Their strategy included learning the language, culture, and religion to preach and teach the Gospel. They translated the Bible, established churches, and trained pastors to lead the churches. Carey never returned to England.

Adoniram Judson (1788-1850) went to Burma in 1813. His strategy was also based on the principle of learning the local language, culture, and religion. He translated the "Judson Bible" directly from Hebrew and Greek into Burmese. Intense discipleship training was given to new converts and missionaries were challenged to lifetime service.

Robert Moffatt (1795-1883) went to South Africa in 1816 and later to Botswana. His strategy was similar to the other Protestant missionary pioneers. Moffatt established a mission station at Kuruman that became a standard feature in Protestant missions. The mission station was a headquarters compound that supported the comprehensive work of missions in the region. At Kuruman, there was missionary and local staff housing, a school, printing press, medical clinic, farm, dairy, workshops, orphanage, and other facilities. The mission station model has been criticized when it has been a variation of the extraction method, where converts withdraw from their indigenous communities. However, at Kuruman and elsewhere, mission stations served as necessary and appropriate centers from which local workers could move into surrounding areas to plant local churches and schools.

Strategy of Faith Missions

Hudson Taylor (1832-1905) founded the China Inland Mission (CIM) in 1865 as one of the first "faith missions." The CIM focused on the interior of China, far away from the coastlands where most other mission agencies worked. Instead of depending on denominational structures or making direct appeals for support, CIM missionaries prayed in faith for their support. Taylor did not require formal theological or medical education of his missionaries, like most agencies did, and he recruited single missionaries, usually women. China Inland Mission was interdenominational and its administrative headquarters were located in China. Missionaries identified closely with the Chinese, learning their language and culture, wearing Chinese clothing, using their hairstyles, eating their food, and living in their houses. To start with, CIM used the "diffusion strategy" of fast, itinerant evangelism as opposed to the "concentration strategy" of church planting. Taylor was eventually forced to concede that church planting was an essential strategy for lasting results. China Inland Mission followed Paul's example by starting in urban centers and then spreading to surrounding villages.

Other examples of the faith mission strategy include Christian Missionary Alliance (1887), Evangelical Alliance Mission (1890), Central African Mission (1890), Sudan Interior Mission (1895), and African Inland Mission (1895). Over the years, names have changed and some agencies have merged.

Strategy on the American Frontier

In the eighteenth century, the First Great Awakening (c. 1730-1755) swept through Protestant Europe and the American colonies, bringing great spiritual renewal. The movement included pastors like Jonathan Edwards and Gilbert Tennent but George Whitefield was the leading light. Whitefield preached to large open-air revival meetings throughout the American colonies and in Europe. Numerous churches were planted and in New England an estimated 40,000 new members joined new or existing churches (Terry and Payne 2013:97).

The Second Great Awakening (c. 1790-1850) brought another wave of revival. The central feature was the camp meeting revival. The Methodist strategy was to conduct evangelism and plant churches, which were then led by lay people and served by "circuit rider" pastors. The pastors used their horses to travel from church to church on their assigned circuits, performing weddings, funerals, and communion. Bishops supervised the circuit riders. Members were organized into societies that were divided into classes to study the Bible, pray, and provide fellowship. Churches gathered for regional camp meetings. The Baptists used farmer-pastors to lead local congregations. The Adventist pioneers used the Methodist camp meeting and other methods borrowed from their mostly Methodist roots.

Strategy of Indigenous Mission

In the nineteenth century, mission thinkers started promoting an intentionally indigenous strategy based on Paul's methods. Their goal was to plant churches that reflected local cultural traits and could reproduce themselves in other church plants. Several leaders were famous for developing and promoting the indigenous strategy.

Henry Venn (1796-1873) was director of the Church Missionary Society in England while Rufus Anderson (1796-1880) led the American Board of Commissioners for Foreign Missions. Together, Venn and Anderson provided leadership for a major part of nineteenth century Protestant missions. They advocated the "three-self" model of planting churches that were self-supporting, self-governing, and self-propagating. The three-selves should be implemented as quickly as possible and missionaries should move to other unevangelized areas. Venn advocated "euthanasia" in missions, meaning that missionaries should depart as quickly as the local church was able to fulfill the three-self model.

John Nevius (1829-1893) was a Presbyterian who expanded the three-self model and applied it in China and Korea. His model was not very influential in China because not many missionaries accepted and used it. But historians give his plan credit for much of the expansion of Christianity in Korea. The "Nevius Plan" can be summarized as follows (Terry and Payne 2013:105).

1. Christians should continue to live in their neighborhoods and pursue their occupations, being self-supporting and witnessing to their co-workers and neighbors.
2. Missions should develop only programs and institutions that the national church desires and can support.
3. The national churches should call out and support their own pastors.
4. Church buildings should be built in the native style with money and materials given by the church members.
5. Intensive biblical and doctrinal instruction should be provided for church leaders every year.

Roland Allen (1868-1947) served as an Anglican missionary in China and Korea. He is known for his two books, *Missionary Methods: St. Paul's or Ours* (1912) and *The Spontaneous Expansion of the Church* (1927). Allen affirmed the three-self model and said missionaries should follow Paul's model of mission. They should trust the Holy Spirit to care for the churches they planted and move on to plant new churches. Converts should be taught in a way that was easy for them to understand and replicate. Instead of establishing complex organizations, like colleges, schools, and hospitals that locals would struggle to maintain, missionaries should keep church structures simple. Local churches should raise and manage their own money. Local believers, rather than missionaries, should minister to human needs to avoid the "rice Christian" problem where people join the church to get food. Local believers should be encouraged to use their spiritual gifts quickly in ministry.

Allan Tippett (1911-1988), anthropologist and missiologist, expanded the Venn and Anderson three-self model to a six-self model.

1. *Self-image*. The church sees itself as being independent from the mission, that is, the church has self-identity It is serving as Christ's church in its locality.
2. *Self-functioning*. The church is capable of carrying on all the normal functions of a church—evangelism and missions, worship, discipling, fellowship, and ministry —without the missionaries.
3. *Self-determining*. The church can and does make its own decisions (described as "self-governing" in earlier writings). The local churches do not depend on the missionary to make their decisions for them; rather, they rely on the guidance of the Holy Spirit and the Holy Bible. Tippett echoes Venn in saying that expatriate mission must die for the local church to be born.
4. *Self-supporting*. The church bears its own financial burdens and finances its own service projects. The national church supports itself with the tithes and offerings given by its own members rather than with financial assistance from abroad.
5. *Self-propagation*. The national church sees itself as responsible for carrying out the Great Commission. The church gives itself whole heartedly to evangelism and missions—locally, nationally, and internationally.
6. *Self-giving*. An indigenous church knows the social needs of its community and endeavors to minister to those needs. (Terry and Payne 2013:107-108)

Paul Hiebert (1932-2007) is noted for adding "self-theologizing" to the list of "selves" in mission strategy (1985:195). While Tippet's six-selves are expansions of Venn and Anderson's three-selves, Hiebert's self-theologizing made a new contribution to missiological thinking. Hiebert did not mean that members of a denomination in one area should develop doctrines that depart from the shared doctrines of their denomination. He meant that believers in every culture have both the responsibility and privilege of addressing their own issues by the principles of the Bible. For example, some peoples have traditions of polygamy or ancestor worship. If so, they must work through those issues for themselves, with the support and guidance of a missionary in the early stages of their Christian journey. Mature church communities will do self-theologizing with more independence, though in harmony with the "global hermeneutical community" of their own denomination. Hiebert recommends that believers from different cultures should be constantly linked in a multicultural dialogue so that they can share their perspectives for the sake of a more unified and enhanced theology (216). He describes a process for self-theologizing that he calls "critical contextualization" that is discussed in chapter 11 (Hiebert 1994:75).

In summary, leading mission thinkers and practitioners in the early stages of the modern missionary movement intended to plant culturally appropriate, biblically faithful churches. Their good intentions were not always fulfilled because they lacked the insights of cultural anthropology and better developed missiology that are now available. The missiological theory for faithful contextualization was not well developed until the 1990s by people like Charles Kraft and Paul Hiebert.

Achieving self-support has always been an issue when missionaries come from relatively wealthy economies to serve among relatively poor peoples. If the local church is required to be self-supporting from the very beginning, its growth can be very slow. On the other hand, if new churches receive subsidies from abroad for their own pastoral salaries and other expenses, they develop habits of dependency that inhibit maturity in the long term. Adventists have traditionally given more support during the early stages, making dependency an issue.

The development of institutions like colleges, hospitals, and publishing houses presents another challenge. On one hand, such institutions support the wholistic, comprehensive mission that is so needed in the developing world. But institutions often require continued subsidies and outside support to maintain quality operation. Mission history makes some things clear:

First, the desired outcome needs to be in clear focus from the very beginning of a mission initiative. When the end-goal is in sight, the methods used along the way can be planned more accurately to achieve the goal. With regard to self-support, some kind of compromise between requiring self-support from the very beginning and providing complete funding from abroad must be made. As churches mature, they need to be gradually weaned from operating subsidies.

Second, methods must be reproducible and sustainable by local believers at their educational and economic levels to the fullest extent of their capacity.

Third, Adventist ecclesiology of a global church fellowship means that local churches and institutions must not be abandoned at a sub-functional level as the congregationalist model might suggest. Adventist missiology encourages continued support and participation by the world church where local churches have a limited capacity. However, the danger of long-term dependency needs to be kept in focus.

To illustrate these points, because Adventist mission is wholistic, medical ministry in economically challenged nations is appropriate. Outside assistance is sometimes offered to hospitals to enhance their effectiveness because of the high costs associated with medical care. On the other hand, local churches and administrative units are generally self-supporting. Educational institutions have played a vital role in Adventist missions by providing long-term, in-depth discipleship training. Education is also a part of wholistic mission that provides educated professionals in many disciplines in economically challenged nations.

Mission Station Strategy

In the nineteenth century, when many mission stations were opened, the large urban centers that exist today were often small villages or towns. Populations were relatively small and mostly rural. In that era, mission stations were often significant centers of activity in rural areas, similar to the monasteries of the

Middle Ages. During the twentieth century, transportation networks were developed and many small towns became large urban centers. These shifts have required a change in mission strategy. Some mission stations, like the Presbyterian Livingstonia Mission of northern Malawi, have become completely isolated from transportation networks and population centers. Other mission stations have remained viable in their areas. Broadly speaking, mission strategy must now focus on urban centers with an appropriate range of wholistic ministries.

Strategy and the Church Growth Movement

Donald McGavran (1897-1990) was one of the most influential missiologists of the twentieth century, whose work gave birth to the Church Growth Movement (McIntosh 2015). He was born in India and served there for thirty-four years, in the footsteps of his parents and grandparents. He was perplexed by the very different rates of church growth in adjacent missionary districts. The work of J. Waskom Pickett caught McGavran's attention. Pickett had studied "mass movements" to Christ in India and McGavran continued the research. McGavran's seminal volume, *The Bridges of God*, summarized his findings and was revolutionary in its time (1955; 2005).

McGavran objected to the mission station approach when it extracted individual converts from among their natural cultural affinity groups and placed them into artificial communities. "People movements" into the church could happen, he said, when appropriate methods for specific groups were used. Individuals within natural affinity groups could be well instructed and the whole group could become Christian. The natural ties that bind people's hearts together were the "bridges" to be used to make disciples, not just converts. "Large numbers" would become disciples "by the conversion of small groups over a period of years" (McGavran 2005:13). New converts would use their social networks as natural bridges to draw relatives and friends into the faith. To be clear, McGavran did not advocate sweeping large groups into the church with only superficial individual conversions.

The Church Growth Movement that came from McGavran's pioneering concepts continues to be influential, although its influence peaked in the 1980s. In 1965 he became the dean of the School of World Missions at Fuller Theological Seminary, where he recruited outstanding faculty like Arthur Glasser, Ralph Winter, Alan Tippett, Peter Wagner, and Charles Kraft. Elmer Town and Gary McIntosh (2004) have edited an excellent evaluation of the Church Growth Movement, which includes some criticisms.

The Church Growth Movement has a number of principles that can be summarized as follows (Terry and Payne 2013:119-123):

1. The evangelization of God's lost sheep is central. McGavran did not reject social ministries but believed that the improvement of people's social-material lives comes as a natural by-product of "Gospel lift." When people

come to Christ, the change they experience in their lifestyles benefits their families and communities. Adventists can affirm the reality of "Gospel lift" that happens when converts receive education, give up bad habits, and live better lives. However, Adventists have historically been more intentional with social ministries than McGavran advocated. People can become active Christians but remain in dire need of intentional humanitarian aid even when they abandon any harmful lifestyle habits they may have.

2. Nation-states, cities, and other politically defined groupings are actually "cultural mosaics of people groups" (120) that must be systematically identified, researched, and evangelized using appropriate methods for each group. Cities with well-established churches usually have people groups that are hidden from the churches until they search for them. A wide variety of methods are needed to reach the wide variety of people groups in every place.

3. The discipling, teaching, and nurturing of new converts must continue, along with evangelization of new people groups. Evangelization should not pause while converts are "perfected" because growth in Christ occurs in the act of sharing the Gospel with others. The opposite mistake is to rush on with evangelism with little or no attention to teaching and nurturing new converts.

4. Cultural anthropology is a powerful aid for mission that should be used in training, planning, and implementation.

5. McGavran identified a number of hindrances to mission that must be identified and avoided. Inadequate mission statistics prevent the continual evaluation needed for effective mission. Poor administration that rewards high and low effectiveness equally hinders mission. Failure to adapt to local cultures is a hindrance. Fuzzy language in discussing mission hinders its effectiveness. Simply saying that a "work" or "witness" or "fellowship" was "initiated" may not describe anything of real significance. High-sounding phrases are often meaningless. Overly optimistic promotions and reports hinder mission. Certain theological hindrances are to be avoided. Universalist theology, that believes all humans will somehow be saved, directly contradicts the call of conversion to Christ. Pluralist theology, that believes all religions lead equally to salvation, undercuts the uniqueness of Christianity and Adventism.

6. The theory of "presence evangelism," that Christians should only mingle with people to show God's love without overtly witnessing to them, was against the Great Commission, said McGavran. A Christlike presence and loving relationship are important, but at the right time and in the right way Christians should make an intentional witness for Christ.

7. Resources and personnel should be concentrated among responsive people groups. The Parable of the Sower or Soils teaches that the Gospel seed should be planted in good soil, said McGavran. Peoples become uniquely

receptive at certain times and should be reached at those times. Conditions among unreceptive peoples should be monitored for movements toward increased receptivity.

8. "Missionaries should use reproducible methods" (122) instead of importing methods and technologies that locals cannot afford or maintain. Local churches should be able to continue effective ministries without the direction or financial support of missionaries.

9. Planting new churches is the most effective method of church growth because "new churches are more evangelistic than older churches and more active in church planting" (122).

10. Culturally homogenous churches grow faster that culturally diverse churches. McGavran was criticized as a racist for this "homogeneous unit principle." However, he "was simply making a sociological observation. He noted that people like to worship with people like themselves, and they are more likely to come to Christ if they can do so without crossing language, racial, or cultural barriers" (123). He did not intend to plant churches that would remain permanent, ethnocentric conclaves. Part of becoming a disciple of Christ includes understanding and embracing the universal fellowship of the body of Christ.

11. Methods and programs should be constantly and rigorously evaluated for their lasting, long term, intended, and unintended results.

The Lausanne Movement

A great movement in Christian mission was launched in 1974 at the Lausanne Congress on World Evangelization. Under the leadership of Billy Graham, John Stott, Donald McGavran, and others, 2,430 mission leaders gathered for ten days to "pray, study, plan, and work together for the evangelization of the world" (Moreau et al. 2000:563). The conference focused on issues like the relationship of evangelism and social action, the uniqueness of Jesus, the continued validity of missions in a post-colonial world, the work of the Holy Spirit in mission, religious liberty and human rights, and the relationship of the Gospel and culture (564). The delegates issued "The Lausanne Covenant" at the conclusion of the conferences.

The Lausanne Congress II on World Evangelization convened in Manila in 1989 and issued "The Manilla Manifesto." In 2010, the Lausanne Conference III convened in Cape Town and issued "The Cape Town Commitment." In between the three main conferences, a number of smaller conferences convened and a series of Lausanne Occasional Papers was published. The complete archives of the Lausanne Movement are available online and offer a rich library for missiological study (www.lausanne.org).

As already mentioned, Adventists share many missiological commitments and positions with evangelical Protestants. The Lausanne Movement is interdenominational but not ecumenical in the sense of seeking to negotiate a lowest-common-denominator theology that draws everyone into a common set of doctrines. The study of mission strategy in the contemporary world has been greatly advanced by the Lausanne Movement.

Strategy for Unreached People Groups

While Donald McGavran and the Church Growth Movement were emphasizing mission among the most receptive peoples, a parallel emphasis developed in the twentieth century on mission among unreached people groups (UPGs). Unreached peoples exist both as hidden groups within nations with well-established Christian communities and in nations with a weak Christian presence. In either case, the focus of mission to UPGs has abandoned the nation-state as the main factor in planning mission strategy.

The Joshua Project provides continuously updated information about unreached people groups under the banner, "Bringing definition to the unfinished task" (see joshuaproject.net). Online resources, social media, smartphone apps, and printed resources are provided.

"An unreached people is a people group among which there is no indigenous community of believing Christians with adequate numbers and resources to evangelize this people group without outside (cross-cultural) assistance" (Terry and Payne 2013:129). One of the strongest evidences of the power of the Gospel is that it can cross all human barriers through the ministry of cross-cultural missionaries as the history of Christian missions has demonstrated. But indigenous witnesses are the ideal.

A number of factors are responsible for the existence of unreached people groups. Some exist in nations with laws intended to keep Christianity out. In other nations, Christianity is legal but heavy religious and social pressure is exerted against Christian mission. In some places, where the relationship between Christians and a non-Christian majority has been historically difficult, the local church is actually opposed to mission among non-Christians. Geographical location, poor communication, and poor transportation keep some peoples in isolation. Some peoples are oral learners who are semi-literate or illiterate and need to be reached with oral strategies. Others have simply been outside of the mission vision of the church.

At Lausanne II in Manila in 1989, Luis Bush introduced the concept of the "10/40 Window," which has endured as a tool to locate and identify UPGs. The window starts in North Africa and extends through Asia, running along the 10 and 40 degrees north of the equator lines. Although it excludes UPGs elsewhere and is not really precise, the 10/40 Window does include about 90% of the world's UPGs. Included in the window are the majority of Muslims, Hindus, Buddhists, and Chinese peoples of different religions.

Figure 13.1
The 10/40 Window

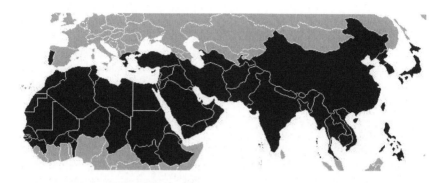

As the population of the 10/40 Window has grown ever larger since the concept was introduced, the combined Christian investment in mission has also increased. In 1989, Luis Bush reported that only 3% of the evangelical missionary work force was in the 10/40, but by 1999 the total was reported to be 8%, and in 2008 it was 15% (Terry and Payne 2013:130). In the last decade, Adventists have worked intentionally to shift resources and missionaries into the world's least-evangelized places included in the 10/40 Window.

Strategy of Rapid Church Planting

David Garrison and others have led a Church Planting Movement (CPM) defined as "a rapid multiplication of indigenous churches planting churches that sweeps through a people group or population segment (2004:21). The philosophy of CPM is to trust the guidance of the Spirit to oversee new churches that multiply themselves rapidly, with minimal oversight or financial support from cross-cultural missionaries. Emphasis is placed on extraordinary prayer, abundant evangelism, the authority of the Bible, local lay leadership, house churches, bold faith, signs and wonders, and on-the-job leadership training (2004:172, 221).

CPM has worked well where cross-cultural missionaries cannot enter or have had little success in the past, as among Muslims in South East Asia. The points of emphasis listed above are all good. There are, however, warnings that come from observing CPM in action. The rapidly planted churches have sometimes had a short life span because new converts have become leaders too soon, with inadequate training. A weak doctrine of the church as "where two or three are gathered" has led to poor congregation-building work. Lay and pastoral leadership are essential elements for any strategy that will produce strong, healthy congregations.

Strategies for Contextualization

Almost everyone who attempts to cross boundaries for Christ intuitively adapts their approach in some way. When the barrier is linguistic, the missionary resorts to hand signals, or finds a translator, or learns the language. When the barriers are cultural, the missionary usually tries to adapt in some way. Sometimes locally appropriate pictures and stories are used in audio-visual presentations.

One of the most significant benefits from the increased use of cultural anthropology in mission study and practice during the twentieth century was the understanding that cultural differences run very deep. Superficial adjustments or adaptations that are made instinctively when encountering a different culture are not adequate. Rather, the missionary needs to learn the other culture deeply and intentionally shape their methods to the other culture. The eternal, universal Gospel is the same for all peoples, but the way it is communicated, applied, and lived-out in daily life gives Christians distinctly different cultural styles. To reach another culture deeply, missionaries must be intentional about contextualizing their methods. Other chapters discuss principles that guide contextualization that is biblically faithful and culturally appropriate.

Receptivity and Resistance

The factors of receptivity and resistance to evangelization have to be addressed in any realistic discussion of mission strategy. Receptivity and resistance are both individual and group phenomena. Social, political, legal, and historical factors shape what whole groups of people think about Christianity, while individuals in every group have different receptivity levels from their groups.

The visible responses to the Gospel among different people groups can be monitored through church growth statistics. Broadly speaking, sub-Saharan Africa, Latin America, Oceania, and parts of Asia are the world regions where Adventist missions encounter the highest levels of visible receptivity. Europe, the Middle East, North Africa, and much of Asia are the regions where mission encounters the lowest levels of visible receptivity. Each of these large regions can be broken down into smaller regions for analysis. The 10/40 Window concept seeks to identify the regions with the least visible receptivity levels.

Church growth statistics for particular regions provide portraits of visible receptivity and resistance over periods of time; however, they do not tell the whole story. Spiritually receptive people do not always respond to evangelization in the same ways or at the same time. Saying that a region or nation with low membership is "resistant" may be inaccurate; but even if it is accurate, the label may prevent the church from doing its missional duty.

Defining Resistance

Labelling a person or people group as "resistant" because they did not visibly accept Christ in the way we wish, at a particular time, in response to a particular style of evangelization is disobeying Christ's command, "Do not judge, or you too will be judged" (Matt 7:1).

The "resistant" are "those who [1] have or are receiving an adequate opportunity to hear but [2] over some time [3] have not responded positively" to the Gospel (Pocock 1998:5). The operative phrases in this definition are "adequate opportunity" and "over time."

Adequate opportunity is a qualitative factor involving how the Gospel presentation is shaped to fit the cultural and religious background of the recipients. Time is a quantitative factor that deals with the length of the journey toward Christ.

A relatively brief period of instruction dealing with key doctrines may give adequate opportunity for a well-informed and committed Christian to accept the Adventist message; however, the adequate opportunity threshold is much higher for a Muslim, Hindu, Buddhist, or a nominal, poorly informed Christian. Even though the Holy Spirit can change any person's heart and mind in a moment, the time and effort needed to lead people to Christ is generally much greater for those who are not already committed Christians.

True resistance levels are known only to God. People may seem to be resistant and yet have a deep level of receptivity that they conceal. Some people who are labelled as resistant would be better understood as neglected or ignored. Other people may have never received a truly adequate opportunity. Still others reject the Gospel when it is presented in a non-contextualized way.

Pocock warns that we "may be using the idea of 'resistant' to comfort ourselves from engaging and living among the unreached when in reality we simply do not know what the disposition of these people may be to the presentation of the Gospel" (Pocock 1998:5).

Defining Receptivity

As with resistance, true inner receptivity is known only to God. "Receptivity is a description of the responses to individuals, peoples, and societies to the Gospel message when they are confronted with this truth through a contextually appropriate method and in a way that can be understood" (Terry and Payne 2005:176).

The concept of ample opportunity and ample time apply also to receptive people. Highly receptive individuals in some contexts require much more time than in other contexts to accept Christ.

Among peoples with the most restrictive rules or pressures against Christian missions, there are always some individuals with high but invisible receptivity.

Receptivity and Resistance in Perspective

The Receptivity and Resistance Scale of figure 13.2 seeks to put the two factors into perspective for the sake of understanding the missional task.

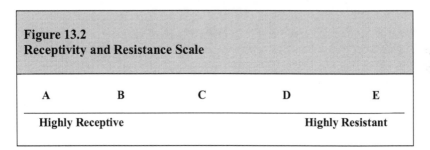

**Figure 13.2
Receptivity and Resistance Scale**

A	B	C	D	E

Highly Receptive   **Highly Resistant**

Point A: High Receptivity

For highly receptive people (Point A) almost any method will work. A non-contextualized, simple tract, radio program, TV program, or the witness of a poorly prepared Christian will cause such a person to almost fall into the church. To use a colloquialism, Point A people are like "low hanging fruit" just waiting to be plucked for the Kingdom.

Almost every community on earth has some Point A people who will attend meetings, make decisions, be baptized, and join a local church if it is available. In fact, the number of highly receptive people is probably greater than ever before because Earth's population is greater than ever. Their value to God is in no way diminished by the fact that they are highly receptive and the work of leading them to Christ should never be diminished. As for the church's resources, praise God that the conversion of Point A people is relatively inexpensive.

Some cautions are raised with regard to highly receptive people: (1) beware of over-estimating the spiritual progress of highly receptive people at baptism, when they probably need much more discipleship training; (2) beware of justifying poor methods because of the easy success with highly receptive peoples; (3) beware of making Point A people the sole focus of evangelization.

Point E: High Resistance

Sadly, there are highly resistant people at the other end of the scale (Point E). The very best contextualized, skillfully used, and Spirit-led methods will not be effective for these highly resistant persons. All one can do is to pray that some influence or event will change the hearts and minds of such persons. That is why prayer ministry is a vital element of mission strategy. High resistance is no justification for staying away from people because they can and do change.

Points B, C, D: Intermediate Receptivity

The persons for whom using the best possible methods in mission is most critical are those in the intermediate ranges of receptivity represented by Points B, C, and D. The model does not attempt to calibrate specific levels of receptivity but to illustrate that there is a range in between highly receptive and highly resistant. In other words, people must not be separated into just two groups—the "receptive" (Point A people) and the "resistant" (Point E people). Rather, people occupy a spectrum of spiritual receptivity that changes with time and circumstances. Identifying and quantifying the degree of receptivity is something only the Spirit can do accurately. The mission task is to seek and use the very best approaches to maximize an adequate opportunity for every person to accept the Gospel within whom the Spirit has awakened interest.

Spiritual receptivity, of all degrees, is an asset to be deeply treasured and nourished. A mechanical "win-some-lose-some" attitude toward the treasury of spiritual openness squanders efforts and investments in mission and potentially drives away receptive people. Because almost every place of work has some Point A people, the careless evangelist happily "plucks" them and moves on. With appropriate methods, some of the Point B, C, and D people can also make decisions for Christ. Inappropriate, non-contextualized approaches that do not give an adequate opportunity potentially immunize or vaccinate people with some degree of spiritual receptivity against future encounters with the Gospel. Adding additional tragedy to this sad scenario, the careless missionary concludes that even though a few people responded to his efforts, the area and its people are very "resistant" and not suitable for much future effort. Workers who might have resulted in the conversion of persons with intermediate receptivity are assigned elsewhere.

The dynamics of evangelization in areas dominated by the world religions are typically more complicated than where Christians are in the majority. In some places the most receptive Point A person cannot be reached directly or cannot make a public confession. People with lesser degrees of receptivity (Points B, C, D) cannot be easily attracted and nurtured in the faith. Even where public conversion and church membership are possible, using the same methods as those used among more Christian populations risks squandering their spiritual receptivity. The goal of mission is always the same—to lead persons to biblically faithful and culturally appropriate life in Christ—but there are different pathways to that goal.

A Theology of Resistance and Receptivity

Charles Van Engen emphasizes the need for a theological perspective of resistance and receptivity and outlines some major points (1998:37-68).

God Loves All, Always

"All humans are loved always by God" (37). God's love (John 3:16) embraces the most receptive and the most resistant. God has a universal love for all peoples, cultures, races, tribes, and language groups that can be called his macro-love. His particular love for each person can be called his micro-love. The particularity and universality of God's love are complimentary and must be well understood for the sake of full-fledged mission.

> Too strong an emphasis on universality will drive us toward uniformity and blind us to cultural distinctives—and the differences in the particular response/resistance represented by a particular people group. Too strong an emphasis on particularity will push us to narrow our mission endeavor to only certain groups of people whom we have tagged "receptive," ignoring or neglecting others. (41)

The church is called to show God's universal, macro-love through a broad missional engagement with all peoples, but not to think all peoples can be reached with a one-size-fits-all methodology. God's particular, micro-love is expressed by making the extra effort to contextualize the Gospel presentation for specific people groups, more resistant ones.

All Are Receptive

"All humans are receptive: They have a profound spiritual hunger to know God." The constant multiplication of religions shows that people are "incurably religious." "God has implanted in us all an innate tendency...to believe in God." All humans have a "God-shaped vacuum" that only He can fill (Van Engen 1998:42-46).

The implication for mission is that the apparent resistance that people show to the Gospel may not be an accurate expression of their true spiritual condition at all. The hunger of the soul is best addressed by receptor-oriented communication of the Gospel that uses culturally appropriate contact points and approaches. The innate spiritual hunger of all people is a cause of valid optimism for mission, even where visible receptivity is low.

All Are Resistant

"Because of sin and the Fall, all humans are resistant to God all the time" (Van Engen 1998:50). "All have sinned and fall short of the glory of God" (Rom 3:28).

Humanity is not neutral, needing only a gentle nudge toward God. Resistance is an inner, spiritual stance, not merely the historical, social-cultural conditioning of having had non-Christian ancestry for millennia. Even missionaries are resistant to God in certain ways, implying that mission involves the resistant calling the resistant to God. This reality is a cause for great humility on the part of the missionary and the realization that the very best methodology will fail without the life-giving power of God the Holy Spirit. Humanity's universal resistance to God is a realistic cause for some pessimism about mission.

Some Are Always Resistant

"Some humans are resistant all the time, to all missional approaches" (Van Engen 1998:53). The parable of the soils (or sower) suggests different receptivity of the soils themselves (Matt 13). The farmer planted the good seed indiscriminately, knowing that some of it would yield no harvest.

The stewardship of resources requires some selective seeding, as suggested by other biblical passages. Jesus told his disciples to "shake the dust off" (Matt 10:1-14) when they met rejection and to go only to the "lost sheep of Israel" (Matt 15:24). Paul chose his places of work carefully and selectively. However, the parable of the soils implies both realism and generosity without promoting irresponsibility. The very best methods must be used to share the Gospel freely, knowing that some people will never respond positively. However, the parable encourages optimism because of the good soils.

Some Are Resistant Sometimes

"Some humans are resistant some of the time to some things" (Van Engen 1998:57). People are resistant both for their own internal reasons and because of external factors.

Contextual factors related to religion, legal systems, politics, history, and culture produce resistance. Factors within the church can produce resistance to the Gospel. Lack of spirituality, hypocrisy, and unethical relationships diminish the church's witness. The church may have lost its missional intention toward its own community. Occasionally, local churches function within a social-religious bubble that makes them hostile to mission in their own community. Unwillingness to contextualize the message for the receivers increases their resistance. Insisting on changes at conversion that are more cultural than biblical raises unnecessary barriers.

Conclusion

It may be that a people [group] is not so much "resistant" as "neglected." Too easily we are tempted to label a group that does not respond to our form of evangelization as "resistant," when in fact it may be the church's lack of cultural and spiritual sensitivity that has increased resistance through neglect.... Maybe the "resistant" are this because we have not prayed in such a way that the Holy Spirit may convert us to be fit instruments of Gospel proclamation. (Van Engen 1998:65, 68)

Chapter
14

A Model for Strategic Adventist Mission

~·∽

Multi-Focal Mission Vision

One of the most important topics in the study of Christian mission is vision (Terry and Payne 2013:193; Malphurs 2005:145). Christ's farewell words provide a good starting point for defining a strategic mission vision.

> Then they gathered around him and asked him, "Lord, are you at this time going to restore the kingdom to Israel?" He said to them: "It is not for you to know the times or dates the Father has set by his own authority. But you will receive power when the Holy Spirit comes on you; and you will be my witnesses in Jerusalem, and in all Judea and Samaria, and to the ends of the earth." After he said this, he was taken up before their very eyes, and a cloud hid him from their sight. (Acts 1:6-9)

After Christ's ascension, the Apostles and their colleagues followed the pattern outlined in his words. The Jerusalem, Judea and Samaria, and ends of the earth pattern provides the basis for an integrated mission vision that I call multi-focal mission vision.

Jerusalem: Near Distance

Every believer needs to have a near-distance (Jerusalem) missional focus. For the majority of believers, Jerusalem represents the local church where their membership is recorded. The local church is the primary location at which God's mission is accomplished through the spiritual gifts of its members. Jerusalem may also represent ministry assignments made by the church like pastoring, teaching, or administration. Even when that is the case, all members have a local church role of some kind, whether as a member of the church pew or as a member serving in another role, Jerusalem represents the work of mission close at hand. Every believer has this personal responsibility to play in God's mission that should receive their wholehearted commitment. Looking elsewhere, at another person's role, and not giving one's best service to one's personal, God-give role, hinders God's mission.

In the multi-focal mission vision model, Jerusalem also represents a believer's home town, mother tongue, birth culture, and personal religion. Every believer must have a mission vision for places and peoples that are nearest and dearest and with whom relationships are easy and natural. Natural affinity is a great asset for missions that needs to be used to the maximum. For example, Argentinians talk easily with other Argentinians about their football rivalry with Brazil and South Africans reminisce pleasurably about the 2010 World Cup in their country. Adventists share their spiritual journeys easily with other Adventists or former Adventists who need to grow in faith or be invited back into fellowship.

Judea and Samaria: Medium-Distance

Judea and Samaria represent the medium-distance of multi-focal mission vision. The Adventist who has multi-focal mission vision has a missional interest and concern for the mission of other local churches in their conference, union, and division. To illustrate, members in Korea are supportive of work in China, while those in California highly value the work of Adventists in New York. Latin Americans who speak both Portuguese and Spanish and share certain cultural traits have a vision for mission in each other's territories. Adventists have a keen sense of their mission among Christians of other denominations.

Ends of the Earth: Far-Distance

Mission at a far-distance is represented by Christ's phrase "to the ends of the earth." Within the church, that means members in Chile having a mission vision for the Middle East/North Africa Union and those in Namibia having a vision for the work of fellow Adventists in India. Every Adventist with multi-focal mission vision has a focus on mission in distant nations, among people with languages they do not know, and with very different cultures and religions. That means having a mission focus on Muslims, Hindus, and Buddhists, either in their traditional homelands or in places to which they have immigrated.

Overlapping Perspectives

In the past, people of very different languages, cultures, and religions lived "over there somewhere," at the geographical "ends of the earth." Most Christians were in Europe or North America and those needing to be reached were in India, China, or Africa. Three things have changed: (1) about two-thirds of all Adventists now live in Latin America and sub-Saharan Africa; (2) globalization has spread Muslims, Hindus, and Buddhists (and others) around the world so that many or most Adventist churches have them within their local communities; (3) many nations that were once centers of active Christianity have become secularized and postmodern.

Because of globalization, local churches frequently have "Judea and Samaria" and "ends of the earth" people groups living within their own communities as part of their geographic "Jerusalem." The boundaries of language, culture, and religion that were once crossed only geographically by missionaries going "over there" must now be crossed by local churches, almost everywhere. In other words, "the ends of the earth" are no longer defined only by geography.

Geography does continue to define the contemporary mission challenges very significantly. "The ends of the earth" needing effective cross-cultural missionaries remain geographical locations that are concentrated in the Middle East and North Africa, Asia, and Europe. For example, there are many Muslims in North America and Europe who speak English or various European languages, but the great majority are still in Indonesia, Middle East and North Africa, and India.

When a Christian has multi-focal mission vision, they perceive mission in its many dimensions with clarity and accuracy wherever they look. Conversely, a believer who has mono-focal mission vision is like a person who has either reading glasses or distance glasses but needs them both. They perceive some aspects of the mission task well but not others.

Mono-Focal Mission Vision

The Apostle Peter had mono-focal mission vision until God opened his eyes to a broader vision with a strange dream of wild beasts and then gave him a missionary encounter with Cornelius (Acts 10). Until that point, Peter was converted to Jesus Christ, but not to Christ's comprehensive mission that included both Jews and Gentiles. On that eventful day, Cornelius was converted to Christ and Peter to Christ's comprehensive mission.

The major Protestant reformers had tunnel mission vision focused only on reforming the Catholic Church of Europe. Three centuries passed after Luther's 95 Theses of 1517 before Protestant mission vision embraced the whole world. Likewise, early Adventists took some time before embracing global mission and sending J. N. Andrews to Switzerland as the first official missionary in 1874.

The contemporary Adventist Church is in a very different place with global mission than it was only a few decades ago. Globalization and the changing location of the Adventist membership have changed the situation of Adventist mission. When I was a boy growing up in Malawi, there were a little more than one million Adventists, of which about one-third lived in North America. Most cross-cultural missionaries were from North America, Europe, or Australia. When my family returned to the United States for a furlough, my father spoke in about 75 churches and three camp meetings. The Doss family was welcomed and sometimes idealized as "real" missionaries from the "real" mission field overseas. The people among whom we worked in Malawi were the "receivers" of mission and the North Americans were the "senders." If people thought of the Doss family as "real" missionaries, they were demonstrating mono-focal mission vision because they did not have the mission of their local churches well in focus.

In the intervening years, the membership has grown to about 20 million with only about 7% in North America. The former receivers have become senders of missionaries and fewer missionaries are North Americans. North American Adventists read glowing reports of membership growth elsewhere. In contrast, evangelism is increasingly difficult in postmodern America, especially among certain groups. Americans correctly assert that America is also a mission field. However, if they think that America is the only "real" mission field needing their focus, they have the opposite kind of mono-focal mission vision than in past eras. Sometimes the thought is expressed that North America should pull back some of its support for global mission to better address the American mission challenge. Among the 93% of Adventists outside of North America, the thought is sometimes expressed that the North American church is rich enough to give ever-increasing, unlimited support. These contrasting views are a normal part of adjusting to the changing demographics of the world church, but they are both wrong.

Multi-Focal Mission Vision in Action

The Adventist church, in all of its world divisions, has a role to play in all dimensions of its shared mission. Some of the roles the various sectors of the church play are the same or similar to past eras and some are very different. The large sectors of the church in Latin America and sub-Saharan Africa are increasingly becoming major contributors of money for missions and senders of missionaries. The cry of the unevangelized billions calls both the traditional givers and senders to give even more money and send even more missionaries. What has changed is that the main direction of money and missionaries in this era must be toward the least evangelized of the Middle East, North Africa, Asia, and Europe instead of to sub-Saharan Africa or Latin America. The shared mission focus of the church needs to become fully multi-focal through deliberate, intentional, prayerful strategizing, and implementation.

To understand where the church is and where it needs to go in today's world with global mission requires a perspective that will unify and focus its mission vision. The multi-focal mission model attempts to provide that unified focus. Figure 14.1 presents some of the many dimensions that need to be contained in a unified focus. Two metaphors are used to illustrate the process of obtaining a unified mission vision—cameras and eyeglasses.

Figure 14.1
Multi-Focal Mission Vision

	Near Distance	Medium Distance	Far Distance
Acts 1:8	"Jerusalem"	"Judea and Samaria"	"Ends of the earth"
Metaphor: Manual Camera	Photographing a flower	Photographing a house	Photographing a distant mountain
Metaphor: Progressive Lenses	Reading a book	Looking across the street	Looking at a far mountain
Church	Local, particular ministry assignment	Nearby local churches, conferences, unions, division	Distant local churches, conferences, unions, divisions
Geography	Home town	Home state or nation	Distant nations
Language	Mother language	Second or third known languages	Unknown languages
Culture	Birth culture	Cultures similar to birth culture	Very different cultures
Religion	Personal religion, fellow Adventists	Related religions, other Christians	Very different religions, non-Christian religions
Receptivity Levels	Strong	Moderate	Weak

Today's digital single lens reflex cameras are highly automated. Older cameras required several manual settings. The old manual cameras illustrate the intentionality needed for multi-focal mission vision. Effective mission strategy cannot be planned and implemented by a "click the button" or "auto-focus" approach. The "just get out there to do missions" approach misuses limited resources and diminishes effective outcomes in mission.

To illustrate, a local Mexican church that is planning outreach to a mostly Mexican Catholic community has only one factor to plan for—the different type of Christianity. That same church adds missional complexity when it plans to witness to English speakers or Muslims or Hindus in its own community. When the Mexican church decides to send cross-cultural missionaries to Indonesia or Lebanon or Mongolia, many more factors are added and even more deliberate planning and training are needed.

Progressive spectacle lenses illustrate multi-focal mission vision in another way. Progressive lenses have a near-distance prescription at the bottom for reading and seeing nearby objects and a far-distance prescription at the top of the lens for distant objects. In between, the prescription gradually changes to give the best possible vision for any distance.

Progressive lenses illustrate the intuitive missional insight that comes from the gifts of the Spirit, the guidance of the Spirit in specific situations, natural abilities, study, training, and experience. The long-term cross-cultural missionary who knows the local language and understands the culture develops multi-focal mission vision that facilitates effective, instantaneous responses and interactions.

The best possible multi-focal mission vision happens when deliberation and intentionality (like a manual camera) and instantaneous response and interaction (like progressive lenses) work together harmoniously. At the local church that means experienced and committed believers using every available tool for deliberately studying their community. At the global church level, people of training and experience use the best possible analytical tools to plan effective strategies.

Defining Success in Mission

Defining success in mission is one of the most challenging aspects of thinking about mission strategy. Car dealers define success as selling cars and mountain climbers define it as reaching the top of the mountain, but what does it mean to succeed in mission? In one sense, the only true measure of success is faithfulness to God's calling and only God can measure that. People who are equally faithful in their work have widely differing responses to their very best efforts in mission. Because of this reality, should the church even attempt to define or measure success in mission? If the church should attempt to measure success in mission, what measures should be used?

> In missions much of what we do is "spiritual." Almost by definition, it proves difficult to know when we have done well, when we have done enough, when we have really finished a task. When have enough people come to Christ? When are believers mature enough? When are leaders adequately trained? And what about our colleagues who labor faithfully in less responsive or nonresponsive areas? How do we measure effectiveness and success? (Terry and Payne 2013:39)

In spite of the challenge of quantifying spiritual matters, there are good reasons to hold ourselves and each other accountable and to assess the effectiveness of mission endeavors. Most importantly, being effective in God's mission potentially involves the eternal destinies of fellow human beings. Individual believers need to hold themselves accountable and administrators who direct and evaluate the work of others need good measures of accountability. The stewardship and management of money requires good assessment of how it is used.

Given the complexity of assessing spiritual matters, the great variety of contexts in which mission is conducted, and the diversity among God's servants who are doing the work, multiple-markers of success are needed. Using a single marker of success for missionaries from any continent serving in any other continent among all of the varied people groups is not effective. Yet, that is what many Christians, including Adventists, have traditionally done. That single marker of mission success is the number of baptisms.

The Journey Toward Discipleship (figure 14.2) illustrates the complex and lengthy spiritual journey to be taken by a person who is in complete rebellion against God to becoming a mature disciple. The model implies that a positive movement of even a single step is to be highly valued, even if the person is not baptized quickly. Long-term commitment is needed to keep the person moving toward Christ. The model also suggests that the journey is far from over at the baptistery. Long-term commitment is needed to lead a person to mature discipleship. Therefore, multiple markers of success are needed in mission.

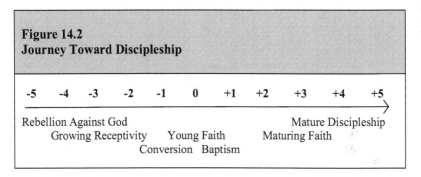

Figure 14.2
Journey Toward Discipleship

-5	-4	-3	-2	-1	0	+1	+2	+3	+4	+5

Rebellion Against God   Mature Discipleship
     Growing Receptivity   Young Faith   Maturing Faith
                     Conversion   Baptism

The Modified Engel Scale (figure 14.3) is valuable because it adds detail to the pre-baptism spiritual journey. When well-informed, committed fellow Christians become interested in the Adventist message, the journey is relatively short. For secular and postmodern people or adherents of the other world religions, the journey toward Christ is longer and more complicated. Because more people are in the latter category than the former, Adventist mission strategy needs to be patient and long term. Multiple markers are needed all along the spiritual journey.

Figure 14.3
Modified Engel Scale

+3 Experiencing lifetime growth in belief and behavior, maturing discipleship
+2 Becoming incorporated into the body of Christ as a member
+1 Making a post-decision evaluation of costs and benefits
 0 Baptism, becoming a new believer
-1 Repenting and having faith in Jesus Christ
-2 Decision to take action
-3 Recognition of personal problems and need
-4 Positive attitude toward the Gospel
-5 Grasp of the implications of the Gospel
-6 Awareness of the fundamentals of the Gospel
-7 Initial awareness of the Gospel
-8 Awareness of a supreme being, but no effective knowledge of the Gospel

A Single-Marker Model of Mission Success

The standard index or marker of mission success for Adventists and many other denominations is the number of baptisms. This approach can be called the "baptism model of mission." Baptism is unquestionably a vital step in the believer's journey with Christ (Rom 6:1-7). However, problems arise when baptism is made the single marker of success in mission.

A Theological Critique

Adventists do not share the Roman Catholic sacramental theology of baptism. In Catholic theology, the church is the reservoir of God's grace that it bestows upon lost sinners through the sacraments. The sacrament of baptism saves the eternal soul from eternal hellfire. Newborn babies or unrepentant sinners who are dying but have not been baptized are in urgent need of the sacrament of baptism to escape hell. The Catholic theology of baptism implies that the most important work has been done when a person has been baptized.

The Adventist theology of baptism also differs from a Protestant "believer's baptism" that disconnects baptism from church membership. Accepting Christ and being baptized must be understood as becoming a part of the body of Christ, the local community of believers (1 Cor 12; Eph 4). Salvation comes only from Jesus Christ, not from the entry of one's name into a church membership list; but integration into the fellowship of believers is an essential part of the biblical pattern. When mission success is declared at the baptistery, full integration into the body of Christ is assumed to be an automatic outcome and inadequate attention is paid to facilitating that outcome.

In Adventist theology, baptism is an outward sign of an inward change (see "Baptism," Fundamental Beliefs, www.adventist.org/en/beliefs). One is saved not by baptism, but through inner repentance and the acceptance of the grace of Jesus Christ. Adventists do not believe that the church bestows eternal life in the baptistery. The newly baptized person can and should feel secure in their salvation in Christ, but from the church's perspective, the person is a newborn spiritual baby at the beginning of a lifetime journey. The church's missional responsibility is to lead the new member toward mature discipleship within the community.

Another theological critique involves sanctification. The baptism model of mission implies an emphasis on justification to the neglect of sanctification. Adventists emphasize the development of a truly Christlike life. "We are called to be a godly people who think, feel, and act in harmony with biblical principles in all aspects of personal and social life" (see "Christian Behavior," Fundamental Beliefs, www.adventist.org/en/beliefs).

A Practical Critique

Several practical critiques can be made of using baptism as the sole marker of mission success. When success is declared at the baptistery, there are some actual or potential unintended consequences that inhibit comprehensive mission: (1) Leaders place heavy pressure for large baptisms on pastors, evangelists, and lay people; (2) pastors neglect their other work, do not develop complete pastoral skill sets, and are promoted solely on the basis of baptismal numbers; (3) converts are brought to the baptistery prematurely, without adequate preparation; (4) individuals are rebaptized multiple times, sometimes without adequate nurture; (5) the "follow up" after the evangelistic meeting is not adequately funded, planned, or implemented; (6) drop-out rates can be very high; (7) those who drop out are potentially vaccinated against future evangelization; (8) Adventist membership statistics are inaccurate and representation on decision-making committees and sessions is distorted.

A Missiological Critique

Certain historical factors may make the baptism model part of early Adventist mission. Like the Adventist pioneers themselves, early converts were often highly committed Christians who were already familiar with the Bible. Winning well-informed Christians meant only teaching unique Adventist doctrines. The Adventist message was a Christian-to-Christian, "value added," or "finishing truth" message that offered a more biblical way of being a Christian.

The world of this century is very different from nineteenth-century America. Biblical literacy has declined in most historically Christian nations and the populace has become more secular. Even more significantly, the greatest numerical challenge confronting Adventist mission is among Muslims, Hindus, Buddhists, and others who may be spiritually receptive, but are completely uninformed about the Bible and the Christian life. For them, the Adventist message is not a "finishing truth" but a "starting truth" message where the basics of the Gospel need to be taught. Using the baptism model of mission among Buddhists in Thailand, Hindus in India, or Muslims in Egypt is ineffective and irresponsible.

The Christian-to-Christian approach does not work where the other world religions or secularism dominate. The single-marker model of mission success does not fit mission in the twenty-first century.

Many Adventists are aware of the high drop-out rate following evangelistic campaigns. Anecdotes about manipulative techniques used to increase baptismal numbers are frequently shared. However, many Adventists seem to be caught in the habituated model. The solution is not to make vows to improve the old model, but to take a bold step into a new model. Like all paradigm shifts, changing the Adventist mission paradigm will take a lot of reflection, dialogue, intentionality, and prayer.

A Multiple-Marker Model of Mission Success

The discipleship model of mission is a multiple-marker alternative to the single-marker baptism model. The discipleship model sees baptism as a major step and rite-of-passage on the spiritual journey of a lifetime. In this model, the church's missional engagement with the individual starts at birth, if the parents are members, or when the church first becomes aware of a person's interest. From the point of first spiritual engagement, the church ministers intentionally with the goal of guiding the person to mature discipleship. In one way, there is nothing new in the discipleship model. Adventists have church schools, Sabbath School for every age group, and many other ministries that are actually discipleship ministries. However, these valuable ministries, into which the church invests many resources and energies, are ignored or forgotten in the vital process of defining and evaluating success. The discipleship model of mission seeks to integrate all that the church already does into a multiple-marker system of mission success.

Actually, the traditional Adventist approach is a discipleship model of mission when Christian education is part of the package. Students enrolled in a church school have regular Bible classes, teachers who model and teach the Christian life in the other classes, Pathfinders, church programs, interaction with local pastors, baptismal classes, and baptism. Some Adventists underestimate the discipleship value of Christian education.

Figure 14.4
Defining a Disciple

A disciple is one who experiences continual transformation toward the fullness of Christ ...
- in a biblically faithful way
- in a culturally appropriate way
- at the worldview level
- in personal spirituality
- in emotional wholeness
- in personal life style
- in family relationships
- as a member of the body of Christ
- as a witness to others

In the discipleship model the church is successful with a baby born into an Adventist home when it facilitates growth in Christlikeness at every age. The church is a success with converts who show an interest, decide to be baptized, and then continue to grow in Christlikeness for the rest of their lives. The discipled member thus lives as a growing Christian in matters of lifestyle, marriage, parenting, relationships, employment, service in the church, and old age until they are laid to rest.

The discipleship model is both punctiliar and process focused. At certain stages of the spiritual journey, including baptism, the person makes punctiliar decisions that are useful markers. Those punctiliar decisions are embedded in a lifelong process of spiritual maturation. Using theological language, the believer is justified daily and growing in sanctification over a lifetime.

Baptism is a punctiliar marker of mission success that marks a unique step. Participation in the Lord's Supper, which is a renewal of the baptismal vows, is a marker. Adventists have recently added church attendance as an official marker. Attendance at other church functions can be useful punctiliar markers. These and other markers can be tabulated to notice trends and assess the process of discipleship in the congregation.

Because the composition and context of every local church is different, a package of markers needs to be identified by local leaders and the pastor. Conference leaders can require the development of a contextualized set of markers for every congregation. One size does not and cannot fit all.

To illustrate some multiple-markers of mission in action, mission could be seen as a success for individuals when: (1) the child attends Sabbath School and Vacation Bible School and is seen to enjoy happy fellowship with other children and adults; (2) the family participates regularly in church services and outreach and enjoys good relationships with the church family; (3) the newly baptized person becomes integrated into the life of the church, participates regularly in church services, uses their spiritual gifts in service and outreach, and enjoys good relationships with the church family; and (4) members experience victory over personal issues of behavior or addiction.

The congregation as a whole can be considered a missional success when showing the following markers: (1) church services are appropriate for the age mix, educational level, and cultures of the members; (2) members are trained for service for which their spiritual gifts prepare them; (3) members participate regularly in outreach; (4) outreach is appropriate for the community; (5) the number of baptisms is appropriate for the general receptivity of the community; and (6) there is a high long-term retention rate for newly baptized members. Retention at the one, two, and five-year marks is celebrated along with new baptisms.

The multiple-markers, discipleship model of mission: (1) produces a more nuanced, accurate assessment of the individual's spiritual journey, the pastor's effectiveness, and the local church's effectiveness than the single-marker model; (2) takes seriously the many ministries of the church and integrates them into mission assessment; and, (3) changes the church's perspective in a way that can enhance missional effectiveness among today's most challenging people groups.

Missional Capacity and Context

Planning and implementing mission in a church of about 20 million members, located in 215 nations, to the 237 nations of earth, that make up over 7 billion people is a complex and demanding task. The reason for faith and optimism is that God the Holy Spirit is the superintendent of mission. The church's responsibility is to use the very best Spirit-empowered methods and to work strategically.

While the Spirit has unlimited power, two important factors shape how the church must make its strategy. First, missional capacity includes the human and material resources available within the church in a given area. The qualities of its members are the church's most important missional resources. Material resources are valuable because they can support the church's members in various ministries.

Second, the context of mission defines how the church's missional capacity must be employed. Missional contexts are incredibly different, meaning that the methods used must also be different.

Figure 14.5
Capacity and Context

Medical Capacity	Missional Capacity
• Number of health care workers • Training and qualification of health care workers • Internal culture of hospital • Hospital equipment and supplies • Administration of hospital	• Number of members • Number of congregations • Quality of discipleship • Quality of leadership • Quality of missional skills • Commitment to missions • Attitudes toward community • Finances, buildings, and equipment
Medical Context	**Missional Context**
• Population served • Number and nature of patient illnesses treated • Hospital relationships with community	• Population size • Religious, legal, cultural, economic, political conditions • Degree of religious freedom • Receptivity to the Gospel

Medical triage is an excellent metaphor for strategic planning in mission. When patients arrive at the hospital, they are evaluated (or triaged) for the seriousness of their condition and the available care-givers treat them accordingly. A patient with a life-threatening condition is treated before those with less serious conditions. The staff matches available health workers with particular patient needs in their order of priority. A medical team may enjoy treating people with lesser problems and may regret making them wait, but they must treat people with major problems first.

The medical triage model is helpful for understanding mission strategy, even if it does not fit in every respect. Applying the triage model to mission strategy implies that (1) every human being who has not accepted Christ must be given an adequate opportunity to do so; (2) people groups that know little or nothing about the Bible and Jesus Christ are in the most urgent need; therefore, (3) mission strategy must give those who have not had opportunity to accept Christ high priority. If the church had unlimited resources, it would simply assign its workers everywhere to witness to everyone, but that is obviously not the case. Instead, it must make hard decisions about allocating its limited resources strategically to maximize effectiveness.

The church is well established and people are generally receptive to the Gospel in some places. In other places, the church is not well established and people do not generally respond well to evangelization. If mission is done strategically, a higher level of priority will be given to people groups among whom the church is poorly established because they are in most dire need of the Gospel. When mission is not done strategically, the church resembles a hospital emergency room that treats all the common cold and flu patients first and makes the brain damage and heart attack patients wait.

Missional Capacity

Missional capacity is the ability of the church in a particular region to witness effectively among the people groups in their area. No local church or conference possesses all of the factors that contribute to optimal missional capacity, but some are much better prepared for effective outreach than others.

Some quantitative and material factors contribute to missional capacity. These include (1) the number of members and the ratio of members to the population, (2) the number of congregations, (3) financial resources, (4) buildings and equipment, (5) the availability of contextualized materials.

Several spiritual, qualitative factors contribute to missional capacity. These include (1) the discipleship maturity of the members, (2) the quality of lay and pastoral leadership, (3) the commitment of the congregation to local outreach, (4) the mission-related skills of the membership, and (5) the relationship of the members with the local community.

Missional Context

The missional context is largely determined by factors beyond the control of the church. These include (1) the degree of freedom to worship and evangelize publicly, (2) the general receptivity of the community and larger society to Christianity in general and to the Adventist message in particular, and (3) the general religious, legal, cultural, economic, and political conditions.

The missional context is also shaped by the way the church has conducted missions in the past. The church may be partly responsible for creating or perpetuating an unfavorable context. Where methods have been uncontextualized and inappropriate for the cultural and religious setting, receptivity may have been diminished or not encouraged. For example, the traditional Christian-to-Christian model of mission may perpetuate low receptivity in contexts where the other world religions predominate.

Capacity, Context, and Strategic Missional Need

Every living person has the right to hear the Gospel, but the task costs more for some than for others. In strictly financial terms, the cost of leading one person to Christ may be $100 in one area but $1,000 in another. On what basis would $1,000 be spent for one convert when it might bring ten converts to Christ in another place? The coordination of missional capacity and context provides a conceptual framework to address that and other hard questions in a way that maintains good stewardship.

Strategic missional need is defined by capacity and context. The church in a particular area has high strategic need when both its missional capacity and its missional context are low. This means that the church in that region needs help from outside itself to be effective in a challenging missional context. If mission costs are relatively high in areas with high strategic need, they can be justified because they facilitate mission in an area of great need and challenge.

Strategic need is low when missional capacity is high and missional context is high. In other words, the church is reasonably well prepared for mission within its local context that is generally favorable. The church in a low strategic need is thus prepared to provide assistance outside of itself to members of the sisterhood of churches who have high strategic need.

There are degrees of strategic need that cannot be precisely calibrated. Strategic need is moderate when missional capacity is high but the context is low or when capacity is low but context is high.

The general goal of strategic planning by the world church should be to engage the parts of the Adventist family with lower strategic need in support of those with higher strategic need. The main way to do that directly is by building missional capacity. The missional context cannot generally be improved directly, but it may improve when the best possible missional methods are used and attitudes toward the church and the Gospel improve. For example, if the world church works strategically in a predominantly Muslim area, both the capacity of the local church and its relationship with the community may be improved to raise the missional context.

Missional capacity can be built by (1) providing training of various kinds for local leaders and church members, (2) educating indigenous pastors, (3) sending cross-cultural missionaries, (4) funding mission initiatives, and (5) funding building projects. Local situations differ a great deal and capacity building plans must always be appropriate for every locale.

Framing the Strategic Task of Adventist Mission

What does focusing on "the ends of the earth" mean at the level of the whole Adventist denomination? Seventh-day Adventists need a big-picture, broad-stroke model to conceptualize global mission in the twenty-first century. Like every big-picture model, the one that follows leaves out some of the finer details and does not apply to every situation.

In the early days of Adventist mission, strategic planning may have been less necessary than today. Church leaders could almost throw a dart at a world map on the wall to select the next mission initiative because the challenge was huge everywhere. Every region had high strategic need. Leaders allocated meager funds and deployed a small work force as best they could for a whole world that needed the Adventist message.

Today, the church has a far greater storehouse of gifted members and material resources to invest in missions, but it does not always work strategically. The successes of Adventist mission in some areas have provided the luxury of pressing for more quick and easy successes in those very same areas. But the sower in Christ's parable (Matt 13) flung his seed everywhere, not only into the good soil.

When Adventists first launched into global mission, the task rested primarily on the shoulders of one division, North America. Later, the church in Europe, Australia, and New Zealand joined as early missionary senders. These early sponsors supported mission in every corner of the earth with open hearts and pocketbooks.

The picture has changed dramatically in the 140-plus years of Adventist global mission since J. N. Andrews went to Switzerland. Some of the early initiatives became great success stories, while others never fully blossomed. Broadly speaking, the most successful initiatives were in Latin America and sub-Saharan Africa.

As the denomination seeks to address its mission challenge in a strategic way, the challenge has two dimensions: (1) each of the divisions needs to plan and implement the very best mission strategies within its own territory because mission always starts at home, in "Jerusalem," whether for every division, union, conference, or local church; (2) all parts of the world church where the membership is concentrated, where missional capacity and context are relatively high, need to unite in coordination with the General Conference in mission outside of their own territories to build the missional capacity of the sisterhood where capacity is lower and the context is more challenging.

When the thirteen world divisions are compared by their missional capacity and context, they can be grouped in two clusters—the Big Seven and the Diverse Six Plus (see table 15.2). The historical, cultural, religious, political, and economic factors within the two groupings are extremely diverse. That means the generalizations that follow do not apply to all or in the same way.

The elements of missional capacity already discussed vary greatly between local churches and every other part of the church. Every church administrator longs for more missional capacity. In fact, many administrators would assert that their particular territory presents the sternest missional challenge. Yet, considering all the factors, the Big Seven divisions have comparatively low strategic need while the Diverse Six Plus divisions have comparatively high strategic missional need.

Table 14.6
The Global Strategic Challenge

Divisions Union Field	Members	% of Members	Population (millions)	% of World Pop	Pop per Member
"Big Seven" Divisions: Low Strategic Need					
E/Central Africa	3,502,462	17.5%	351.4	4.9%	100
S/Africa In/Ocean	3,747,573	18.7%	181.1	2.5%	48
W/Central Africa	725,045	3.6%	386.9	5.3%	534
Sub-Total	**7,975,080**	**39.9%**	**919.4**	**12.7%**	**115**
Inter-American	3,726,421	18.6%	287.4	4.0%	77
North American	1,237,004	6.2%	353.7	4.9%	286
South American	2,479,452	12.4%	330.6	4.6%	133
Sub-Total	**7,442,877**	**37.2%**	**972.0**	**13.4%**	**131**
South Pacific	490,294	2.5%	38.2	0.5%	78
Total	**15,908,251**	**79.5%**	**1,929.3**	**26.7%**	**121**
"Diverse Six Plus" Divisions: High Strategic Need					
Euro-Asia	111,531	0.6%	318.4	4.4%	2,855
Inter-European	178,339	0.9%	335.4	4.6%	1,881
N/Asia-Pacific	719,766	3.6%	1,600.5	22.1%	2,224
Southern Asia	1,580,614	7.9%	1,324.5	18.3%	838
S/Asia-Pacific	1,418,551	7.1%	994.4	13.7%	701
Trans-European	87,193	0.4%	203.7	2.8%	2,336
Israel Field	752	0.004%	8.2	0.1%	10,904
MENA Union	3,782	0.019%	518.9	7.2%	137,203
Total	**4,100,528**	**20.5%**	**5,342.0**	**73.3%**	**1,293**
Grand Total	**20,008,779**		**7,233**		**362**

Source: GC Annual Statistical Report 2017. Data for 12/2016.

The "Big Seven" Divisions

The Big Seven division cluster is made up of the three American divisions, the three African divisions, and the South Pacific Division. The South Pacific Division has a smaller population and membership than the others, but its member-to-population ratio (1:78) is among the most favorable of all divisions.

These seven divisions are where Adventist mission initiatives have been most fruitful and where about almost 80% of Adventists now reside. However, the Big Seven embrace only about 27% of humanity. The overall population-to-member ratio is 1:121, which is better than the global ratio of 1:362. The most favorable ratio is in the Southern African Indian Ocean Division (1:48) and the most challenging in the West Central Africa Division (1:534). The North American Division's ratio (1:286) is somewhat less favorable than the Big Seven average (1:121), but more favorable than the world average (1:362).

Missional capacity among the Big Seven divisions differs notably in material resources. The group includes both the United States and some of the world's weakest economies. Missional context factors also vary a great deal. The factor of religious freedom is generally high and some peoples are quite receptive to evangelization. However, secularism and pluralism make some peoples indifferent or unresponsive. Nevertheless, this cluster of divisions has relatively high missional capacity and context that together comprise low strategic need. These divisions have the capacity to reach beyond themselves to the world field.

The "Diverse Six Plus" Divisions

The Middle East/North Africa Union (MENA) and the Israel Field are administered separately and directly by the General Conference, instead of being part of a division. In this model, they are grouped with the "Diverse Six" divisions because they constitute a similar missional challenge for the church. The "Plus" refers to MENA and Israel.

This cluster of church organizations is even more diverse than the Big Seven cluster, if that is possible. The largest non-Christian religions (Islam, Hinduism, Buddhism) are centered here. The mega-nations of India and China are located here. The 10/40 Window is also located here. Europe, once the hub of Christianity and Christian missions, now presents a major missional challenge, with secularism and large immigrant groups.

The group has only 20.5% of the Adventist membership, but 73.3% of the world population. The member-to-population ratio for the whole group is 1:1,293. The ratios range from 1:701 in the Southern Asia Pacific Division to 1:137,203 in the MENA Union. The three European divisions have an average ratio of 1:2,274, while the three Asia divisions have an average ratio of 1:1,054 members-to-population.

The factors that make up missional capacity and context vary greatly in the Diverse Six Plus group. However, the broad picture is one of comparatively high strategic challenge. As a group, these organizations need the mutual partnership of the world church.

Strategic Vision Applied

When Adventist world mission commenced, the GC and the NAD were virtually the same organization. The missional capacity of the church was based mostly within the NAD. As the church grew, other world divisions were established. As the world divisions grew, the church's missional capacity became widely distributed. The NAD remains the division with the most material resources, but it has only about 7% of Adventist members and the economic capacity of the other divisions has grown steadily. The NAD is now more of a collegial partner in the sisterhood of divisions than the "mother," who should be expected to nourish the whole church as it did a century ago.

The new partnership will see all divisions working harmoniously to blend their missional capacities in the shared tasks of global mission. In this model for action, the Big Seven understand themselves to have a special calling for coordinated action to build the missional capacity of the Diverse Six Plus. This does not imply a strictly one-way flow of resources in the direction of the Diverse Six Plus because they also have resources to share with the world church. Neither does it imply the development or continuation of a dependency on outside resources.

Strategic thinking will include some adjustments. Some Adventists who have been accustomed to being on the receiving end will shift toward seeing themselves as being givers to world mission. On the other hand, people who have seen themselves as givers and supporters will shift their giving and support to different places and projects. Some who have come to understand short-term mission as a virtual replacement of long-term mission will come to understand mission service of many years to be the foundation and short-term service as a supporting, supplemental activity.

The shared goal of the partnership will be to build local missional capacity so that local churches and administrative units will be empowered in mission. That capacity building will be highly contextualized to suit the great variations of cultural, political, economic, and religious environments.

Multi-Focal Mission Vision to Work

Combining People Group and Geographic Focus

Adventist strategic mission needs to have both a people group and a geographic focus. The people group focus will lead every local church and every administrative unit to study and understand the people groups in their communities. The people group focus opens the church's eyes to the people next door, in their own communities, who are culturally and religiously different from those they traditionally reach. In particular, people group thinking identifies Muslims, Hindus, Buddhists and others who were once "over there" somewhere, but have migrated to nearby communities. The people group focus also identifies local nationals or citizens who have been overlooked.

The geographic focus remains essential for engaging the world in mission. The 10/40 Window concept is a geographic model that helps to focus mission vision. The Big Seven and Diverse Six Plus model is an Adventist organizational and geographic model that focuses the denomination's global mission. The geographic focus reminds the church of the billions of people who still live "over there," far away, upon whom the church's missional vision must never waver.

Giving Special Priority to Non-Christians

About two-thirds of humanity do not self-identify as Christians in any way, even though many admire Jesus Christ. A hundred years ago, Adventists had the "luxury" of giving priority to other Christians with a "value added" message and to traditional animistic peoples who were receptive. That earlier work was fruitful and it produced today's membership in the Big Seven group. Today's major challenge is with non-Christian people groups.

To be more effective among non-Christians, Adventists need a broadly held consensus that mission among Christian and non-Christian groups is very different. The goal or destination of evangelization is the same for both groups but the spiritual journey starts at different places. For example, Christians of any kind can receive the biblical teaching of the Second Coming easily because they base it on what they already believe about the First Coming. Non-Christians must first understand and believe the biblical teaching about the birth, life, teachings, atoning death, resurrection, ascension, and heavenly mediation of Jesus Christ before they can understand the blessed hope of the Second Coming in its full significance.

Conclusion

Humanly speaking, the most challenging days of Adventist mission are ahead as it contemplates addressing the most daunting strategic missional challenges. But Adventist eschatology includes the Latter Rain of the Holy Spirit that provides the essential missiological key to human hearts. The church never controls the Spirit because he blows when and where he wishes (John 3:8). But the church can seek to use its God-given capacities in the very best possible way. Those capacities must be focused with utmost intentionality on areas with the greatest strategic need so that the Holy Spirit can do his most dramatic work.

Chapter 15

Encountering the World Religions

~•~

Introduction

When Christians encounter Muslims, Hindus, Buddhists, or the followers of any other religion, they must have some specific knowledge of the particular religion. They also need to reflect on what kind of encounter is most effective with other religious groups.

Missionary Encounter

What is the best way to characterize the encounter a Christian might have with a Muslim, Hindu, Buddhist, or a follower of another world religion? Two approaches to inter-religious encounters are common. First, the comparative religions approach seeks a scholarly, neutral, objective analysis of religious options. Second, the pluralist approach assumes that all religions are equally valid, that they are all incomplete revelations, and that the other religions have the potential to bring completion to Christianity.

Neither the comparative religions nor the pluralist approaches are suitable based on the theology of religions discussed in chapter 6. The approach that fits with the Adventist theology of religions can be called a "missionary encounter" (Goheen 2014:334). The many biblical examples of inter-religious missionary encounters include Jesus with the woman at Jacob's well (John 4), Philip with the Ethiopian eunuch (Acts 8), and Paul in Athens (Acts 17).

The interreligious contact will be "missionary" because it is invitational, appealing, persuasive, and gentle, as opposed to coercive, abrasive, manipulative, or violent. Other religions may practice forced conversion, but Christians honor the God-given right of humans to decline the Gospel invitation. The Christian will seek an authentic human-with-human relationship building encounter rather than a meeting with a stereotypical caricature of a person who is "one of them."

Christlike attitudes of respect, humility, and love characterize the believer's words and deeds.

The interreligious meeting is an "encounter" because it brings together people who differ with each other at the deepest worldview assumption levels. The parties who meet come from traditions often held by their ancestors for many generations. Both bring deep commitments to different scriptures, beliefs, worship practices, and lifestyles. Understanding the encounter as merely an exchange of ideas trivializes it. Coming in search of a lowest common denominator which all can support risks syncretism.

Interreligious Dialogue

Another way to characterize the encounter is as dialogue. The concept of inter-religious dialogue is controversial for some. The reason for the controversy is that some who practice dialogue do so from the comparative religions or pluralist perspectives. Their goal is to reach ecumenical conclusions with which all can agree. In doing so, they may be willing to surrender certain unique Christian commitments and the goal of conversion may be abandoned.

A thoughtful examination of the practice of interreligious dialogue shows that it is not incompatible with Christian witness and evangelization. Rather, it is a valid approach that is modeled in Scripture (see examples in the previous section). Dialogue is a normal part of healthy human interaction, with mutual give and take. A monologue is not a healthy form of human interaction and to use a one-way approach with a Muslim, Hindu, or Buddhist mispresents the Christian faith. Authentic missional encounters are always highly relational and relationships always include mutual dialogue. The real question is not whether to use dialogue but what kind of dialogue should be used in interreligious encounters.

Missional dialogue should have several characteristics: First, "It is not permissible to suspend our commitments or to hide or relativize the faith commitments that shape us....There is no neutrality in the public square, only faith stances" (Goheen 2014:366). Followers of the other religions are perplexed and irritated by Christians who pretend to be neutral because they respect a candid expression of faith commitments.

Second, dialogue presupposes that Christians have good things to learn from people of other religions that do not impinge on their faith commitments. For example, the regularity and commitment to prayer seen among Muslims is a valuable example for Christians. Relational bonds deepen when a Christian expresses admiration to a Muslim friend regarding Islamic faithfulness in prayer.

Third, dialogue assumes the need to know and understand something about the other religions. This does not mean that one needs to become an expert before entering a dialogue; however, Christians need to be curious and willing to be taught about the other religion in the course of the dialogue. Willingness to learn can be reciprocated by the others so that the Christian bears witness to them.

Fourth, interreligious dialogue usually requires a longer-term engagement, a different style, and a different mindset than many Adventists are accustomed to with work among other Christians. Many Adventist Bible studies use a monologue or teaching style. Mutual exploration and explanation characterizes effective interreligious meetings. Christians believe, as an article of faith, that the Word is powerful (Heb 4:12). In the interchange of ideas, the Word rises to the top and draws people to Christ.

Fifth, dialogue assumes that the Holy Spirit can bring conviction (John 16:7-11) to all people in different and mysterious ways (John 3:8). Dialogue partners from the world religions have spiritual journeys to make that start at different places, but the Spirit moves on the hearts of all people as he draws them to Christ.

Introduction to the Three Largest Non-Christian World Religions

This brief introduction to the three largest non-Christian world religions provides only an awareness building summary of their main beliefs and practices. Many excellent resources are available, including Paul Dybdahl (2017), Muck, Netland, and McDormatt (2014), Partridge and Dowley (2013), Corduan (1998), and Smart (1998). The General Conference Global Mission Centers website has materials from an Adventist perspective at www.globalmissioncenters.org.

Understanding the other religions requires hearing their own voices speaking about themselves. Partridge (2005) is used frequently because his edited book has chapters written by practitioners of the different religions. Many print resources written by practitioners are available. An excellent Islamic resource can be found at www.islamreligion.com. Information about Hindus is found at www.hinduismtoday.com. For Buddhism, www.buddhanet.net is helpful.

An adequate missiological response to the beliefs and practices of the other world religions requires bearing constantly in mind the scale of worldview transformation required to become a disciple of Jesus Christ. The other religions hold worldview assumptions about the nature of reality that are, in many cases, very different from those of the Christian faith. One other important reminder is that Christian mission addresses real human beings, not cogs in large religious machines. To illustrate, mission is concerned primarily with real Hindus as individuals and members of their cultural groups rather than with Hinduism as a religious system. A discussion of Hinduism is helpful to help locate real humans within the family of humanity.

Introduction to Islam

Islam is the second largest world religion, after Christianity. In the last century, the Muslim share of the world's population has grown from 12.6% to 22.4% (Johnson and Ross 2009:10-11). Islam originated in Mecca, Saudi Arabia, and the founder of Islam was Muhammad (570-632). Muslims believe that Muhammad started receiving messages from God in AD 610. The messages were later collected to make up the Qur'an. The Islamic era started when Muhammad and his followers made the move (*Hijrah*) from Mecca to Medina in 622. The Islamic religion took shape in Medina, where Muhammad had contact with Jews and Christians. After a period of hostilities with pagan opponents, the Muslims moved back to Mecca and made it their headquarters, with the *Kabaah* as its sacred center. The *Kabaah* is a black cubed structure, said to have been built by Abraham and Ishmael to worship God. Mecca is considered a holy city that cannot be entered by non-Muslims.

Indonesia, India, and Pakistan are the nations with the largest Muslim populations. The Asian continent has 70% and Africa has 27% of all Muslims. The Middle East and North Africa have some nations with over 98% Muslim populations. Immigration is increasing Muslim populations on the other continents.

Sunni Muslims make up about 85% of Islam. Sunnis accept Abu Bakr as the appropriate replacement of Muhammad and first caliph, even though he was not a biological relative. They believe that the caliphs did not have his prophetic qualities, but served only as the stewards of his legacy. Sunni *imams* are spiritual leaders who lead the mosque in prayers but lack Muhammad's prophetic authority.

Shi'a Muslims make up about 12% of Islam and Iran is the nation with the largest Shi'a concentration. The Shi'a majority countries are Iran, Iraq, Azerbaijan, and Bahrain. Shi'as believe that Ali, a biological relative of Muhammad and the fourth caliph (656-66), should have been the first caliph instead of Abu Bakr. When 'Ali and his son Husayn were assassinated, Shi'a became a part of Islam that focuses on suffering and martyrdom. Shi'as believe that *imams* serve with the potential for continued divine revelation and are inspired interpreters of the Qur'an.

Sufi Muslims, who are found in all branches of Islam, seek spiritual purification through mystical forms of worship, music, and dance. Through their mystical approach to Islam, they seek to internalize the faith.

The Six Articles of Faith

Goheen finds that "the orienting core of Islam is to proclaim one transcendent God and to found a community ruled by God and his prophet." In Islam "we hear a cry for a God who is holy, transcendent, and just" (2014:355, 356).

Muslims have a core of beliefs with six points: The oneness of God, angels and spirits, prophets, revealed books, the last day judgment, and the foreknowledge of God (see www.islamreligion.com/articles/4/what-is-islam-part-3/).

The Oneness of God

The central Islamic belief is that God is One. The Islamic understanding can be summarized by one word, *Tawhid*, which refers to the absolute unity of God. The Qur'an uses 99 names for the Sovereign, Creator God, each representing divine attributes. For example: *ar-Rahmân*, the All-Merciful; *ar-Rahïm*, the All-Compassionate; *al-Jabbär*, the Irresistible; *al-Khäliq*, the Creator.

Angels

Angels are seen as a special creation of God, made from light to perform specific duties. They always obey God, sing praises to him, communicate his messages to the prophets, and strengthen everything that is good in humanity. Gabriel (*Jibril*) is mentioned several times as one who brings special messages from God, including the announcement to Mary concerning the birth of Jesus (3:45; 19:17-21). *Jibril* also brought revelations (*wahy*) to Muhammad that later became the written Qur'an. Guardian angels are responsible for protecting believers throughout life.

The devil is an evil angel who has many evil spirit associates called *jinn*. Evil angels are relatively weak, but bring trouble to humans and seek to weaken their obedience to God. Believers must constantly be on guard against the *jinn*. Folk Muslims place heavy emphasis on the activities of the *jinn*.

Prophets

Muslims believe that throughout history God has sent messengers to point people back to the "straight way." Twenty-five prophets are named in the Qur'an, twenty of which appear in the Bible. Muhammad is understood to be the "seal of the prophets," meaning that by receiving and transmitting the Qur'an in written form, he summarized all that humans must know from Allah's revelation.

Holy Books

The Qur'an is the Muslim holy book. "For Muslims the Qur'an represents the supreme revelation of God's word in written form. It is unique among revealed books, universal in its application, and eternal in its relevance" (Partridge 2005:368; Malik 2008:12-13). The Arabic words of the Qur'an are understood to be the literal words spoken by God to Muhammad. Translations into other languages exist but only the Arabic Qur'an carries authority. The Qur'an has 114 chapters called *surahs*. The Hadith are a supplementary, voluminous collection of prophetic traditions that guide Muslims in their daily lives.

The Qur'an recognizes the Torah as revealed by God to the prophet Moses (3:3; 5:44), the Psalms (*Zabur*) as revealed to the prophet David (17:55), and the Gospel (*Injil*) as revealed to the prophet Jesus (5:46; 57:27). Jews and Christians are the "people of the book" and Muslims should not reject the Christian book (4:136). However, Muslims believe that the original texts of the Bible were lost and that Christians have polluted those writings that remain.

The Last Day Judgment

Muslims believe in a final day of judgment in which everyone will be summoned before God to account for their deeds. The Qur'an refers to the day of judgment as the "final hour" and calls Jesus "the sign of the final hour" (43:61). Only God knows the time of the "final hour" (7:187; 16:77). Most Muslims agree with the idea of the coming of Jesus (*Isa al Masih*) to judge the world and give rewards. At the resurrection, the righteous will think that they have been dead but for only a moment (22:5; 50:2, 21; 75:1-4; 17:52). To unbelievers, the resurrection is a fearful thing (83:1-6) because hell fire awaits them.

God's Foreknowledge

God knows and has power over everything that happens (4:78; 36:38-39). Humans have a free will to obey or disobey God, but he knows what they will choose and their destiny. People should trust God no matter what happens to them because everything is his will (Malik 2008:4).

The Five Pillars of Islam

Muslims show their complete submission to God through the Five Pillars or practices: Confession of faith, prayers, fasting, charitable giving, and pilgrimage (see www.islamreligion.com/articles/3/what-is-islam-part-4).

Confession of Faith: Shahadah

The *Shahadah* is the most basic, two-part statement of Islamic faith: "I bear witness that there is no god but God and Muhammad is the apostle of God" (37:35; 48:29). The first part declares that God is One and the second that Muhammad is his most important messenger. The first sound a newborn baby and the last sound a dying person must hear is the *Shahadah*. A Muslim is expected to recite this statement out loud, in Arabic, with total sincerity, fully understanding its meaning.

Prayers: Salat

Salat is the obligatory set of prayers, performed five times each day: (1) at sunrise, (2) at noon, (3) in midafternoon, (4) at sunset, and (5) between sunset and midnight. On Fridays the *Salat* is prayed at the mosque. The prayer timetable provides a daily pattern for personal spirituality. In Islamic societies, the call to prayer from the mosque sets a rhythm for the whole society. Muslims prepare for prayers by special ablutions that involve rinsing hands, feet, eyes, ears, nose, and mouth three times. On Friday, the noon prayers are performed in the mosque with the community, the *Umma*.

Charitable Giving: Zakat

Zakat is the giving of a set proportion of one's wealth to charity. It is regarded as a type of worship and of self-purification. *Zakat* does not refer to spontaneous charitable gifts, but to the systematic giving of 2.5% of net profit each year to benefit the poor.

Fasting: Sawm

Muslims are required to fast during Ramadan, which in 2018 came between May 15 and June 16. During the 29/30 days of Ramadan, all adult Muslims must give up food and drink, smoking, and sexual activity during the hours of daylight. The whole Qur'an is recited during the course of the month and Muslims are to diligently avoid all evil thoughts and deeds. A meal is eaten just before dawn and in the evening. The evening meals are occasions for special family and community fellowship. The month of Ramadan ends with the festival of *Eid ul-Fitr*. This festival is marked by visiting the mosque for prayer, visiting and sharing gifts with family and friends, and celebratory meals.

Muslims who are physically or mentally unwell can be excused from some or all of the requirements. Children under twelve years old, the elderly, women who are pregnant, breast-feeding, or menstruating, and travelers may be exempted. Adults who miss the fast can make it up later or make a donation to the poor instead.

Pilgrimage: Hajj

At least once in a lifetime, every adult Muslim who is healthy enough and can afford the trip, must make the Hajj to worship Allah before the *Kabaah* in Mecca. The *Hajj* occurs during the month of *Dhul Hijjah*, which in 2018 was August 19-24. The *Hajj* unites Muslims of every ethnic group, social status, and culture. Pilgrims wear simple white clothes called *Ihram* and perform acts of worship that renew their sense of purpose in the world.

Islamic Practices

Islam prohibits the eating of pigs as well as animals like lions, tigers, leopards, cats, dogs, wolves, hyenas, rodents, and reptiles because eating them would make people impure and violent (Malik 2008:21-22). Gambling and drinking alcohol are forbidden (5:90-92)

Although some Islamic nations require specific forms of dress, Islam requires modest dress for everyone, including both women and men. Women should dress in a way that does not call public attention to their beauty (24:31). Men generally prefer long trousers because they are more modest than short trousers.

"Family in Islam is the foundation of society. The family provides security and opportunity for the spiritual and material growth of its members" (Malik 2008:23). Children and the aged are treasures to be given special care. Men can marry as many as four wives, but must love them and provide for them equally (4:3). A wife is divorced when her husband says "I divorce you" three times

Introduction to Hinduism

With about 1 billion adherents who make up about 14% of the world population, Hindus comprise the majority religion of India and a significant portion of humanity. The name "Hindu" is ancient, referring to the people of India with its Indus river. "Hinduism" is a modern term coined by European scholars of the nineteenth century to name a cluster of very diverse beliefs and practices on the Indian subcontinent.

Hinduism has no single founder, no unified system of beliefs, no single doctrine of salvation, and no centralized authority. In this sense it is different from the other "world religions." Diversity is a characteristic feature of Hinduism, yet most scholars would agree that there are unifying strands that run through the diverse traditions that constitute it. Although the term Hinduism is recent, the diverse traditions that it encompasses have very ancient origins that extend back beyond the second millennium BCE. (Partridge 2005:134)

Hinduism is best understood as a complete way of life in which religion and culture are fused together. Philosophical Hindus focus on philosophical questions and the meaning of human existence. Popular or folk Hindus emphasize a great variety of rituals in the home or at the temple that are directed to the many gods of the Hindu pantheon. Goheen suggests that "the orientating core of Hinduism is the quest to escape from the endless and meaningless cycle of finite existence." In Hinduism "we hear the longing to find what will endure" (2014:355, 356).

Hindu Scriptures

The Hindu scriptures are a large collection of writings, mostly written in Sanskrit, and dating from as early as 1300 BCE to more recent times. The main Hindu canon is the Veda. Other scriptures, including the Bhagavad Gita, tell the great epic narratives of Hinduism.

Hindu Deities, Avatars, and Images

Sometimes Hindus are said to have 330 million gods, although the number has not been confirmed. "Hindus may be polytheistic, monotheistic, or monistic (believing that all reality is actually one)" or even atheistic. "Many Hindus believe there is one God (*Brahman*) who can be worshipped in many forms." God can "appear as a baby, a friend, a king, a mother, or a lover." God can be manifested "as male or female or in nonhuman form, be worshipped as without form or with form." God appears "through icons and images, or in human shape as a living saint or guru" (Partridge 2005:146).

Hindus have three main gods—Brahman, the creator; Vishnu, the sustainer; and Shiva, the destroyer. Sometimes the group is broadened to five—Vishnu, Shiva, Devi, Surya, and Ganesha. Shiva and Vishnu are the preeminent gods worshipped by Hindus everywhere.

Avatars are manifestations of God who intervene to fight against evil and make sure the universe functions according to the *dharma*. Krishna and Rama, both avatars of Vishnu, are famous and much loved.

Hindus worship before images of the gods made of many different materials. Some believe that images only represent the gods and others that images actually embody the gods.

Hindu Concepts

Hindu thought has three central presuppositions: First, that time is cyclical. The "universe has neither beginning nor end. It issued forth from *Brahman* (the ultimate, divine 'ground of being') and will eventually return to *Brahman*, only to repeat the cycle again" (Partridge 2005:141). Life is an unending cycle of birth and rebirth called *samsara*.

Second, because of *samsara*, the microcosmic level of individual life, the seasons of nature, and the generations of life are linked with the macrocosmic level. The macrocosmic level includes the great eras of history and the creations and dissolutions of the whole cosmos.

Third, "the causal principle of *karma* connects each event in *samsara*, so that events in this cycle effect subsequent cycles" (141). To illustrate, one's destiny combined with one's choices cause one to live in a certain way; one's way of life results is a particular kind of rebirth in the cycle of time; and the aggregate of the individual rebirths of all humanity gives the whole cosmos a particular character.

Dharma and Moksha

Dharma is the "moral and metaphysical foundation of the universe" and the duty which individuals must perform. *Moksha* is the ultimate liberation and freedom from the *samsara* cycle of rebirth that every human seeks. *Moksha* comes from fulfilling one's *dharma* or duty (Partridge 2005:141).

Karma

Karma is the combined activities that determine the nature of one's rebirth in the coming *samsara* cycles of rebirth. One can be reborn as a member of a higher or lower caste or be demoted to life as an animal. People perform many rites and rituals during life and their funerals are planned to improve their *karma*. Individuals are not aware of the details of their past lives or able to know about their future lives after death.

Three Paths

Hindus are supposed to concentrate on one of three paths (*margas* or *yogas*) leading to *moksha* (liberation), although some link the three paths together. The Three Paths come from the Bhagavad Gita.

Jnana Yoga: The Path of Knowledge and Wisdom. On this pathway, one overcomes the problem of ignorance and achieves oneness with *Brahman*. "The pursuit of wisdom implies religious practice, meditation, self-purification, and above all the study of the scriptures" (Partridge 2005:151).

Karma Yoga: The Path of Work. People on this pathway perform their duty (*dharma*) selflessly, "without the desire for status or reward" (151).

Bhakti Yoga: The Path of Loving Devotion. This path is characterized by an intense, loving relationship and communion with the deity. *Bhakti* is manifested by rituals, pilgrimages, and other acts of worship and devotion.

Four Goals

Hindus pursue major goals in search of spiritual and social harmony. "Some Hindus believe that these goals are interconnected and that no goal is primary. Others believe they form a hierarchy with *moksha* transcending and even opposing the other three."

"*Artha* (worldly wealth and success) is a proper goal if pursued without desire, anger, and greed. Pursuing an occupation, accumulating wealth, governing and so on are justified if they do not violate *dharma*."

"*Kama* (pleasure, desire) is also a legitimate goal if it accords with *dharma*. This is the pursuit of pleasurable activities, including sexuality, play, recreation, and arts and literature."

"*Dharma* (virtue, morality) has two levels. It is both one's own particular set of duties ... and absolute morality, valid universally."

"*Moksha* (spiritual liberation) is the ultimate Hindu quest. It is the release from the bondage of suffering and rebirth (*samsara*)" (Partridge 2005:151).

Astrology

Although the sacred texts are not well known by many Hindus, the use of astrology is very common. Decisions about the minor and major events of daily life are made with the help of astrological charts and almanacs.

The Caste System

Many Hindus believe that God divided humanity into different castes. *Brahman* are the priestly caste who are better schooled. *Kshatriya* is the warrior caste, many of whom were ancient kings. *Vaishya* is the merchant caste. *Shudra* is the low caste that includes people of menial occupations who work alongside social outcasts in impure duties like handling corpses. The *Dalit* are the lowest class who perform the least desirable jobs. The caste system has many sub-castes in between these major types. Modern India has tried to equalize educational and professional opportunities for the lower castes.

Hindu Ritual Practices

Many Hindus highly value the rituals and practices that are part of their daily lives and yearly cycle. Innumerable temples and shrines appear both in densely populated urban centers and peaceful rural settings. Rituals accompany all of the events of normal life as well as times of special difficulty and disaster.

Puja

Puja is "a ritual of devotional worship regularly conducted at temples, usually by Brahman priests, and often observed privately at household shrines" (Partridge 2005:153). *Puja* addresses the gods of the Hindu pantheon who are represented by images. The priest ritually purifies himself and the shrine and invokes the presence of the deity by bathing, adorning, and feeding the image. Householders perform similar rituals at home shrines.

Pilgrimage

There are innumerable sites in India that are considered to be sacred. Because the sacred is so ubiquitous, common things like stones, trees, mountains, or rivers can become pilgrimage destinations. These destinations draw countless Hindus from nearby, from all of India, and from the world. Taking a bath in the Ganges river is one of the most valued pilgrimage rituals.

Certain pilgrimage sites are considered most sacred: *Varanasi* and *Hardwar*, located on the Ganges river, receive thousands of pilgrims every year; *Ayodhya* is believed to be the birth place of Lord Rama; *Mathura* is believed to be the birthplace of Lord Krishna; *Dwarka* is the city where Krishna ruled as king; *Kanchipuram* is a temple city in South India; and *Ujjan* is the site of the *Kumbh Mela* festival.

Festivals

The Hindu year is punctuated by a series of festivals honoring specific deities and remembering events in Hindu mythology. For example, *Janmashtami* celebrates the birthday of Krishna; *Diwali* is the festival lights, during which Hindus exchange gifts and illuminate their homes with special lights; and *Holi* during which people throw brightly colored powder and water on each other. The *Kumbh Mela* festival is one of the most popular that draws pilgrims from around the world.

Introduction to Buddhism

The almost 500 million Buddhists in the world make up about 7% of the world population. China, Japan, and Thailand have the largest Buddhist populations. Thailand, Cambodia, and Myanmar have the highest Buddhist concentrations (Johnson and Ross 2009:14).

> Buddhism has been described as a very pragmatic religion. It does not indulge in metaphysical speculation about first causes; there is no theology, no worship of a deity or deification of the Buddha. Buddhism takes a very straightforward look at our human condition; nothing is based on wishful thinking, at all. Everything that the Buddha taught was based on his own observation of the way things are. Everything that he taught can be verified by our own observation of the way things are. (www.buddhanet.net/e-learning/intro_bud.htm)

Goheen says that "the orienting core of Buddhism is the pursuit of deliverance from transient existence." In Buddhism "we hear a cry to be liberated from a suffering world" (2014:355, 356).

"The Buddha": Siddhartha Gautama

Siddhartha Gautama, later called "The Buddha" ("the enlightened one"), was born in the fifth century BCE into a wealthy royal family near the Himalayas. He married, had a son, and seemed destined to succeed his father as king.

One day Gautama slipped out of the palace and saw four scenes that changed his life. He saw an old man, a sick man, a corpse, and an ascetic. The first three scenes brought home to his heart the striking reality that age, sickness and death come to all. The fourth scene gave him a hint of a possible escape from the cycle of death and rebirth.

Gautama left the luxuries and privileges of the palace, renouncing everything in order to search out a way of escape from suffering and death. He diligently practiced self-mortification and meditation until he almost died. While nearly starving, Gautama recognized that extreme asceticism was as useless as pleasure seeking. So he ate then sat down beneath a Bodhi tree and determined to meditate until he could find a better way.

According to the story, on his 35th birthday he attained enlightenment, destroying all mental impurities and gaining perfect understanding into all realities, therefore called "the Buddha," "fully awake" or "enlightened." He continued to reflect on his insights for seven weeks and determined to spend the rest of his life helping others move toward the same.

The Buddha sent out 60 disciples to teach others and spent 45 years in active ministry. He died at age 80. His last words were "Verily do I say unto you: Perishable are all conditional things. Work out your way with diligence." (cear.globalmissioncenters.org/buddhism)

One Buddha, Many Variations

There are two major divisions in Buddhism: Theravada and Mahayana. Theravada Buddhism is more conservative in its beliefs, claiming to hold more closely to the Buddha's original teachings. It is primarily practiced in Sri Lanka and Southeast Asia. Mahayana Buddhism is considered to be more liberal and is practiced more in China, Japan, and Korea. Mahayana is further divided into various sects such as Pure Land, Nichiren, and Zen. Some people classify a third division as Vajrayana, which is practiced primarily in Tibet and Mongolia as well as in parts of China and Russia. However, others recognize Vajrayana as a part of the Mahayana branch.

Tibetan Buddhism has been popularized in the West by the Dalai Lama with his emphasis on moral and ethical elements that foster tolerance and peace. His focus has greatly down-played the Tantric elements and magic central to the Tibetan belief which has made it very appealing to Westerners searching for peace in this age of chaos.

Wherever it has gone, Buddhism has been tolerant of folk beliefs and has invariably been mixed with indigenous religious practices. For example, Hindu ceremonies and celebrations are practiced in many Buddhist countries. And in other countries, animistic and ancestral worship practices play a central role in people's lives (cear.globalmissioncenters.org/buddhism).

Buddhist Scriptures

After the Buddha's death, the leading monks who had achieved enlightenment recited what they remembered of his teachings. The teachings were transmitted orally until about 100 BCE when they were written. The Buddhist canon has two main parts. The *Sutras* record the Buddha's teachings and those of his main followers. The *Vinayas* contain materials related to Buddhists monastic structures and disciplines.

Buddhist Beliefs

There are various types of Buddhists with different beliefs and practices. However, generally speaking, the Three Gems, Four Noble Truths, and the Eightfold Path are the foundation of the Buddhist belief system.

Three Gems

The Three Gems comprise the only creedal statement for Buddhists: "I go to the Buddha for refuge; I go to the *Dharma* for refuge; I go to the *Sangha* (the Buddhist community) for refuge" (Partridge 2005:199).

The Four Noble Truths

The Four Noble Truths are: (1) The Noble Truth of *Dukkha*: Suffering and emptiness are at the heart of human existence; (2) The Noble Truth of the Origin of *Dukkha*: Cravings and desires (*tanha*) are the causes of *Dukkha*; (3) The Noble Truth of the Escape from *Dukkha*: By overcoming cravings and desires, people can move beyond *Dukkha*; (4) The Noble Truth of the Eightfold Path to the Cessation of *Dukkha*: Though "people are trapped in mental prisons of their own making ... liberation waits for all who can change the way they look at the world and work towards freedom from cravings" (Partridge 2005:200). The cessation of *Dukkha* is referred to as nirvana.

The Eightfold Path

The Eightfold Path helps put the Noble Truths into practice and is often summarized as "mindfulness," or awareness of one's inner self and motives.

- Right Understanding
- Right Thought
- Right Speech
- Right Action
- Right Livelihood
- Right Effort
- Right Mindfulness
- Right Concentration

Five Precepts of Morality

"Morality is the bedrock of the Buddhist path. It involves 'the avoidance of evil and the understanding of good. Without moral discipline the holy life cannot be lived" (Partridge 2005:201). Being a moral person means abstaining from:

- harming or killing any living things.
- taking what is not given.

- sexual misconduct.
- false speech.
- anything that clouds or intoxicates the mind.

The Law of Karma

Most Buddhists believe in the law of karma, which teaches that every good deed will have a good result and every evil deed will have an evil result. This belief in karma and the desire to escape suffering motivates many Buddhists to meditate, perform ceremonies, and do good deeds to obtain good merit, the currency of the karma system (cear.globalmissioncenters.org/buddhism).

Chapter

Mission Among Creative Access Peoples

∿•⌇

Introduction

C hristian mission is particularly challenging in contexts where the other world religions predominate. The nature and degree of the missional challenge cannot be generalized to all places because of major social, legal, and religious differences between nations. For example, the main barriers to mission in Japan and Thailand are social and religious, while in parts of the Middle East and North Africa, Christian mission encounters the additional barriers of legal prohibition.

In the past century, resistance to Christian mission has become more intentional and structured. The philosophy and methods of Christian mission are studied and strategies are developed to oppose them. Muslims have their own form of evangelism, called *Dawah*. The beliefs and practices of specific Christian groups are studied for the sake of effective *Dawah*.

Those of us who live and work in countries where the freedom of worship is guaranteed by law sometimes have trouble accepting the reality of limited religious freedom. We may want to protest and demand our right to go into any nation to proclaim the Gospel in any way we wish; however, just like Jesus and Paul, we have to do the work of mission in the world just as it is. Our only choice is to use Spirit-guided, biblically faithful, creative methods that may not always suit our habituated and favored patterns.

The term "creative access people" is used to identify people groups who cannot be reached in a typical, open, public manner. In some contexts, conversion to Christianity is legal but converts face major social disapproval. That disapproval can be relatively minor, causing irritation and upsetting relationships temporarily. Or it can be serious enough to cause converts to be disinherited, thrown out of the family, or divorced. In other places, conversion is against the law. Sometimes converts can manage their disobedience of the law and avoid legal penalties with appropriate care and discretion. In other places, converts inevitably receive legal penalties that can be as serious as execution.

Some legal systems permit any type of Christian meeting, including evangelism, on officially registered church property but nowhere else. In such places, non-Christians can attend meetings, but they will face whatever social or legal sanctions if they are converted. In other places, Christian witnessing of any kind is forbidden and must be restricted to secure places and small groups.

Some nations have ancient Christian communities that exist as sub-cultures within larger cultures. For example, Egypt has Coptic Orthodox Christian communities that predate Islam and are a recognized part of society. Other nations have no publicly recognized indigenous Christian communities.

In this age of globalization, expatriate Christians from places like Africa or the Philippines work throughout the Middle East and North Africa. In some countries they are able to worship publicly in registered churches while elsewhere they must worship secretly in house churches. Local, indigenous people are often forbidden to attend the expatriate churches. The house church phenomenon is well known from the Communist era and continues today in China.

How does Christian mission function in creative access countries? The two scenarios that follow illustrate different patterns.

Scenario 1: Extraction or Isolation

A Muslim university student meets a foreign fellow student in one of his classes who is a Christian. They start having religious discussions and the Muslim is attracted to the Bible and Jesus Christ. The foreigner contacts friends at home and they arrange to sponsor the Muslim to study in America. Once in America, the Muslim is baptized and becomes a member of a local Adventist Church. He marries an American, becomes a dentist, physician, or engineer, and takes American citizenship. Aside from occasional contacts with his immediate family back home, he has no contact with his native people and his conversion has negligible missional impact with them. He is an example of mission by emigration or extraction.

Alternatively, the Muslim student might join a local Christian church that exists in a social-cultural bubble. The church members are part of a sub-culture that has little interaction with the larger culture. Their presence is tolerated, but they have no effective mission in their own community. The convert is an example of mission that produces isolation.

Scenario 2: Staying Home and Engaged

A group of Muslims comprises a cultural sub-group within their larger people group. They worship in several mosques and are led by several imams. Their nation has strict laws against conversion to Christianity or any other religion.

Public evangelism and personal witnessing by expatriates is outlawed. Planting publicly functioning, formally organized churches is impossible.

One night one of the imams has a dream that puzzles and amazes him. A figure appears in the dream calling himself *Isa Al Misah* (Jesus the Messiah). The imam has a deep peace in his heart. Jesus tells the imam that he has a special message for him that will be carried by a special messenger. As the dream closes, Jesus shows the imam an image of the special messenger.

A few weeks later, the imam recognizes the special messenger on the street and approaches him. Mutual trust is established and they start talking about the Qur'an and the Bible in private. The imam brings his fellow imams into the Bible study. Over a period of time, the imams accept Jesus Christ and the Bible, including all of the Adventist message. The special messenger arranges private meetings between the imams and Adventist leaders outside their country.

As time passes, the two imams use bridges within the Qur'an to introduce Bible truth to their members. The members come to love Jesus and look forward to His Second Coming. They believe that the Law of the Prophet Moses should govern their lives. They confess their sins and accept forgiveness from Jesus. They add weekly Sabbath worship to their Friday prayers in the mosque.

Other Muslims think of the group as being somewhat deviant but there are many factions within Islam and this group is tolerated. Members of the group continue to self-identify as Muslim and not Christian because they identify "Christian" with the Crusades, colonialism, Western immorality, Hollywood movies, and decadence. They call themselves followers of *Isa Al Masih* and know they are different because Jesus and the Bible have replaced the Qur'an and Mohammed as their primary spiritual centers. The group is not organized as a church in the typical way and reports about them are not published. Continued contact is maintained between the church headquarters in a nearby nation and the group leaders for the sake of counsel and guidance.

Mapping the Challenges

The two scenarios are both success stories of doing mission in different ways among creative access peoples. They give only two illustrations along a wide spectrum of how mission functions in challenging places. The problem with the first scenario is that the convert does not have a continuing witness in his motherland. The limitation of the second scenario is that the world church lacks normal access to fully support and nurture the newly birthed congregation, even though there is some contact.

Because of the spectrum of the missional challenge, the church must exercise appropriate flexibility in its methods, with obedience to the unchanging Word of God. Jesus worked among people of varying levels of openness and hiddenness, carefully managing message and methods to suit his audience. The world in which the Apostles worked was hostile and oppositional. With this hostility as a backdrop, Paul said

> Though I am free and belong to no man, I make myself a slave to everyone, to win as many as possible. To the Jews I became like a Jew, to win the Jews. To those under the law I became like one under the law (though I myself am not under the law), so as to win those under the law. To those not having the law I became like one not having the law (though I am not free from God's law but am under Christ's law), so as to win those not having the law. To the weak I became weak, to win the weak. I have become all things to all men so that by all possible means I might save some. I do all this for the sake of the gospel, that I may share in its blessings. (1 Cor 9:19-23)

For most of Christian history there have been believers who have had to work and worship in secrecy. In the Middles Ages, the Waldensians hid in mountains and caves and ventured out in disguise to witness using handwritten Scripture portions concealed in their clothing.

The freedom of worship enjoyed in much of the contemporary world may actually be an historical oddity. Governments of the colonial era, when Adventist global mission was beginning, generally upheld freedom of worship. But the world has changed because many governments now give only lip service to religious freedom, at best. Mission to non-Christians in the twenty-first century requires many shifts in thinking and methods—all under obedience to the Word.

The Travis C1 to C6 Model

Conceptual models help to understand the multiple missional challenges and formulate responses to them. John Travis (a pseudonym) was a long-time missionary in Asia working among Muslims. He observed congregations of Christians in the Muslim context who adapted to their varied environments in different ways. From his observations on the field, he developed the "C1 to C6 Model" to describe how "Christ-centered communities" function in different Muslim contexts (1998;2015).

> The C1-C6 Spectrum describes six types of fellowship (or "Christ-centered communities," represented by the letter C) that Muslims either join or form when they follow Jesus. The six types are differentiated in terms of language, culture, religious forms, and religious identity....Points along the Spectrum are meant to be descriptive rather than prescriptive, and dynamic rather than static. A given Jesus fellowship or movement may take on different expressions over time. (Travis and Woodberry 2015:35)

Travis does not intend to prescribe how mission *should* function among Muslims, but rather to describe different ways Christ-centered communities are *already functioning*. The groups he observed existed because of many different mission initiatives, the guidance of the Spirit, and the guidance of the Bible. He believes his model broadly describes Christian communities among Buddhists, Hindus, and other religions, even though the specific ways of adapting are different than in the Muslim context.

In a fifteen-year retrospective, Travis offers some clarifications about the C1 to C6 Model (2015:360-364). First, the model should be viewed as "a range of colors placed side by side," where the characteristics of congregations are not fixed into rigid patterns. In other words, the differences between the C1 to C6 patterns are like colors in a spectrum that blend into each other.

Second, the way communities express their Christianity in their challenging contexts evolves and morphs with time and circumstances. Some churches move toward a more public presence and others have to be more secretive, as circumstances become either easier or harder.

Third, communities at every point on the spectrum can be either more faithful or less faithful to the Bible. Thus, a C1 congregation that is a more traditional can be more syncretistic than a C5 or C6 group that is non-traditional but is more faithful to the Bible. Conversely, a C5 or C6 group could be highly syncretistic and a C1 very true to the Bible. Assuming that traditional congregations are faithful to Scripture may be unwise, while assuming that non-traditional groups are unfaithful may be unfair.

Factors in the C1 to C6 Model

The Travis C1 to C6 Model is adapted for the Adventist perspective using John Travis (1998; 2015), Kurt Nelson (2009), and Nate Irwin (2011). The reader will benefit by visualizing a setting where another world religion is dominant and Christians are a small minority. An Islamic context is used in this discussion.

The model does not offer precise definitions or prescriptions. Rather, it demonstrates how the components of being a congregation and doing mission are adjusted to accommodate the exceedingly wide variation of religious, cultural, political, and legal factors that cannot be changed. This section discusses the factors and the next section shows how they are linked in C1 to C6 congregations.

Language

The most basic factor needing contextualization is language. Even for Christians, the Gospel sounds the sweetest in one's mother tongue. The appeal of the Gospel to non-Christians is greatly magnified when the Gospel is heard as a local message rather than a foreign one. The C1 churches are valuable because they serve a multicultural, international community with a shared language, but their potential for reaching local Muslims, Hindus, or Buddhists is limited. Starting with C2, a local language is used.

Religious Forms

Typical Adventist forms are derived mostly from American culture. If the rest of the world wants to borrow Western-styled architecture, church seating, hymn tunes, or prayer postures, they are free to do so. Borrowed forms are suitable for C1 and C2 churches. Starting with C3, local cultural forms are used to convey the accurate meanings about worship. For example, some societies sit on chairs in school or at work, but on the floor to worship. When local non-Christians observe Christians sitting on the floor in church, they say, "Those people are worshipping." Some societies leave their shoes at the door to show reverence.

Membership

The model describes a range from mostly expatriate to completely local memberships. In very restricted access contexts, expatriates are not even able to visit. Even where there is freedom of worship, locals will often not visit a church where most members are foreigners.

Places of Worship

The local context determines whether official church buildings, neutral halls, or house churches are best. In very restricted access contexts the only viable places of worship are house churches or in random places "where two or three are gathered in my name" (Matt 18:20).

Self-Identity

Ideally, every congregation has an official church sign, website, and phone book entry, and every member publicly declares a Seventh-day Adventist Christian self-identity. Sadly, the ideal is not always possible. In creative access contexts the degree of public openness that is possible varies greatly. Some converts self-identify as "followers of *Isa Al-Misah*," or as "Adventists" instead of as "Christian," because "Christian" makes Muslims think of the Crusades, Western colonialism, Hollywood movies, immorality and decadence. Some even retain a Muslim self-identity. The reasons for using a particular self-identity need thoughtful reflection.

The followers of Jesus Christ did not call themselves "Christians" until the church at Antioch had become the main hub of mission in about AD 42, almost a decade after Christ's ascension (Acts 11:26). The term "Christian" did not make Early Church believers who they were. What they believed and practiced made them who they were. They might have chosen some other name for themselves. There are particular reasons some converts from Islam do not call themselves "Christians," as already mentioned, but this does not indicate a rejection of Jesus Christ.

The "Seventh-day Adventist" name was chosen in 1860, sixteen years after the Great Disappointment, and after the new denomination had developed its major beliefs and was well on its way to formal organization. The name was chosen intentionally to convey core beliefs and to serve as part of the Adventist mission; however, the core beliefs and practices behind the name are more important than the name itself. Converts from Islam or another religion who believe, accept, and practice Adventist beliefs can rightly be considered to be fellow Adventist Christians, even if their circumstances prevent them calling themselves by the name. If circumstances change, they can be led to accept the name and see themselves as part of a world community.

The reason some converts continue to call themselves "Muslim" is that culture and religion are almost impossible to separate. They often live in societies that are 90%-plus Islamic and every part of their cultures are shaped by Islam. They can change their beliefs about the Qur'an, Mohammed, and God and make other changes required by the Bible, but they still remain members of their culture. Being Christian makes them live within their culture differently, but they are still a part of their culture. Remaining within their restricted culture makes them valuable in God's mission to their own people. As cultural insiders, they have unique access to witness by their lives, words, and deeds where no foreigners can enter.

The Early Church in Jerusalem was made up of followers of Jesus who retained their Jewish cultural identity. Other Jews rejected Jesus Christ as Messiah. The Early Church believers had the same cultural identity, but a new religious identity. The situation in Jerusalem changed, especially after the temple was destroyed in AD 70, and Jewish Christian self-identity evolved into a more universal Christian identity as Gentiles joined the church. That evolving self-identity also occurs among Muslims who become Christians.

Community Assigned Identity

The ideal is that governments and societies would give Adventists the identity they have chosen for themselves. The local community, in some contexts, makes room for all Christian churches with their full denominational identities, but that does not and cannot happen everywhere. Starting with C4, the identity of Christians is somewhat fuzzy in the eyes of the local community. Christians may be seen as atypical Muslims, deviant Muslims, sectarian Muslims, or just Muslims. The reason Christian identity is allowed in some places is that the Qur'an says many positive things about Jesus, the Second Coming, the Bible, and the People of the Book. The assigned identity depends on factors within the local community and how Christians present themselves.

Relationship with Culture

Indigenous Christians in C1 congregations are seen by the local community as outsiders who have taken a foreign religion. They may even be seen as traitors, although many are viewed with indifference. The model charts a progression until, by C5, they are complete cultural insiders. Being a cultural insider is a major missional asset. Christians in restricted access contexts cannot witness as freely as where there is freedom of religion, but they have access, cultural affinity, and credibility that no foreigners can ever have.

Potential Outreach

Humanly speaking, the potential for outreach is limited in all creative access contexts. C1 churches seem so foreign to local people that their effective outreach is minimal, even if there is freedom to evangelize. At the other end of the spectrum, C6 believers are so hidden from society that their outreach is negligible. Believers who are C3, C4, or C5 have the best potential for outreach because they have access to Muslims and Muslim Background Believers (MBBs), or Christians of other denominations, because they are cultural insiders.

Relationship with World Church

The limited access to C4 to C5 groups by the global church makes administrative oversight challenging. This difficulty corresponds somewhat to circumstances during the cold war. The conference or field serving a particular area cannot implement everything in the normal administrative package, including official record keeping; administrative offices may be in neighboring countries; however, with creativity and adaptability, oversight arrangements can be made. Administrators serving creative access contexts need special competence and understanding. Visits from short-term mission groups and others who lack orientation can undermine C4 to C6 groups and are risky for all. Reports of work among C4 and C5 groups usually cannot be published in church media.

Discipleship

The challenge of doing effective discipleship applies to all congregational types. The Adventist tendency to follow the baptism model of mission, that by default considers the task of mission complete in the baptistery, needs to be changed for every context, but especially so for creative access contexts. Even in C1 and C2 congregations, where public worship, evangelism, and baptism are possible, the dominant surrounding culture makes the discipleship model of mission essential. Leading a spiritually receptive Muslim, Hindu, or Buddhist to full conversion and mature discipleship is a much longer journey than leading one who is already a Christian. With C3 to C6 groups, the challenge of full discipleship is complicated by limited access to the resources of the world church. Basic materials, like translated Bibles, Sabbath School lessons, and Ellen White publications may be difficult to supply. Contextualized materials for specific people groups may not even exist.

Honesty and Integrity

Being hidden, insider, or underground Christians raises an ethical consideration. Is it ethical for Christians to be less than fully transparent and open about their identities, beliefs, and practices? Examples from Jesus, the Apostles, and church history indicate that withholding information strategically for the sake of God's mission is indeed highly ethical. Jesus withheld his Messianic identity until he reached the best place in his mission to reveal it (Matt 16:20; Mark 8:30). When he sent the Twelve on their first mission trip he instructed them "Behold, I send you out as sheep in the midst of wolves; so be shrewd as serpents and innocent as doves" (Matt 10:16). Believers have taken refuge in catacombs, while the Waldensians, Communist-era believers, and many others have lived and witnessed as hidden, underground Christians. Those who are guilty of unethical behavior are the rulers and governments who restrict a person's freedom of choice and worship.

Martyrdom

Christian martyrdom is related to honesty and integrity. Untold thousands have died as martyrs throughout the history of the church, including in the twenty-first century. Does being a true Christian require a public confession of belief in Jesus Christ, even when martyrdom is a possible or likely outcome? Does the Travis C1 to C6 model make being a Christian "too easy" by letting converts "off the hook"? Definitely not. The decision to make a public confession that could lead to martyrdom is between the individual believer and their Lord. In God's eternal wisdom, the public testimony of a Christian martyr may be of great value; however, in this age of terrorism, a martyrdom may be just one more gruesome killing like many seen in the media. Martyrdom should not be glamorized. In most circumstances, God's mission is best served by a living Christian whose life and witness in very trying circumstances testifies for God. Those who live in the blessed state of full religious freedom should beware of laying heavy burdens on others that they might be unable to bear, themselves (Matt 23:4).

The C1 to C6 Model in Action

The C1 Group

Language: usually English, occasionally French, Spanish, or Portuguese in some contexts

Religious Forms: typical Adventist music, order of service, furniture styles, architecture, and prayer postures

Membership: multicultural expatriates and indigenous people who are Westernized and know English or another global language; indigenous members are part of a small sub-culture

Place of Worship: official church building

Self-Identity: Seventh-day Adventist Christian

Community Assigned Identity: Seventh-day Adventist Christian

Relationship with Culture: foreign religion, a social-religious island

Potential Outreach: to expatriates and MBBs (Muslim Background Believers) in other Christian denominations who know English; limited outreach to Muslims in the community

Relationship with World Church: standard

The C2 Group

Language: local language

Religious Forms: typical Adventist music, order of service, furniture styles, architecture, and prayer postures

Membership: indigenous people and expatriates who know the local language

Place of Worship: official church building

Self-Identity: Seventh-day Adventist Christian
Community Assigned Identity: Seventh-day Adventist Christian
Relationship with Culture: foreign religion, a social-religious island
Potential Outreach: to MBBs in other Christian denominations; limited outreach to Muslims
Relationship with World Church: Standard

The C3 Group

Language: local language.
Religious Forms: religious terms familiar to Muslims (like *Isa* for Jesus, *Yahya* for John the Baptist, *Ingil* for the Gospels, and *Zabur* for the Psalms); local Muslim cultural forms are used (shoes left at door, worshippers seated on carpets, Bible read from wooden stands, etc.); unbiblical meanings purged from forms where necessary and replaced by biblical meanings
Membership: MBBs and a few expatriates who know local language, adopt cultural forms, and are engaged in mission among Muslims
Place of Worship: official church buildings or neutral locations, like rented halls
Self-Identity: Seventh-day Adventist Christian
Community Assigned Identity: Seventh-day Adventist Christian
Relationship with Culture: religiously different, culturally familiar
Potential Outreach: to MBBs or Muslims, not to expatriates
Relationship with World Church: standard

The C4 Group

Language: local language
Religious Forms: local religious terms and cultural forms used as in C3
Membership: MBBs and a few expatriates who know local language, adopt cultural forms, and are engaged in mission among Muslims
Place of Worship: official church buildings or neutral locations, like rented halls
Self-Identity: believers no longer self-identify as "Christian" but as "followers of *Isa Al Masih*" or "Adventists"
Community Assigned Identity: not typical Muslim
Relationship with Culture: culturally alike, religiously more similar than C3
Potential Outreach: to MBBs or Muslims, not to expatriates
Relationship with World Church: somewhat limited

The C5 Group

Language: local language
Religious Forms: local religious terms and cultural forms used as in C3 and C4
Membership: MBBs
Place of Worship: small fellowships, house churches
Self-Identity: "Messianic Muslims," "Muslim believers," "Muslim followers of *Isa Al-Masih*," or just "Muslims"
Community Assigned Identity: deviant or atypical Muslims but not "Christians"
Relationship with Culture: cultural insiders
Potential Outreach: to MBBs or Muslims, not to expatriates
Relationship with World Church: limited

The C6 Group

Language: local language
Religious Forms: no group worship services or communal Bible reading and prayer
Membership: MBBs
Place of Worship: unable to meet or meeting in small secret fellowships
Self-Identity: "Messianic Muslims," "Muslim believers," "Muslim followers of *Isa Al-Misah*," or just "Muslims"
Community Assigned Identity: not known by community as a group
Relationship with Culture: cultural insiders; "salt and light"
Potential Outreach: extremely limited, to Muslims as Spirit gives opportunity
Relationship with World Church: none

Conclusion

The C1 to C6 Model defines how groups of believers are functioning in difficult circumstances. The model arises from the visible working of the Spirit, where the church has the obligation to be as flexible as necessary under the guidance of scriptural principles. The model has the potential of keeping the church's mission vision open to new circumstances and opportunities as they develop. In creative access contexts, many aspects of church life are far from ideal because of limitations imposed by societies and governments; however, the Great Commission applies equally to every human context and the church has an obligation to be intentionally creative so that, with Paul, we might by all possible means save some (1 Cor 9:23).

Chapter

Mission and Animism

~•~

Introduction

Some religious beliefs and practices that involve interaction with the evil beings and powers of darkness are found in the earliest records of antiquity and persist to the present day. Those beliefs and practices are often identified as spiritism, spiritualism, witchcraft, shamanism, voodooism, or animism. This chapter uses "animism" as a single, inclusive term.

Animism is a diffuse but comprehensive religious system that uses various forms, rituals, and beliefs that are attractive to many societies, whether they be traditional, modern, or postmodern. Animism is found on every continent, in countries at all stages of economic development, among both rural and urban peoples, and among both illiterates and the highly educated elite. There are animistic tribal peoples who have had little outside influence, but that group has shrunk dramatically in the last century with globalization. Animistic practices flourish in today's great urban centers, notably in the slums. Some urban dwellers who work in high rise offices and drive expensive cars also participate in sensational rituals. Other modern, well-educated people have nothing to do with sensational rituals, but hold animistic beliefs and assumptions.

The largest presence of animism is where it is intertwined with the world religions—Christianity, Islam, Hinduism, and Buddhism being the largest. Every world religion has formal and folk sectors. People in the formal sectors tend to follow the official teachings and practices of their respective religions more closely. Those in the folk sectors, who make up the majority of all the world religions, tend to depart further from the official, orthodox positions. Their own religious leaders often disapprove of them and seek to correct them. Broadly speaking, people in the folk sectors of all world religions tend toward animistic beliefs and practices.

In Christianity, the formal sector is made up of theology teachers, administrators, clergy, and local church leaders. Christians of the church pew make up the folk sector. Some Christians, of both the formal and folk sectors, continue animistic practices. Some denominations reject while others embrace animistic beliefs and practices. To illustrate, some denominations officially reject voodoo-ist practices, while others embrace them; some members of voodoo-rejecting denominations, including both formal and folk sectors, practice variations of voodoo. While all Christians are susceptible to the attractions of animism, those attractions seem stronger in the folk sector among members who are poorly grounded in the faith.

Animistic adherents of all the religions share a significant body of beliefs and practices, even though their official beliefs and practices are very different from each other. These shared practices frequently include the use of amulets or charms for protection, the use of curses and counter-curses, and appeals for help to spirits and ancestors. Some who do not identify with any established religion participate in similar practices.

One of the major dividing lines between Adventist beliefs and many other people groups, including many fellow Christians, is the doctrine of humanity. Adventists have a worldview assumption that humans (1) were created by God; (2) are a wholistic unity of body, mind, and spirit; (3) are fully unconscious and inactive in death; (4) are waiting in death for God's final judgment either to conscious immortality or unconscious eternal extinction. Most Christians and non-Christians, alike, teach that humans have a dualistic nature of body and spirit. At death, the spirit leaves the body to participate with the spirit world in the afterlife. The Adventist doctrine of humanity thus presents a direct challenge to animistic beliefs and practices at the deepest worldview level. Worldview transformation at the deepest level is needed to successfully abandon animistic beliefs and practices.

Herein rests the unique challenge and opportunity for Adventist mission. Adventists have a mission to address animism (1) where it exists among ourselves, (2) with other Christians, and (3) with the other religions or secular people. If Adventist mission can understand animism and address it effectively with the Gospel, a huge portion of humanity will be potentially reachable.

Animism as False Religion

The impulse to worship comes from the inner longing for God that he implants and cultivates in all people; however, that impulse to worship God is distorted by sin. The origin of false religion can be traced back to the Fall and to Cain's perversion of the God-given sacrificial system that foreshadowed the saving work of Jesus Christ. As humans departed from faithful worship of the only God, they developed elaborate idolatrous substitutes. At the core of false religion was human self-sufficiency. As Ellen White wrote,

> The class of worshipers who follow the example of Cain includes by far the greater portion of the world; for nearly every false religion has been based on the same principle—that man can depend upon his own efforts [or merits] for salvation. (PP:73)

Through the centuries, the manifestations of false worship in the Great Controversy between Christ and Satan fit the broad profile of animism. Many of its features (like sorcery, divination, séances, magic, witchcraft, etc.) are sensational and dramatic. However, animism is best understood as a comprehensive system of opposition to God rather than as just a collection of sensational practices. Ellen White's frequent references to "spiritualism" (a data base search yielded 410 references) and its role in end-time events refer to much more than sensational phenomena. For example, she says

> spiritualism asserts that men are unfallen demigods; that "each mind will judge itself;" that "true knowledge places men above all law;" that "all sins committed are innocent;" for "whatever is, is right," and "God doth not condemn." (Ed:227)

Spiritualism teaches "fanciful views of God" (8T:291). The doctrines "of consciousness after death, of the spirits of the dead being in communion with the living" (Ed:603) and of "eternal torment" (GC:588) are part of spiritualism. Spiritualism "numbers its converts by hundreds of thousands, yea, by millions" (GC:556). In summary, White's discussions of the features of spiritualism suggests a large, false religious system. Gailyn Van Rheenen notes that

> in the animist context the message must center on the cosmic conflict between God and the gods, between Christ and the demons, between the church and the principalities and powers....In this great confrontation with the forces of Satan, Christians will overcome because Christ, who dwells in them, is greater "than he who is in the world." (1991:61)

One common but unfortunate approach to animism in its many expressions is to glamorize it by repeating sensational stories. Another mistaken approach is to exclude, ignore, or deny its reality and to refuse to confront manifestations of evil power with prayer in the name and power of Jesus Christ.

This chapter suggests that (1) sensational, glamorizing stories be avoided because they trivialize satanic evil; (2) Christians be always prepared to confront manifestations of evil in the name of Christ; (3) animism is best challenged by understanding it as a complex religious system that undercuts the core assumptions of the Christian faith.

Worldview Assumptions of Animism

Van Rheenen defines animism as "the belief that personal spiritual beings and impersonal spiritual forces have power over human affairs and, consequently, that human beings must discover what beings and forces are influencing them in order to determine future action and ... [to] manipulate their power" (2000:20).

Animism is based on a set of worldview assumptions that differ from those of the Bible. Hiebert provides a helpful way to understand different worldviews as being made up of upper, middle, and lower zones. (This chapter relies on Hiebert, Shaw, and Tienou 1999 and Hiebert 1994).

Figure 17.1 Worldview of Animism	
UPPER ZONE • High God	• Wholly transcendent. • Little or no interaction with humans. • Unseen by humans.
MIDDLE ZONE • Lesser gods • Good and bad spirits • Saints • Ancestors • Impersonal forces	• Main focus of human religious life. • Highly interactive with Lower Zone, both for good and evil. • Provides linkage and mediation between Lower and Upper Zones. • Sometimes seen or experienced by humans.
LOWER ZONE • Humans • Animals • Plants • Inanimate objects	• Many explanations of human origin. • Many explanations of human predicament and its solution. • Lower Zone has constant interaction with Middle Zone. • Humans retain consciousness and move to Middle Zone at death. • Sub-human animals, plants, and inanimate objects interact with humans and Middle Zone.

For many animists, the upper zone is occupied by the High God, who is the Creator. The High God is distant and uninvolved with humanity and the religious life of humans typically has little to do with him.

The middle zone is occupied by personal beings like lesser deities, good and bad spirits, saints, and ancestors. Impersonal spiritual forces, that can be compared to electricity or gravity, make up an important part of the middle zone. The middle zone is directly accessible to humans, unlike the High God. Middle zone beings have similar passions and weaknesses and make mistakes like humans. They are more powerful than humans, but less powerful than God. Because they understand humanity, they are good mediators between humans and God.

The lower zone is made up of humans, animals, plants, and inanimate objects. Unborn, living, and deceased human beings constitute a unified family that interacts within and beyond itself. Many different explanations for the origin of humanity and the central predicament of humanity are made. The remedy for the human predicament is defined by different kinds of merit-producing good deeds. The deceased move to the middle zone at their death, where they continue to exert influence on living humans. The animals, plants, and inanimate objects that share the lower zone with humans have spiritual interaction with humans and with the middle zone.

Animistic peoples value spiritual explanations of causation and attribute everything that happens to spiritual beings or forces. There are no "accidents" in the modern scientific sense. Car crashes are caused by spiritual forces, no matter what the technical explanations may be. The nail that punctured the tire that made the car crash was only the secondary cause. The primary cause was the spiritual being or power that placed the nail in the right place and caused the nail to cause the crash. An enemy consulted a practitioner who made a curse that directed spiritual power to cause the car crash. The families of crash victims use practitioners to identify the source of the curse and to make retaliatory or preventative curses in response.

The forces and beings of the middle zone must constantly be made to work for human good so that they will not cause harm; therefore, a successful life strategy is one that manipulates the beings and powers (and, by implication, the High God) in a way that wards off evil and brings blessing. For example, car owners put amulets or charms in their cars to protect themselves against potential curses that cause crashes.

Public manipulation of spirits and powers is usually intended to be beneficial for the whole community, while private or secret manipulation is often intended to harm individuals or the community. For example, during times of drought and famine, animistic practitioners perform public rituals to "call" the blessing of rain for the good of everyone. Individuals with a grudge against someone meet secretly with a practitioner to place a curse on them. If a person thinks they have been cursed, they may arrange a stronger counter-curse upon the one bringing the curse. Humans are completely alone and self-dependent in successfully ma-nipulating the animistic religious system; thus, the system produces generalized fear of being cursed and of not manipulating the spirits and powers successfully.

When people suffer calamity or misfortune, others assume they have neglect-ed their duty to manipulate spirits and powers or have done so unskillfully; thus, human suffering sometimes receives little sympathy or empathy. The suffering person is believed to have brought the problem on themselves and potentially upon their whole family and community.

When an animist practitioner is paid to make a curse or blessing, it simply "must work" because it has power (Donkor 2015). After all, when one puts a match to gasoline, it burns and when one plugs a light into the electricity, it shines. When practitioners harness spiritual powers, they work because their power is viewed mechanistically. If spiritual power does not work, the failure is blamed on incorrect procedure, incompetence by the practitioner, or stronger counter-balancing magic by another practitioner. Animists usually do not sub-ject the whole animistic system to a critique when it fails, but keep thinking, "Maybe next time it will work," or "Let me try a different practitioner." When one remedy fails, animists feel fully justified and even obligated to seek alterna-tive remedies. If both the treatments of modern medicine and the prayers of the church fail, the parent with a sick child feels justified and obligated to consult an animist practitioner.

Animism posits an unfailingly accurate, impersonal, cosmic recording system of good and bad deeds that gives every person precisely what they "deserve," no more and no less, either in this life or the life to come. There is no solution for a low merit score other than to add more meritorious deeds to the cosmic scales. People who apparently suffer in excess of their known bad deeds are assumed to be suffering for hidden bad deeds in this life or in a previous life. Those who seem to have easier lives than they deserve can be assured of receiving their just rewards eventually. There is no forgiveness or grace in the mechanical moral-ethical system of animism.

Animists have a pragmatic focus on obtaining immediate, practical benefits for the here-and-now, for "me" and "us." Ethics are relativistic—"If it works and I don't get caught, it's OK." There is no room for absolute laws or principles.

A religious system that lacks both absolute ethics and saving grace is a vastly different system from Christianity with the Decalogue and the Cross. Leading an animistic person of any religion to become a disciple of Christ involves a worldview transformation at the deepest level. Animistic Christians are trying to practice two religious systems that are contradictory at the very deepest, worldview level at the same time. They have a dual allegiance, to Christ and to Satan, and are living in the central vortex of the Great Controversy.

Worldview Assumptions of the Bible

The Bible portrays a universe divided into two main categories—Creator and creation. The Triune Creator God is utterly unique and transcendent from his creation; however, God was with humanity during the incarnation of Jesus and is immanent and interactive with humanity through God the Holy Spirit.

The Triune God is highly relational and his absolute Law instructs humanity regarding good relationships with God and fellow humans; thus, righteousness and salvation are offered through a right relationship with the relational God rather than through a mechanical accounting of human merit and demerit.

The realm of creation is divided into a middle zone and lower zone in the biblical model, with the lower zone being subdivided into human and sub-human sectors. The middle zone is occupied by real angels of two varieties. The good or faithful angels are those who remained loyal to God when Lucifer fell. Even though they are good and loyal, angels are not to be placed in the upper zone because they were created by the Creator, like humans. Good angels work for God in the Great Controversy as "ministering spirits sent forth to minister for those who will inherit salvation" (Heb 1:14).

The middle zone also includes really real, evil, fallen angels called demons who rebelled against God with Lucifer as their leader. Demons work with Lucifer in the Great Controversy against God. They tempt and deceive humans and try to ruin God's creation in every way possible by bringing suffering and calamity.

The unnumbered deities, spirits, and powers included in the animistic middle zone are not really real in the biblical worldview. Ancestral spirits do not exist because the dead rest in their graves. Spirits that appear as animals, birds, plants, or inanimate objects do not have a real, independent existence; yet, the spirits are not "mere superstition." Rather, they are impersonations and deceptions done by real fallen angels who serve Satan. In other words, a hyena seen flying over a village is the impersonation of a really real evil angel, not a hyena with inherent powers. An ancestor who appears to a séance is the impersonation of really real demons, not the real ancestor who rests in the grave.

Humans experience the middle zone for their good through encounters with angels, prophecy, visions, dreams, miracles, the inspired Bible, and prayer. Humans encounter the middle zone to their harm through demonic works and deceptions.

Figure 17.2 Worldview of the Bible	
CREATOR	
UPPER ZONE • Triune God	• Both transcendent and immanent • Heavenly mediation provided by Jesus Christ • Guidance and empowerment provided by Holy Spirit • Believer's main focus for faith and practice • Visible to humanity during the Incarnation • Normally unseen by humans
CREATION	
MIDDLE ZONE • Angels • Demons	• Angels: Real, interactive messengers, God's agents in Great Controversy • Demons: Real, interactive deceivers, Satan's agents in Great Controversy • Good: Bible, prayer, angelic appearances, prophecy, visions, dreams, miracles • Evil: Demonic influence, impersonations, deceptions • Angels and demons seen only occasionally by humans
LOWER ZONE • Humans	• Created as moral-ethical beings, with wholistic physical, social, spiritual nature; stewards of God's creation • Predicament caused by sin; salvation by grace through faith in Christ • Death is an unconscious state, awaiting final judgment. • Primary earthly focus of the Great Controversy • Direct access to God, through Christ
• Animals • Plants • Inanimate Objects	• Non-moral-ethical • No independent role in Great Controversy • Sometimes used for good (Balaam's donkey; Apostles' handkerchiefs and aprons) • Frequently used by demons to deceive humans

The Bible describes human access to God through the heavenly mediation of Jesus, the High Priest (Heb 4:14-16). The writer of Hebrews emphasizes that Jesus is a superior High Priest who offers mediation superior to anything that angels can do (Heb 1:5-13). Angels are to be highly valued as "ministering spirits" (Heb 1:14), but humans have direct access to God through the heavenly High Priest. The Bible does not describe the middle zone as the main focus of Christianity. Humans are to be God-fearing, God-glorifying, God-centered, God-serving, and God-loving. The inspired Word and prayer are the middle zone elements that are to be the main focus for Christians because they link humans with God through the Holy Spirit. Angelic interventions, prophecy, visions, dreams, and miracles are provided by God's providential grace only as he sees fit.

The lower zone includes humans, animals, plants, and inanimate objects. Only humans are morally-ethically responsible and capable of relating to the middle and upper zones. Deceased humans exist only in God's eternal memory, not as middle zone ancestors or saints. Neither animals, nor plants, nor inanimate objects possess inherent spiritual powers. Angels and demons sometimes use animals and inanimate objects to accomplish their purposes. The angelic use of animals, like Balaam's donkey (Num 22), and inanimate objects, like the Apostles' handkerchiefs and aprons (Acts 19:12), is relatively rare in Scripture. Demons use animals and inanimate objects more frequently as part of their strategies to deceive humans.

Submission or Manipulation

One of Christianity's strongest critiques of animism is its manipulative posture toward God. The Bible prescribes a posture of humble, faithful submission toward God. The animistic assumption that spiritual exercises and remedies "must work" implies that when Christians live good ethical-moral lives, God is obligated to grant their prayer requests. If prayers are offered correctly and with adequate emotion and conviction, the prayers "must work." If God does not grant prayer requests, the animistic Christian may feel justified in seeking alternative remedies through animistic practitioners. "What else can I do? I must help myself or my loved ones somehow." Thus, a pathway to dual allegiance is opened. Such a Christian has an allegiance both to God and to the evil spirits and powers of the middle zone.

The Bible teaches that no good deed nor the avoidance of any bad deed can create an obligation which coerces God to act in a certain way. The quality of human life is not related to human behavior as a direct equation because some good people suffer much more than some bad people. The message of the book of Job is that no direct relationship exists between human ethics and morality and the human quality of life. The truly Christian posture is to submit oneself humbly to the providence of God, whatever the condition of one's life may be. Nothing justifies the dual allegiance of one who seeks remedies both from God and the spirits and powers of the middle zone.

Many non-Christian people have an unabashedly manipulative posture towards their deities, spirits, and powers. They openly declare their intentions to perform good deeds that produce merit so that those deities will give them a good future. The spirits are openly manipulated and tricked to avert disaster and attract prosperity. The missiological challenge of leading such people into a submissive posture toward God, that depends wholly of the grace of God, and offers obedience as the response of gratitude is profound.

God-Centered or Human-Centered

Animists are human-centered and me-oriented instead of God-centered. They seek a church and religion primarily to "meet my needs." This perspective implies that they are justified to change allegiances if their needs are not met. To clarify, Christ's ministry did focus on human needs and wholistic missiology follows his example; however, the Bible and church history are full of examples of people of authentic faith whose deep human needs were never met. The heroes of faith named in Hebrews 11 were persecuted, starved, and martyred because their lives were God-centered instead of self-centered. Being a follower of Jesus Christ is not "about me," its "about God."

Right or Wrong View of Power

Animists are obsessed with power and understand power wrongly. First, they depersonalize God's power and make it into something that can be used mechanically. This view distorts the biblical view of God, who is intensely relational and always exerts his power within his relationships. God's power is always used Person-to-person. The much beloved song "Give me oil in my lamp, keep it burning" must not be misunderstood to suggest that the Holy Spirit's power can be obtained and used in a mechanical way, like literal lamp oil.

Second, animists see power as being theologically, morally, and ethically neutral—like electricity or gasoline. Successful living requires staying "plugged in" or "tanked up," with power from any source. The biblical view is that power always has a theological, moral, and ethical character, depending upon its source. Demons have real power that they use for evil purposes. Sometimes demonic power brings temporary benefits to humanity, but the ends are always destructive. Christians can rejoice in God's power and receive his power, but should choose suffering and even death itself over any benefits from an evil power source.

Third, animism underestimates the malignity and power of Satan. The evil spirits and beings of the middle zone seem human-like in their passions, behaviors, and powers. They deceive each other and are often portrayed as clownish tricksters. Humans think they can enlist the help of practitioners to trick and deceive the spirits, making life into a high stakes game with the powers of darkness. Some modern people even doubt the existence of a personal Devil and Satan. Paul wrote, "Our struggle is not against flesh and blood, but against the rulers, against the powers, against the world forces of this darkness, against the spiritual forces of wickedness in the heavenly places" (Eph 6:12).

The missiological challenge is to lead people to experience the authentic power of God in the warfare of life, while avoiding the animistic distortions.

Modern Scientific Worldview Assumptions

The culture of modernity arose in the North Atlantic nations under the influence of the Enlightenment. Through the process of globalization, the scientific worldview of modernity has spread far beyond Europe and North America. Modernity has been reshaped by postmodernity but the modern, scientific worldview persists.

Figure 17.3
Worldview of Modernity

SUPERNATURAL ZONE	
• High God • Angels • Demons • Lesser gods • Good and bad spirits • Impersonal forces • Saints • Ancestral spirits	• Unknowable by scientific study, therefore, unknowable to humans • Part of pre-scientific folklore and superstition • Not really real • Faith • Miracles • Sacred
MIDDLE ZONE: EXCLUDED, DENIED, IGNORED	
NATURAL ZONE	
• Humans • Animals • Plants • Inanimate objects	• Knowable by scientific study • The only knowable realm for humans • Only really real part of universe • Everything exists on the natural level • Evolution produces everything, including humans • Human predicament caused by ignorance, solved by education and development • Death is a return to dust without a future

The Western scientific worldview divides the whole cosmos into two zones—natural and supernatural. There would not be a major problem if this two-part division was only between what is visible and invisible, but the categories are much deeper than that.

The supernatural zone includes the High God, angels, demons, and spirits of all kinds. These beings are said to be part of pre-scientific folklore, superstition, and individual conviction, but are not really real. Only the scientific method can discern what is really real and the supernatural zone is beyond science.

The middle zone is completely excluded, denied, or ignored in the modern two-part worldview. All of the elements of the middle zone are pushed into the supernatural zone because they are outside of scientific study.

The natural zone is open to scientific study and is, therefore, really real. All of nature has emerged from the evolutionary process and humans are the most highly evolved part of nature.

Christians have related the claims of the Bible to the modern natural-supernatural model in different ways. Some give priority to modern science and deny the reality of everything that science cannot prove. The Bible then becomes merely a human document and spirits, angels, miracles, the virgin birth, the resurrection, and God himself become matters of individual opinion or superstition. The Bible is studied in the same way as all other ancient literature, not as the inspired Word of God. Theologies on the liberal side of the spectrum give privilege to the modern scientific worldview.

Others straddle the fence by adopting the natural-supernatural model, but asserting the reality of the High God, other supernatural beings, miracles, and the inspiration of the Bible. They are perhaps unaware that they are trying to merge contradictory worldviews and accepting the implications of doing so. Placing the Creator God into the same category as the created angels implies that they exist on the same qualitative level with God. Placing Lucifer and his demons into the same qualitative category with God is blasphemy. The Creator and all parts of his creation must be seen as radically different from each other because nothing exists without the Creator.

Both options, either denying the reality of whatever science cannot prove or affirming the reality of the Creator, but placing him on the same level with his creation, are wrong. Both mistakes arise from a biblically unfaithful contextualization of modern Western culture. Both mistakes make believers powerless in their confrontations with temptation, illness, and evil powers.

Modern Missions and the Middle Zone

Every missionary has cultural worldview commitments, some of which help and others that hinder their cross-cultural service. During the modern missionary movement (c.1750-1950), most missionaries were from Europe and North America. Their modern scientific worldview made it difficult for them to address issues raised by animistic peoples.

Hiebert coined the phrase "the flaw of the excluded middle" to describe the problem people of the modern scientific worldview have when they encounter the animistic worldview in action (1994:189). When a missionary among a traditional people group is approached for help with a problem related to the middle zone and its evil spirits, the response the modern scientific worldview supports is to deny, exclude, or ignore the problem. The missionary may say, "That is all superstition. Just stop believing in evil spirits and they won't bother you. I don't believe in them and they never bother me." Responses like this are unacceptable because (1) they are biblically inaccurate and (2) they hinder ministry among people who live in animistic societies, where issues related to the middle zone are confronted regularly. The best way to address animistic issues is through the process of faithful contextualization.

Animism and a Globalized Church

Christians are sobered when they recognize that their own practice of the faith is syncretized by their cultural perspectives. Each person should accept Paul's exhortation to "Examine yourselves to see whether you are in the faith" (2 Cor 13:5). Every true believer is called to be countercultural in some ways, depending on their culture. Globalization has intermingled peoples from traditionally animistic societies with those of modern and postmodern societies. Most people are cultural hybrids of some variety. Those on the side of modernity might be less inclined to engage in animistic practices, but they are also less experienced in engaging the powers of darkness. Christians all worship and work together in God's mission and have a great deal to learn from each other.

The hold that animism has on Christians differs in nature and intensity. Some participate in none of the rituals and use none of the symbols of animism, but hold animistic theological assumptions that deform their Christian faith. The animist concept of an impersonal cosmic scale of merit was implicit in a recent story that originated in North America. A tornado swept through a large Adventist community, leaving some houses untouched but demolishing others. The Adventist who reported the event explained that the Adventists whose houses were destroyed were not living good lives, while those whose homes were untouched were true Adventists. Did this person ever read the book of Job?

Some believers use things like good luck charms or horoscopes in ways that do not intrude into their Christian lives, even though these items may not be advisable. Some people who use animistic forms do not participate in the dark meanings of spiritual warfare. Christians should avoid a judgmental attitude that causes them to label everyone who wears a good luck charm as an animistic Satan worshipper; yet, every believer should examine themselves and their influence upon others.

Other believers bring animistic meanings into Christian forms, like using the Bible or the communion bread and wine or anointing oil in magical ways. One pastor told me about a church member in North America who maintains a bedroom shrine where she regularly communes with Jesus, whose image appears to her on the wall. Some Christians place the Bible on a sick part of the body in a magical way. Others put themselves intentionally into perilous situations where Satan is directly at work through various manifestations.

Animism persists in the global church because of various factors. Some younger Christian groups lack an adequate biblical foundation and stray into animistic practices because of their appeal to the masses. Other groups are committed to biblical doctrine, but lack adequate faith, or courage, or procedural skills to lead the church away from animism.

Shortcomings in missionary practice can leave converts unprepared to face the powers of evil; yet, even the very best missionary theory and practice are not enough to avoid the cosmic battle between good and evil. Converts from animistic traditions will face particular challenges. Adventists who can understand and address animism with insider cultural knowledge have a special advantage.

Conclusion

The wide reach of animism makes it one of the great mission challenges and opportunities of this century. The challenges are among fellow Adventists, among other Christian groups, and among non-Christians. The similarities that unite the diverse animistic people groups who otherwise have little in common present a great opportunity. A deep understanding and an effective approach to animistic people groups potentially opens the door to much of the world population.

Modes of Mission Service

~•~

Long-Term Mission Service

Introduction

In the Adventist Church, a long-term cross-cultural missionary sent by the General Conference is called an International Service Employee (ISE). The minimum period of service is five years, with annual leaves of a month. Thus, in this book, "long-term" refers to service of five years or more.

The church's ISE program is administered by the General Conference Secretariat (www.adventistmission.org). Within the GC Secretariat, the International Personnel Resources and Services (IPRS) administers about 900 ISEs. The exact number of ISEs in service varies as they leave and return. The GC annual budget allocates about US$30 million for ISEs. Once on the field, ISEs report to the local organizations and administrations where they serve. The main categories of ISE service include pastoral/ministerial, educational, health-care, treasury and auditing, aid and development, information technology, and administration.

Missionary Education

The Institute of World Mission (IWM) provides education for out-going missionaries and re-entry debriefing when they return. The IWM has five goals for missionary education. An Adventist missionary should be one who is (1) growing spiritually, (2) thinking biblically, (3) reasoning missiologically, (4) living wholistically, (5) serving incarnationally. The IWM serves mostly ISEs and Adventist Volunteers but also trains missionaries sent by Adventist supporting ministries, tentmakers, and other types of missionaries. The IWM currently conducts its three-week Mission Institutes several times a year, once at Andrews University, and the other times locations with a non-Christian majority religion. Typical

Institutes have 30 to 50 adults and 10 to 20 children. Attendees typically come from a dozen or more nations and are going to a dozen or more different nations. Most attendees are professional people going to serve in the varied dimensions of Adventist mission.

Missionary Trends

The high point of total ISEs in service came in 1983, when the total approached 1,600 and the world membership stood at 4.1 million. By 2015, the membership had increased to 19.1 million, but the number of ISEs in service had decreased to about 900 (Trim 2017a:10). In other words, about 2,500 Adventists were needed in 1983 to send one ISE, but 20,000 members were needed in 2015. If the 1983 ratio of members to ISEs had been the same in 2015, Adventists would now have about 7,600 ISEs in service. As this is written, the total remains at about 900. Today's ISE work force comes from about 70 different nations and serves in about 90 different nations. About 30% are from the North American Division (NAD) and that group is very multi-cultural (C. Doss 2018).

Some explanations can be given for the decline in total ISEs since the high point in 1983: (1) Some positions formerly held by ISEs are now held by locals; (2) the world divisions now send more cross-cultural missionaries between the unions in their territories; (3) some divisions send missionaries directly to other divisions and to the Middle East North Africa Union; (4) the number of unofficial, supporting ministries sending missionaries has increased; (5) the number of short-term volunteers and people in other categories of service has increased. Compiling statistics for the different categories is difficult and they are not included in the GC ISE numbers. However, it seems doubtful that the different categories of full-time, long-term missionaries serving today equal as many as the 700 needed to be combined with today's 900 ISEs to equal the 1600 of 1983.

However valid these and other explanations may be, the dramatic growth of the church and the corresponding growth of the world's unevangelized population render the explanations inadequate. A church with 19.1 million members should send more GC ISEs than one with 4.1 million members, not less. Millions of unreached people await the Gospel that can be brought only by cross-cultural missionaries because the local church lacks the missional capacity.

Fulfilling God's mission requires the church to cross boundaries of language, culture, religion, and geography that can only be done in many places by long-term cross-cultural missionaries who have the requisite training, skills, and church support. To reawaken and enhance the church's commitment to long-term missionary service, some steps seem appropriate:

First, to reaffirm the essential role of long-term missionaries who learn the language and culture of unevangelized people groups for extended periods of service. The five-year commitment that ISEs make is truly just the minimum. Young Adventists need to be recruited, trained, and supported who will make a lifetime commitment to serve among specific people groups. Other modes of service are valid, but long-term service is at the core of mission for today's challenging unevangelized people groups. The challenge of reaching the unevangelized requires specialization and professionalism.

Second, to intentionally disconnect the image of today's cross-cultural missionary from the stereotypical image of "the missionary" of colonial times. One common misconception could be stated thus: "The day of the long-term cross-cultural missionary is gone. These are the days of the indigenous worker." This misconception overlooks the history of the Phase IV period of Adventist Mission, Mission to All the World. During that phase, cross-cultural missionaries built the missional capacity of indigenous believers so that they progressively assumed leadership roles. The Malawian case study in chapter 8 illustrates the process. The thorough work of the early decades prepared Malawian Adventists to assume almost all leadership roles by 1980.

Third, to differentiate between world regions with low strategic need and those with high strategic need. As already noted, the Big Seven divisions are those with low strategic need, while the Diverse Six Plus divisions have high strategic need. Regions with low strategic need are well served by a small number of ISEs who fill specialized roles and help to maintain the unity-in-diversity of the global church. Regions with high strategic need are helped through partnership with the world church that provides higher numbers of ISEs. The type of ISEs needed and the duration of their service varies with the local context and the missional capacity of the church in different regions, but they are still needed. One serious pitfall to avoid is assuming that the early stages of missional capacity building can be skipped or rushed. Good missional capacity building cannot be done with a few short seminars conducted by outside instructors.

Fourth, to correct the possible misconception that alternative modes of service, including short-term volunteer service, are adequate replacements for long-term service. Volunteers can and do provide excellent service, but they cannot replace long-term service. Long-term missionaries, along with local personnel, are needed to train and coordinate those providing other forms of service.

Fifth, to encourage the world divisions to send and support their people as long-term missionaries, in coordination with the GC. All the divisions included in the Big Seven group, with their combined 15 million members, have the capacity to send and support missionaries.

Sixth, to encourage the Adventist supporting ministries to work in partnership with the official church in sending long-term missionaries.

Missionaries and Strategic Missional Need

Adventist missionaries serve in the varied capacities named above because of Adventist ecclesiology, or doctrine of the church, and a wholistic theology of mission. Adventists see their church as a worldwide fellowship, linked together organically as the body of Christ (1 Cor 12:12). The metaphor of a body indicates that every member of the church contributes to the functioning of the church in different ways. Local churches are planted that become part of a global sisterhood of churches and linked with local fields/conferences that oversee pastors and the comprehensive work of the church. ISEs build the missional capacity of the local church and guide it to spiritual maturity and unity as part of the global Adventist Church. Denominations with congregationalist ecclesiology send church planters who establish new, free-standing congregations and then move on to plant more free-standing churches.

Adventists understand mission to include both evangelization and ministry to the physical, emotional, and social needs of humanity. This missiology leads Adventists to send ISEs who provide a wide range of ministries to the comprehensive needs of humanity. Other denominations whose missiology includes only evangelization send only pastors and evangelists.

As the Adventist Church in particular regions grows and develops, the kinds of ISE needed to put Adventist ecclesiology and missiology into action changes. For example, in Malawi, the first missionaries were pastors, teachers, and nurses. The very first evangelization and church planting was done by missionaries, but Malawians were soon educated to be the primary teachers, evangelists, and pastors. The service of missionaries evolved into teacher training, pastoral education, healthcare and healthcare worker education, and administration. Today, ISEs serve only in certain technical, specialized capacities, as requested by Malawian Adventist leaders. The Malawi Union has low strategic mission need and the world church is facilitating Adventist mission in Malawi appropriately, in a selective, strategic way.

One common and often repeated perception among Adventists is that the ISE program has become unbalanced because it sends mostly "institutional" workers, instead of "frontline" workers. Several responses are needed to address that perception: (1) The church in particular regions needs the partnership of the world church in different ways, at different stages of its development, as illustrated by the Malawi Union case study; sending ISEs that match the need at the particular stage of development is practicing good strategic mission; (2) the distinction between "institutional" and "frontline" is artificial, in many cases; "institutional" ISEs are truly "frontline" workers when they serve in needed capacities in a context with high strategic need; for example, an ISE who serves as a school principal, or medical director of a hospital, or treasurer of the field in a Buddhist nation, where the strategic missional need is high, is a true frontline missionary; (3) having made these clarifications, more pastoral, evangelistic, and church planting ISEs are needed in unevangelized regions, where strategic need is high; some ISE budgets do need to be moved away from regions where strategic need is low and the GC is in the process of making adjustments in that direction.

Short-Term Mission Service

In this era of globalization, with its easy and affordable travel, Christians are able to personally participate in mission projects far from home. The new mode of service has come to be called Short-Term Mission (STM). The length of STM varies from two or three weeks to a year or two. Trips of a few weeks are typically made by church or school groups to perform work projects, provide health services, lead vacation Bible school, or conduct evangelistic meetings.

Short-Term Mission has become an important part of American Christianity's continued missional engagement with the rest of the world. Authors like Philip Jenkins (2002), Robert Wuthnow (2009), and Mark Noll (2009) have documented the fact that the majority of Christians now reside in the global south instead of in the global north, as in former times. Yet, American Christianity continues to exert a significant influence on global Christianity in various ways. One of those modes of interaction is STM, which carries over a million Americans abroad each year, spending an estimated US$1 to 2 billion. Of this number, two-thirds travel for fourteen days or less (Priest et al. 2006:432). STM teams are sent from many nations but the largest cohort comes from the United States and Canada.

The nature of North America's continued mission engagement with the world has produced what Wuthnow calls a "huge debate" in leadership and missiological circles (2009:8). In the last decade, a great volume of research on STM has produced a rich literature. What is the character or missional quality of that engagement? What will be the long-term consequences, both intended and unintended, of the methods being used, including STM? For example, what impact does STM from a wealthy nation have on the capacity of fellow believers in a less-wealthy nation to fulfill their God-given mission among their own people? Do STM travelers think more about achieving their immediate trip goals or facilitating the on-going work of their hosts? Wuthnow found that most Americans somewhat naively assume that the outcomes of their STM work abroad are wholly beneficial to everyone involved (2009:8).

In contrast to the "celebratory rhetoric" sometimes heard in America about STM, Gary Corwin believes that its inherent limitations cause it to produce results that "seem to be less than meets the eye" (2008:144). Comments Gene Daniels, "The dark little secret" that long-term missionaries and indigenous people who host STM groups are reluctant to articulate is that "the average short-term missionary takes far more than he or she gives. The time invested to host the person, the resources he or she drains from the church's world mission budget, the problems the person sometimes causes ... all-too-often ... cost more than whatever benefit the visitor brings to the field" (2008:152). Research with multiple denominations in the USA indicates that STM does not produce the assumed benefits for all of the parties involved or increase support for long-term mission service (Priest et al. 2006: 431-450).

Some STM leaders and participants will be startled by the challenging assessments coming from experienced missionaries and missiological researchers. But with every form of service, the church is obligated to assess its ministries candidly. There are low-end, "missio-tourist" STM groups who never seriously try to enter the perspective of the hosts; who assume anything and everything they do will automatically be good for their hosts; and who consider the trip a success if the logistical tasks (like transportation, food, and accommodation) of the trip are managed acceptably. In contrast, STM teams at the high-end of the spectrum do their best to enter the perspective of the hosts, follow best practices to maximize the missional value of the trip for all, and candidly assess the outcomes of their trips. There is a consensus among missiologists that high-end STM that adheres to best practices is a valid mode of service for twenty-first century missions.

Adventist Short-Term Mission

Adventist STM provides many kinds of service. There are groups frequently sent from local churches or schools for a few weeks. Student missionaries take a school year away from college to teach English or general subjects. The Adventist Volunteer Service (AVS) sends people with a variety of skills for a year or two.

Adventist STM volunteers are sent from all divisions, but the NAD probably sends the most. Complete figures are difficult to obtain because STM is decentralized. The NAD and General Conference AVS offices provide coordination but many STM groups do not utilize it.

A recent NAD survey of 65 organizations reported that 4,491 STM volunteers, from 9 unions, had been deployed to 210 mission projects in 2016. The NAD itself received 30% of the deployments, Inter-American Division (IAD) 40%, and South American Division (SAD) 9%. The remaining 21% were spread among seven other divisions and the Middle East North Africa Union (MENA). The NAD uses the terminology of "Long Term Missionary" for its AVS workers who serve a year or two. In 2016, a total of 434 AVS workers served in NAD and 546 served in other divisions (Bryant 2017).

Observation and anecdotal evidence suggest that the actual number participating in STM is far greater than the numbers in the NAD survey. Estimates have been made that as many as 30,000 Adventists from the NAD give various kinds of STM service outside the division annually. If that estimate is accurate and if the average total cost per person is between $1,000 and $2,000, the total annual expense of STM would be between $30 million and $60 million. The funding generally comes from those making the trips and their friends and relatives rather than from the budgets of church organizations. As already noted, the GC spends about US$30 million annually to support its 900 ISEs.

The decentralized character of STM facilitates personal involvement and participation from every part of the church. Committee votes and protocols are not required to "get out there and do something." The NAD Secretary's Report (Bryant 2017) highlighted some of the challenges of decentralization. Only a fraction of STM travelers are covered by trip insurance offered by Adventist Risk Management. When uninsured teams encounter emergencies of various kinds in distant places, they assume that the Seventh-day Adventist Church there and back home will come to their rescue.

Adventist STM benefits from the global organization of the church. Establishing the initial linkage with potential hosts, planning trip activities, negotiating logistics, finding common ground upon arrival, performing planned activities, and maintaining long-term partnerships benefit from the sisterhood of the church.

Although STM is used as a broad term to include longer periods of service, there is a significant difference between spending a year or two and spending a week or two in service. Student missionaries and AVS workers who spend a year or more usually have well defined job descriptions and serve under long-term missionaries or local administrators. STM of a week or two functions in a very different way. Most of what follows focuses on STM of a few weeks.

The goal of every STM group should be to maximize the missional value of their service by understanding and implementing the very best practices. Best practices for STM rest upon appropriate assumptions about mission in general and STM in specific. There are three assumptions or starting points for an excellent STM trip: (1) Defining the priorities of STM, (2) being prepared to relate to wealth and power imbalances often inherent to STM, and (3) providing excellent training.

Figure 18.1
Standards of Excellence for Short-Term Mission

1. GOD-CENTEREDNESS
An excellent short-term mission seeks first God's glory and his kingdom and is centered on God's redemptive purposes for all nations and modeled after Christ's mission to the world.
2. EMPOWERING PARTNERSHIPS
An excellent short-term mission establishes healthy, interdependent, ongoing relationships between sending and receiving partners sustained by a willingness to grow together while serving God.
3. MUTUAL DESIGN
An excellent short-term mission collaboratively plans each specific outreach for the benefits of all participants and uses methods and activities aligned with the long-term strategies of sending and receiving partners.
4. COMPREHENSIVE ADMINISTRATION
An excellent short-term mission exhibits integrity through reliable set-up and thorough administration for all participants in order to glorify God and to exercise good stewardship of time, talents and funds.
5. QUALIFIED LEADERSHIP
An excellent short-term mission screens, trains, and develops capable leaders for all participants who possess the character, competency, and commitment needed for each particular outreach.
6. APPROPRIATE TRAINING
An excellent short-term mission prepares and equips all participants to be effective in the mutually designed outreach with biblical, timely, and relevant training suitable for the planned service and culture.
7. THOROUGH FOLLOW-THROUGH
An excellent short-term mission assures debriefing and appropriate follow-up for all participants because these are crucial elements for achieving significant lasting change.

Source: www.soe.org

The Priorities of Short-Term Mission

Some potential benefits are similar for both STM travelers and their hosts. These could include broadening global perspectives, developing appreciation for other cultures, developing inter-cultural skills, having good fellowship, developing long-term trans-cultural relationships, experiencing spiritual renewal, deepening commitment to Christian mission, and more.

Some potential benefits are different for the two groups. The pilgrimage character of STM gives the travelers a heightened sense of drama and awareness that can facilitate dramatic learning. Travelers from wealthier nations often observe poverty in a concrete, new way. The hosts frequently receive material benefits for personal and ministry needs. This list of potential benefits could be expanded.

Maximizing the missional value of STM requires paying attention to its primary purposes and priorities. Glenn Russell (2017) names four priorities that must shape the entire STM process: (1) The impact on individuals and groups in the church, school, orphanage, or other entity that acts as host; (2) the impact on the community surrounding the host organization; (3) the impact on the STM travelers; (4) the impact on the sending church, school, or other organizations back home. Notice that every party in the STM process is given an important and vital role.

Priority 1: The Hosts

Russell's order of priorities is a helpful corrective for an unhealthy arrangement of priorities that is sometimes operative, whether articulated or not. One mission pastor attending an interdenominational mission conference stated that his large church had decided simply to be honest and forthright by defining the benefits for the travelers as primary. His goal was to give every member of his church a "STM experience," not necessarily at the expense of the hosts, but with the recognition that the visitors might benefit most. At the same conference, speakers from both Asia and Africa expressed resentment that their congregations were being used as "guinea pigs" to give Americans a wonderful spiritual experience. As already mentioned, Wuthnow's research found that many STM travelers assume that their hosts automatically benefit from anything and everything they do (2009:8). This implies that the impact on STM hosts does not even need to be seriously considered and that only the impact on the travelers must be intentionally planned.

If, by contrast, the short- and long-term impact on the hosts is made first priority, the entire STM process comes into biblical focus. STM leaders and planners walk in the footsteps of Jesus and Paul as trainers of missionary teams; however, the top priority for Jesus, Paul, and their teams was to impart the blessings of the Gospel to those for whom they labored. Paul referred to mutual blessings for himself and the Roman church. "For I long to see you, that I may impart to you some spiritual gift to strengthen you—that is, that we may be mutually encouraged by each other's faith, both yours and mine" (Rom 1:11-12). But the personal blessings of service were secondary and derivative. In other words, Paul did not take Silas and Timothy on a mission trip primarily to give them a "mission experience," even though their service was a blessing to themselves.

Several things are implied by giving STM hosts top priority. First, potential hosts have the right to decline to receive a proposed visit. Hosts are sometimes overwhelmed by the task of entertaining numerous STM groups, or they believe a particular group would not match their needs. Whatever the case may be, host churches or church organizations should give themselves permission to decline trip proposals. Second, when a host does accept a proposed visit, they have the leading role in negotiating what tasks the visitors will perform. Finally, the hosts should feel free to guide and shape the team activities during the visit.

Priority 2: The Host's Community

The second priority is that the combined ministry of the STM travelers and hosts will have a missional impact on the local community that is appropriate and contextualized. Some projects are very outward-reaching to the community and others are on an enclosed campus but every team makes contact with the community in some way. The nature of an appropriate community impact is as diverse as the millions of communities in the world. Only intentional planning between STM travelers and hosts will ensure positive encounters. Some Roman Catholic communities in South America are more open to home visits from foreign Protestants than from local Protestants. On the other hand, STM teams can unintentionally do great harm to community relations when they are not well trained and if they lack adequate coordination with their hosts. When the STM group departs, their hosts must always feel empowered for better service.

Priority 3: The STM Team

Ranking the STM team as third in priority does not minimize their value but rather enhances and elevates the missional quality of their service. The self-centered "IMission" or "SelfieMission" motivation is replaced by the model of Christ's incarnational mission (Phil 2:4-8). Christ's motivational posture can then shape everything. Best practices for STM require a great deal of planning and intentionality to maximize the learning experience for every team member. How will the trip become a legacy of learning one, five, or ten years in the future?

Priority 4: The STM Home Community

Sometimes the benefits for the sponsoring church or school back home receive scant attention, even though they make the trip possible. At best, a brief and breathless report may be given that flashes pictures of poorly clad people across the screen. But what did the team learn that enhanced their cross-cultural competence, understanding of God's mission in a different place, God's mission back home, and the walk with God? How might all that benefit the community that sent them? The mission trip needs to enhance the sponsor organization's mission in every possible way.

Wealth and Power Imbalances

To maximize the missional quality of STM, travelers need to be prepared to serve in a truly Christlike way in the context of a wealth and power imbalance. Most STM trips bring relatively wealthy people into contact with people who are less materially wealthy. In this kind of encounter, there are inherent power and wealth imbalances. American teams, with their good clothing, computers, cameras, iPhones, sound equipment, and money simply "reek" of riches that local people can only dream about.

Even though partnership is the often-repeated goal and theme for STM, Corwin suggests that it is generally more of a "power trip" than a partnership (2008:144). Edwin Zehner critiques the "Delta Force" model (2006:512) and Hunter Farrell (2007:69) critiques the "Paratrooper Incursion" model, both of which view the STM trip as a military-like operation of spiritual power projection. Oscar Muriu (2009), a pastor in Nairobi, says that Kenyans know when its summer in America because the color of Nairobi's streets changes as STM groups appear in full tourist regalia.

Relationships are unavoidably warped in different ways when there is a wealth and power gap. If you are from North America (or another wealthy country), put yourself into the picture by visualizing how you would respond if you lived in a declining rural community when a group of very wealthy philanthropists came to spend two weeks working with your church. Sadly, the more wealthy tend to view themselves and their contributions more favorably than can always be justified and the less wealthy tend to be more agreeable and less evaluative than can always be justified. The valid desire for a new church or school building can cause local leaders to support almost any suggestion made by the STM team while the STM team may think that every idea they express is contextually appropriate because the leaders never disagree.

Recently, a multicultural STM group arrived at a Christian university with plans to hold a week of revival meetings and do some construction work. When the indigenous university provost asked who was to be the revival speaker, he was shocked to discover that the speaker had a gold earring and hairdo that were strictly forbidden on his campus and by the local Christian community. Using his best diplomacy, he told the group that no one looking like that could preach on his campus. The group responded that, unless "pastor earring" was allowed to preach, they would take their donation and themselves back home. Much conflict ensued with frantic calls to denominational executives and board members. In the end, the provost preached the revival himself and the donation was received. Had the provost been weak-kneed, the STM group would have presented a very negative view of Christianity in the local context.

The reality of relational warping caused by wealth and power imbalance places the obligation upon the travelers to be what Jonathan Bonk (1991) calls the "righteous rich" and practice what Miriam Adeney calls "Godly tourism" (2006:464). Human encounters involve the exchange of both material and non-material assets (such as friendship, loyalty, esteem, and reputation), sometimes consciously and other times unconsciously. Healthy encounters bring roughly equal benefits to the parties, while unhealthy encounters exploit one or both parties. Both parties can be exploited when they use each other to achieve material or non-material ends. In a worst case scenario, STM visitors use hosts as ecclesial "Disney World employees" to give them a spiritual-cultural-missional high while the hosts say and do almost anything to milk dollars from the visitors.

When STM teams visit the developing world, they are usually in a "power-up" position in both material and non-material capital. The material advantage comes from their obvious wealth, while the non-material advantage comes from being seen as more modern, sophisticated, educated and socially/politically powerful. The obligation for Christians on the "power-up" side is to make every possible effort to ensure that those on the "power-down" side receive equitable benefits from the encounter, even if not all of their issues and needs can be resolved. Adeney has noted that STM involves several kinds of encounters or exchanges (2006:464-472).

A Physical Encounter

First, there is a physical encounter. Tourists consume local resources and place a burden on the local economy, ecology and infrastructure without always benefitting the local people. An ethical physical encounter will bring at least as much good to the hosts as the visitors receive. "Godly tourists" will intentionally seek to benefit the local community by directing spending toward local businesses and minimizing any negative "footprint" on the ecology and infrastructure.

A Social-Cultural Encounter

Second, there is a social-cultural encounter. The temptation to feel culturally superior can be overwhelming for visitors from wealthy, powerful countries. A STM "power trip" can bring a team of task-oriented human "bulldozers" into a community in a way that is culturally disorienting and disruptive. Completion of the task can completely eclipse relationship-building activities. One church building team virtually refused to interact with the locals as they sought to complete the task on time. The training for one group of student evangelists included instruction to stay in the hotel room each day studying the evening's sermon instead of associating with the people. STM must be understood as a highly relational ministry. Visitors must work cooperatively and respectfully within local cultural norms so that whatever initiatives they make will be sustainable when they are gone.

A Spiritual Encounter

Third, STM involves a spiritual encounter. Without trying to assume an overly pious, saintly persona, a STM visitor needs to be recognized as a spiritual person. Wise visitors will respect the fact that the spiritual environment of the hosts may be quite different from their own. Worship, music, and preaching styles may be very different. The exercise of spiritual gifts also differs between cultures. If local patterns are not respected, the character and quality of worship in the host church can be so changed by the visitors that it bears no relationship to regular life and worship. Visitors should arrive as spiritual seekers and learners, willing to be served spiritually and willing to have their service shaped by and for the local spiritual environment. Visitors should not be the only ones singing, preaching, and witnessing during the visit.

A Material and Non-Material Exchange

In encounters where power and wealth are imbalanced, it is important that the assessment of the exchange be accurate and that it include both material and non-material assets. Unless care is taken, visitors could make an inaccurate assessment of the net material benefits they bring to their hosts. Visitor travel expense should not be counted as a contribution to the hosts—because it is not. The full cost of hosting the STM team, including hidden costs, needs to be assessed. Pastor Muriu, of Nairobi (2009), reported that his own church often provides a "reverse subsidy" to visiting groups, of which the visitors are oblivious. In other words, hosting STM teams is a net expense for his church. Ethical STM teams will ensure that their hosts do not suffer from hidden costs. This will require tact and diplomacy because accepting hospitality is part of being a good visitor, especially where showing hospitality is a strong traditional value. Making sure that hosts do not suffer a net loss is the lowest, minimal standard.

Non-material assets must also be included in the assessment of an encounter. One of the issues for STM visitors from the West is that their culture can predispose them to under-value the non-material assets that are part of human encounters. When seen in their true scale, the non-material gifts host communities give to their STM guests are to be greatly valued. These gifts can include a warm welcome, personal time and energy needed to facilitate the visit, patience with cultural unfamiliarity, forgiveness for cultural blunders, advocacy with government authorities and business people, protection from thieves, general social guidance needed to negotiate an unfamiliar culture, loyal support of visitors' ministries, and accepting their suggestions. In many places, hospitality is such a strong value that hosts often over-extend themselves in non-material ways to make visitors welcome.

On the other side of the encounter, the visitors also convey important non-material gifts. The hosts often receive social capital in their communities by hosting foreign guests who are often given celebrity status. Being the intermediaries for the celebrities elevates the status of the hosts. When genuine friendships are established, they carry great significance for "power-down" hosts. Such social capital can enhance mission and ministry in the local community.

Understanding the importance of the mutual non-material exchange is very important for Westerners. The hosts stand to benefit greatly from the fellowship and relational dimensions of STM, which travelers sometimes undervalue because of their task-oriented, materialistic approach. Material gifts are valued, but the gift of true friendship and the building of long-term relationships are greatly treasured. The travelers often benefit more than they realize from the generous non-material benevolence of the hosts. Ethical travelers will value and intentionally facilitate a generous and equitable non-material exchange.

Leading, Selecting, and Training for Short-Term Mission

The missional value of STM is greatly enhanced through careful leadership, team selection, and training for all who are involved in the project.

Traveler Leadership Tasks

Perhaps the first leadership task is to study some of the rich literature about STM that is available. Leading STM groups is a specialized ministry that needs specialized study.

When planning a trip to a destination for the first time, the leader needs to obtain permission to come. When the potential host has approved the visit, a planning trip by the STM leader is highly recommended because planning is so much more complex for first-time than with for return-visits.

A cluster of responsibilities surrounds the task of planning a trip with the potential host organization. These tasks include (1) determining what services best facilitate the ministries of the host organization; (2) developing a detailed action plan; (3) obtaining guidance on logistical matters, like food, transportation, and accommodation; and (4) identifying local medical care contacts for potential problems.

A second cluster of responsibilities involves planning at home and includes (1) planning a realistic trip budget; (2) selecting team members; (3) making travel bookings; (4) registering with Adventist Volunteer Services; (5) obtaining trip insurance; (6) providing team training, including matters of passports, visas, and immunizations; and (7) developing a mission statement for the group. The importance of having trip insurance cannot be over-stated.

Host Leadership Tasks

The first leadership task for those who host STM groups is to assess the match between the needs of their organization and the capacity of the proposed visiting team. What are the local needs and does the group who wants to come have the interest and capacity to meet them? A detailed action plan is then negotiated between the traveler and host leaders.

The second task for host leaders is to carefully define their own responsibilities and assess their capacity to fulfill them. Do the hosts have the money and personnel to perform their part of the project? The hosts want to express warm hospitality while avoiding overwhelming unexpected costs left behind by the visitors.

Finally, host leaders have the responsibility to fulfill their negotiated roles during the visit. Bringing unexpected charges and obligations to the guests is as bad as being left with unexpected costs when they depart.

Team Selection

The selection of team members is an important leadership task, with implications for everyone involved. The destination and projects of the trip require particular skills. For example, a group that will provide healthcare needs medical professionals to either perform or supervise medical work, as is ethically appropriate. Trip leaders need to have adequate experience and skills. All team members must be screened to provide protection for minors, both on the team and among the hosts. In a worst-case scenario, a team is made up without a selection process of members who have no training for the trip, get the money, passports, and visas at the last minute, and lack the necessary skills to do the work.

Russell (2017) uses a selection process with six elements: (1) Submission of an application form; (2) providing references; (3) submitting an essay describing motivations for the trip; (4) having an interview with team leaders; (5) obtaining passports, visas, and immunizations; and (6) completion of all required steps by a stated deadline.

Team Training

STM travelers go with high expectations of having a "whole-life-changing-experience" that makes a significant contribution to God's mission among the trip hosts. Therefore, training before, during, and after the trip is essential. Without such training, some travelers will step onto the aircraft without even the most basic concepts about Christian mission in place; they will not be prepared to observe and interpret accurately what they see and experience; they will not be able to relate to the hosts and minister among them effectively; and once back home they will not be able to retain and apply the lessons of the trip to their lives. Russell recommends 7 to 10 required training sessions (2017).

At the minimum, pre-trip training should include the following:

- Overview of Christian mission, past and present.
- Introduction to the concept of culture and cross-cultural missions.
- Basic skills of being a good learner and guest in a cross-cultural setting.
- Introduction to the host people and the progress of Christian missions among them.
- Guidelines for culturally appropriate dress and behavior among the host people.
- Guidelines for personal safety and health on the trip.
- Development of trip goals for the hosts.
- Development of trip goals for the group.
- Development of individual trip goals.

Training during the trip should include regular debriefing and the discussion of particular topics or issues that arise during the trip.

Post-trip debriefing needs to include the following:

- A narrative review of the trip, including high points and low points, to see how God worked in and through the hosts and the travelers.
- Assessment of team goals and their achievement with a cataloging of valuable lessons learned for the benefit of future trips.
- Assessment and sharing of individual's goals and their achievement with planning for the implementation of valuable lessons learned.
- Application of valuable lessons learned to individual and corporate plans for service in the local church and community.

Tentmaking Mission Service

A "Tentmaker" is a cross-cultural worker with a secular identity, called to make disciples within a closed or restricted access country, who supports themselves with their own employment (Moreau et al. 2000:939). The title is borrowed from Paul's work in Corinth with Aquila and Priscilla, where he supported his ministry by making tents (Acts 18:3).

Tentmakers gain access to places where cross-cultural missionaries cannot enter in the typical way. They can serve in almost any profession, including healthcare, academics, travel and tourism, diplomacy, development, engineering, and many more. They are intentional about witnessing for Christ in every possible and appropriate way. Their witnessing comes in addition to the normal work load of their profession. Their service may be lonely and their successes often cannot be published. Yet, tentmaking missionaries can be seed-planters whose work bears fruit for the Kingdom.

CONCLUSION

This book began by noting that the story of God's mission to lost humanity is the greatest story ever told. That amazing story is recounted in the biblical canon, from Genesis to Revelation. Adventists are "canonical Christians," rather than only "NT Christians," and they understand their mission through the lens of the whole Bible. A biblical understanding of mission is not to be built on collections of "missionary texts" or "proof texts," but on the whole narrative of the Bible. That grand narrative of God's mission was discussed as a series of God's missional acts, each of which instructs today's church.

Another presupposition of Adventist mission is that it is Trinitarian. God the Father initiated mission after the Fall. God the Son embodied mission as the incarnated Christ who provided the atonement for humanity on the Cross. God the Holy Spirit empowers and supervises mission and will bring God's mission to a glorious conclusion. The church's role is to submit to the Spirit's guidance in all things.

Adventist mission is also strongly eschatological, blending the Great Commission and the Three Angels' Messages. Eschatology gives Adventist mission special urgency that enhances commitment and effectiveness.

Another presupposition is that God's followers are always members of particular societies who experience and live out the religion of Jesus Christ in different cultural styles. The principles of the Bible are eternal and universal and those principles judge all cultures. The application of biblical principles differs in time and place. Thus, Adventist mission is guided by the process of faithful contextualization, where being faithful to Scripture is always primary and being appropriate for culture is secondary, but essential. One great need for Adventist mission is to produce more contextualized materials and approached.

The book repeats the point that Adventist mission is largely a Christian-to-Christian endeavor. In other words, Adventists offer a "finishing truth" or "value added" approach designed for other Christian groups that is ineffective among non-Christians. Most of humanity is not Christian and thus needs a "Christian-to-non-Christian" approach that takes a "starting truth" approach. The first Advent and its meaning must be understood and experienced before the second Advent and other biblical truths can be understood.

A final major point, among many others that could be mentioned, is the need for Adventist mission to be strategic. The missional capacity of the world church is spread unevenly, being concentrated in the American and African divisions. The bulk of the world's exploding population is located in Europe and Asia, where the Adventist presence is small. The world church, including divisions once primarily receivers of mission resources, needs to direct more resources of all kinds to the least evangelized world regions.

If Adventists have a single favorite song, it is probably "We Have this Hope." Our name proclaims hope in the imminent return of Jesus Christ. God is on his throne, directing his mission to humanity, empowering his servants through the Holy Spirit, and joyously planning the soon return of Jesus Christ in glory. God's mission to lost humanity and all of creation will be victorious.

REFERENCES

Adeney, Miriam. 2006. "Shalom Tourist: Loving Your Neighbor While Using Her." *Missiology* 34, no. 4:463-476.

Adeuyan, Jacob. 2011. *The Journey of the First Black Bishop: Bishop Samuel Ajayi Crowther 1806-1891*. Bloomington, IN: Author House.

Allen, David Lewis and Steve W. Lemke. 2010. *Whosoever Will: A Biblical-Theological Critique of Five-Point Calvinism*. Nashville: B & H Academic.

Allen, Roland. 1962. *Missionary Methods: St. Paul's or Ours?* Grand Rapids, MI: Eerdmans.

_____. 1962. *The Spontaneous Expansion of the Church and the Causes Which Hinder It*. Grand Rapids, MI: Eerdmans.

Anderson, Gerald H., ed. 1994. *Mission Legacies: Biographical Studies of Leaders of the Modern Missionary Movement*. Maryknoll, NY: Orbis.

Barrett, David, Todd Johnson, and Peter Crossing. 2008. "Status of Global Mission, Presence, and Activities, AD 1800-2025." *International Bulletin of Missionary Research*, 32 (January): 30.

Bavinck, J. H. 1960. *An Introduction to the Science of Missions*. Philadelphia: Presbyterian and Reformed Publishing.

Beer, Jennifer E. 2003. "High and Low Context" Culture at Work: Communicating Across Cultures. Accessed Sept. 28, 2016. http://www.culture-at-work.com/highlow.html.

Blauw, J. 1974. *The Missionary Nature of the Church: A Survey of the Biblical Theology of Mission*. Grand Rapids, MI: Eerdmans.

Bonk, Jonathan. 1991. *Missions and Money: Affluence as a Western Missionary Problem*. Maryknoll, NY: Orbis.

Bosch, David J. 1991. *Transforming Mission*. Maryknoll, NY: Orbis.

Boyd, Gregory A. 1997. *God at War: The Bible and Spiritual Conflict*. Downers Grove, IL: InterVarsity.

_____. 2001. *Satan and the Problem of Evil: Constructing a Trinitarian Warfare Theodicy*. Downers Grove, IL: InterVarsity.

Brasil de Souza, Elias. 2015 "The Hebrew Prophets and Literature of the Ancient Near East," *The Gift of Prophecy in Scripture and History*, edited by Alberto Timm and Dwain N. Esmond, 117-136. Silver Spring, MD: Review and Herald.

Brown, Colin. 1975. *The New International Dictionary of New Testament Theology*. 3 vols. Grand Rapids, MI: Zondervan.

_____, ed. 1976. *The New International Dictionary of New Testament Theology*. 3 vols. Grand Rapids, MI: Zondervan.

Bryant, Alexander G. 2017. *Secretary's Report: North American Division 2017 Year End Meeting*. PowerPoint Presentation.

Chavez, Stephen. 2010. *Mission Matters: Global Mission—20 Years After its Birth*. Accessed December 15, 2017. http://archives.adventistworld.org/issue.php?id=861&action=print

CIA World Fact Book. 2018. Accessed December 15, 2017. www.cia.gov/

Corduan, W. 1998. *Neighboring Faiths: A Christian Introduction to World Religions*. Downers Grove, IL: InterVarsity.

_____. 2006. *Pocket Guide to World Religions*. Downers Grove, IL: InterVarsity.

Corrie, John, Samuel Escobar, and Wilbert R. Shenk. 2007. *Dictionary of Mission Theology: Evangelical Foundations*. Nottingham, England: InterVarsity.

Corwin, Gary. 2008. "Of Partnerships and Power Trips." *Evangelical Missions Quarterly*, 44 no. 2 (April):144-145.

Crockett, William V., and James G. Sigountos. 1991. *Through No Fault of Their Own?: The Fate of Those Who Have Never Heard*. Grand Rapids, MI: Baker Book House.

Daniels, Gene. 2008. "The Character of Short Term Mission." *Evangelical Missions Quarterly*, 44 no. 2 (April):150-156.

Daniells, A. G. 1905. "Remarks to the General Conference Session." *Review and Herald*, 82 no. 19 (11 May 1905):9.

Dayton, Edward R., and David A. Fraser. 2003. *Planning Strategies for World Evangelization*. Eugene, OR: Wipf & Stock.

Donkor, Kwabena. 2015. Private conversation.

Doss, Cheryl, ed. 2009. *Passport to Mission*. 3rd ed. Berrien Springs, MI: Institute of World Mission.

_____. 2018. Institute of World Mission resources. Silver Spring, MD: General Conference.

Doss, Gorden. 1993. "George James Pioneer in the Malawi Work. "*Adventist Review*, 170 (Nov 11): 17-18.

Dybdahl, Jon, ed. 1999. *Adventist Mission in the 21st Century*. Hagerstown, MD: Review and Herald.

Dybdahl, Paul. 2017. *Before We Call Them Strangers: What Adventists Ought to Know About Muslims, Buddhists, and Hindus*. Lincoln, NE: AdventSource.

Dyrness, W. A. and V. M Kärkkäinen. 2008. *Global Dictionary of Theology: A Resource for the Worldwide Church*. Downers Grove, IL: Inter-Varsity.

Engen, Charles van. 1996. *Mission on the Way: Issues in Mission Theology*. Grand Rapids, MI: Baker.

_____. "Reflecting Theologically About the Resistant." *Reaching the Resistant: Barriers and Bridges for Mission*. Edited by J. Dudley Woodberry, 22-75. Pasadena, CA: William Carey Library.

Erickson, Millard J. 1991. "The State of the Question." *Through No Fault of Their Own?: The Fate of Those Who Have Never Heard*. Edited by William Crockett and James G. Sigountos, 23-33. Grand Rapids, MI: Baker Book House.

Eriksen, Thomas. 1996. "Ethnicity, Race, Class, and Nation." *Ethnicity*. Edited by John Hutchinson and Anthony D. Smith, 28-31. Oxford, UK: Oxford University Press.

Farrell, Hunter. 2007. "Short Term Missions: Paratrooper Incursion or 'Zaccheus Encounter'"? *Journal of Latin American Theology*, 2 no. 2:69-83.

Flemming, Dean. 2005. *Contextualization in the New Testament*. Downers Grove, IL: InterVarsity.

Fortin, D., and J. Moon. 2013, eds. *The Ellen G. White Encyclopedia* (2nd ed.). Hagerstown, MD: Review and Herald Publishing Association.

Fortin, D. 2017. Private conversation.

Garrison, David. 2004. *Church Planting Movements, How God Is Redeeming a Lost World*. Midlothian, VA: WIGTake Resources.

_____. 2014. *A Wind in the House of Islam*. Midlothian, VA: WIGTake Resources.

Gay, Craig. 1998. *The Way of the (Modern) World*. Grand Rapids, MI: Eerdmans.

Gilliland, Dean S. 1998. *Pauline Theology & Mission Practice*. Eugene, OR: Wipf and Stock.

Glasser, A. F., and C. E. van Engen. 2003. *Announcing the Kingdom: The Story of God's Mission in the Bible*. Grand Rapids, MI: Baker Academic.

Goheen, M. W. 2014. *Introducing Christian Mission Today: Scripture, History, and Issues*. Downers Grove, IL: InterVarsity.

Halverson, Dean. 1996. *Compact Guide to World Religions*. Minneapolis, MN: Bethany House Publishers.

Hart, Trevor A. and Richard Bauckham. 2000. *The Dictionary of Historical Theology*. Grand Rapids, MI: Eerdmans.

Hiebert, Paul G. 1982. "The Flaw of the Excluded Middle," *Missiology: An International Review*, vol. X, no. 1 (January): 35-47.

_____. 1983. *Cultural Anthropology*. Grand Rapids, MI: Baker.

_____. 1985. *Anthropological Insights for Missionaries*. Grand Rapids, MI: Baker.

_____. 1994. *Anthropological Reflections on Missiological Issues*. Grand Rapids, MI: Baker.

_____. 2008. *Transforming Worldview*. Grand Rapids, MI: Baker.

Hiebert, P. G., R. D. Shaw, and T. Tiénou. 1999. *Understanding Folk Religion: A Christian Response to Popular Beliefs and Practices*. Grand Rapids, MI: Baker.

Howell, Brian M., and Jenell Williams. Paris. 2011. *Introducing Cultural Anthropology: A Christian Perspective*. Grand Rapids, MI: Baker Academic.

Hutchinson, John, and Anthony D. Smith. 1996. *Ethnicity*. Oxford: Oxford University Press.

Irwin, Nate. 2011. "Muslim Churches? Another Perspective on C5." *Evangelical Missions Quarterly*, 47 no. 3 (July): 328-334.

Jenkins, Philip. 2002. *The Next Christendom: The Coming of Global Christianity.* Oxford, UK: Oxford University Press.

Jobes, Karen H. 2005. *1 Peter: Baker Exegetical Commentary of the NT.* Grand Rapids, MI: Baker Academic.

Johnson, Todd M. and Kenneth R. Ross, eds. 2009. *Atlas of Global Christianity 1910-2010.* Edinburgh, Scotland: Edinburgh University Press.

Johnstone, Patrick J. 2011. *The Future of the Global Church: History, Trends and Possibilities.* Downers Grove, IL: IVP.

Knight, George R., ed. 2005. *Historical Sketches of Foreign Missions.* Berrien Springs, MI: Andrews University Press.

Knitter, Paul F. 2002. *Introducing Theologies of Religions.* Maryknoll, NY: Orbis.

Kraft, Charles H. 1996. *Anthropology for Christian Witness.* Maryknoll, NY: Orbis.

_____. 2005. *Appropriate Christianity.* Pasadena, CA: William Carey Library.

Ladd, George Eldon.1993. *A Theology of the New Testament.* Grand Rapids, MI: Eerdmans.

_____. 2001.*The Gospel of the Kingdom: Scriptural Studies in the Kingdom of God.* Grand Rapids, MI: Eerdmans.

Latourette, Kenneth Scott. 1970. *A History of the Expansion of Christianity.* 7 vols., Contemporary Evangelical Perspectives. Grand Rapids, MI: Zondervan Pub. House.

Lausanne Movement Archives. Accessed December 1, 2017. http://www.lausanne .org/

Malik, Muhammad Farooq-i-Azam. 2008. *What Is Islam? Who Are the Muslims?* Houston, TX: Institute of Islamic Knowledge.

Malphurs, Aubrey. 2005. *Advanced Strategic Planning: A New Model for Church and Ministry Leaders.* Grand Rapids, MI: Baker.

Mbiti, John. 1980. "The Encounter of Christian Faith and African Religion." *Christian Century*, August 27- September 3, 1980: 817-820.

McDermott, G. R. and H. A. Netland. 2014. *A Trinitarian Theology of Religions: An Evangelical Proposal.* New York: Oxford University Press.

McEdward, Richard. 2012. "Adventist Best Practices of Contextual Mission in South East Asia." DMiss diss., Fuller School of Intercultural Studies.

McGavran, Donald A. 2005. *The Bridges of God: A Study in the Strategy of Missions.* Eugene, OR: Wipf & Stock.

McGavran, Donald A., and C. Peter. Wagner. 1990. *Understanding Church Growth.* Grand Rapids, MI: Eerdmans.

McIntosh, Gary. 2015. *Donald A. McGavran: A Biography of the Twentieth Century's Premier Missiologist.* Boca Raton, FL: Church Leader Insights.

Moreau, A. S., H. A. Netland, C. E. van Engen, and D. Burnett. 2000. *Evangelical Dictionary of World Missions.* Grand Rapids, MI: Baker.

Moreau, A. S., G. Corwin, and G. B. McGee. 2004. *Introducing World Missions: A Biblical, Historical, and Practical Survey*. Grand Rapids, MI: Baker Academic.

Moreau, A. Scott. 2012. *Contextualization in World Missions: Mapping and Assessing Evangelical Models*. Grand Rapids, MI: Kregel Publications.

Muck, Terry C., and Frances S. Adeney. 2009. *Christianity Encountering World Religions*. Grand Rapids, MI: Baker Academic.

Muck, Terry, Harold Netland, and Gerald McDermott, eds. 2014. *Handbook of Religion a Christian Engagement with Traditions, Teachings, and Practices*. Grand Rapids, MI: Baker Academic.

Muriu, Oscar. 2009. "Short-Term Mission from a Kenyan Pastor's Perspective." Paper presented at Being There: Short-term Mission and Human Need Conference, July 31, Deerfield, IL: Trinity Evangelical Divinity School.

Myers, Bryant L. 1996. *The New Context of World Mission*. Monrovia, CA: MARC.

Neill, Stephen. 1986. *A History of Christian Missions*. New York: Pelican.

Nelson, Kurt. 2009. "Establishing the Church in the Midst of Islam: A Flexible Contextual Approach." Occasional Bulletin (Evangelical Mission Society) 22 (2) Spring 2009.

Newbigin, Lesslie. 1954. *The Household of God*. New York: Friendship Press.

_____. 1995. *The Open Secret*. Grand Rapids, MI: Eerdmans.

_____. 1996. *The Missionary Movement in Christian History*. Maryknoll, NY. Orbis.

Niebuhr, H. Richard. 1951. *Christ and Culture*. New York: Harper.

Noll, Mark A. 2009. *The New Shape of World Christianity: How American Experience Reflects Global Faith*. Downers Grove, IL: IVP Academic.

Olson, Roger. E. 2006. *Arminian Theology: Myths and Realities*. Grand Rapids, MI: IVP Academic.

Ott, C., S. J. Strauss, and T. C. Tennent. 2010. *Encountering Theology of Mission: Biblical Foundations, Historical Developments, and Contemporary Issues*. Grand Rapids, MI: Baker Academic.

Partridge, Christopher, ed. 2005. *Introduction to World Religions*. Minneapolis, MN: Fortress Press.

Partridge, Christopher H., and Tim Dowley, eds. 2013. *Introduction to World Religions*, 2nd ed. Minneapolis, MN: Fortress Press.

Pierson, Paul Everett. 2009. *The Dynamics of Christian Mission: History through a Missiological Perspective*. Pasadena, CA: William Carey International University Press.

Peters, G. W. 1972. *A Biblical Theology of Missions*. Chicago: Moody Press.

Pettifer, Julian, and Richard Bradley. 1991. *Missionaries*. New York: BBC/ Parkwest Publications.

Pfandl, Gerhard. 2012. "Jesus Only." *Perspectives Digest*, vol. 17, no. 1.

Plummer, Robert L., and John Mark Terry. 2012. *Paul's Missionary Methods: In His Time and Ours*. Downers Grove, IL: IVP Academic.

Pocock, Michael. 1998. "Raising Questions about the Resistant," *Reaching the Resistant: Barriers and Bridges for Mission*, edited by Dudley Woodberry, 3-10. Pasadena, CA: William Carey Library.

Priest, Robert J. 2008. *Effective Engagement in Short-term Missions: Doing It Right*. Pasadena, CA: William Carey Library.

Priest, Robert, Terry Dischinger, Steve Rasmussem, and C.M. Brown. 2006. "Researching the Short-Term Mission Movement," *Missiology* 34, no. 4, (October): 427-429.

Richardson, Alan, and John Stephen Bowden. 1983. *The Westminster Dictionary of Christian Theology*. Philadelphia: Westminster Press.

Robert, Dana, ed. 2008. *Converting Colonialism: Visions and Realities in Mission History, 1706-1914*. Grand Rapids, MI: William B. Eerdmans Pub.

Rodriguez, Angel M. 2013. "World Religions and Salvation: An Adventist View." In *Message, Mission and Unity of the Church*. 429-442. Silver Spring, MD: Biblical Research Institute.

Russell, Glenn. 2017. "Short Term Mission: Toward Greater Effectiveness." Unpublished PowerPoint. Berrien Springs, MI.

Schmidt, Wilhelm. 2014. *The Origin and Growth of Religion: Facts and Theories*. Proctorville, OH: Wythe-North Pub.

Schnabel, Eckhard J. 2004. *Early Christian Mission*. Downers Grove, IL: IVP Academic.

Schnabel, Eckhard J. 2008. *Paul the Missionary: Realities, Strategies and Methods*. Downers Grove, IL: IVP Academic.

Seventh-day Adventist Encyclopedia. 1996. Hagerstown, MD: Review & Herald.

Seventh-day Adventist Yearbook. Hagerstown, MD: Review & Herald.

Sire, James. 2004. *The Universe Next Door*. 4th ed. Downers Gove, IL: IVP Academic.

Skreslet, S. H. 2012. *Comprehending Mission: The Questions, Methods, Themes, Problems, and Prospects of Missiology*. Maryknoll, NY: Orbis.

Smart, Ninian. 1998. *The World Religions*. 2nd ed. Cambridge, UK: Cambridge University Press.

Spicer, W. A. 1930. "I Know Whom I Have Believed." *Review and Herald* vol. 107, no. 37, (June 26, 1930): 1-3.

Staples, R. L. 1999. *Community of Faith: The Seventh-day Adventist Church and the Contemporary World*. Hagerstown, MD: Review and Herald Pub. Association.

Stefanović, Ranko. 2009. *Revelation of Jesus Christ: Commentary on the Book of Revelation*, 2nd ed. Berrien Springs, MI: Andrews University Press.

Stott, John. 2012. *The Lausanne Covenant: Complete Text with Study Guide*. Peabody, MA: Hendrickson.

Stott, John R. W., and Christopher J. H. Wright. 2015. *Christian Mission in the Modern World*. Downers Grove, IL: IVP.

Sunquist, S. 2013. *Understanding Christian Mission: Participation in Suffering and Glory*. Grand Rapids, MI: Baker.

Talman, Harley and John Jay Travis, eds. 2015. *Understanding Insider Movements: Disciples of Jesus within Diverse Religious Communities*. Pasadena, CA: William Carey Library.

Tennent, Timothy. 2002. *Christianity at the Religious Roundtable: Evangelicalism in Conversation with Hinduism, Buddhism, and Islam*. Grand Rapids, MI: Baker Academic.

_____. 2007. *Theology in the Context of World Christianity*. Grand Rapids, MI: Zondervan.

_____. 2010. *Invitation to World Missions*. Grand Rapids, MI: Kregal.

Terry, John Mark, Ebbie C. Smith, and Justice Anderson. 1998. *Missiology: An Introduction to the Foundations, History, and Strategies of World Missions*. Nashville: Broadman & Holman Publishers.

Terry, John Mark, and Jervis David Payne. 2013. *Developing a Strategy for Missions: A Biblical, Historical, and Cultural Introduction*. Grand Rapids, MI: Baker Academic.

Tompkins, Andrew. 2016. *A Fresh Look at Ellen G. White's Statements within their Original Context on the Heathen Being Saved*. Unpublished paper. Berrien Springs, MI.

Towns, Elmer L., and Gary McIntosh. 2004. *Evaluating the Church Growth Movement: 5 Views*. Grand Rapids, MI: Zondervan.

Travis, John. 1998. "The C1 to C6 Spectrum: A Practical Tool for Defining Six Types of 'Christ-centered Communities' ('C') Found in the Muslim Context." *Evangelical Missions Quarterly* 34, no. 4: 407–408.

Travis, John. 2015. "The C1-C6 Spectrum after Fifteen Years." *Evangelical Missions Quarterly* 51, no. 4: 358-365.

Travis, John, and J. Dudley Woodberry. 2015. "When God's Kingdom Grows Like Yeast." In *Understanding Insider Movements: Disciples of Jesus within Diverse Religious Communities*. Edited by Harley Talman and John Jay Travis, 31-40. Pasadena, CA: William Carey Library.

Trim, David. 2017a. "Foreign Missionary Program of the Seventh-day Adventist Church." Unpublished paper. Silver Spring, MD: General Conference Office of Archives, Statistics, and Research.

Trim, David. 2017b. "General Conference Secretariat and Foreign Missions." Unpublished paper. Silver Spring, MD: General Conference Office of Archives, Statistics, and Research.

Tucker, Ruth. 2011. *Parade of Faith: A Biographical History of the Christian Church*. Grand Rapids, MI: Zondervan

Turner, M. 1998. *The Holy Spirit and Spiritual Gifts: In the New Testament Church and Today* (Rev. ed.). Peabody, MA: Hendrickson Publishers.

Van Engen, Charles. 1996. *Mission on the Way*. Grand Rapids, MI: Baker.

Van Rheenen, Gailyn. 1991. *Communicating Christ in Animistic Contexts*. Pasadena, CA: William Carey Library.

Walls, A. F. 1996. *The Missionary Movement in Christian History: Studies in the Transmission of Faith*. Maryknoll, NY: Orbis.

_____. 2002. *The Cross-Cultural Process in Christian History: Studies in the Transmission and Appropriation of Faith*. Maryknoll, NY: Orbis.

Wagner, C. P. 1974. *Your Spiritual Gifts Can Help Your Church Grow*. Glendale, CA: Regal.

Wagner, C. P. 2012. *Discover Your Spiritual Gifts*. Ventura, CA: Regal.

Waters, Malcolm. 1995. *Globalization*. London, UK: Routledge.

Watts, Kit. 1989. "Progress Toward a Global Strategy," *Adventist Review*, 31 August, 1989, 8-10.

Wesley, John. N.d. "The General Spread of the Gospel," *Wesley's Sermons*, Sermon 63. Accessed Feb 2017. http://www.godrules.net/library/wsermons/wsermons63.htm.

_____. N.d. "Without God in the World," Sermon 125. Accessed Feb 2017. http://www.godrules.net/library/wsermons/wsermons63.htm

Whidden, W. W., J. Moon, and J. Reeve. 2002. *The Trinity: Understanding God's Love, His Plan of Salvation, and Christian Relationships*. Hagerstown, MD: Review and Herald.

White, Ellen G. 2002. *Education* (ED). Nampa, ID: Pacific Press.

_____. 2003. *Sons and Daughters of God* (SD). Hagerstown, MD: Review and Herald.

_____. 2007. *Life Sketches* (LS). Hagerstown, MD: Review and Herald.

_____. 2009. *Christ's Object Lessons* (COL). Hagerstown, MD: Review and Herald.

_____. 2009. *Ministry of Healing* (MH). Hagerstown, MD: Review and Herald.

_____. 2013. *Desire of Ages* (DA). Hagerstown, MD: Review and Herald.

_____. 2013. *Prophets and Kings* (PK). Hagerstown, MD: Review and Herald.

_____. 2013. *Patriarchs and Prophets* (PP). Hagerstown, MD: Review and Herald.

_____. 2015. *Great Controversy* (GC). Hagerstown, MD: Review and Herald.

_____. 2016. *Story of Redemption* (SR). Hagerstown, MD: Review and Herald.

_____. 2017. *Steps to Christ* (SC). Hagerstown, MD: Review and Herald.

_____. 2017. *Testimonies* (Vols. 1-9). Hagerstown, MD: Review and Herald.

Winter, Ralph and Steven C. Hawthorne, eds. 2009. *Perspectives on the World Christian Movement*. 4th ed. Pasadena, CA: William Carey Library.

Wright, Christopher. 2006. *The Mission of God*. Downers Grove, IL: IVP Academic.

Woodberry, J. Dudley, ed. 1998. *Reaching the Resistant: Barriers and Bridges for Mission*. Pasadena, CA: William Carey Library.

Woodberry, Robert D. 2012. "The Missionary Roots of Liberal Democracy." *American Political Science Review*. Vol. 106, no. 2 (May): 244-274.

Wuthnow, Robert. 2009. *Boundless Faith: The Global Outreach of American Churches*. Berkeley, CA: University of California Press.

Van Rheenen, Gailyn. 1996. *Communicating Christ in Animistic Contexts*. Pasadena, CA: William Carey Library.

Yong, Amos. 2003. *Beyond the Impasse: Toward a Pneumatological Theology of Religions*. Grand Rapids, MI: Baker Academic

Zehner, Edwin. 2006. "Short-Term Missions: Toward a More Field-Oriented Model." *Missiology* 34, no. 4: 509-521.

Made in the USA
Columbia, SC
21 April 2019